NEW Let's Meet up!

2de A2/B1

W0215138

DIRECTION D'OUVRAGE ET AUTEUR

Erwan GOURAUD
Formateur
Enseignant au lycée Jean-Jacques Rousseau, Sarcelles (95)

AUTEURS ET AUTRICES

Bryce ANGOT
Collège Jacques Prévert, Chambly (60)

Julia BEHAR
Lycée Gustave Eiffel, Rueil-Malmaison (92)

Aline CHARLES
Lycée Descartes, Rabat (Maroc)

Véronique DORGET
Lycée Louis Lapicque, Épinal (88)

Sylvie DOUGLADE VAL
Lycée Claude Gellée, Épinal (88)

Charlotte FLOCMOINE
Collège du Sacré Cœur, Nancy (54)

Sue GALAND-JONES
École Navale, Lanvéoc (29)

Frédéric GULDNER MONIER
Groupe scolaire Fénelon Sainte-Marie, Paris (75)

Mathilde HENRIOT
Lycée Montgrand, Marseille (13)

Axel JACOBIN
Lycée Montalembert, Courbevoie (92)

Sophie MATHIEU
Lycée Jean Baptiste Poquelin, Saint Germain en Laye (78)

Jean-Marck MOLIGNIER
Lycée Saint-Michel de Picpus, Paris (75)

GRAMMAIRE ET PHONOLOGIE

Sylvain GATELAIS
Maitre de conférences
Université de Tours (37)

Hatier

Les auteurs et l'éditeur remercient chaleureusement tous les enseignants et enseignantes qui les ont aidés à élaborer ce manuel en testant les séquences, notamment :

Rebecca Ahmed, Lycée Notre Dame de la Providence, Thionville (57) / Laurence Altibelli, Lycée Jules Verne, Limours (91) / Colette Badinier, Lycée Charlie Chaplin, Décines-Charpieu (69) / Samira Berqoqi, Lycée Jacques Brel, La Courneuve (93) / Catherine Campaner, Lycée des Graves, Gradignan (33) / Muriele Charrier, Lycée Sainte Marie Grand Lebrun, Bordeaux (33) / Marie-Odile Cothias, Lycée Voltaire, Paris (75) / Estelle Coutris, Lycée polyvalent Albert de Mun, Paris (75) / Catherine Dolet, Lycée Marc Chagall, Reims (51) / Nadine Fessmann, Lycée Robert Schuman, Haguenau (67) / Céline Gaspar, Lycée François Joseph Talma, Brunoy (91) / Sarah Le Baron, L'Externat-Chavagnes, Nantes (44) / Sandra Leclerc, Lycée Guy de Maupassant, Fécamp (76) / Christophe Marty, Lycée Pierre de la Ramée, Saint-Quentin (02) / Patrizia Mione, Lycée Saint Joseph, Avignon (84) / Mickael Monier, Institut Notre Dame, Bourg-la-Reine (92) / Sophie Morales Cuella, Lycée Olympe de Gouges, Montech (82) / Sandra Murphy, Lycée Louis Armand, Eaubonne (95) / Annie Papin-Champion, L'Externat-Chavagnes, Nantes (44) / Marie Rocher, Institut Fédération Française de Golf (IFFG), Magny-les-Hameaux (78) / Anne Wiener, Lycée Nicolas Appert, Orvault (44) / Laurent Zaninetti, Lycée Jean-Baptiste de Baudre, Agen (47) / Pascale Huteau, Lycée NDTA, Nantes (40) / Mathieu Kersse, Lycée Bellevue, ALBI (81) / Soâade Merazka, Lycée Notre Dame de la Providence, Thionville (57) / Stéphanie Saunier, Lycée Blaise Pascal, Charbonnières-les-Bains (69)

Les auteurs tiennent également à remercier leurs élèves qui, en expérimentant avec enthousiasme les activités, ont permis de les ajuster, notamment les Escape Games.

Enfin, les éditeurs remercient Ann Elkington pour la qualité et la précision de sa relecture.

Conception de la couverture : Primo & Primo

Conception maquette intérieure : ADN

Mise en page : Anne-Danielle Naname, Juliette Lancien

Édition : Claudine Varin, Catherine de Bernis, Elisabeth Coquidé

Illustrations : Parko Polo (p. 25), Marie-Hélène Van Tilbeurgh (p. 94), Mojo Wong (p. 217)

Cartes : Légendes Cartographie (p. 190, 211 et 298-301)

Infographies : Vincent Landrin (p. 296-301)

Iconographie : Véronique Foz

Droits : Andréa Freire

ISBN : 978-240-1-09679-0

Bienvenue en 2de !

Dans *New Let's Meet Up*, tout est conçu pour votre réussite :

- **un ancrage culturel fort**, à travers des documents authentiques et originaux afin de découvrir la richesse et la diversité du monde anglophone. Cette année de lycée vous permettra ainsi de voyager de l'Écosse au Kenya, de Londres à Bangalore en passant par la Jamaïque ou l'Australie… Un large choix de lieux et de thèmes pour s'adapter à toutes et tous !
- **un travail sur la langue clair et accessible**, dans les unités et dans les précis des annexes, afin d'acquérir les outils lexicaux, grammaticaux et phonétiques essentiels pour mieux vous exprimer à l'oral et à l'écrit.
- **une approche différenciée** par des travaux de groupe, avec des fiches pour permettre à tous de réussir les activités et les projets.
- **une méthodologie accompagnant les tâches finales** afin d'acquérir des savoir-faire que vous pourrez réutiliser.

Organisé de manière progressive, le manuel propose des unités de longueurs différentes qui reprennent les jalons du collège tout au long de l'année, afin que chacun soit en situation de réussite.

Parmi toutes ces nouveautés, vous aurez aussi le plaisir de découvrir **les vidéos *Tyron's Tips*** : conçues par un maître de conférences en linguistique, ces courtes capsules vidéo reprennent, façon réseaux sociaux, l'un des points de grammaire ou de phonétique de chaque unité de manière amusante et décalée.

Toute l'équipe des auteurs espère que vous apprécierez ce manuel autant que nous avons apprécié le créer, en ayant toujours comme motivation votre réussite et le plaisir d'être ensemble en cours d'anglais.

Les auteurs

découverte
réfléchir
communiquer
consolider
s'amuser
culture
différenciation
musique
s'exprimer
art
s'impliquer
monde
PROGRESSER

Sommaire

21 unités pour découvrir les 8 axes du programme de 2de

L'art de vivre ensemble

1 Welcome to high school

▶ To what extent is choosing a club shaping your identity at school?

Club de théâtre, manga, cuisine... Au Royaume-Uni, les établissements scolaires offrent une palette d'activités très variée pour permettre aux élèves de se découvrir au travers de nouveaux centres d'intérêt.

Représentation de soi et rapport à autrui

→ p. 16-23

Pictures
- Wordcloud: clubs at the British School of Paris
- Brochure and posters: clubs and activities at Arran High and other schools in the UK
- Student newspaper frontpage

Texts
- Presentations of clubs and activities

Videos
- Clubs of the British School of Paris
- Clubs and activities of the British School of Brussels

Success boxes
- Décrire et présenter un club ou des activités
- Les adverbes de fréquence
- Indiquer des horaires
- Exprimer ses goûts et ses désirs
- Exprimer la cause
- Donner son opinion et convaincre
- Exprimer le souhait
- Donner un conseil
- Indiquer des objectifs
- L'ordre des mots dans les questions

YOUR PROJECTS

Shoot a promotional video for two school clubs.

Prepare a leaflet of extracurricular activities for open day.

2 Scotland: land of legends

▶ How does Scotland keep its legends alive?

Créatures fantastiques et fantômes inquiétants peuplent les légendes d'Écosse. Un patrimoine culturel unique, dont l'Écosse a fait un atout pour développer son tourisme et son économie.

Le passé dans le présent

→ p. 24-37

Pictures
- Map of Scotland's myths and legends
- Pictures of Scottish legends

Texts
- 3 Scottish legends
- How the Loch Ness Monster became a force in Scotland's economy
- Beware of Kelpies
- *Visit Scotland* Instagram post

Videos
- Scotland's year of stories campaign
- A night in a haunted castle
- Visit Inverness Loch Ness promotional campaign
- A tribute to the Kelpies

Entraînement à l'évaluation

Scotland myths & legends podcast

The Ghost Piper of Clanyard Bay

YOUR PROJECTS

Join the #TalesOfScotland contest!

Record a podcast about Scottish myths and legends.

Write an Instagram post to promote tourism based on Scottish legends.

Method
How to write an Instagram post

+ prof Évaluation

Grammar
- Le prétérit simple
- Les superlatifs de supériorité

Pronunciation
- La terminaison *-ed*
- Le schwa /ə/

Vocabulary
Les mythes et l'héritage culturel

Remember how to
- Boost your memory
- Tell a story in the past

Flash

3 Acting Teens

▶ How do celeb teens fit into the entertainment industry?

Séries, films, comédies musicales... L'industrie du spectacle permet à de jeunes artistes talentueux de vivre leur rêve et parfois de connaître la célébrité à un très jeune âge. Mais à quel prix ?

Les univers professionnels, le monde du travail

→ p. 38-43

Pictures
- Fame and work – Pictures of celeb acting teens

Texts
- *Stranger Things* is breaking one dangerous (and deadly) hollywood pattern
- A quick curtain call, then bed
- The not so cursed child: did Harry Potter mark the end of troubled young actors?
- There is no book of rules: how theatres aim to safeguard child actors

Video
- Playing *Matilda* on the West End – Lara Wollington

YOUR PROJECTS

It's Career Day!

As a teen actor, explain the pros and cons of being in the entertainment industry for Career Day.

+ prof Évaluation

Grammar
- Le *present perfect*

Pronunciation
- La voyelle longue /iː/

Vocabulary

Le monde du travail et l'industrie du spectacle

Remember how to
- Compare and contrast two facts
- Choose between active and passive voice

Escape Game

4 Mission Museum

▶ How do the Washington DC Smithsonian Museums celebrate American history?

Des hackers ont verrouillé l'accès au préambule de la constitution américaine, conservé au *Lincoln Memorial* ! Parcourez la *Smithsonian Institution* pour déjouer le complot et découvrez l'histoire américaine.

Le passé dans le présent → p. 44-53

Pictures
- Map: the Smithsonian Institution in Washington DC
- 6 portraits of American Presidents

Texts
- The Declaration of Independence
- Timeline: the History of African Americans

Videos
- Introduction to the Smithsonian
- Hidden clues you may have missed in Washington's portrait

Audios
- Mary Pickersgill and the story of the Star-Spangled Banner
- *The Star-Spangled Banner* (anthem)

5 The future of American STEM jobs

▶ How is science conquering the job market in the USA?

Marcher sur la lune, trouver un vaccin, étudier les animaux… Aux États-Unis, les études scientifiques sont de plus en plus valorisées car les besoins sont immenses et les perspectives de carrière nombreuses.

Pictures
- Poster: STEM careers - where might science take you?
- Infographic: STEM in numbers

Textes
- Dr. Meredith Grey from *Grey's Anatomy*: a talented surgeon
- Richard Hendricks from *Silicon Valley*: the creator of an innovative music app
- Shuri from *Black Panther*: genius-level engineer
- Dr. Charles Edward Eppes from *Numbers*: a young mathematical genius

Videos
- STEM professionals
- We don't need more Lebrons
- The STEM queen

Entraînement à l'évaluation

The importance of STEM education in schools

Lab Girl, by Hope Jahren

YOUR PROJECTS

It's National STEM Day in the USA!

Create a poster to promote STEM Day in your school.

Make a short video presenting a STEM job.

Method

How to create a poster

+ prof Évaluation

Grammar
- L'absence d'article (l'article Ø)
- Le présent simple

Pronunciation
- La diphtongue /aɪ/
- Quelques terminaisons accentuées

Vocabulary

Le monde du travail et les sciences

Remember how to
- Say what you prefer
- Give your opinion
- Write and say numbers
- Ask questions

Flash

6 Save the waves

▶ How are Australian surfers protecting their coastline?

La culture du surf fait partie intégrante de la société australienne. Alors que les espaces côtiers sont de plus en plus menacés, la communauté des surfeurs se mobilise pour sauver les vagues.

Pictures
- Print campaign for the *Surfrider Foundation*

Texts
- The battle to protect Australia's surf breaks
- Endangered waves
- Surfing to save the world

Videos
- GC World Surf Reserve
- Save the Waves App: take action today

YOUR PROJECTS

It's Career Day!

Write a guide to help the *Surfrider Foundation* volunteers protect Australian coastlines!

+ prof Évaluation

Grammar
- L'expression du but

Pronunciation
- L'accentuation des mots se terminant par *-ion*

Vocabulary

La protection de l'environnement et des océans

Remember how to
- Talk about a possible or probable future
- Describe a scene

7 British cities go foodie!

▶ To what extent do food halls transform British cities?

La folie des *food halls* s'est emparée des villes britanniques ! Si la « nourriture de rue » est une tradition bien anglaise, ces nouveaux lieux de consommation sont en train de modifier les quartiers. À quel prix ?

Le village, le quartier, la ville → p. 74-87

Pictures
- Advert: Market halls in Victoria
- Infographic: The 3 components to a successful food hall

Texts
- The evolution of street food in London
- Spoilt for choice
- Reusing iconic buildings
- Gentrification in British cities

Videos
- Best London markets to visit – Mercato Metropolitano
- The future of Smithfield Market in London

Entraînement à l'évaluation
- Discover the team from Pergola Paddington
- The best neighbourhoods for foodies in London

YOUR PROJECTS
- Present your food hall project for a British city.
- Write a letter to a British city council to react to a new food hall project.

Method
How to deliver a speech

+ prof Évaluation

Grammar
- La voix passive
- Exprimer la conséquence

Pronunciation
- La voyelle longue /ɔː/
- L'accentuation des mots en *-ic* et *-ical*

Vocabulary
Renouveau dans la ville et restauration de rue

Remember how to
- Make compound nouns
- Express necessity

Flash

8 From garbage to garden in Kenya

▶ How does Nairobi transform its waste?

Dans la ville de Nairobi, artistes, ingénieurs et communautés se mobilisent pour recycler les déchets de l'une des plus grandes décharges à ciel ouvert d'Afrique. Éveiller les consciences et améliorer la vie des habitants est leur principal objectif.

Sauver la planète, penser les futurs possibles → p. 88-93

Pictures
- The beauty of waste materials, by artist Joan Otieno
- Infographic: Waste in Kenya
- Cartoon: Recycling plastic waste... at what cost?

Texts
- Creating green spaces amid Kenya's largest dumpsite

Videos
- Lords of the trash
- Transforming Nairobi's mountain of plastic waste

YOUR PROJECTS
- Create a piece of art to raise awareness about plastic waste and present it to the Nairobi City Hall.

+ prof Évaluation

Grammar
- Les indénombrables

Pronunciation
- La consonne /ŋ/

Vocabulary
Virage écologique

Remember how to
- Write a dialogue

9 Symbolising America

▶ Do American symbols still represent the USA?

Drapeau, hymne national, statue de la liberté… Le sentiment national des Américains s'est toujours appuyé sur des symboles fédérateurs. Alors que la société se divise, comment évoluent les regards sur ces icônes ?

Le passé dans le présent → p. 94-107

Pictures
- Map: American symbols
- The American flag: a pride or a burden?
- Cartoon: *Rethinking American symbols*
- Infographic

Texts
- Uncle Sam
- *The Star-Spangled Banner:* America's national anthem
- Pro & Con

Videos
- The Statue of liberty
- Colin Kaepernick

Audio
- "How do you feel about the U.S. flag?"

Entraînement à l'évaluation

Ruth Bader Ginsburg's comments about Colin Kaepernick

Our flag tells a lot about who we are

YOUR PROJECTS

Take part in a televised debate.

Write to the Editor of the *New York Times*.

Method
How to debate and win!

+ prof
Évaluation

Grammar
- Le *past perfect*
- Exprimer la concession et la contradiction

Pronunciation
- Les consonnes muettes
- La prononciation du *r*

Vocabulary
- Les symboles des États-Unis
- L'expression d'un point de vue

Remember how to
- Write a paragraph expressing contrasts
- Interpret symbols

10 Being Irish

▶ How is the Irish heritage passed on?

Jeunes ou anciens, Irlandais du bout du monde ou nouveaux venus, que veut dire aujourd'hui « être Irlandais » ?

Vivre entre générations → p. 108-121

Pictures
- Pictures of Irish symbols
- Infographic: Irish population and migration

Texts
- Famous Irish people statements: Ola Majekodunmi (journalist), Niall Horan (musician), Mary Lou McDonald (politician), Sonia O'Sullivan (athlete)
- *Don't Drink the Bathroom Water: A Guide to Living in Ireland,* by Robin Castle

Videos
- What it means to be Irish
- What's it like to be a 16-year-old in Dublin today?

Entraînement à l'évaluation

#IAmIrish

Growing up Irish: traditions of an Irish-American family

YOUR PROJECTS

Create an infographic about Irish culture and identity.

Shoot a video to talk about Irish teenagers.

Method
Create an infographic

+ prof
Évaluation

Grammar
- Les comparatifs
- Le gérondif

Pronunciation
- La consonne *h*
- Les terminaisons inaccentuées

Vocabulary
Culture irlandaise et identité

Remember how to
- Present and discuss data

Flash

11 Art for all

▶ To what extent is Kadir Nelson making African American Art accessible to all?

À travers ses tableaux, illustrations de presse et ouvrages pour la jeunesse, l'artiste Kadir Nelson rend aux Afro-Américains leur place dans l'histoire des USA.

La création et le rapport aux arts → p. 122-127

Pictures
- *American Uprising*: cover illustration for the magazine *Rolling Stone*
- Book cover: *Heart and Soul*

Texts
- Award-winning artist, author Kadir Nelson to speak at Norman Rockwell Museum
- Kadir Nelson: proudly black, pointedly positive

Videos
- Kadir Nelson: the birth of an artist
- Painting their story
- Kwame Alexander reads *The Undefeated*

Audio
- The audience reacts

YOUR PROJECTS

Present Kadir Nelson in a video for Black History Month.

+ prof Évaluation

Grammar
- Le présent en *be* + V-*ing*

Pronunciation
- La voyelle longue /ɑː/

Vocabulary

Les arts graphiques et leur message

Remember how to
- Analyse a picture
- Express your feelings and emotions

12 Australia: winning together

▶ How is sport bridging the gap between communities in Australia?

En Australie, athlètes et fédérations sportives œuvrent pour une meilleure reconnaissance des personnes aborigènes afin que le sport devienne un facteur d'inclusion et de réconciliation.

Sports et société → p. 128-141

Pictures
- Mural: *Coming together*, by Warwick Keen
- Champion Patty Mills' portrait
- A new jersey – Cricket Australia (Tweet)

Texts
- Johnny Mullagh, an Indigenous sports icon
- Football Australia launches Indigenous Reconciliation Action Plan

Videos
- Patty Mills: Aboriginal and proud
- Lionel Rose
- Cathy Freeman
- Our reconciliation statement

Entraînement à l'évaluation
- Reconciliation through sport
- Cathy Freeman's tribute to granddad

YOUR PROJECTS

Record a video promoting an Australian Aboriginal athlete for the Australian Book of Records.

Write an article about sport and reconciliation in Australia for your school website.

Method
How to shoot a video

+ prof Évaluation

Grammar
- L'expression de la capacité
- *By* + gérondif

Pronunciation
- La diphtongue /eɪ/
- Les liaisons

Vocabulary

Le sport et l'inclusion

Remember how to
- Express cause

13 Let's get musical!

▶ How do musicals mirror society?

Spectacles complets au croisement de la danse, du chant et du théâtre, les comédies musicales permettent de transmettre des messages engagés et d'appeler au changement.

Pictures
- Posters and stills from famous musicals: *Dear Evan Hansen, Hamilton, West Side Story, Rent*

Texts
- Reviews: *Dear Evan Hansen, From & Juliet, Hamilton, The Color Purple*
- The power of musical theatre
- Lyrics: *America* (*West Side Story*)

Videos
- *Hamilton*, official song clip
- Trailers: *The Color Purple, Glasgow girls*
- *West Side Story*, Steven Spielberg's remake
- Song: *America*

Entraînement à l'évaluation
- *In the Heights* review
- *Rent:* struggling to survive in New York City

YOUR PROJECTS
- Rap to promote a musical on your social media account.
- Create a brochure for a musical.

Method
How to rap a song for a musical

+ prof Évaluation

Grammar
- Le discours rapporté
- Les adjectifs

Pronunciation
- La diphtongue /əʊ/
- L'accent emphatique

Vocabulary
Les spectacles et leurs thèmes

Remember how to
- Express enthusiasm

Flash

14 The uniting states of football

▶ How is American football bringing people together?

Le football américain, notamment lors du Super Bowl, rassemble chaque année des millions d'Américains dans la fièvre du sport. Mais il permet aussi d'afficher au grand jour certaines inégalités et ainsi de lutter contre les discriminations.

Texts
- What's so super about the Super Bowl?
- Reactions to the 2022 half-time show

Videos
- Super Bowl: What does it mean to Americans?
- Colin Kaepernick
- Carl Nassib

+ prof Évaluation

YOUR PROJECTS
- Take part in a discussion on an NFL online forum.

Grammar
- La phrase exclamative

Pronunciation
- L'accentuation des mots en *-ity* et *-ety*

Vocabulary
Événements sportifs et gestes politiques

Remember how to
- Express your enthusiasm
- Express your opinion

15 Being born-free in South Africa

▶ How is the new generation building post-apartheid South Africa?

30 ans après la fin de l'apartheid, comment les jeunes Sud-Africains vivent-ils avec cet héritage ? Quels sont leurs espoirs et leurs révoltes ?

Vivre entre générations → p. 162-175

Pictures
- Portraits of South African youth
- Cartoon: *Happy Youth Day*

Texts
- Timeline: the apartheid
- The changing youth of South Africa
- Being part of a new generation
- Born free
- *Born a Crime: Stories From a South African Childhood*, by Trevor Noah

Videos
- 'The Rainbow Nation'
- Mandela's Generation of Hope
- Is 'black tax' a help or a burden?

Entraînement à l'évaluation

Hopes and dreams about South Africa

No Rainbow Nation for today's youth

YOUR PROJECTS

Write an article about the South African youth.

Deliver a speech on South Africa's future.

Method
How to write an article

+ prof
Évaluation

Grammar
- Les propositions relatives
- Exprimer l'interdiction

Pronunciation
- La prononciation de *th*
- La terminaison *-ate*

Vocabulary

Héritage et action politique

Remember how to
- Express certainty
- Describe past habits

16 Youth voices, youth power!

▶ How are American teens fighting to be heard?

De quelle manière les jeunes américains affirment-ils leur identité et portent-ils leurs revendications ?

Représentation de soi et rapport à autrui → p. 176-189

Pictures
- Youth protests in American cities
- Portraits of American young activists

Texts
- Can high school students make a real impact?
- Luka Galle, reconnecting with Feminity
- Xiuhtezcatl Martinez, the Earth Guardian
- The fate of the world is in their hands

Video
- Young activists on why they march

Audios
- Supporting a teen activist
- How to be a meddling kid with Isabel Hope

Entraînement à l'évaluation

Interview with teen climate activist Jamie Margolin

X González about to snap

YOUR PROJECTS

Take part in an interview.

Write a teen activist's profile story.

Method
How to take part in an interview

+ prof
Évaluation

Grammar
- Exprimer le conseil
- Les propositions infinitives

Pronunciation
- L'anglais américain
- Les mots inaccentués

Vocabulary

Les actions collectives et l'émancipation

Remember how to
- Say if you agree or disagree
- Express blame

Flash

17 Jammin' in Jamaica

▶ To what extent does reggae represent Jamaican culture?

Une musique pour évoquer ses racines, protester, unifier… Le reggae et le rastafarisme sont le cœur vibrant de l'âme jamaïquaine.

Pictures
- Jamaica and the reggae culture
- Portrait of Bob Marley

Texts
- Soul rebels
- *Get Up, Stand Up* (lyrics)

Videos
- Roots, rock, reggae
- *Get Up, Stand Up* (song)
- Trailer of a documentary about the legendary group Inna da Yard

YOUR PROJECTS

Shoot a video to promote "International Reggae Day".

+ prof Évaluation

Grammar
- Les verbes à particule

Pronunciation
- La voyelle brève /ʌ/

Vocabulary
Musique et engagement politique

Remember how to
- Make a statement

18 The London Tube

▶ What is the role of the Tube in Londoners' lives?

Construit à l'apogée de l'Empire britannique, abris pendant la guerre, galerie d'art aujourd'hui, le métro de Londres porte de mille manières l'identité de la ville et de ses habitants.

Pictures
- Painting: Mind the gap
- Posters: A multicoloured Tube, Visit the Empire
- The Underground and the Blitz

Texts
- Taking shelter in the Underground
- The Elizabeth Line
- Mind the gap: London Tube opens new doors
- *Our Meetings* (poem)

Videos
- The Underground brand
- Elizabeth Line
- Art on the Underground commission
- "Rats" attack in the Underground! – Banksy

Audio
- Tube map covers

Entraînement à l'évaluation
- What I (dis)like about the Tube
- Why is art important in public places?

YOUR PROJECTS

Create a brochure about art events in the underground.

Prepare a presentation for the reopening of a Tube station.

Method How to create a brochure

+ prof Évaluation

Grammar
- Le génitif
- Les prépositions *in*, *on* et *at*

Pronunciation
- La diphtongue /aʊ/
- La terminaison -(e)s

Vocabulary
Le métro et les réseaux de transport

Remember how to
- Pronounce dates

Flash

19 Bangalore, the city of tech

▶ How has Bangalore created a new urban identity?

Au carrefour de la tradition et de la modernité, Bangalore est devenue le fer de lance de l'innovation et le royaume des start-ups en Inde.

Le village, le quartier, la ville → p. 210-215

Pictures
- Map of India
- Art project: the Story of Bangalore

Texts
- Bangalore, city of high tech
- A place called home

Videos
- Bangalore: India's own Silicon Valley?
- Guide to living and working in Bangalore

YOUR PROJECTS

Host a radio show: 'Why is Bangalore the ideal place to set up a startup?'

+ prof Évaluation

Grammar
- Le *present perfect* avec *for* et *since*

Pronunciation
- La voyelle brève /ɪ/

Vocabulary

La ville et ses mutations

Remember how to
- Compare the past with the present
- Describe an image

20 From Asia to America

▶ How have Asian immigrants been welcomed into the USA?

Immigrés chinois et japonais aux États-Unis ont dû faire face à de grandes difficultés. Un passé peu connu, que leurs descendants essaient aujourd'hui de remettre en lumière.

Le passé dans le présent → p. 216-229

Pictures
- *Price of Gold,* by Mojo Wang
- Infographic: New U.S. permanent residents 1820-2019
- Movie Star Anna May Wong

Texts
- The Chinese Exclusion Act
- Illinois becomes first state to mandate teaching Asian American History

Videos
- Angel Island, the Ellis Island of the West
- Camps of shame – The early life of Aki
- The myth of the model minority

Audio
- Paper daughters and sons

Entraînement à l'évaluation
- Anna May Wong's legacy
- Then and Now - Two immigration stories

YOUR PROJECTS

Write a biography of a famous Asian American personality.

Record a podcast on Asian immigration history.

Method: How to write a biography

+ prof Évaluation

Grammar
- *Present perfect* ou prétérit ?
- Les propositions de temps

Pronunciation
- La consonne /ʒ/
- L'accentuation des mots en *-ate*

Vocabulary

Immigration et histoire

Remember how to
- Describe and debunk stereotypes

Escape Game

21 Alice's quest for identity

▶ How does Alice's journey through Wonderland help her grow up?

Vous voici projetés dans le monde virtuel de *Wonderland* ! Au fil des rencontre et des énigmes, aidez Alice à partir en quête de son identité et à retrouver son chemin vers la réalité.

Représentation de soi et rapport à autrui

→ p. 230-239

Pictures
- Lewis Carroll and the real Alice
- Illustrations from *Alice in Wonderland* (books and movies)

Textes
- *A Boat Beneath a Sunny Sky*, by Lewis Carroll (poem)
- *Alice in Wonderland*, by Lewis Carroll (extracts)

Videos
- Extracts from *Alice in Wonderland* movies (1999 and 2010)

Audios
- Lewis Carroll and the story of Alice
- *Alice in Wonderland*, by Lewis Carroll (extract from the audiobook)

Annexes

Representation de soi et rapport à autrui

UNIT 1 Welcome to high school

YOUR PROJECTS

Shoot a promotional video for two school clubs!

OR

Prepare a leaflet of extracurricular activities for open day!

Clubs in British schools

A Clubs and activities in a British school **Video** 23lmu2101

1. Watch the video and find as many clubs as possible. Place them in the right category: **sports**, **art**, **languages**, **academic**, **others**.

2. Spot when and where the clubs usually take place.

PAIR WORK 3. Pick a club, present it and tell a classmate why you would like to join.

SUCESS BOX

- **Pour décrire, je peux utiliser :**
  There is + nom singulier
  There are + nom pluriel
- ***a club*** = an extracurricular activity
  /ʌ/ /ə/ /ə/ /ə/ /ə/

- **Pour donner des indications de temps :**
  It takes place + temps/lieu… ***It happens…***
- ***never sometimes often usually always*** + présent simple

at + heure	***on*** + jour (*on Mondays*)
in + mois	***in*** *the morning/the afternoon*

→ *Manga club usually takes place on Tuesdays at 4.30pm.*

- **Exprimer le souhait :** *I **would like/love** to join…* /wʊd/
- **Exprimer la cause :** *because, seeing that, as…*

Online practice makes perfect! **Activities** 23lmu2102

▶ To what extent is choosing a club shaping your identity at school?

B Clubs of the British School of Paris Video 23lmu2103

1. Choose a word cloud and guess the club's activities. Fiche 23lmu2104 (GROUP WORK)

2. Watch the video associated with your cloud. Take as many notes as possible about the club.

3. Write a short description of your club including activities, time and frequency. Share it with your classmates.

SUCESS BOX

- Donner son opinion : *To me, ... / In my opinion, ... / Personally, I think... /As far as I understand, ...*
- Faire des suppositions : *They **must** meet in the art bloc. The members **may** learn how to play instruments.*

- Concentrez-vous sur les chiffres et déterminez s'il s'agit d'**heures**, de **nombres** ou de **dates**.
- Repérez les mots des nuages dans les vidéos.

- Dire l'heure : *1.30pm = **half past one in the afternoon / one thirty in the afternoon***
- Parler d'une plage horaire : ***from** 1.00pm **to** 1.30pm*

Online practice makes perfect! Activities 23lmu2105

Signing up for a club

Clubs and activities

We have some fantastic clubs and activities on offer at Arran High. We certainly make the most of our fantastic location.

You can also take part in trips, productions and help with fundraising for charity.

We think that taking part is so important for you that we have arranged extra school transport to take you home after your clubs. You will also get house points for coming to an after-school club. Clubs run at lunchtime and after school Mondays to Thursdays.

Try something you love already, try something new or try something that is out of your comfort zone. You may discover something you will love for the rest of your life and make new friends!

6

A Clubs and activities at Arran High

Culture Tip **Arran High** is a state-funded secondary school at Lamlash, on the Isle of Arran, Scotland. It is the only secondary school on the island and has around 250 pupils.

SUCESS BOX

1. Choose two clubs or activities available at Arran High: draw each one in the style of the poster, then say why you would like to join them.

Dire ce que l'on aimerait : *I would like to* + V
→ *I would like to join the futsal club because I love playing football.*

2. Read the text and find the following information: activities • timing • advantages. Fiche 23lmu2106

activities	timing	advantages
Focus on 1st paragraph	Look for days / time indications	Look for adjectives / verbs expressing likes and dislikes

3. Try something new! Convince your friend to join your favourite club. Use the advantages listed in the poster.

Donner un conseil : *you should* + V
→ *You should join the futsal club because you should try something new.*

Online practice makes perfect! Activities 23lmu2107

Master chef semi-final in Prince Henry's High School

B High school clubs

FICHE GROUP WORK **1.** Choose a club and write down the following information about it: name • time • place • goal and events.
Then, describe your poster. Fiche 23lmu2108

SUCESS BOX

Pour décrire ce que je vois :
j'utilise le **présent *be* + V-*ing***
→ *In my poster a teenager is dancing.*

2. Prepare questions to ask the other students (name of the club, time, place, goal and events). Go see your classmates to find information about the other clubs.

L'ordre des mots dans les questions :
(WH- word) + Auxiliaire + S + V + (OBJECT) ?
→ *What time does your club start?* (does = Aux., your club = S, start = V)

3. Create a poster for a club of your choice.

Online practice makes perfect! Activities 23lmu2109

Find the right club for you

GROUP WORK

1 Model United Nations club

2 UNICEF club

A In this club you must represent a country honestly and convincingly. You will have to negotiate with other countries that may have different views and reach compromises on such topics[1] as climate change, children's rights, poverty reduction, public health, gender equality and human rights... You will demonstrate your talent for debate and develop a collaborative spirit. You will improve[2] your communication and problem-solving skills.

1. subjects – 2. make better

B Joining this club is an ideal opportunity to get more involved[1] in making our school more environmentally friendly. It provides opportunities for pupils to communicate their feelings as well as influence decisions that are made. You will encourage teachers and students to recycle. The members of the club have the opportunity to develop skills[2] such as confidence, communication and negotiation.

1. engaged – 2. competences

C In this club you will learn to write and express your thoughts, ideas, and voice your opinions. You will understand the importance of good journalism and always question where the information they want to publish has come from. It will make you feel much more confident about interviewing people and seeing your work published.

D If you join this club, you will have a unique opportunity to involve members of your community in global humanitarian issues. Your club will combat global injustice, help save children's lives and give back to those in need. You will organise fundraising events[1] in order to help finance actions. You will learn about issues you've never heard of and how to fight these critical crises.

1. when you collect money

3 Eco warriors club at Frogmore Junior school

Blue & White
Serving Wharton High students since 1997
@NewspaperWHS
February 2021 — 20150 Bruce B. Downs Blvd. Tampa, FL 33647 — Volume 24 Issue 3

WHAT'S INSIDE
Junglelife: Speech and Debate continue to excel during COVID-19 Pg. 3
Hotspot: Satisfy your sweet tooth at Cookie Crumbl Pg. 10
Gameday: Frank Micallef commits to USF for baseball Pg. 15
News: 1-3
Education: 4
Health: 5
Feature: 6-7
Centerspread: 8-9
Entertainment: 10-12
Editorial: 13-14
Sports: 15-16

Biden implements new COVID-19 policies
vladapitner, news editor
PHOTO COURTESY OF • THE WHITE HOUSE

U.S. vs. Australia, tale of two lockdowns
peterchandler, staff writer
PHOTO BY • AUDREY BEST

Hillsborough County Public Schoo (Tampa, Florida)

4 High school newspaper

1. Match each document (1 → 4) with the corresponding club description (A → D).

2. Explain the objectives of the club with words from the description.

PAIR WORK

3. Choose a club you would like to join. There are only two places left: convince the president of the club to choose you.

Student A: you want to join the club. Explain the reasons why it is important for you.

Student B: you are the president. Ask questions, give your decision and explain it.

SUCESS BOX

Pour donner les objectifs, on peut utiliser :
The goal/objective of this club is ***to + V*** */*
it aims to + V
→ *The goal of this club is to bring students together around a charity that fights for people's rights.*

- **Pour parler de soi / de ce que l'on aime :**
  → *I* ***love*** *helping people / I* ***hate*** *injustice*
  (V-ing ou groupe nominal)
  → *I* ***am interested in*** *charity work.*
  (V-ing ou groupe nominal)
- **Pour donner son opinion :**
  → ***To me / in my opinion,*** *helping people is important.*

Online practice makes perfect! Activities 23lmu2110

Path to success

Start

Choose two clubs.

List the information about your clubs: activities, events, outings and practical information.

Path 1

Organise your notes with **link words**: *first, second, third, in addition, for example...*

Use the **present simple** to speak about your clubs' activities. Check the endings of your verbs.

Use **adverbs of frequency** to say how often your meetings take place.

Use ***should*** to invite others to join.

Use ***because*** to explain why they should join your clubs.

Choose 5 keywords for each club.

Find a creative way of shooting your video: a poster presentation, acting your own role in the school...

Record yourself and check your pronunciation.

Path 2

List original arguments to convince new students to join.

Write an introductive paragraph.

Use the **present simple** to speak about your clubs' meetings and activities. Check the endings of your verbs.

Invite people to try new things with ***should***.

Design your leaflet and choose illustrations. You can use Canva.com.

Improve your Vocabulary

Lexique 23lmu2111

PROJECT 1

Shoot a promotional video for two school clubs!

You are the president of two clubs in a British high school.
Present them in a video to the new students.

- Choose your two clubs. — Pick two from the unit or find others that exist in a British school on the internet.
- List all the information about the club. — Make sure you use adverbs of frequency and the correct prepositions of time and place.
- Explain what students will be able to do. — Use ***will*** to present the different activities.
- Prepare your notes and check your pronunciation. — Make a list of five keywords for each club and check your pronunciation of difficult words.
- Record your 1'30 video. — Be creative to promote your clubs and speak at least for one minute and thirty seconds.

PROJECT 2

Prepare a leaflet of extracurricular activities for open day!

You are a student in a British high school. Prepare a leaflet about two clubs you will present on open day.

- Choose your school. — Choose a British school in the unit or on the internet, and imagine the clubs and activities it might offer.
- Select two clubs. — Introduce their activities and important information such as time, location and supervisor.
- Use images and/or drawings. — Find a photo or an illustration in order to motivate students to join.
- Show the school's objectives. — Explain the impacts / opportunities your clubs can have on students, using *should: "You should join because you will..."*

Le passé dans le présent

UNIT 2 Scotland: land of legends

▶ How does Scotland keep its legends alive?

YOUR PROJECTS

Join the #TalesofScotland contest!

Write an Instagram post to promote tourism based on Scottish legends.

OR

Record a podcast about Scottish myths and legends.

visitscotland.com

A Scotland's year of stories **Video** 23lmu2201

WORD BOX

- an **em**blem = a **sym**bol
- a **land**scape /ˈlændskeɪp/
- a myth /mɪθ/ = a **leg**end, a tale /teɪl/
- **sun**set: when you last see the sun before the night
- **Scot**land / **Scot**tish
- tell a **sto**ry
- **vis**it, dis**cov**er

PAIR WORK

1. Watch the video with the sound off and take notes.
2. Watch it again with the sound on and guess the purpose of this video.
3. Sum it up in a tweet.

Pronunciation Listen to these words and repeat them. Pay attention to the pronunciation of the underlined letters: *Scotland, loyal, wonder, protect, discover*.
Audio 23lmu2202

Capital city: Edinburgh

Largest city: Glasgow

Official languages: English, Scots, Scottish Gaelic

Union with England: 1707

Currency: Pound Sterling

Politics: Scotland is part of the United Kingdom. It is represented in both the Scottish Parliament and the Parliament of the UK.

B

1. Brainstorm what you know about Scotland with your classmates.
2. Look at the map and the information card for one minute. Close your books and tell your classmates what you remember.
3. Guess the motivations for creating this map.
4. Explain why Scotland is a land of "myths and legends".
5. Leave a voice note to your friend listing the reasons why they should visit Scotland.

Remember how to

Boost your memory > Doc B.

- Concentrez-vous sur ce que vous avez besoin de retenir. Répétez-le plusieurs fois à l'oral ou dans votre tête.
- Écrivez tout une ou plusieurs fois.
- Séparez les éléments à retenir en plusieurs catégories qui faciliteront la mémorisation (villes, personnages...).
- Entraînez-vous régulièrement avec des choses du quotidien, par exemple en essayant de retenir les chansons de votre playlist.

1 Once upon a time in Scotland

GROUP WORK

DIFFÉRENCIATION

THE SELKIES

Hopeless romantics, beware[1]. The selkie (Orcadian dialect for seal[2]) is an alluring shape-shifting[3] creature which resembles a seal in the water but assumes human form on dry land. The graceful selkie may look astonishingly beautiful, but they can leave you lovesick forever. Eternally lustful[4], a selkie will capture the hearts of human beings and then disappear forever into the ocean, leaving behind a few broken hearts.

Yes, it is thought that both male and female selkies can elegantly emerge from the water as beautiful people and intense seductive powers over humans. After finding love and spending years on land, 'selkie folk' will always crave a return to the sea, their rightful home. In some tales, humans hide the seal skins to prevent them returning home to the ocean.

Other stories say that selkies have a moral consciousness and return to play with their children at the seashore and visit them regularly once they've gone back to the sea.

visitscotland.com

1. pay attention – **2.** *phoque* – **3.** able to change its form – **4.** sensual

A Group 1

THE HEADLESS DRUMMER OF EDINBURGH CASTLE

Sometimes in the dead of night or at dawn[1] or dusk, the distant sound of drumming can be heard reverberating around the fortress of Edinburgh Castle. [...]

No one knows exactly who or what the source of this ghostly sound is, but legends tell us it belongs to one of Edinburgh Castle's infamous[2] phantoms: the Headless Drummer Boy. His identity and the story behind his decapitation remain a mystery, but it is said he made his first appearance in 1650. This was the fateful year Oliver Cromwell launched his invasion of Scotland which culminated in the capture of the castle following a three-month siege. Ever since then the drummer has been seen as a bad omen[3] whose apparition foretells imminent disaster for the castle.

Even now, during quiet times of the day, the unmistakable 'rat-a-tat-tat' sound of drums is heard, seemingly emanating from all directions, without a mortal drummer to be seen or found.

visitscotland.com

1. when the sun appears in the morning (≠ dusk) – **2.** famous – **3.** sign of a future event

B Group 2

WORD BOX

- a spot = a place
- the best ≠ the worst
- brave = courageous
- **spooky** /'spu:ki/ = **terrifying**
- **cultural** /'kʌltʃərəl/
- known for = **famous** for
- take place = **happen**
- get **goose**bumps /'gu:sbʌmps/ = be scared
- ring a bell = **remind** you of sth, sound **familiar**

THE GREEN LADY OF CRATHES CASTLE

Within the walls of the 16th century Crathes Castle stalks the Green Lady. [...] But who is she?

The Green Lady always appears in the same room, pacing back and forth from the fireplace, sometimes cradling an infant in her arms. Some say that she is an apparition of a servant girl who fell pregnant out of wedlock[1] and fled the castle never to be seen again. But a grisly[2] discovery allegedly[3] unearthed while the castle was being renovated in the 1800s tells a far more sinister story. It is said that beneath the hearthstone of the fireplace workmen uncovered the skeletal remains of a woman and child. She may not have been sighted in many years, but one thing is certain: an unspeakable sense of dread is felt by all who dare to step foot in the room of the Green Lady.

visitscotland.com

1. out of marriage – 2. horrible – 3. supposedly

C Group 3

FICHE GROUP WORK

1. Work on your document (A, B or C).
Read your group's legend and take notes about: place • action • time Fiche 23lmu2203

2. Fill your grid to exchange information about your legend with the other groups. Be ready to answer your classmate's questions.

3. Watch the video and take notes.

A Night in a Haunted Castle, BBC Scotland
Video 23lmu2204

4. Discuss which legend it resembles and justify your answer.

Grammar Read text B. Identify the verbs in the simple past. Are they regular or irregular? What is this tense used for?

Remember how to

Tell a story in the past

Vous pouvez utiliser :

- **le prétérit** pour faire avancer le récit :
  → *She **fell** pregnant out of wedlock.*
- le prétérit *be* + V-*ing* pour apporter des explications :
  → *She **was haunting** the castle when visitors came in.*
- **des marqueurs de temps :**
  → *years ago, a long time ago, in the 17th century, on December 15th 1625...*
- **Le présent simple** pour parler des conséquences de votre histoire dans le présent :
  → *All visitors **feel** dread when they **visit** the castle.*

PREPARE YOUR PROJECT

Host a radio show

You and your group are hosting a radio show about Scottish myths and legends. Discuss which legend you prefer, explain why and what places tourists should visit to learn more about it.

2 And the legends live on!

Culture Tip A "loch" /lɒx/ is a Scottish Gaelic word for lake, but you can also see lochs in England and Ireland.

A "Discover Our Stories at Visit Inverness Loch Ness"

1. Watch the video and focus on how Nessie appeared.
   Video 23lmu2205
2. Explain how Nessie is described and why it is described this way.
3. List the elements showing that Nessie is a legend.
4. Make hypotheses on why this video was created.
5. Now, your turn! Imagine the story of how you first spotted Nessie.

Many tourist reviews of Loch Ness on travel websites like TripAdvisor note that they came away from their visit without having spotted the lake's most famous resident, Nessie. Some have posited the creature is just a tourism ploy[1] — and give the Loch five stars anyway.

Whether they view the Loch Ness Monster as a fun story, an elaborate hoax[2], or an undiscovered species, millions of tourists flock to the cryptid's[3] alleged home each year. "You can see that people come to Loch Ness simply because of Nessie," Gary Campbell, a chartered accountant based in Inverness, Scotland, and founder of the Loch Ness Monster fan club, tells Mental Floss. "It's lovely and the scenery is nice and all, but they come because of the Loch Ness Monster." Campbell released a study in 2018 analyzing the number of tourist dollars Nessie generates for Scotland. He determined the monster adds roughly £41 million to the Scottish economy in a typical year. Not bad for a mythical creature.

mentalfloss.com

1. strategy – 2. something false, a trick – 3. the creature's

Culture Tip The Loch Ness monster's story dates back to the 6th century but became known worldwide in the 1930s when many people reported having seen a monster. Sea monsters have always been popular in Scotland. Children were even forbidden to swim into deep rivers for fear of these creatures!

B

1. Find elements characterising Nessie and draw conclusions about what she represents for people.
2. Look for numbers and figures in the text and explain what they reveal about Nessie.
3. You went to Loch Ness and did not see the monster, which disappointed you. Write a review on Tripadvisor entitled *"Nessie is only about business!"*.

BEWARE OF KELPIES!

A Kelpie is the most common water spirit in Scottish folklore and is said to haunt the deep pools in rivers and streams, usually in the form of a lost horse. This mythological transforming beast allegedly has the strength and endurance of a hundred horses. But beware… this is not some gentle pony but a malevolent spirit who will eat you for dinner! [...]

The Kelpie is apparently particularly attractive to children, yet once on its back, their hide[1] becomes sticky, trapping the child which it promptly drags into the water, then eats. A tale is recounted of ten children who were out playing when they discover a "pony" on the banks of a river. Nine of the siblings climb onto its back, but one child strokes[2] its nose and his finger becomes stuck[3]. He escapes by managing to cut off his finger. However, the other children are pulled into the water, never to return!

spookyscotland.net

1. skin – 2. caresses – 3. glued

C

1. Describe where you can encounter a Kelpie.
2. Note down the physical characteristics of that creature.
3. Recap what happens if you come too close to one.
4. Use the text and the Culture tip to prepare your own comic strip of the Kelpie legend.

D A tribute to the Kelpies Video 23lmu2206

Culture Tip Kelpies are very popular in contemporary literature: J.K Rowling herself used this legend in both *Harry Potter* and *Fantastic Beasts*.

WORD BOX

- a **her**itage
- a sou**venir**
- a **trib**ute /ˈtrɪbjuːt/ = recog**ni**tion
- com**mer**cial = **ad**vert
- fi**nan**cial /faɪˈnænʃəl/
- at**tract** = tempt, lure /lʊər/

1. Watch the first part of the video (→ 0'20) and take notes: what the statues represent • their name • their characteristics • date • place
   Use Fiche 23lmu2207
2. Watch the second part (0'20 → end). Recap what Andy Scott's ambition was when he decided to make these sculptures.
3. List the elements that show the social importance of horses in Scotland.
4. Record the audio guide for Andy Scott's Kelpies. Describe the sculptures, then explain how they link the past to the present.

PREPARE YOUR PROJECT

Participate to a group chat

Visit Scotland, the Scottish tourist office, wants to create a new hashtag: #LegendsOfScotland.
In groups, decide which legend you want to launch the hashtag with on your WhatsApp group chat. Discuss and explain which legend should be promoted and why.

IMPROVE YOUR Grammar

Activités en ligne
23lmu2208

Le prétérit simple

Tyron's Tips
23lmu2209

- Le prétérit se forme de la façon suivante :

verbe + *-ed* (verbes réguliers) : → *I worked*	**Forme affirmative**	forme à apprendre (verbes irréguliers) : → *I ran*

Forme négative	**Forme interrogative**
DID NOT ou ***DIDN'T*** + V → *I **didn't work***	***DID*** + sujet + V → ***Did** you **work**?*

- Le prétérit est **le temps du récit** : il est employé pour raconter des événements révolus sans lien avec le moment présent. On l'utilise dans les romans, les contes, les livres d'histoire, etc.
- On trouve très souvent le prétérit **avec des compléments de temps** qui permettent de dater les événements : *in 2015, last week, in the 19th century, a long time ago*, etc.
  → *The ghost **made** his first appearance **in 1650**.*

> Précis p. 260

1 **Mettez les verbes soulignés à la forme négative puis à la forme interrogative.**

a. We visited Edinburgh Castle two years ago.
b. My grandmother told me this old Scottish tale when I was younger.

2 a) **Mettez le verbe entre parenthèses au prétérit. Attention aux verbes irréguliers !**

The modern legend of the Loch Ness Monster *(be)* born in 1933, when a couple *(see)* a huge animal near Loch Ness. A few days later, a Scottish newspaper *(report)* the incident, and numerous sightings *(follow)*. Later that same year, a man allegedly *(take)* the first photo of the monster.

b) **Repérez les compléments de temps qui déclenchent l'emploi du prétérit.**

Les superlatifs de supériorité

- Le superlatif permet d'indiquer qu'un élément d'un groupe surpasse tous les autres. On le traduit en français par ***le / la / les plus* + adjectif**.
  → *Loch Ness is **the most mysterious lake** in the world.*
- On peut le construire de deux façons :

adjectifs longs (une syllabe)	***the*** adjectif + ***-est*** → ***the** old**est** castle*
adjectifs longs (deux syllabes ou plus)	***the most*** + adjectif → ***the most** frightening story*

On double la consonne dans : *big → **biggest**, sad → **saddest**, hot → **hottest**.*

- Les adjectifs de deux syllabes se terminant par ***-y*** forment leur superlatif en ***-iest*** : *scary → **scariest**, happy → **happiest**.*
- Il existe quelques superlatifs irréguliers : *good → **the best*** *bad → **the worst***

> Précis p. 255

3 **Mettez l'adjectif entre parenthèses à la forme du superlatif de supériorité.**

a. What is ... *(large)* city in Scotland?
b. Loch Ness is ... *(famous)* lake in the UK.
c. This is ... *(dark)* and ... *(sad)* legend I've ever heard!
d. Some people believe Edinburgh Castle is one of ... *(haunted)* and ... *(spooky)* castles in the UK.

4 a) **Quels sont les contes ou légendes de l'unité qui évoquent le plus les adjectifs suivants ?**

scary • romantic • pessimistic • weird • bad

b) **Rédigez 5 phrases pour en parler, en utilisant des comparatifs de supériorité.**
Ex : *The legend of the Kelpies is **the spookiest story** I know.*

IMPROVE YOUR Pronunciation

La prononciation de la terminaison *-ed*

Audio 23lmu2210

- La terminaison ***-ed*** du prétérit et du participe passé peut avoir trois prononciations possibles en fonction du dernier son du verbe :

Après une voyelle ou les consonnes /b/, /g/, /z/, /v/, /l/, /m/, /n/, /ʒ/, /dʒ/, /r/	/d/ *loved, called, continued*
Après les consonnes /p/, /k/, /s/, /f/, /ʃ/, /tʃ/	/t/ *passed, pushed, looked*
Consonne /d/ **et** /t/	/ɪd/ *wanted, decided*

La terminaison *-ed* ne se prononce **jamais** /ed/ comme dans *bed* !

1 a) **Classez ces verbes au prétérit en fonction de la prononciation de *-ed*.**

tried • walked • renovated • determined • stopped • used • crowded • bewitched • arrived

/t/	/d/	/ɪd/

b) **Écoutez pour vérifier vos réponses et répétez.**
Audio 23lmu2211

La voyelle *schwa* /ə/

Audio 23lmu2212

- On appelle « schwa » le son voyelle que l'on trouve dans les articles ***an*** et ***the***. Ce son ressemble au e de « petit » en français. On le représente par le symbole /ə/. Il s'agit de la voyelle la plus fréquente de l'anglais.
- Cette voyelle apparaît toujours dans **une syllabe inaccentuée.**

Scotland ◯○ /ə/ *legend* ◯○ /ə/ *famous* ◯○ /ə/

Les voyelles des syllabes inaccentuées sont souvent prononcées /ə/.

Le schwa peut être représenté par des graphies très diverses (*a, o, e, u, ...*)

2 a) **Écoutez les mots suivants, recopiez-les puis répétez-les.**
Audio 23lmu2213

ago • malevolent • phantom • attract • forever • distant • cultural

b) **Soulignez les syllabes accentuées. Les voyelles inaccentuées sont-elles prononcées /ə/ ?**

3 **Dans la phrase suivante, notez les voyelles prononcées /ə/.**

In Scottish mythology, a Kelpie is a dangerous shape-shifting water creature who haunts a river or a stream, usually in the shape of a horse.

Écoutez et répétez. **Audio** 23lmu2214

IMPROVE YOUR Vocabulary

Activités en ligne 23lmu2222

Cultural heritage

TRADITIONS

Audio 23lmu2219

- a **her**itage = a **leg**acy
- an adap**ta**tion
- a re**vi**val
- **cus**toms = **hab**its
- be proud of
- pass on = trans**mit**, share
- con**serve** = pro**tect**
- stand up for = de**fend**

TOURISM

Audio 23lmu2220

- **tra**vel **in**dustry
- a tour
- a **pack**age **hol**iday
- an ad**van**tage ≠ a **draw**back, a **down**side
- a**broad**
- go **sight**seeing = visit **tour**ist sights
- at**tract tour**ists
- have a **pos**itive/**neg**ative **im**pact

DESCRIBING TOURISTIC PLACES

Audio 23lmu2221

- a **sce**nery = a **land**scape
- a **fa**mous site
- a view
- a **must**-see
- ma**jes**tic
- **breath**taking = **stri**king, **stun**ning
- **tour**isty
- **crowd**ed ≠ **peace**ful, **qui**et

Myths and legends

CREATURES

Audio 23lmu2215

- a ghost, a **spir**it
- a **fair**y / **fair**ies
- a **mer**maid
- a **were**wolf
- a **lep**rechaun
- a **gob**lin
- a **wa**ter horse

PLACES AND SETTINGS

Audio 23lmu2217

- a loch /lɒx/ = a lake
- a creek
- a cave = a **cav**ern
- a lane = a small road
- a **chap**el
- a ruin
- a tomb /tuːm/ = a grave
- a **grave**yard = a **cem**etery

DESCRIBING SCARY PLACES

Audio 23lmu2216

- **ee**rie /ˈɪəri/ = mys**te**rious
- **chill**ing = **scar**y, **creep**y, **spook**y
- **des**olate
- **din**gy = dark, **gloom**y, grim
- **grue**some = **hor**rible

SUPERNATURAL

Audio 23lmu2218

- an appa**ri**tion
- a curse = a bad spell
- a **flick**er = a flame, a light
- sur**real** /səˈrɪəl/
- **wick**ed /ˈwɪkɪd/ = evil, **dan**gerous
- moan /məʊn/ = cry, groan
- be**witch** = charm, **cap**tivate
- chop off = cut, slice

1 ***Time's Up!*** **Make your group guess as many words as possible using definitions, synonyms, and mime.**

2 **Pick 5 words from one of the texts p. 26-29. Use them to describe the legend so that your friend can deduce which creature you are talking about.**

3 **Use at least 10 words from the mind map above to explain why Scottish myths and legends have a strong impact on today's Scotland.**

Let's RECAP

Faites le point ! Complétez la fiche bilan avec les documents que vous avez étudiés. **Fiche** 23lmu2223

AXE 8

The past in the present

How does Scotland keep its legends alive?

#mythsandlegends
What are the most famous myths and legends in Scotland?

#yearsofstories
How are Scottish people passing on their tales and legends nowadays?

#scottishheritage
Why are Scottish myths and legends part of Scotland's cultural heritage?

#scottishtourism
How are Scottish myths and legends used to attract tourists?

GROUP WORK Choose a question and discuss.

Quiz 23lmu2224

Become AN EXPERT

Lisez et écoutez de l'anglais en dehors de la classe

Music

- *Blackbriar*, "Selkie" (2021)

Books

- *An Illustrated Treasury of Scottish Folks and Fairy Tales*, Theresa Breslin and Kate Leiper

- *Ivanhoe*, Sir Walter Scott (1819) vers **LLCER**
- *Luckenbooth*, Jenni Fagan (2021)
- *The Outlander*, Diana Gabaldon (1991) vers **LLCER**
- *Scottish Folk and Fairy Tales from Burns to Buchan*, Penguin Classics (1992) vers **LLCER**

Series & films

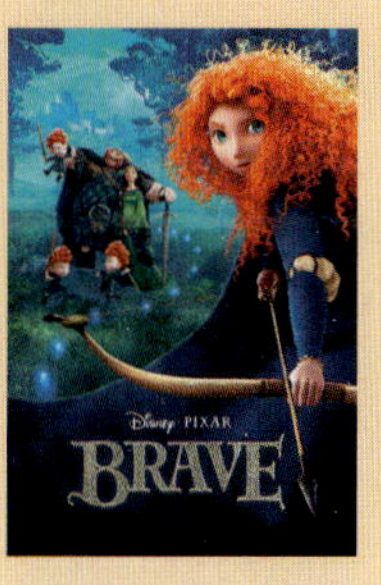

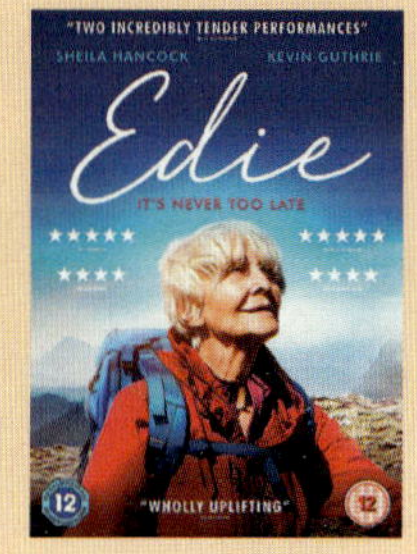

YOUR PROJECTS

Join the #TalesOfScotland contest!

Write an Instagram post

You work for Visit Scotland, the Scottish tourist office.
Using #TalesOfScotland, promote tourism in the country.

- Pick a Scottish myth or legend. — Choose a legend from the unit or do some research on the internet to find another one.
- Sum up the story. — Use the preterite to talk about the legend and present simple to talk about its impact.
- Give examples on the way this myth represents Scotland. — Use superlatives to show this legend gives the best image of the country.
- Give tourists some advice about where they should go and what they should do. — You can suggest places, museums or shops.
- Pick a picture to illustrate your post and use hashtags.

OR

Record a podcast

Choose a myth, present it, then explain why it is still alive in today's Scotland. Vote for the best podcast!

- Pick a Scottish myth of legend. — Choose a legend from the unit or do some research on the internet to find another one.
- Tell the story. — Use the correct tenses to narrate your story. Add adjectives to make it catchy!
- Explain why it is a good story. — Use superlatives to show this story is the most fascinating or the scariest.
- Give proof to show that this story still has an impact today. — Explain how this story may have influenced art, tourism, the economy, etc.

BUILD UP YOUR SKILLS

How to write an Instagram post

Visitscotland • **Follow**
Orkney
...

Visitscotland Oh, Orkney!
With around 70 islands & nearly 600 miles of coastline, there's no denying this part of Scotland has some absolutely stunning natural landscapes! Loving this collection of snaps by @rachelvisual taken across the islands

📍 Rousay
📍 Hoy
📍 Stromness
📍 Rackwick Bay

@visitorkney #Orkney #Rousay #Hoy #Stromness #RackwickBay #Scotland #VisitScotland #VisitOrkney

4 weeks

11 304 Likes
October 13, 2022

www.instagram.com

1. Pour le préparer

- Identifiez l'objectif de la publication : faire la promotion d'un lieu, d'un patrimoine culturel, d'un artiste, d'un site naturel...
- Listez les arguments à présenter pour convaincre les lecteurs.
- Trouvez une image qui attire l'oeil.
- Employez des formulations accrocheuses.

2. Pour le réaliser

- Pensez aux applications gratuites pour générer des posts Instagram tels que Canva ou Zeoob.
- Vérifiez que vous avez bien respecté les consignes de la tâche.
- Utilisez des émojis.

Are you ready?

+ prof Évaluation

Entraînement à l'évaluation

Compréhension orale

Faites un compte-rendu en français de l'audio.

history.org

Podcast: Scottish myths and legends Audio 23lmu2225

- Analysez le titre du document pour repérer sa thématique.
- Repérez les mots clés en lien avec l'unité pour comprendre le sujet.
- Repérez les noms propres pour identifier les lieux mentionnés.

Production écrite

You have just listened to this podcast from history.org.
React on their website, explaining what you learnt. (120 words)

Compréhension écrite

THE GHOST PIPER OF CLANYARD BAY

The unmistakable blast of the bagpipes is a common sound in Scotland, particularly in our cities and at festivals and celebrations. But what happens when the piper himself vanishes into thin air? There are several stories of phantom pipers throughout Scottish history and folklore. In days gone by, a dark network of tunnels was said to extend from the Cove of Grennan to the cliffs* of Clanyard Bay, near Stranraer.

Locals believed that fairies lived in these tunnels and caves, and no one dared to go inside and disturb them until one day, a piper boldly entered the caves. He played his pipes loudly, accompanied by his faithful brown dog. The music droned on for hours, slowly fading away until it couldn't be heard. Suddenly, the dog ran out of the cave terrified and howling, without any of its hair! The piper was never seen again.

Although the caves are now long gone, on summer nights, passers-by have heard the distant sound of bagpipes coming from deep under the ground.

Perhaps it's the wind whistling through the old underground caves, maybe it's just a trick of the mind, or maybe… just maybe, it's the spirit of the piper, playing his Scottish melodies forevermore.

www.scotland.org

* a precipice, often on a coast

1. Identify and describe where this tale takes place.
2. Pick out elements about the characters and the events from this tale.
3. Comment on the atmosphere of this tale.
4. Show how this tale could be used to attract tourists to the area.

> **Analysez la source du document : à qui s'adresse ce texte ?**
> **Relevez les adjectifs décrivant l'atmosphère de cette légende pour exprimer ce qu'elle vous fait ressentir.**

Production écrite

Using elements from this tale, write an article for #VisitScotland to invite people to come visit Clanyard Bay. (120 words)

Flash UNIT 3

Les univers professionnels, le monde du travail

Acting teens

How do celeb teens fit into the entertainment industry?

YOUR PROJECT

It's Career Day. As a teen actor, talk about the pros and cons of being in the entertainment industry.

1 Teen artists

Goalcast

Stranger Things Is Breaking One Dangerous (And Deadly) Hollywood Pattern

The cast[1] *of 'Stranger Things' consists mainly of children. They have grown up in the spotlight but managed to stay out of the tabloids and break the negative pattern*[2] *typically seen in child acting. Has Hollywood changed or are the kids just… alright?* [...]

How Have The Cast of *Stranger Things* Handled Life Under a Spotlight?

According to sources, the B-tier cast, which is made up of the child stars, cash in at around $250,000 per episode. That's a lot of money for anyone, let alone children who most likely haven't learned the true value of money yet. And then there's the fame dilemma[3].

So, how are this new generation of child actors handling their immense stardom? According to an interview they did in Teen Vogue, they're doing quite well. "The show is so well-received, and we're just very grateful," Millie Bobby Brown said, "We really couldn't have done this without Netflix and the Duffers[4]."

When asked about how they felt about their fame, the theme really was appreciation. "It's a great feeling to know that so many people appreciate your work," Gaten Matarazzo stated, "It makes me feel good that people will go out of their way to follow me and message me."

It was Finn Wolfhard who truly acknowledged the craziness of it all. Very candidly, he said, "For me it's sort of surreal… My Twitter followers went up and my Instagram followers went up, and I'm getting recognized on the street, which is also very weird for me." [...]

1. performers – 2. system – 3. difficult choice – 4. *Stranger Things*' creators, directors and producers

A

Bianca Mercuri, *Goalcast*, 2022

Culture Tip

Actors are usually classified into categories called A/B/C/D/...-lists.
A-list actors are considered extremely famous and bring millions to the box office. These categories also help determine how much money these actors earn.

Face to Face, YouTube

B Playing *Matilda* on the West End | Lara Wollington

Video 23lmu2301

1. Read lines 1-5 [Doc A]. Pick out two things the cast of *Stranger Things* managed to do.
2. Create a mind-map:

   the terms used by the journalist
   ↑
   child stardom
   ↓
   the terms used by *Stranger Things* actors

3. Explain lines 28-29: *"It was Finn Wolfhard who truly acknowledged the craziness of it all."*.
4. Email an American agent to convince him/her you can become a teen actor in Hollywood.

---

1. Read the Culture tip and watch the video. Pick up information about: career • fame • experience.
2. List Lara's positive and negative experiences.
3. Explain what allowed Lara to pursue her goals in this industry.
4. Act out! You are two teen artists:
   - one of you is having a difficult time in the entertainment industry,
   - the other one isn't.

Culture Tip

The West End of London is famous for its many theatres where multiple shows and musicals are playing.

Remember how to

Compare and contrast two facts > Docs A/B

- Pour montrer que **deux situations sont similaires** : ***likewise*** ou ***similarly***.
  → *Lara became famous when she was 9. **Likewise**, Millie had to handle celebrity at the age of 12.*
- Pour marquer **un contraste** entre deux propositions, on peut utiliser :
  - ***while*** *et* ***whereas*** *[alors que / tandis que]*
    → *Lara is a stage performer, **while** Finn is a TV actor.*
  - ***unlike*** *et* ***contrary to*** *[contrairement à / à la différence de] :*
    → ***Unlike*** *their grownup co-stars, they have to get up for school.*
    (their grownup co-stars : groupe nominal ou pronom)

WORD BOX

- an **act**or
- a cast = the perform**er**s
- a **com**pany
- a re**hear**sal /rɪ'hɜːsəl/
- the **au**dience = the **pub**lic
- recog**ni**tion
- ac**claim**ed
- re**mark**able = **won**derful
- be in the **pub**lic eye
- re**hearse** = **prac**tise
- per**form**

2 Being too famous, too soon?

GROUP WORK

DIFFÉRENCIATION

Lennie and Ellie do a particular, and quite peculiar, job: they are child actors who perform in a wholly adult environment, in shows their parents would never take them to see. It requires them to stay up well past bedtime – and, unlike their grownup co-stars, they also have to get up for school the next day. [...]

There are plenty of other disruptions. Under-16s (actors are classed as adults when they hit 16) can't stop going to school just because they're in a show: Lennie keeps up with missed lessons by going over work backstage[1], but Wesley, five years his senior, will spend half his weekend on additional homework when he's performing. Tiredness is another issue: Lennie usually goes to bed at 8pm, Ellie at 9.30pm, yet their curtain calls[2] aren't until 10pm – and then they have to travel home. "When I first started in Enron, I was almost falling asleep in my lessons, because I wasn't used to it," Ellie admits. But complaints have to be prised out of the children because for them, acting is simply a thrill[3]. [...] Ellie gets closest when she says: "I like the attention, the fact everyone is looking at you." [...]

Maddy Costa, The Guardian

1. out of the public view – 2. end of the show – 3. a strong emotion

A **A quick curtain call. Then bed: Child actors in adult theatre**

As we reach the 20th anniversary of the magical British blockbusters, the real magic lies in the way its young stars have stayed on the rails – unlike many before them. [...]

Daniel Radcliffe, Emma Watson and Rupert Grint – are still alive, apparently content, and not noticeably addicted to class A drugs. [...]

Their post-Potter lives could so easily have been different. [...] Chris Columbus, director of the first two instalments[1], [expressed] "a need to protect these kids against what can eventually go wrong if you star in a film of this magnitude."

He would know. After all, he directed the biggest child stars of the previous decade: Macaulay Culkin, who was nine when he shot *Home Alone*, and Mara Wilson, just six during the making of *Mrs Doubtfire*. Both are now synonymous with the trauma and turbulence that can befall a child actor. Culkin became embroiled[2] in legal disputes with his parents. "I was just a machine," he said in 2000. "I had been wanting to stop since I was about 11." Wilson, later the star of *Matilda*, felt washed-up before she hit adolescence, and came to resent[3] her success. "It felt very out of control to have everybody know my name," she says in the recent HBO documentary *Showbiz Kids*. "I didn't feel like I could trust anybody. And that's still a problem I have now." [...]

Ryan Gilbey, The Guardian

1. episodes – 2. involved – 3. feel angry about

B **The not so cursed child: did *Harry Potter* mark the end of troubled young actors?**

Zoe Brough was just 10 when she was cast as Iris in Jennifer Haley's dystopian drama *The Nether* [...] – scenarios to summon a parent's worst nightmares. "When I got the part," Brough explains, "the director, Jeremy Herrin, had a sit-down meeting with my parents, discussing any concerns my mum and dad had about the project, and they each had a chat with me. They felt I was in a completely safe pair of hands. I could not have asked for a better team." Despite the grim[1] subject matter, Iris's scenes are framed as golden-lit fantasy, which made it easier to protect the young actors. In rehearsal, Brough and Isabelle Pappas, who shared the role, were "separated from some scenes that were deemed[2] indecent for our age. Jeremy would direct us then send us away with a chaperone." Herrin confirms that "we were rigorous in making sure they weren't around. If you're really careful, there's no osmosis[3]."

David Jays, The Guardian

1. dark – 2. considered – 3. transfer/influence

C **'There is no book of rules': how theatres aim to safeguard child actors**

FICHE GROUP WORK

1. Work on one of these texts (A, B or C).

a) Pick out elements to show that being a teen performer is a risky business. Use **Fiche** 23lmu2302

b) Describe how these teen performers were kept safe in the entertainment industry.

c) Explain how adults who supervise child actors play a significant part in their well-being.

2. Act out the scene: your British friend is worried about your experience in the entertainment industry. Reassure them about your well-being.

Grammar In text B, pick out a verb in the present perfect. How is it formed?

WORD BOX

- compe**ti**tion
- expec**ta**tions
- **pres**sure
- **spot**lights
- **men**tal health
- **wea**riness = **tired**ness
- **safe**guard = pro**tect**

Remember how to

Choose between active and passive voice GROUP WORK A/B/C

- Lorsqu'on veut faire porter l'attention sur le sujet grammatical, mais que ce n'est pas lui qui est à l'origine de l'action, on peut utiliser la voix passive :

  BE* + participe passé du verbe + *by

  → *Children* ***were kept*** *safe* ***by*** *the director of the film.*
  Sujet — complément d'agent (= à l'origine de l'action)

- Parfois, il n'est pas nécessaire de mentionner le complément d'agent :
  → *The two young actors* ***are separated*** *from inappropriate scenes.*

MEMORY CHALLENGE

1-minute challenge: give as many adjectives as you can to define teens' experience in the entertainment industry.

IMPROVE YOUR Grammar

Activités en ligne 23lmu2303

Le *present perfect*

Tyron's Tips 23lmu2304

	Toutes les personnes	3e personne du singulier
Forme affirmative	***HAVE*** ou ***'VE*** + participe passé → *You **have worked***	***HAS*** ou ***'S*** + participe passé → *He's / **has worked***
Forme négative	***HAVE NOT*** ou ***HAVEN'T*** + participe passé → *You **haven't worked***	***HAS NOT*** ou ***HASN'T*** + participe passé → *He **hasn't worked***

Le participe passé des verbes réguliers se construit en ajoutant *-ed* (*worked*). Les verbes irréguliers ont une forme qu'il faut apprendre (*take* → *taken*, etc.). → p. 275

- Le *present perfect* permet de **faire un bilan ou parler de son expérience.** Il est souvent employé avec les adverbes ***never*** (jamais), ***ever*** (déjà, employé dans des questions), ***always*** (toujours), ***already*** (déjà).
  → *She's only 15 but **has already appeared** in three films.*

Yet (déjà/encore) est employé dans les phrases négatives et interrogatives. Il est souvent placé en fin de phrase. → *Those teenagers **haven't learned** the true value of money **yet**.*

> Précis p. 262

1 **Mettez les verbes entre parenthèses au *present perfect* simple.**

a. I ... (*always / dream*) of becoming an actor. But I ... (*not / take*) any acting classes yet.

b. Teen actors ... (*always / be*) very popular in Hollywood.

c. We ... (*never / see*) an episode of *Stranger Things.*

d. This young actress... (*grow up*) in the spotlight but her parents ... (*manage*) to keep her safe.

2 a) **Préparez 5 questions au *présent perfect* pour interviewer une jeune actrice. Utilisez les verbes et adverbes ci-dessous.**

meet sb • audition for sth • appear in sth • be harassed by sb (être harcelé) • have a passion for sth

b) **Imaginez 5 réponses à vos questions.**

IMPROVE YOUR Pronunciation

La voyelle longue /iː/

Audio 23lmu2305

- La voyelle de ***teen*** est une voyelle longue proche du *i* français. On la représente par le symbole /iː/. Elle correspond à plusieurs graphies :

ee	*teen, keep, feel*
ea	*beat, dream*
ie	*believe, piece*
dans les terminaisons **-*e*se, -*e*te**, -***e****de*, -***e****me*	*Japanese, complete, precede, theme*

Il ne faut pas confonde le i long /iː/ avec la voyelle brève /ɪ/ de *big*, un son plus bref intermédiaire entre le *i* et le *è* de *père* (la bouche est un peu plus fermée). La voyelle /ɪ/ est souvent représentée par la graphie *i* : *kid, bit.*

1 a) **Recopiez les paires de mots suivantes. Soulignez en vert le mot qui contient la voyelle longue /iː/ et en rouge celui qui contient la voyelle brève /ɪ/.**

a) hit/heat b) tin/teen c) sheep/ship
d) bit/beat e) live/leave

Écoutez l'enregistrement pour vérifier vos réponses et répétez. Audio 23lmu2306

b) **Trouvez trois autres paires de mots du même type.**

2 a) **Trouvez les homophones (des mots qui se prononcent de la même façon mais s'orthographient différemment) des mots suivants.**

scene • meet • sea • peace • steal

b) **Écoutez l'enregistrement et répétez.**
Audio 23lmu2307

IMPROVE YOUR Vocabulary

Activités en ligne 23lmu2308

The world of work

Opportunities

Audio 23lmu2311

- creativity
- fame = stardom, recognition
- a blockbuster = a hit, a success
- the audience = the public
- in the spotlight = in the public eye
- acclaimed

Drama

Audio 23lmu2309

- a company
- a studio
- a theatre
- on stage/ backstage
- a rehearsal /rɪˈhɜːsəl/

Showbiz

Audio 23lmu2310

- an actor / an actress
- a dancer
- a director
- a stage manager
- a producer
- a TV host
- a cast = the performers
- a contract
- a fee = a commission
- a negotiation

Dangers

Audio 23lmu2312

- competition
- expectation
- inappropriate = indecent
- mental health
- pressure
- safeguarding = protecting
- weariness = tiredness

Skills

Audio 23lmu2313

- talented = gifted
- artistic
- confident
- hardworking
- resourceful

Let's RECAP

Faites le point ! Complétez la fiche bilan avec les documents que vous avez étudiés. Fiche 23lmu2314

AXE 2

Professional fields, the world of work

How do celeb teens fit into the entertainment industry?

#stardom

Is celebrity a goal for teen actors?

#dangers

What are the risks linked to teen stardom?

#career

To what extent can teens make a career out of performing?

GROUP WORK Choose a question and discuss.

Quiz 23lmu2315

YOUR PROJECT

A special guest for Career Day!

It's Career Day! As a child actor, you have been invited to speak about the pros and cons of being in the entertainment industry.

- Think about your character and prepare your resume: *age – country – talent – ...*

  Use the present perfect to speak of your experience as a performer.

- Explain why you became a teen actor.

  Use examples from the documents.

- Draw a word cloud with the pros and cons.

  You can use it as notes to present your arguments.

Escape Game

UNIT 4

Le passé dans le présent

MISSION MUSEUM

Fiche 23lmu2401
Le fichier d'activité

Vidéo 23lmu2402
Le trailer de l'escape game

You need to help us while we are with the President but no worries, we will be here to guide you!

▶ How do the Washington DC Smithsonian Museums celebrate American history?

THE SMITHSONIAN INSTITUTION

The Smithsonian Institution is too large, you need to know where to go!

Smithsonian @smithsonian

Planning a visit to the Smithsonian, the world's largest museum complex? We look forward to welcoming you. Plan your trip, check our schedule, and explore all we have to offer at our many museums and National Zoo:

Three hours before the President's speech, hackers blocked the safe in which the Declaration is locked. Security guards are in the Situation Room with the President and do not have time to break the code, you must help them.

Video 23lmu2403

- Watch the video and identify the different museums mentioned.
- Complete the ID card of the Institution.
- Draw the track you must follow on your map to identify the museums you will go to. Use this official map to understand where you will have to stop.

Fiche 1 23lmu2404

MUSEUM OF AMERICAN HISTORY

Escape Game

HOURS 03 MINUTES 00 SECONDES 00

Solve the two challenges added by the hackers and collect the first part of the code.

Discover my story to learn more about the flag that inspired our national anthem…

Mary Pickersgill

Hackers' challenge #1

Your national anthem is about to be erased in … 3… 2… 1… Listen to the anthem and put the sentences back in the correct order.

Fiche 2 23lmu2405

Audio 23lmu2412

Hackers' challenge #2

You are American, aren't you? Do you really know the history behind your national anthem? Listen to Mary Pickersgill's story and answer questions to unlock the computer. We don't mess around with the national anthem: you can have a maximum of two bad answers otherwise you will have to try again.

Fiche 3 23lmu2406

Audio 23lmu2413

DID YOU KNOW ?

The flag has changed 27 times as new states were included in the country! The last time it was changed was on August 26th 1959 when they added a 50th star celebrating the arrival of Hawaii as an American State.

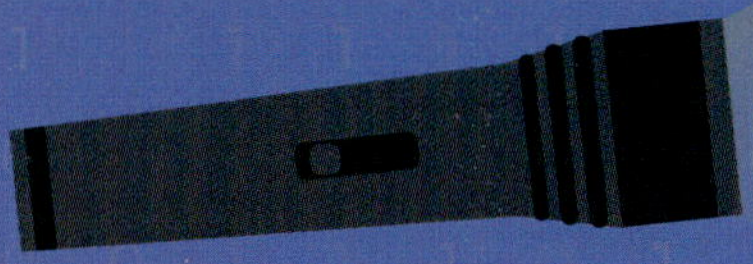

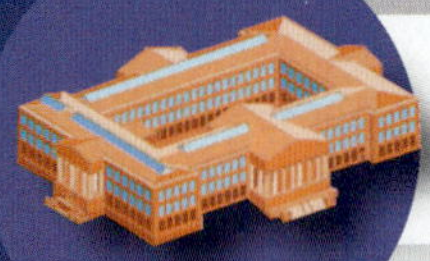

NATIONAL PORTRAIT GALLERY

Watch the video and complete the presidents' biographies to collect the second part of the code.

AGHINNOSTW

The exhibition "American Presidents" lies at the heart of the Portrait Gallery's mission to tell the story of America through the individuals who have shaped it.

Video 23lmu2407

Hackers' challenge #3

Let's have fun... What do you know about the symbols on this famous painting? Watch the video and complete the analysis of the *Lawnsome Portrait*.

Fiche 4 23lmu2408

Escape Game

Hackers' challenge #4

Not that bad... But knowing one president is not like knowing five more...! Read the biographies of the Presidents and find their names. Fiche 5 23lmu2409

1 EEFFJNORS

2 CILLNNO

AMERICA'S PRESIDENTS

3 EELOORSTV

4 EEDKNNY

5 AABMO

MUSEUM OF AFRICAN AMERICAN

It seems that for this museum, the hackers want you to explore the painful history of African Americans.

The NAACP Becomes a Force for Change

African American and white activists establish the National Association for the Advancement of Colored People (NAACP) to secure voting rights, equal access to education and employment, and due process under the law. One year later, the NAACP creates Crisis magazine to report national and international news and publish creative works by African American writers.

The CRISIS

...

School Segregation Deemed[1] Unconstitutional

In *Brown v. Board of Education of Topeka, Kansas*, the Supreme Court rules unanimously against school segregation, overturning[2] its 1896 decision in *Plessy v. Ferguson*. Thurgood Marshall, who is protégé of civil rights legal strategist Charles Hamilton Houston, is the lead attorney[3] for the case.

1. judged, considered – **2.** cancelling – **3.** main lawyer

...

...

The President Signs Civil Rights Act

President Lyndon B. Johnson signs the Civil Rights Act, which gives the federal government far-reaching* powers to prosecute discrimination in employment, voting and education.

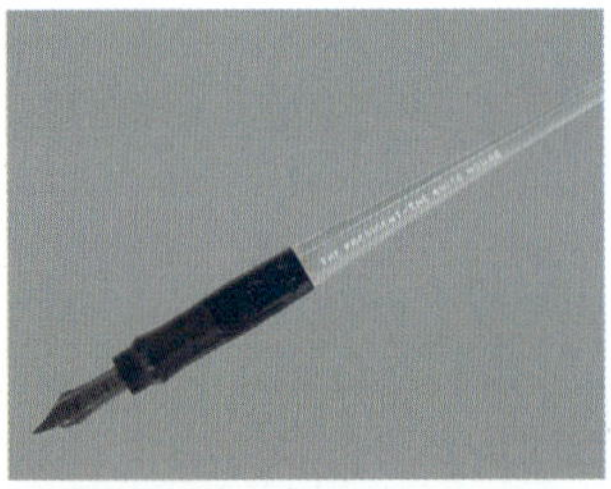

* that has a great influence

...

Dr. Martin Luther King Jr. is Assassinated

HISTORY AND CULTURE

Escape Game

Hackers' challenge #5

Your wonderful timeline... does not exist anymore!
You want to open the last computer? Use these elements to recreate the timeline! Fiche 6 23lmu2410

Daisy Bates Preps the Little Rock Nine

For the first time since Reconstruction, the federal government uses the military to uphold* African Americans' civil rights, as US Army troops escort nine students to desegregate a school in Little Rock, Arkansas. Daisy Bates, a NACCP leader, advises and assists the students. She eventually has a state holiday dedicated to her.

* defend

...

Four African American college students 'sit-in' at a Woolworth's* lunch counter in Greensboro, North Carolina, leading to the counter's desegregation five months later and launching similar protests across the South. On April 15, Ela Baker organizes students at Shaw University in Raleigh to help them form the Student Nonviolent Coordinating Committee (SNCC) to facilitate the growing sit-in movement.

* American store

...

...

The United States Elects its First African American President

Barack Obama, the only sitting[1] African American in the US Senate, is elected President of the United States, becoming the first African American to fill this office[2].

1. elected
2. to become president

LINCOLN MEMORIAL

Do you have the code? Hurry up! Unlock the safe! The President is on his way, the attack is now under control. The American President is counting on you!

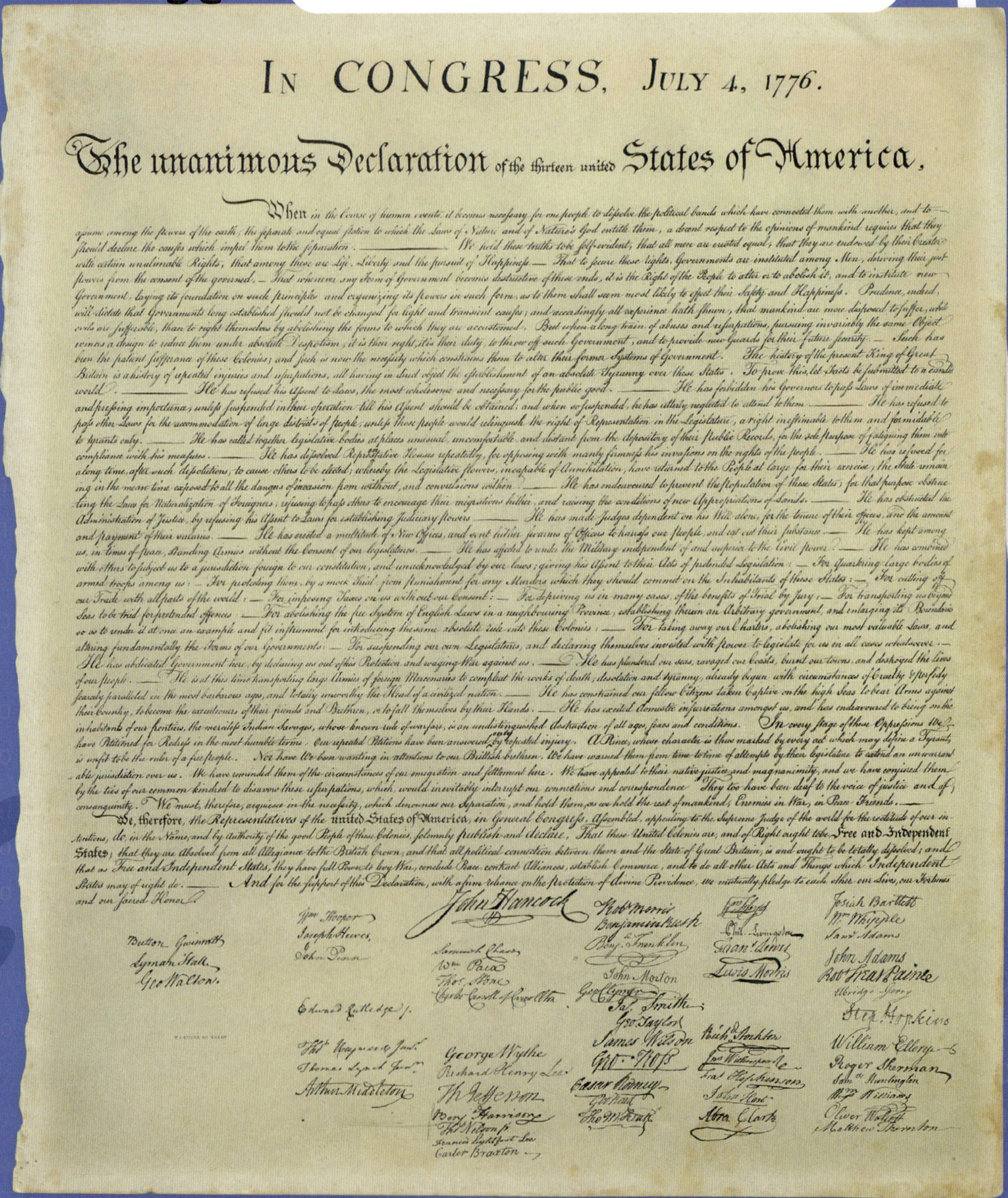

IN CONGRESS, JULY 4, 1776.

The unanimous Declaration of the thirteen united States of America,

When in the Course of human events, it becomes necessary for one people to dissolve the political bands which have connected them with another, and to assume among the powers of the earth, …

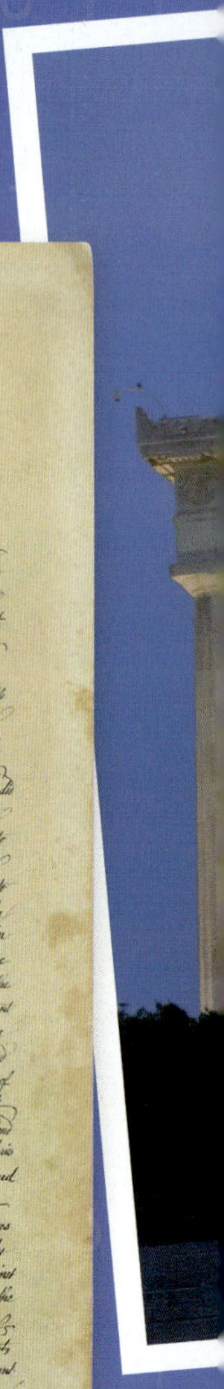

Escape Game

Hackers' challenge #6

Will you manage to break the code and open the vault in which the Declaration of Independence is locked?

Fiche 7 23lmu2411

“We hold these truths to be self-evident, that all men are created equal, that they are endowed by their Creator with certain unalienable Rights, that among these are Life, Liberty and the pursuit of Happiness.”

Good job comrade! In your honor, the President wants you to read the opening of the declaration to begin the festivities!

Les univers professionnels, le monde du travail

UNIT 5 The future of American STEM Jobs

YOUR PROJECTS

It's National STEM Day in the USA!

Create a poster to promote STEM Day in your school.

OR

Make a short video presenting a STEM job.

▶ How is science conquering the job market in the USA?

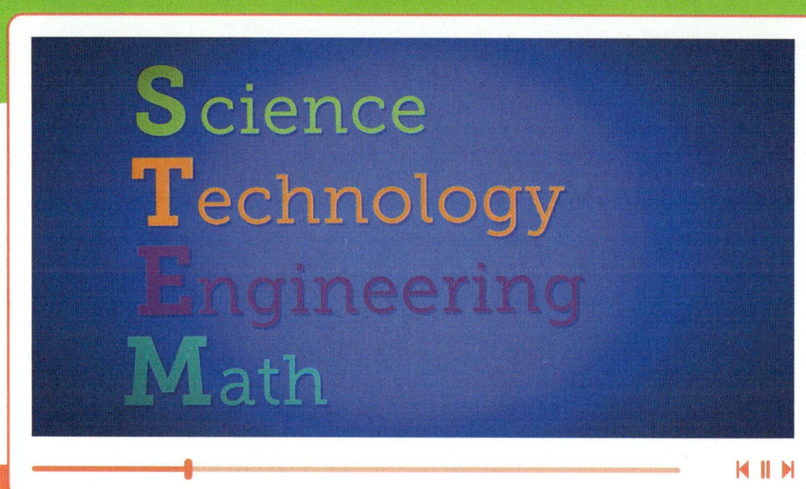

McGraw Hill Education

A STEM carreers Vidéo 23lmu2501

PAIR WORK

1. Watch the video.
Student A works on Mrs Montano and Dr Jackson
Student B works on Dr Fippin and Mrs Markers
Identify the jobs of your STEM professionals, then pick out scientific vocabulary to show science is important to their jobs. Use Fiche 23lmu2502

2. Find out why STEM is important for them and from whom they got their inspiration.

3. Exchange your findings with your partner. Explain which job you prefer and why.

Grammar What tense is mainly used to describe the characters' jobs and daily routines? How is it formed?

Remember how to

Say what you prefer
> Doc A

- On peut dire :
  → *My favourite [US: favorite] job is...*
  → *The job I like [the] most/ best is...*
- Avec des verbes, on peut employer :
  I prefer **+ V-*ing*** **:**
  → *I prefer becoming a vet.*
  I would/'d prefer to **+ V :**
  → *I'd prefer to become a vet.*

B

Pearson UK

1. Look at the poster and select three jobs you find interesting.

2. Find three key words for each job. Use them to show #whysciencematters.

WORD BOX

- a **career** /kəˈrɪə/
- health
- **in**novative = ori**gin**al
- **chal**lenging
- **unique** /juːˈniːk/
- im**prove** = make **bet**ter
- find a cure /kjʊə/

1 STEM nation

Verizon / weneedmore.com

A We don't need more Lebrons Vidéo 23lmu2503

Remember how to

Give your opinion

> Doc A - question 4.

On peut utiliser :

- des expressions
  - → *For me, ...*
  - → *In my opinion/view, ...*
  - → *As far as I am concerned, ...*
  - → *From my point of view, ...*
  - → *To my mind, ...*
- des verbes d'opinion :
  - → *I **think** / **believe** / **consider** / **feel** that...*
  - → *It **seems** to me that...*

1. Watch the first part of the video. Imagine why we don't need more of these jobs.
2. Watch the second part of the video and explain what type of jobs is needed and why.
3. Imagine why Verizon, an American telecom company, is sponsoring this ad.
4. You saw the video on Lebron James' Instagram page, write a comment explaining whether you agree or not with this ad campaign.

STEM Queen | TODAY

B The STEM queen Vidéo 23lmu2504

1. Watch the video.
   Describe the situation using the following key words:
   science • school • girls • love • STEM • change • underprivileged.
2. List the goals of this initiative.
3. Write a tweet to the STEM queen complimenting her on her initiative. Use some of the key words as hashtags.

Pronunciation Listen to the video (until 1'08) and pick out the words containing the diphthong /aɪ/ (like in *my*, *pie* or *buy*). Classify them according to their spellings.

The US Bureau of Labor predicts **15%** growth across healthcare professions by 2029.

The average yearly salary for all STEM workers is **$100,900**.

The average median hourly wage for STEM jobs is **$38.85**.

Employment in STEM occupations has grown **79%** since 1990.

STEM jobs are projected to grow **8.8%**. → Specifically, software development employment is projected to grow **22%**

C STEM in numbers

1. Use the numbers to explain in your own words how STEM jobs and salaries are evolving.

2. You are in charge of promoting STEM in your school. A student comes to you with doubts about studying STEM for his/her future career. Convince him/her using some key figures and arguments from the documents.

WORD BOX

- a role **mod**el
- a **sal**ary = a wage /weɪdʒ/
- a **pass**ion /ˈpæʃən/
- a**maz**ing = in**cred**ible
- in**spir**ing /ɪnˈspaɪərɪŋ/

MEMORY CHALLENGE — PAIR WORK

Look at page 55 and take one minute to memorise as many jobs as possible. Close your books and see who can remember the most!

Remember how to

Write and say numbers > Doc C.

- *hundred, thousand, million, billion* : pas de -s au pluriel
  → *five thousand dollars, ten million people*
- Les nombres en *-teen* et en *-ty* ne sont pas accentués de la même manière : *thir**teen*** / ***thir**ty*
- Les milliers sont séparés par une virgule :
  → *10,000 = ten thousand*
  Les décimales sont séparées par un point :
  → *1.4 = one **point** four*
- % se dit ***percent*** /pəˈsent/ et est invariable :
  → *Women make up only **19% (percent)** of people in the STEM field.*

PREPARE YOUR PROJECT

Record a WhatsApp message

Convince your best friend to study STEM with you next year!

- Prepare your arguments.
- Record a 1-minute message.

1 American stem heroes

GROUP WORK

DIFFÉRENCIATION

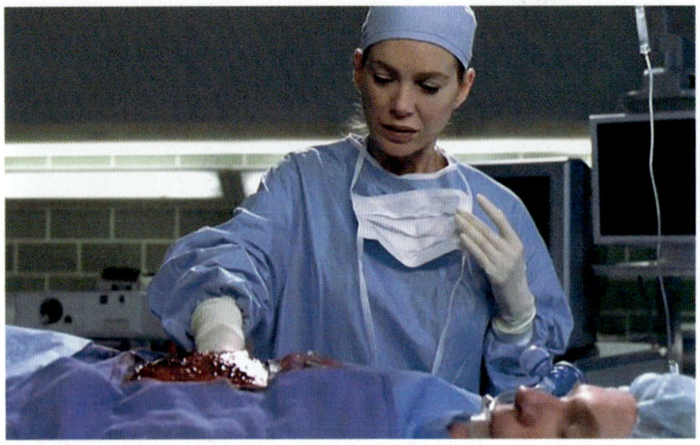

DR. MEREDITH GREY

STEM: Science

JOB: Surgeon

TV SHOW: Grey's anatomy

DR. MEREDITH GREY is a graduate of *Dartmouth College*. She starts as a surgical intern at the fictional Seattle Grace Hospital where she shows immense natural talent. She possesses a remarkable calm and ease during medical procedures and emergencies, and is a natural observer of people. She eventually becomes a surgical resident, and obtains the position of Chief of General Surgery.

A

Adapted from www.charactour.com

RICHARD HENDRICKS

STEM: Technology

JOB: Application designer and coder

TV SHOW: Silicon Valley

RICHARD HENDRICKS is the CEO and founder of *Pied Piper*, a music app that lets songwriters know if they are infringing any copyrights. Richard learns that the algorithm he wrote to compress data files does so without degrading the quality of the data giving it a variety of very valuable potential applications. In fact, it could make Richard a billionaire

B

Adapted from charactour.com

SHURI

STEM: Engineering

JOB: Innovation Engineer

FILM: Black Panther

Profession… genius-level engineer. **SHURI** is arguably the smartest scientist on the planet, with knowledge and technology that far surpasses the work of better-known geniuses like Tony Stark and Bruce Banner. She designs everything from weaponry and defences to communications and transportation.

C

Adapted from charactour.com

D

DR. CHARLES EDWARD EPPES

STEM: Mathematics

JOB: Cryptanalist

TV SHOW: Numbers

DR. CHARLES EDWARD EPPES is a young mathematical genius and professor of applied mathematics at the fictional California Institute of Science, CalSci. As a world-class mathematician, Charlie helps his brother Don Eppes solve many of his perplexing FBI cases. Charlie has consulted for the National Security Agency (NSA), in part as a cryptanalyst, for nearly five years.

sharetv.com

FICHE GROUP WORK

1. Work on one of these characters. Find the following information:
- *name*
- *TV show/film*
- *job*
- *STEM subject*
- *accomplishment*

Use **Fiche** 23lmu2505

2. Exchange information with your classmates to gather details about each job.

PAIR WORK

3. Discuss with your partner which character inspires you the most and why.

Remember how to

Ask questions > Question 2.

- Attention à l'ordre des mots dans les questions :

Mot interrogatif	Auxiliaire	Sujet	Verbe...
What	*do*	*You*	***prefer**?*
Why	*did*	*You*	***choose** this job?*
-	*Are*	*You*	***looking** for a new job?*

- Dans une question fermée [*Yes – No question*], la question commence par l'auxiliaire :
  → ***Do** you like your job?*
- Si la question porte sur le sujet de la phrase, le verbe suit directement le mot interrogatif :
  → *Who **inspired** you?*

WORD BOX

- an ad**van**tage
- **per**sonally
- **mo**tivated
- make/earn **mon**ey /ˈmʌn.i/
- dis**cov**er
- ex**cit**ing = **thril**ling, **mind**-blowing

PREPARE YOUR PROJECT

Write a short article

Present a STEM job or career of your choice in a short article for the blog STEMx:
job • salary • tasks • possible evolutions...

IMPROVE YOUR Grammar

+ Activités en ligne
23lmu2506

L'absence d'article (l'article Ø)

Tyron's Tips
23lmu2507

- **Pour évoquer des généralités**, on ne met pas d'article devant le nom (on parle parfois de déterminant Ø). Ceci se produit :
  - avec des noms au singulier qui désignent des abstractions (sentiments, disciplines scientifiques ou concepts).
    → ***Technology** plays a major role in our everyday lives.*
  - avec des noms au pluriel quand on désigne tous les individus d'une catégorie.
    → ***Children** are often interested in science.*
- On ne met pas d'article devant **les noms de langue**
  → *She speaks **French** very well.*
  ou de pays → *She lives in **France**.*

Il existe quelques exceptions :
→ ***the** United States / **the** United Kingdom.*

> Précis p. 247

Le présent simple

- **Le présent simple se forme de la façon suivante :**

Toutes les personnes		3ᵉ personne du singulier
Verbe à sa forme nue → *I **like** science.*	**Forme affirmative**	Verbe + -S ou -ES → *She **likes** science.*
DO NOT ou **DON'T** + V → *I **don't like** science.*	**Forme négative**	**DOES NOT** ou **DOESN'T** + V → *She **doesn't like** science.*
DO + sujet + V → ***Do** you **like** science?*	**Forme interrogative**	**DOES** + sujet + V → ***Does** she **like** science?*

- **On utilise le présent simple :**
  - pour évoquer des vérités générales :
    → *The sun **rises** in the East.*
  - pour donner une caractéristique d'une chose ou d'une personne (par exemple, dire ce qu'elle fait dans la vie) :
    → *She **works** as a lab technician.*
  - pour parler d'une habitude :
    → *Every day, she **wakes up** at 6 o'clock.*

> Précis p. 258

1 Complétez avec l'article *the* ou *a(n)*. Si aucun article n'est nécessaire, utilisez le symbole Ø.

a. In ... United States, you have to study ... mathematics in ... high school. They also study ... physics, ... chemistry, and ... biology.
b. In ... Britain, ... career prospects in ... computer science are excellent.
c. She found ... new job in ... lab in ... UK.

2 Quelles sont les qualités ou les compétences nécessaires pour exercer ces professions ?

lab technician • engineer • surgeon

Rédigez deux phrases pour chaque profession en utilisant Ø.

Ex. : *Laboratory technicians need good organisational skills.*

3 a) Dites pourquoi le présent simple est employé dans les phrases suivantes.

b) Mettez-les à la forme interrogative puis à la forme négative.

a. His new job pays well.
b. Julia wants to become a forensic scientist.
c. They usually work overtime on Fridays.

4 Vous êtes chercheur dans l'un des domaines suivants :

vulcanology • astronomy • robotics

Expliquez en quoi consiste votre métier et décrivez votre quotidien (40 mots). Utilisez le présent simple et des adverbes de fréquence :

always • often • usually • never • seldom / rarely

IMPROVE YOUR Pronunciation

La diphtongue /aɪ/ Audio 23lmu2508

- La diphtongue de *my* ou *night* est représentée par le symbole /aɪ/.
- Elle correspond le plus souvent à la graphie *i* ou *y* :

i, *y* ou *ie* en fin de mot d'une seule syllabe	*my*, *why*, *die*, *hi*
dans la graphie ***-igh***	*night*, *might*, *high*
i dans ***-ind*** et ***-ild***	*behind*, *wild*, *find*
i dans ***-ign*** (le *g* ne se prononce pas)	*design*, *sign*

- Quand la graphie *i* ou *y* est suivie d'une consonne unique suivie d'un « e », elle se prononce très souvent /aɪ/, surtout en syllabe accentuée : *type*, *drive*, *file*...

Les verbes *give* /gɪv/ et *live* /lɪv/ sont des exceptions. Cette règle ne s'applique pas non plus dans certaines terminaisons inaccentuées comme *-ive* (*positive*).

Quelques terminaisons accentuées

Audio 23lmu2511

- **Certaines terminaisons sont accentuées en anglais.** Cela signifie que la dernière syllabe de ces mots est prononcée avec plus de force et est légèrement plus longue que les autres. En voici certaines :

-ee(r)	*engineer*, *career* Exceptions : *coffee*, *employee*
-ette	*cigarette*, *kitchenette*
-oo(n)	*tattoo*, *cartoon* • Exception : *igloo*
-aire	*billionaire*
-ese	*Chinese*, *Japanese*
-ique	*unique*, *technique*

1 **a) Recopiez les mots suivants et entourez ceux qui contiennent la diphtongue /aɪ/.**

right • biology • science • sky • design • child • bright • wise • private • pilot • live (verbe) • final • innovative • horizon

b) Écoutez l'enregistrement pour vérifier vos réponses et répétez.
Audio 23lmu2509

2 **Trouvez les homophones (des mots qui se prononcent de la même façon mais qui s'orthographient différemment) des mots suivants :**

buy • hi • site • eye

Audio 23lmu2510

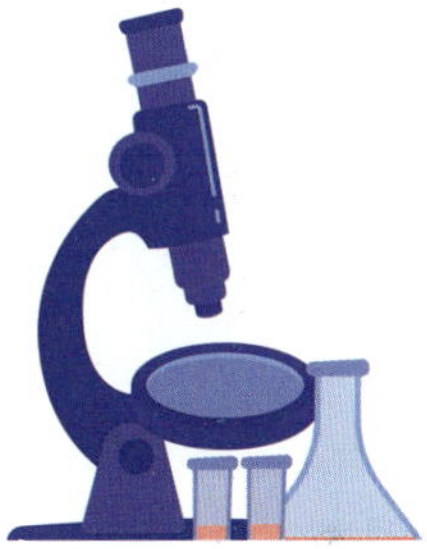

4 **a) Recopiez les mots suivants et soulignez la syllabe accentuée.**

unique • engineer • billionaire • coffee • Waterloo • Japanese • kangaroo • cartoon • volunteer

b) Écoutez l'enregistrement pour vérifier vos réponses et répétez.
Audio 23lmu2512

5 **a) Recopiez le texte suivant et soulignez les mots accentués sur la dernière syllabe.**

Lynette's parents encouraged her in her chosen career. She got a degree at Berkley University and now works for a Chinese company.

b) Écoutez l'enregistrement pour vérifier vos réponses et répétez.
Audio 23lmu2513

IMPROVE YOUR Vocabulary

Activités en ligne 23lmu2514

World of work

MOTIVATION
Audio 23lmu2515

- a role model
- a salary / wages
- inspiring
- stimulating
- sensational
- exciting
- inspire
- change the world
- make an impact
- make/earn money

FUTURE
Audio 23lmu2516

- an evolution
- an advantage
- a career
- amazing
- challenging
- unique
- what lies ahead
- evolve

PERSONALITY & SKILLS
Audio 23lmu2517

- motivated
- tenacious
- curious
- open-minded
- logical
- passionate
- calm
- innovative
- problem-solving
- collaborative
- communicative

Science

MATHS
Audio 23lmu2518

- an algorithm
- a sequence
- measuring
- formulating
- quantifying
- computing

SCIENCE
Audio 23lmu2519

- an evidence
- a hypothesis
- observing
- identifying
- describing
- experimenting

TECHNOLOGY
Audio 23lmu2520

- a program
- software
- big data
- advancing
- progressing
- creating
- achieving

STEM
Audio 23lmu2521

- science
- technology
- engineering
- mathematics

ENGINEERING
Audio 23lmu2522

- a component
- tools
- building
- designing
- making
- constructing

1 **Scan the unit and find three jobs for each category.**

S CIENCE → *marine biologist, …*
T ECHNOLOGY → …
E NGINEERING → …
M ATHS → …

2 **Use 10 words from the mind map to explain why jobs will be developing in STEM in the future.**

3 **The California Institute of Technology is offering summer internships! Write a short email to apply online. Show your motivation and give details about your personality and skills.**

Let's RECAP

Faites le point ! Complétez la fiche bilan avec les documents que vous avez étudiés. Fiche 23lmu2523

AXE 2

Professional fields, the world of work

The future of American jobs: How is science conquering the job market in the USA?

#starsintheireyes
Why are celebrities pushing for STEM careers?

#newcareers
How can young professionals find new career paths in the USA?

#reality&fiction
How are STEM jobs presented in fiction?

#science
How is science promoted to adapt to new jobs?

#STEM
To what extent are STEM jobs the future of work in the USA?

GROUP WORK Choose a question and discuss.

Quiz 23lmu2524

Become AN EXPERT

Lisez et écoutez de l'anglais en dehors de la classe

Books

- *Slay*, Brittney Morris vers LLCER

- *Bad taste in Boys*, Carrie Harris vers LLCER
- *See You in the Cosmos*, Jack Cheng vers LLCER
- *Women in Science: 50 Fearless Pioneers Who Changed the World*, Rachel Ignotofsky vers AMC
- *Calling All Minds: How To Think and Create Like an Inventor*, Temple Grandin

Series

Films & documentaries

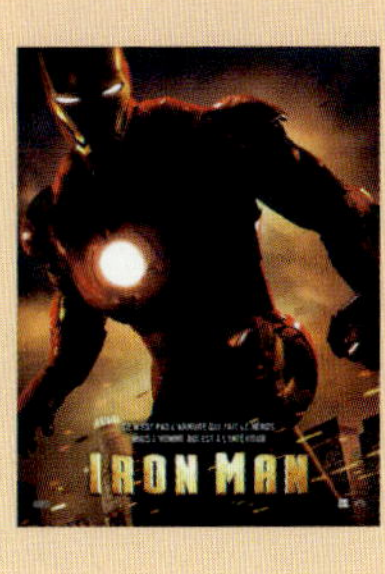

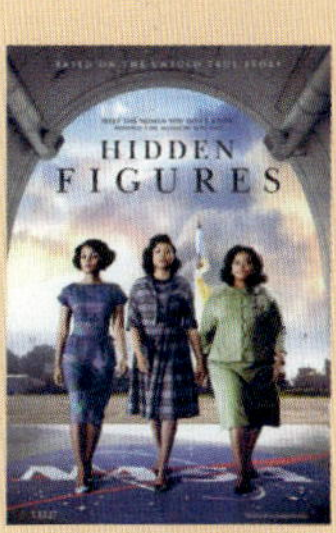

vers AMC

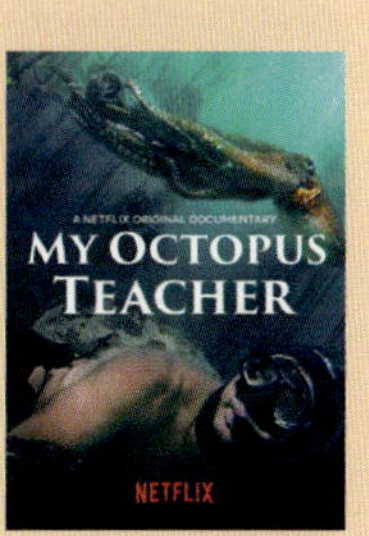

vers AMC

YOUR PROJECTS

Create a poster

Design a poster about a fictional American character who has a successful STEM career in order to promote STEM Day in your school and inspire your fellow students.

- Imagine a slogan that will catch people's attention about STEM careers.
  - Use a short sentence and write it in big bold letters.
- Select a STEM character from an American novel, series or film.
  - Find two pictures best representing him/her doing his/her job so your classmates can visualise it.
- Write a short paragraph describing your character and his/her STEM career.
  - Use adjectives and superlatives to show this job is amazing.
- Include some convincing statistics showing that your character's career is the future of the American job market.
  - Use Doc C p. 57 and make an internet search to find some data.

OR

Make a short video

For National STEM day, make a short video presenting a STEM job and showing why it is the future of work.

- List arguments that will convince students.
  - Give concrete examples of success stories in STEM.
- Use numbers to show STEM jobs are the future.
  - Find useful figures in the unit or on the web.
- Add images to present some jobs.
- Edit the video and add images to illustrate the job.
  - Use free online tools such as Shotcut, Open Shot Video or Videoshop.
- Impersonate a professional and give a testimony.
  - You can act and pass on key messages.

How to shoot a video p. 139

BUILD UP YOUR SKILLS

How to create a poster

1. Pour le préparer

- Réfléchissez à l'objectif du document : faire la promotion d'un événement, présenter une personnalité, dénoncer une injustice…
- Listez vos idées, cherchez des illustrations en rapport avec votre thématique.
- Trouvez un titre et des images accrocheurs.

2. Pour le réaliser

- Pensez aux sites ou applis gratuits : Canva, Calameo, Madmagz.
- Vérifiez que vous avez respecté les consignes.

Are you ready?

+ prof Évaluation

Entraînement à l'évaluation

Compréhension orale

Faites un compte-rendu en français de la vidéo.

The importance of STEM educations in schools, ABC News, 2022 [00 → 1'30] Vidéo 23lmu2525

- Relevez les données chiffrées.
- Concentrez-vous sur les bonnes raisons de faire des études en sciences.
- Prenez en compte l'évolution des métiers depuis les années 1990.

Production écrite

You have just listened to this video and you believe that money should not be the only motivation to join STEM studies. Explain why STEM is also about the future of humanity.

Compréhension **écrite**

Bestselling autobiography* Lab Girl *traces the trajectory of Hope, from a curious child in her father's lab, to her career as a respected scientist and passionate observer of the natural world.

Lab Girl, Hope Jahren © Knopf Doubleday

Lab Girl, Hope Jahren

My desire to become a scientist was founded upon a deep instinct and nothing more; I never heard a single story about a living female scientist, never met one or even saw one on television.

As a female scientist I am still unusual, but in my heart I was never anything else. Over the years I have built three laboratories from scratch, given warmth and life to three empty rooms, each one bigger and better than the last. My current laboratory is almost perfect – located in Honolulu and housed within a magnificent building that is frequently crowned by rainbows and surrounded by hibiscus flowers in constant bloom – but somehow I know that I will never stop building and wanting more. My laboratory is not "room T309", as stated on my university's blueprints; it is "the Jahren Laboratory" and it always will be, no matter where it is located. It bears my name because it is my home. My laboratory is a place where the lights are always on. My laboratory has no windows, but it needs none. It is self-contained. It is its own world. My lab is both private and familiar, populated by a small number of people who know one another well. My lab is the place where I put my brain out on my fingers and I do things. My lab is a place where I move. I stand, walk, sit, fetch, carry, climb, and crawl. My lab is a place where it's just a well that I can't sleep, because there are so many things to do in the world besides that. My lab is a place where it matters if I get hurt. There are warnings and rules designed to protect me. I wear gloves, glasses, and closed-toed shoes shield myself against disastrous mistakes. In my lab, whatever I need is greatly outbalanced by what I have.

1. Explain in your own words what Hope means when she says "As a female scientist I am still unusual".
2. Where did Hope get her inspiration from to become a scientist?
3. Give a description of the location of Hope's lab. Would you say it is a pleasant working environment? Why?
4. Comment on the number of activities in her daily work.
5. What precautions must she take to carry out her daily tasks?

- Repérez le type de texte dont il s'agit. Qui est le narrateur ?
- Relevez le lexique scientifique pour comprendre le métier dont il est question.
- La ponctuation peut vous aider à mieux comprendre le texte.

Production **écrite**

Hope describes her job as a scientist, imagine her daily routine. (100 words)

Flash

UNIT 6

Sauver la planète, penser les futurs possibles

Save the waves

▶ How are Australian surfers protecting their coastline?

YOUR PROJECT

Write a guide to help *Surfrider Foundation* volunteers protect Australian coastlines!

1 A paradise lost?

Gold Coast World Surfing Reserve

A GC World Surfing Reserve Vidéo 23lmu2601

Wave goodbye: the battle to protect Australia's surf breaks

"Surfing brings a wealth of benefits, it makes places more desirable to live in, it is good for the local community, so the question is: when waves are impacted, how is that loss of value going to be accounted for?" There are an estimated 2.5 million recreational surfers in Australia and surf tourism expenditure* was estimated to be about $91bn a year globally before the pandemic.

theguardian.com

* spending

B

1. Observe the photo (Doc A) and imagine what a surfing reserve could be.
2. Read the text (Doc B) and list the benefits of surfing for the Australian economy.
3. Watch the video (→ 1'16) and make a list of the reasons why surfing has become such an important activity.
4. Write a tweet on the importance of creating laws to protect waves and surfing reserves in Australia.

WORD BOX

- a beach /biːtʃ/
- a wave
- a **coast**line /ˈkəʊstlaɪn/
- a **pro**ject
- an **im**pact
- a threat /θret/
- po**llu**tion
- e**ro**sion
- **coast**al de**vel**opment

ENDANGERED WAVES

Many of Australia's best waves are endangered. The Endangered Waves program aims to highlight the many threats endangering a number of Australia's most unique and fragile surfing and coastal environments.

SURFRIDER FOUNDATION AUSTRALIA

ENDANGERED WAVE 1

MARTHA LAVINIA, KING IS, TASMANIA

Threats: polluted water, visual amenity & ecosystem integrity

Martha Lavinia is a world class beach break on King Island in Bass Strait. TASSAL[1] has been granted a permit to establish a salmon farm immediately east of Marthas (potentially 1 million fish in 22 sea pens). Impacts of such a development include: potential impacts on the quality of the surfing waves due to structures within the farm. Potential for the public to lose recreational access to coastal areas on the east side of the island. Pollution in the form of untreated waste (fish faeces[2]) on the seabed which could wash up on the beaches. Disease and parasites from the salmon farm being introduced to the surrounding water. Increase of marine debris from fish pen infrastructure, rope, pipe and nets. Seals may be attracted to the smorgasbord[3] of fish which in turn could increase shark numbers.

ENDANGERED WAVE 2

THE OTHER SIDE (TOS) / THE SPIT, QUEENSLAND

Threats: coastal developments, accessibility & ecosystem integrity

The Queensland's state government considered a proposal for the development of an integrated resort including a casino and cruise ship terminal on Wave Break Island directly adjacent to TOS. The proposal would involve significant dredging[4] through the Nerang River Delta to allow access to mega cruise ships. In addition to the dredging the project involves a massive land reclamation project, the intensification of development on coastal public land and restrictions on access to TOS during cruise ship operations. For TOS surfers the development of an integrated resort development will restrict access across the seaway and risks negative impacts on the wave as a result of changes to coastal processes from dredging.

surfrider.org.au

1. Australia's largest salmon producer – 2. excrement – 3. buffet – 4. removing sand from the bottom of the ocean

C

FICHE PAIR WORK

1. Work on one of these endangered waves.
Find information about: location of the endangered wave • type of threat • details of the project
Use Fiche 23lmu2602

2. Make a list of the potential negative impacts the project could have upon your wave.

3. Exchange with your partner to gather information about the other wave.

4. Give a speech to your school's 'eco reps' about endangered waves.

Culture Tip Tasmania is an island state of Australia. It is located south of Melbourne, 240 km off the mainland. Its capital is Hobart.

Remember how to

Talk about a possible or probable future > Doc C

- Pour évoquer un événement futur hautement **probable**, on utilise ***be likely to*** + V [il est probable que...] :
  → *Because of global warming, sea levels **are likely to** rise.*
- Quand on juge qu'un événement futur est **possible**, on utilise le modal ***might*** ou ***could*** + V [*il se pourrait que...*]
  → *The resort project **could / might destroy** the beach.*

MEMORY CHALLENGE
List as many words as possible linked to the topic of surf reserves.

2 Inspiring surfers

A

Advertising agency Arnold Furnace created a new print campaign for the SURFRIDER FOUNDATION, a non-profit organisation dedicated to the protection of waves and beaches.

1. Describe the photo.
2. Explain the goal of the campaign.
3. Take part in the SURFRIDER FOUNDATION campaign and write a caption for the photo.

Remember how to

Describe a scene > Doc A

- Pour décrire une scène ou une image, on utilise le présent en ***be* + V-*ing*** :
  → *A surfer **is riding** a wave in an ocean of plastic.*
- Pour dire qu'il y a un ou plusieurs éléments dans l'image :
  → *There **is** a man on a surfboard. / There **are** plastic bottles in the water.*
  (a man : nom au sing. ; plastic bottles : nom au plur.)

WORD BOX

- a **surf**er
- a **surf**board
- **plas**tic waste
- **tox**ic
- de**grad**ed
- ride
- float

Save The waves

B Save The Waves App: take action today

Vidéo 23lmu2603

1. Watch the video with the sound off. Describe what you have seen and try to guess what the app is for.
2. Watch the video with the sound on. List all the things which will be protected when people use the app.
3. List all the threats mentioned in the video.
4. PAIR WORK Your friend thinks the app is useless. Convince him/her otherwise. Act out the conversation.

www.geelongtimes.com.au

SURFING TO SAVE THE WORLD

NOVEMBER 19, 2020 • by James Taylor

AUSTRALIAN surfers have banded together to defend Australia's coastline and the surfing lifestyle from the threat of climate change. SURFERS FOR CLIMATE, founded by longboarding champion **Belinda Baggs** and former pro-surfer **Johnny Abegg**, aims to bring the Australian surf community together to protect the coastline from future threats. SURFERS FOR CLIMATE is taking on an even bigger challenge – climate change.

Belinda BAGGS

"For surfers, the ocean is life," Baggs said. "Climate change, fuelled* by the burning of fossil fuels, threatens everyone's way of life. For the surfing community, this is a red alert. Everything we love is under threat."

Johnny ABEGG

"Surfers for Climate will bring surfers together in a positive, fun and inspiring way," Abegg said. "The ocean has shaped our country. And now, we must stand up and do what we can to create the future we want."

* nourished

C

1. Read the introduction and list SURFERS FOR CLIMATE's goals.
2. Focus on Belinda Baggs's and Johnny Abegg's quotes and list what the two surfers have in common.
3. Write an entry for the SURFERS FOR CLIMATE's website saying why we should protect the ocean.

IMPROVE YOUR Grammar

Activités en ligne 23lmu2604

L'expression du but

Tyron's Tips 23lmu2605

- On peut exprimer le but en employant :
  - une proposition infinitive en **to + V** / **in order (not) to + V** ou **so as (not) to + V** :
    → *Australian surfers have banded together **(in order) to protect** Australia's coastline.*
  - une proposition introduite par **so that / in order that** (afin que, pour que). Cette proposition contient alors souvent un modal (*can*, *could* ou *may*) :
    → *I'll get some trash bags **so that** we **can** clean the beach.*
  - le verbe **aim to do sth** (viser à / avoir pour but de) :
    → *This ad **aims to** raise awareness about the climate crisis.*

1 Réunissez les deux phrases en utilisant les expressions entre parenthèses.

Ex : *The government has passed a new law. The purpose of this law is to protect wildlife (so as to + V)*
→ *The government has passed a new law **so as to protect wildlife**.*

a. We have created a non-profit organisation. This organisation aims to protect endangered sea animals. *(to + V)*

b. Hundreds of surfers organised a protest march. They asked the government to take action against marine pollution. *(in order to + V)*

c. We are raising funds. We want to produce a documentary about plastic waste in Australia. *(so that + can)*

IMPROVE YOUR Pronunciation

L'accentuation des mots se terminant par *-ion*

Audio 23lmu2606

- Ils portent leur accent principal sur **la syllabe qui précède cette terminaison** :

  pollution ○◯○
  erosion ○◯○

  Le mot *television* est une exception.

- Cette règle s'applique à d'autres terminaisons commençant pas un *i* :

-ia	*Australia, Tasmania*
-ial	*potential, industrial*
-ian	*Australian*
-ious	*ambitious*

1 a) Recopiez ces mots et soulignez les syllabes qui portent l'accent principal.

solution • information • Victoria • official • Italian • vegetarian • musician • organisation • television

b) Écoutez l'enregistrement pour vérifier vos réponses et répétez. Audio 23lmu2607

2 Écoutez la phrase suivante et répétez-la en faisant particulièrement attention à l'accentuation des mots en gras. Audio 23lmu2608

Australian officials have taken **action** to reduce the water **pollution** caused by **industrial** waste.

THE 3 COMPONENTS TO A SUCCESSFUL FOOD HALL

1. Landmark building

A historical building or unique space adds to the success of foodhalls.

2. Local appeal

Creating the right feel and trend for the neighbourhood is vital.

3. Location

A location close to places of business where people can go at lunchtimes or after work is essential.

Adapted from forsters.co.uk

B

1. Read the title and the three texts. Then present this document.
2. Introduce the food hall concept to the members of your Town Hall Youth Council.

SPOILT FOR CHOICE

It's a Friday night. You're going out with your #squad. You're all hungry for something delicious to kick-start the weekend but, as is always the case with these sorts of things, there's a catch[1]. The catch is that you're all relatively young, trendy, and somewhere between the ages of 18 and 35. That means at least one of you is going to be a vegan; one of you is going to be gluten intolerant; one of you's already eaten at every hyped Instagram eatery in the country; and one of you is going to be a fussy git[2]. Choosing a restaurant that suits everyone in your friendship group can be difficult and nigh-on impossible at such short notice[3]. Thankfully, for times like these, food halls exist.

1. a problem
2. a person difficult to please
3. at the last moment

mob.co.uk

C

1. List the characteristics of the consumers depicted.
2. Deduce what sort of people food halls want to attract.
3. Explain why food halls can be a solution for groups of friends.
4. Message your friends to convince them to grab take-away food from a new food hall!

Remember how to

Express necessity

- On peut utiliser *need*, qui se construit avec un infinitif en *to* :
  → *To create a food hall, you* ***don't need to*** *invest a lot of money.*
- On peut aussi utiliser des adjectifs :
  → *It's* ***necessary/essential/vital*** *to offer a wide range of affordable dishes.*
- La nécessité et l'obligation peuvent aussi être exprimées par *must* et *have to*, et le conseil par *should*:
  → *To create a great food hall, you* ***have to / must / should*** *find a large food venue in a busy area.*

PREPARE YOUR PROJECT

Record a voice over

You have just visited Market Hall Victoria in London. Watch the video (4'00-5'00) and record a 1-minute voice over describing the place and its atmosphere. Video 23lmu2704

2 Transforming the cities

The Mackie Mayor food Hall, Manchester

Reusing iconic buildings

Smithfield Market in the Northern Quarter was once the largest covered market complex in Britain but by the 1970s most of the buildings had closed. The Victorian meat market, announcing its function with a magnificent stone bull's head over the entrance, became in turn a training centre for unemployed youngsters, a shop-mobility centre[1] and a skateboard park, but they all folded[2] and the building was left empty for decades. It was spotted[3] by Nick Johnson, formerly of Urban Splash, the developer that prides itself[4] on regenerating properties that no one else dares touch. With his partner Jenny, he had already created a successful foodie venue[5] at Altrincham Market House and he did it again at the larger Manchester market. Mackie Mayor embraces[6] communal dining at long tables in the centre of the hall served by eight independent kitchens plus beer and wine bars. [...]

The building has been restored with its rough brick walls exposed and a reclaimed wooden foot[7], giving the glass-roofed market hall a touch of contemporary industrial chic.

ilovemanchester.com

1. a shop where people who cannot walk can borrow mobility equipment – 2. closed – 3. discovered – 4. congratulates himself – 5. place – 6. includes – 7. the floor made of wood has been restored

A

1. Read lines 1-9 and list the past functions of the building.
2. Identify what has changed. Draw the new building.
3. Read the end of the text and pick out the characteristics that make it a real food hall.
4. PAIR WORK Present your drawing of the new building, explaining the history and heritage of Mackie Mayor.

B The future of Smithfield Market, London Video 23lmu2705

1. Look at the picture and imagine the place they want to create.
2. Watch the video [→ 1'52] and pick out information about the old building: location • type of building • importance
3. Show how the place and the role of food will be reimagined.
4. Vlog a speech to inform your foodie followers about this new concept.

www.manchesterworld.uk

Manchester World

New £20m bid* for food hall, cinema & culture hub to transform centre of Wythenshawe

2nd Aug 2022

* £20m bid = a £20,000,000 offer of money
Wythenshawe is a rather poor district in the south of Manchester

C

www.tripadvisor.co.uk

●●●○○ Reviewed 13 April 2019

Gentrification at its finest

Over-priced tat[1] and 'street food' for the well-heeled Bristol and Bath toffs[2]. Barbour jackets and Hunter wellies[3] everywhere! Parking was a complete nightmare and badly organised.

1. merchandise – **2** rich or upper-class persons – **3.** boots

E

www.placenorthwest.co.uk

Submit comment

We want shops not over-priced food halls or evening entertainment areas. People of Wythenshawe don't have the money to eat in posh* food halls or go out at night. If we wanted that kind of lifestyle we can get a bus to Sale where the Council have removed all the shops for trendy overpriced food outlets. Leave the shops in Wythie alone, we need cheap shops selling cheap items, that is how we are forced to make ends meet.

October 17, 2022 at 10:14 pm •
By Anonymous

* chic, upper-class

D

Culture Tip

Gentrification: when a poor area in a city changes and becomes a richer one where people from a higher social class come to live.

1. Present each document (C, D, E): type • ideas • location • ...

2. List the criticisms in documents B and C.

3. You are a resident who regrets the gentrification of your neighbourhood. Write a post to denounce the impact food halls have on your life.

WORD BOX

- unaf**ford**able = high-**priced**, ex**pen**sive
- af**ford**able = cheap
- **com**munal **di**ning /ˈkɒmjənəl/
- re**gen**erate = re**new**
- re**stored** ≠ de**re**lict
- en**hance** = em**bel**lish
- **pur**pose-**built** = built for a spe**ci**fic use
- multi**pur**pose = multi**func**tion

PREPARE YOUR PROJECT

Write an article

You are doing your internship at *The Manchester Guardian*. Write a short article about the regeneration of Mackie Mayor or Smithfield Market, presenting the pros and cons of such projects.

IMPROVE YOUR Grammar

Activités en ligne
23lmu2706

La voix passive

Tyron's Tips
23lmu2707

- Elle se construit au moyen de l'auxiliaire ***be*** conjugué suivi du participe passé du verbe :

Présent	***am / is / are*** + participe passé → *The meals are **prepared** by the cook.*
Prétérit	***was / were*** + participe passé → *The meals **were prepared** by the cook.*
Present perfect	***has / have been*** + participe passé → *The meals **have been prepared** by the cook.*
Modal (*will, would, can*...)	modal + ***be*** + participe passé → *The meals **will be prepared** by the cook.*

- Le complément d'objet de la phrase active (*The cook prepared **the meal***) devient **le sujet** de la phrase passive :
  → ***The meal** was prepared by the cook.*
- Dans une phrase passive, **l'agent** (à l'origine de l'action) est introduit par ***by***. Il n'est pas obligatoirement exprimé :
  → *The building was renovated (**by a young entrepreneur**).*
- On utilise souvent la voix passive quand on ne sait pas qui est l'agent ou qu'il n'a pas d'importance :
  → *Fish and chips **was invented** in the 1860s.*

> Précis p. 273

Exprimer la conséquence

- Pour souligner un lien de cause à effet, on peut employer, surtout en début de phrase : ***therefore***, ***consequently***, ***as a result*** (par conséquent), ***that's why*** (c'est pourquoi), ***so*** (donc).
  → *The area has become affluent. **Therefore / As a result / Consequently**, rents have increased significantly.*
- On peut aussi employer **so + adjectif + *that...*** (tellement + adjectif + que...) :
  → *The food in the restaurant is **so expensive that** few people can afford to eat there.*
- Pour imaginer les conséquences d'un fait possible ou qui n'a pas encore eu lieu, on peut utiliser ***if...then...*** Attention aux formes verbales à utiliser :

Proposition en *IF* + Présent simple	**Verbe principal** (= la conséquence) : ***WILL* + V**
→ *If a food hall opens,*	→ *then the neighbourhood **will become** more attractive.*

1 **Mettez le verbe au prétérit de la voix passive. Attention aux verbes irréguliers ! (→ p. 275)**

The warehouse near the port ... (*build*) in the 19th century. It ... (*leave*) empty for decades and ... (*occupy /even*) by squatters. In 2018, it ... (*sell*) to a rich businessman. Then, it ... (*restore*) and ... (*convert*) into a food hall.

2 **Mettez les phrases à la voix passive en commençant par l'amorce proposée. Exprimez l'agent si nécessaire.**

Ex. In this eatery, they serve a wide selection of drinks and pizzas.
→ *A wide selection of drinks and pizzas is served in this eatery...*

a. You can order our tasty dishes online. → *Our tasty dishes...*
b. The owner has redecorated and embellished the bar with trendy furniture. → *The bar...*
c. My friend Susan bought this food truck. → *This food truck...*

3 **Réécrivez les phrases en utilisant les expressions entre parenthèses.**

a. Food halls offer a wide range of food. Even picky eaters can find something to their liking. (*that's why*)
b. The food in this restaurant is cheap and tasty. It is always full. (*so* + adj. + *that...*)
c. I'll get a Chinese takeaway near my workplace because I don't have enough time for lunch. (*so*)

4 **Imaginez les conséquences (positives ou négatives) qu'aurait l'ouverture d'un *food hall* près de chez vous. Utilisez la structure *If... then...* . Produisez 4 phrases en commençant par l'amorce suivante :**

→ If a food hall opens in the neighbourhood, then...

IMPROVE YOUR Pronunciation

La voyelle longue /ɔː/ Audio 23lmu2708

- La voyelle de *hall* et de *court* est représentée par le symbole /ɔː/. Elle ressemble au son du français *eau* mais est légèrement plus longue.
- Ce son-voyelle est le plus souvent représenté par **les graphies suivantes contenant un *r*** en syllabe accentuée :

or	*sh**or**t, inf**or**m, s**or**t*
our	*y**our**, c**our**t, f**our***
oor	*d**oor**, fl**oor**, p**oor***

Le suffixe inaccentué *-or* / *-our* est prononcé /ə/ comme le *-er* de *father* : *neighb**our**, auth**or**...* (anglais britannique).

- On trouve aussi /ɔː/ dans les contextes suivants (anglais britannique) :

aw, au	*l**aw**, s**aw**, c**au**se, s**au**ce*
al(l)	*h**all**, w**all**, t**all**, **al**so*
alk	*t**alk**, w**alk*** (attention, le *l* est muet !)

- On trouve également /ɔː/ dans les verbes irréguliers qui forment leur prétérit en ***-ought*** : *th**ought**, b**ought**.*

1 **Écoutez les mots suivants et répétez, en faisant attention à la prononciation de la voyelle /ɔː/.** Audio 23lmu2709

support • affordable • Northern Quarter • informal • organise • important • court

2 a) **Recopiez la phrase suivante et soulignez le son /ɔː/.**

Four years ago, the Victorian building was carefully restored and transformed into a food hall.

b) **Écoutez et répétez.** Audio 23lmu2710

L'accentuation des mots en *-ic* et *-ical* Audio 23lmu2711

- Les mots qui se terminent par *-ic*, *-ics* et *-ical* portent leur accent principal sur la syllabe qui précède immédiatement cette terminaison :

*e**xo**tic* ○◯○ *i**co**nic* ○◯○ *his**to**rical* ○◯○○

Ne confondez pas *economi**c*** (qui est en lien avec l'économie, le commerce, etc.) et *economic**al*** (peu coûteux).

- Il existe quelques **exceptions** à cette règle. En voici les principales :
  - ***Cath**olic* (mais *Ca**tho**licism* est régulier)
  - ***po**litics* (mais *po**li**tical* est régulier)
  - ***Ar**abic*

3 **Recopiez les mots suivants et soulignez la syllabe qui porte l'accent principal. Écoutez l'enregistrement pour vérifier vos réponses et répétez.** Audio 23lmu2712

organic • public • specific • scientific • demographics • characteristic • authentic

4 **Écoutez et répétez les paires de mots suivantes.** Audio 23lmu2713

a. history → historical
b. economy → economic
c. allergy → allergic

Repérez à chaque fois la syllabe accentuée : que remarquez-vous ?

IMPROVE YOUR Vocabulary

Activités en ligne 23lmu2714

City regeneration

POSITIVE CHANGE

Audio 23lmu2715

- an asset = an advantage
- an upmarket area = a chic, expensive area
- trendy, fashionable ≠ old-fashioned
- vibrant, attractive
- multipurpose = multifunction
- restored ≠ derelict
- rehabilitate = revamp
- enhance = embellish
- upgrade = improve, make better
- modernise

NEGATIVE CONSEQUENCES

Audio 23lmu2716

- gentrification
- a disadvantage = a drawback
- a concern
- a nuisance
- a rent: money paid to live somewhere
- unaffordable = high-priced, expensive
- increase ≠ diminish /də'mɪnɪʃ/
- harm = damage
- displace = move somebody from their place

Food halls

PEOPLE

Audio 23lmu2717

- an inhabitant = a local
- a food vendor
- a customer
- a foodie = a gourmet
- a hipster
- a local community
- hip = cool
- rich = affluent, well-off, wealthy

ATMOSPHERE

Audio 23lmu2719

- convivial = sociable
- casual = informal
- busy, noisy ≠ calm, relaxed
- lively = vibrant, bustling, animated
- crowded ≠ empty

PLACES

Audio 23lmu2718

- a district = a neighbourhood
- a hub = a center of activity
- a location = a place
- an outdoor/indoor market
- a hotspot = a place of lively activity
- a food venue = a place offering food
- an eatery /'i:təri/ = a restaurant
- a stall = a stand
- a food truck
- a warehouse = a distribution center
- communal dining

FOOD

Audio 23lmu2720

- a wide selection ≠ a limited choice
- international cuisine
- a traditional meal
- exotic
- organic = without pesticides
- vegan /'vi:gən/
- healthy = good for you
- tasty = delicious
- spicy /'spaɪsi/ = piquant /'pi:kənt/
- cheap, economical ≠ expensive, costly
- eat on the go: get sth to eat and go

PAIR WORK

1 Sketch it! Draw and make your teammate guess three words from the mind map.

2 Use 10 words from the mind map to explain the main characteristics of a food hall.

Let's RECAP

Faites le point ! Complétez la fiche bilan avec les documents que vous avez étudiés. **Fiche** 23lmu2721

AXE 3

Village, neighbourhood, city

To what extent do food halls transform British cities?

#frompasttopresent

How do food halls reflect a continuity in the British food scene?

#anewconcept

What does it take to create a successful foodie venue?

#gentrifiedfood

To what extent do food halls contribute to the gentrification of an area?

#regeneration

How do new food halls benefit local communities?

GROUP WORK Choose a question and discuss.

Quiz 23lmu2722

Become AN EXPERT

Lisez et écoutez de l'anglais en dehors de la classe

Websites

- *Best street Food in the UK*
  Site 23lmu2723
- *About Battery Power Station*
  Site 23lmu2724
  vers AMC

Books

- *See You Tomorrow at the Food Court*, Shinichiro Nariie
- *Street Food Scotland, A journey of stories and recipes to inspire*, Ailidh Forlan
- *Fish and Chips: A History*, Panikos Panayi vers AMC
- *Street Food, Hawkers and the History of London*, Charlie Taverner vers AMC

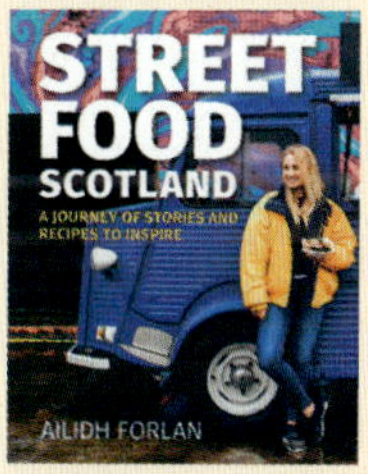

Podcasts

- *Are you a foodie?*
  BBC Learning English
  Audio 23lmu2725
- *Gentrification Through Food*
  The Social Breakdown
  Audio 23lmu2726 vers AMC

Documentaries

- *Tooting's Forgotten*
  Anpu London
  Video 23lmu2727
- *The Street*
  Official UK Trailer
  Video 23lmu2728

YOUR PROJECTS

Deliver a speech

Present your food hall project to the City Hall for a city's participatory budget.

- Think about your project and its location.
  - Type of building, types of food, types of customers, what is done there...
- List the benefits: for the city, for the neighbourhood, for customers...
  - List your arguments and illustrate each benefit with precise examples.
  - Work on the logic of your presentation: *first, second, then, moreover, for example, however, finally...*
- Write notes and practise.
  - Pay attention to your body language.
  - Use gap fillers (*er, hum, well, so...*) when you need time to think!
- Draw a powerful conclusion to win votes!
- Vote for the best project!
  - → *As all the above points have shown/ demonstrated, my project ...*
  - → *Taking everything into account, .../*
  - → *Considering all this, there is no doubt that...*

OR

Write a letter

A new food hall project is about to start in a British city's neighbourhood. Write a letter to the local council and react!

- Choose your side: for or against food halls?
  - You can also have mixed feelings!
- Explain why you are writing this letter:
  - present the food hall project,
  - give details on the advantages and the drawbacks.
  - Use linking words and words expressing consequences: *first, second, then, moreover, however...*
- State your opinion clearly.
  - → *I don't agree / I am against... / Don't let it happen*
  - → *From my point of view, it is a good idea because...*
  - → *It is about time we got...*
- Write a compelling conclusion.
  - Your final sentence should make the reader want to agree with you!

Be convincing! p. 290

BUILD UP YOUR SKILLS

How to deliver a speech

1. Pour se préparer

How street food feeds the soul | Petra Barran | TEDxLondonSalon (4'02 à 5'48) Video 23lmu2729

a Réfléchissez à l'objectif de votre discours :

- Présenter un projet ou une idée
- Défendre un projet ou s'y opposer
- Parler d'une expérience personnelle
- Inciter des personnes à agir ...

b Listez vos idées et arguments, puis organisez vos notes.

c Structurez votre discours :

1 Introduction	2 Arguments	3 Conclusion
• Pour captiver votre auditoire dès l'introduction, posez une question : *'**What if** dining out suddenly became an out-of-this-world experience?'*	• Illustrez vos arguments par des exemples, des anecdotes ou des citations. N'oubliez pas la règle : **1 idée = 1 argument = 1 exemple** • Pour montrer votre maîtrise du sujet, citez quelques statistiques.	• Résumez les idées principales de vos arguments. • Formulez clairement votre opinion.

d Pour commencer ou conclure votre discours, notez quelques tournures idiomatiques :

- *'Good evening ladies and gentlemen,' 'First of all, I'd like to...'*
- *'Thank you for giving me the opportunity to talk to you today.'*
- *'In conclusion, it is clear that...', 'It is important that we...' , 'I hope that ...'*

e Entraînez-vous à parler à partir de vos notes. Pensez à vérifier la prononciation sur un dictionnaire en ligne ! 😊

2. Pour faire votre discours

a Présentez-vous.

b Regardez votre auditoire et adaptez le registre de langue.

c Impliquez vos auditeurs en utilisant l'impératif ou des questions rhétoriques, suscitez leurs émotions, soyez dynamique et convaincant·e.

'Wouldn't you like to ...?', 'What if you ...', 'Imagine going out ...', 'Let's ...'

d N'hésitez pas à répéter certains points importants !

Are you ready?

+ prof Évaluation

Entraînement à l'évaluation

Compréhension orale

Faites un compte-rendu en français de la vidéo.

Meet the team from Pergola Paddington Video 23lmu2730

- Analysez le titre du document et les rôles des deux intervenants pour expliquer à qui s'adresse cette vidéo.
- Relevez les atouts de ce lieu.
- Expliquez quelle expérience ces 2 intervenants ont tenté de créer avec ces atouts.

Production écrite

You are a food journalist for *TimeOut*, an entertainment magazine that informs visitors and helps them plan their stay in London.
Write a review of Pergola Paddington to be published in this magazine.
(100 words)

Compréhension écrite

THESE ARE THE BEST NEIGHBORHOODS FOR FOODIES IN LONDON

Posted on August 8, 2022
by City Experiences

Visitors to the big city might expect to find a preponderance of traditional British fare[1], such as fish and chips (a delicious must!). But there's plenty on offer here beyond the proper Sunday roast. Let's start with Soho, a foodie paradise nestled on the formerly seedy[2] side of West London, now boasting a hipster vibe and the attendant culinary trends you'd expect that crowd to inspire. Then there's Notting Hill, another darling of London's West End. Once one of the capital's most artsy and culturally vibrant neighborhoods, Notting Hill has become quite affluent and has many decades of fine dining under its belt—not to mention some much-coveted Michelin stars. […] Although it's already on its way to being gentrified, gritty Bethnal Green in East London is home to some of the edgiest[3] and most innovative restaurants and wine bars in the city. The neighborhood's historic Brick Lane is an absolute must for excellent Bangladeshi cuisine, served up in countless curry houses rivaling those of Manchester's celebrated Curry Mile. […]

Also scattered about the capital are casual street-food markets with equally good food. At destinations like Brixton Market, Maltby Street Market, Exmouth Market, and Borough Market, you'll discover a wide range of cuisines and dining options, whether it's a quick bite of small plates or something tasty to eat on the go. From highbrow, trendy restaurants where you can go all-in on a splurge-worthy dinner to low-key[4] dining options where meals are served at communal tables, these are the foodie hotspots that cater to locals—and visitors—with adventurous tastes. […]

www.cityexperiences.com

1. food – 2. poor and dirty and with illegal activities – 3. fashionable – 4. relaxed

1. Pick out: the names of the different districts • their atmosphere • their food specificities.
2. Focus on the different markets. Show what type of eating out experience they offer.
3. Conclude on what it shows about London.
4. Explain the London food scene to an American food lover visiting London.

- Analysez le titre du document pour comprendre l'idée clé.
- Repérez les mots et lieux que vous connaissez. Les majuscules peuvent vous aider à repérer les lieux et les noms propres.
- Relevez les adjectifs pour définir l'atmosphère de ces lieux.

Production écrite

You work for *visitbritain.com*. Write and post a text about the foodhall revolution in the UK. Show how food halls have regenerated the local food scene. (120 words)

Flash

UNIT 8

Sauver la planète, penser les futurs possibles

From garbage to garden in Kenya

▶ How does Nairobi transform its waste?

YOUR PROJECT

Create a piece of art to raise awareness about plastic waste and present it.

1 Nairobi's scavengers

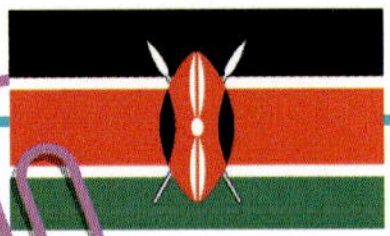

Country: Republic of Kenya

Capital city: Nairobi (4,5 million)
Dandora is a slum in Nairobi

Population: 55,8 million

Independence: 1963 (UK)

Languages: Swahili and English

Politics: Presidential republic

Kenyan Historian

A Lords of the trash Vidéo 23lmu2801

1. Read the information card. Locate and present Kenya and Nairobi. Country Files > p. 299

2. Read the title of the video, look at the image and match these words or expressions with their equivalents:

scavengers •	• people that look for discarded objects
a dumpsite / a landfill •	• source of support
a lifeline •	• gangs
cartels •	• have enough money to live on
make ends meet •	• a place where waste is thrown

3. Watch the video. Spot keywords and say why this place is dangerous.

4. Find information about James Okutoyi.

5. Write an email to the Nairobi City Hall to share your concern about Dandora and ask them for solutions.

Joan Otieno is a Nairobi-based artist inspired by the waste materials on the streets of her city. She incorporates them into her artworks, here a dress worn by a young model. Joan captures the beauty of waste materials by recycling through art.

B

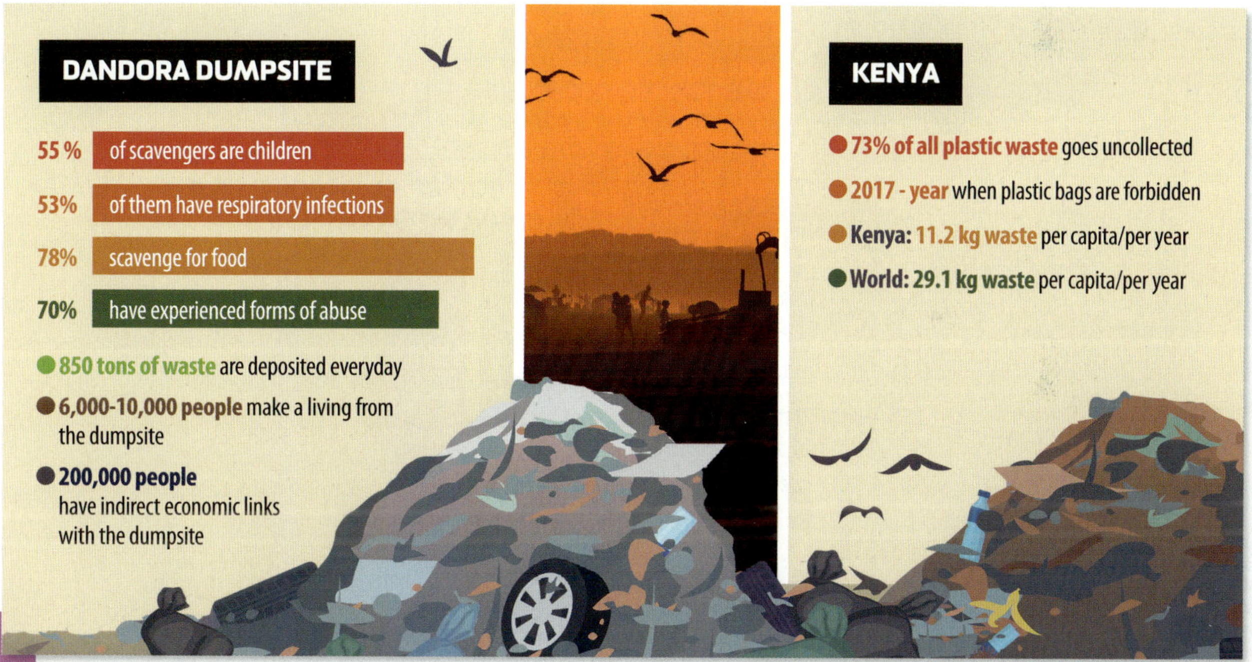

C

1. Look at the photograph (Doc B) and say what surprises you. Explain Joan Otieno's message through art.
2. Read the infographic (Doc C). Using the numbers and figures, say what children are confronted with.
3. Use both documents to show how Kenya is trying to stop pollution.
4. Joan Otieno and you have a project to help the children of Dandora. Prepare a paragraph to explain what you want to do.

WORD BOX

- a **scav**enger = a **pick**er
- a **dump**site = a **land**fill
- a slum = a de**prived** **ur**ban **ar**ea
- a truck (US) / a **lor**ry (UK)
- **de**bris /'debri:/ = waste, trash
- de**ter**gent = **pow**der used for **wash**ing
- rich ≠ **des**titute, under**priv**ileged
- sharp = able to cut
- bring sb up = **ed**ucate sb
- sort = **class**ify
- sew (sewed, sewn) = as**sem**ble with thread

2 Giving a breath of fresh air to Nairobi

CBS News

A Transforming Nairobi's mountain of plastic waste Vidéo 23lmu2802

1. Watch the video (0'56 → 3'05) and identify the negative and positive aspects of plastic.
2. Explain Nzambie Matee's idea.
3. Pick out the advantages of Matee's invention and her aspirations.
4. Post your reaction to the project on Instagram.

B

1. Focus on the 4 people in the foreground. Identify their jobs and comment on their attitudes.
2. Pick out all the negative elements in the cartoon. Explain the journalist's comment and the intention of the cartoonist.
3. Imagine the next drawing. Include a dialogue between the journalist and the factory owner that suggest healthier solutions.

WORD BOX

- a **haz**ard = a **dan**ger
- a com**mu**nity **gar**den = a **gar**den in a **neigh**bourhood
- a de**lin**quent /dɪ'lɪŋkwənt/= a **cri**minal
- a re**cy**cling plant = *usine de retraitement*
- con**cerned** /kən'sɜ:nd/ = **wor**ried
- reha**bil**itate = im**prove**, re**turn** to a good state
- take care of sb/sth = look **af**ter sb/sth
- for**bid** sth = ban sth

www.nextcity.org

CREATING GREEN SPACES AMID KENYA'S LARGEST DUMPSITE

From dumpsite to baby shower venue[1]: green spaces are sprouting up within the endless landfills of Dandora.

MARIE MULLI • AUGUST 3, 2022

Since 2013, Robinson and Dandora community activist Charles Gachanga have joined forces to mobilize communities in Dandora and beyond to rehabilitate slots[2] across the town, creating around 200 gardens that serve as clean lungs[3] amidst the pollution. PSN (Public Space Network) estimates these green spaces serve around 200,000 people in total.

Fighting garbage and crime

[...] Evans Otieno, 31, had been living a life of crime since the age of 18, when he joined one of the countless cartels that have made crime rampant in this part of Kenya. After barely escaping death by an angry mob who killed two of his colleagues, Otieno was ready to start afresh. [...]

Otieno started "Believers Garden," one of Dandora's most innovative gardens. Car tires, old television sets and gumboots[4] were turned into flower pots. Grass was planted, and a sitting space made from recycled material was set up. A fish tank, birds and rabbits, along with a children's play area and a library, kept young visitors entertained.

Otieno charges visitors from outside Dandora a fee[5] of $20 to use the premises, now popular for social functions including weddings and baby showers. But more important to Otieno than the income[6], he says, is the respect he's earned from a community that had once tried to kill him. [...]

Dandora's Officer Commanding Station Mathew Ndogo told media in 2016 that DTL has curbed crime by more than 70% because it created employment opportunities for the youth. According to Mark Ojal, a Kenyan urban designer and PhD researcher at King's College London, the grassroots[7] project did more: it created a sense of belonging and attachment.

1. place to celebrate a birth – 2. small parcels – 3. *poumons* – 4. rainboots – 5. entrance price – 6. salary – 7. from the basis, local

C

1. Read the title and the first paragraph. Imagine the caption of the photo.
2. Read the rest of the article and pick out information about Evans Otieno.
3. Using the text and the photo, describe the "Believers Garden".
4. Find how Otieno finances the project and its impact on the community.
5. You are a radio journalist. Make a news report about Otieno and the positive effects of being green.

Remember how to

Write a dialogue

- En anglais, on n'utilise pas de tirets mais **les guillemets "..."**.
  "Welcome to Radio 4, how are you today?"
  "Fine, thank you."
- Pour rendre votre dialogue vivant et crédible, utilisez du vocabulaire ou des structures grammaticales courantes à l'oral :
  - **exclamations** → *'Great! That's fine!'*
  - ***question tags* ou réponses courtes avec des auxiliaires** → *"Can you?" / "Of course, I can!"*
  - **vocabulaire familier** → *gonna, yeah, awesome....*

IMPROVE YOUR Grammar

Activités en ligne 23lmu2803

Les indénombrables

Tyron's Tips 23lmu2804

- En anglais, il existe deux catégories de noms :

les noms dénombrables (que l'on peut compter avec précision)	*a bottle → **two** bottle**s***
les noms indénombrables (qu'on ne peut pas compter)	*garbage*, *money* Ils désignent souvent des substances (*paper*), des activités (*recycling*), des abstractions (*beauty*)...

- Un indénombrable **n'a pas de forme au pluriel** et s'accorde avec un verbe au singulier :
  → ***The garbage is** collected every day.*
- Ils ne peuvent pas être précédés de l'article *a(n)*. On les emploie souvent avec **l'article Ø ou *some*** :
  → *They collect Ø **rubbish** every day.*
- Avec ces noms, on utilise le quantifieur ***much*** (beaucoup de), ***too much*** (trop de) ou des questions en ***How much* + indénombrable** (combien de...).
  → ***How much rubbish** do you throw away every day?*

  On emploie *many* avec les dénombrables au pluriel :
  → ***How many bottles** do you throw away every day?*

> Précis p. 244

1 Les noms soulignés sont-ils dénombrables ou indénombrables ? Choisissez la forme correcte.

a) The trash can was filled with empty (bottle/bottles, box/boxes, paper/papers) and rotten (tomato/tomatoes).
b) The company dumps toxic (waste/wastes) in the sea.
c) Our (packaging is/packagings are) made of recyclable (cardboard/cardboards).

2 Les noms soulignés sont-ils dénombrables ou indénombrables ? Complétez avec *much* ou *many* :

a) I don't use ... recycled paper.
b) Have they found ... empty shopping bags on the beach?
c) How ... bins are there in the building?
d) How ... plastic do you use in a week?

IMPROVE YOUR Pronunciation

La consonne /ŋ/

Audio 23lmu2805

- Il s'agit d'une consonne nasale qui a la particularité de ne jamais apparaître en début de mot ou de syllabe.
- Le plus souvent, elle est représentée par **la graphie *ng*** : *recycling, strong, young*...

  Quand la graphie *ng* apparaît en fin de mot, on ne prononce pas le *g*. Quand elle apparaît en milieu de mot, le *g* est prononcé (*English, language*).
- La consonne /ŋ/ est aussi représentée par **la graphie *n*** quand celle-ci est suivie du son consonne /k/ (comme dans *cat*) : *thank, link, income, delinquent*...

1 Écoutez et prononcez les paires de mots suivantes. Attention à bien distinguer le son /ŋ/ de *sing* du son /n/ de *sin*.

Audio 23lmu2806

a) sin / sing
b) hand / hanged
c) win / wing
d) thin / thing

2 a) Dites si le *g* en gras est prononcé dans les mots suivants.

lung • wedding • angry • wrong • English • young • packaging • belonging • single-use

b) Écoutez pour vérifier vos réponses et répétez en faisant attention à la prononciation de /ŋ/

Audio 23lmu2807

IMPROVE YOUR Vocabulary

Activités en ligne 23lmu2808

Turning green

SAVING THE PLANET
Audio 23lmu2810
- **healthy** /ˈhelθi/
- a sense of be**long**ing
- to**geth**erness
- **cir**cular e**con**omy
- reha**bil**itate sth = make sth good a**gain**

RECYCLING
Audio 23lmu2812
- a **dump**site = a **land**fill, a **rub**bish dump
- waste = **de**bris (UK), **gar**bage /ˈɡɑːbɪdʒ/
- a **sca**venger = a **pick**er
- **pack**aging = **wrap**pers
- single-**use plas**tic/cups...
- non-re**cy**clable
- **sca**venge (for sth) = pick sth
- dis**card** sth = throw sth a**way**

ENVIRONMENT
Audio 23lmu2809
- envi**ron**mental **is**sues
- **cli**mate change
- well-**be**ing
- an **e**covillage
- **need**y = poor, **des**titute
- sus**tain**able = **e**co-friendly

FUTURE
Audio 23lmu2811
- **green**er = more eco**lo**gical
- **ra**tional = **sen**sible
- take **ac**tion = act

- con**tri**bute to + V-*ing*
- raise a**ware**ness about sth = make **peo**ple **con**scious about sth
- curb pol**lu**tion = try to **li**mit pol**lu**tion

Let's RECAP

Faites le point ! Complétez la fiche bilan avec les documents que vous avez étudiés. Fiche 23lmu2813

AXE 7

Saving the planet, imagining possible futures

How does Nairobi transform its waste?

#circulareconomy
Why does fighting waste also means fighting inequality?

#recycledart
How can art help reduce waste and raise awareness?

#singleuseplastic
Why is it vital for Nairobi to stop plastic pollution?

#betterfuture
How can young Kenyans find a brighter future?

GROUP WORK Choose a question and discuss.

Quiz 23lmu2814

YOUR PROJECT

Raise awareness about waste

Create a piece of art using recycled material to raise awareness about plastic waste and present it to the Nairobi City Hall.

- Use everyday life plastic objects to make your point (bottles, cans, any plastic containers...).
  - Your work of art can take many forms: posters, clothes, sculptures... Be creative!
  - You can use this website to create posters. Site 23lmu2815
- Write a short text to explain your goals.
  - Use what you have learnt in the unit.
  - Describe your piece of art and how you made it.
- Check the pronunciation of the keywords of your speech.
  - Repeat them ten times at least!
- Rehearse your speech so you won't read too much.
  - Think about eye-contact and body language to catch people's attention.

Le passé dans le présent

UNIT 9 Symbolising America

▶ Do American symbols still represent the USA?

YOUR PROJECTS

Take part in a televised debate.

OR

Write to the Editor of the *New York Times*.

A

WORD BOX

- a **sym**bol
= an **em**blem
- a flag, a **ban**ner
- a pa**rade**
- a cele**bra**tion
- a **pro**test
- raise sth
- take down
= disas**sem**ble
- be proud of sth
- be in **fa**vour of sth
≠ be a**gainst** sth
- be di**vi**sive /dɪˈvaɪsɪv/
- stand for sth
= repre**sent** sth
- de**pict** sth = **il**lustrate sth
- o**ri**ginate **from/in sth**

1. Look at the map. You have 2 minutes to identify elements from the following categories: a. buildings and monuments • b. people and sports • c. food • d. animals • e. objects

2. Say where they are situated and explain their importance.

Remember how to

Write a paragraph expressing contrasts > Docs B / C

Organisez votre texte :

- Faites un tableau en 2 colonnes : éléments positifs / négatifs
- Utilisez des expressions pour structurer votre texte :
→ *first and foremost... / then... / lastly..., in a word...*
- Utilisez des termes ou expressions qui expriment le contraste :
→ *although, whereas, despite, even if...*

B

NASA astronauts Christina Koch and Nick Hague on the International Space Station sending a Fourth of July message

C

Independence Day celebrations in Washington, D.C., July 4, 2019

1. Analyse what the American flag shows in the two situations above.

PAIR WORK 2. Listen to the audio and identify the different opinions people have of the flag.
Student A: positive elements
Student B: negative elements

"How do you feel about the U.S. flag?"
NPR, 2020 Audio 23lmu2901

PAIR WORK 3. Together, write a paragraph for the school's website: '*The contrasting opinions of the American flag*'.

1 Decoding the symbols

GROUP WORK

DIFFÉRENCIATION

smarthistory

A | All groups | The Statue of liberty

Video 23lmu2902

1. Watch the video (2'55-4'50) and take notes.
   Find information on the following: the rondels • the rays of the crown • the tablet • the torch • facial expression • engineering
2. Check your findings with your classmates.
3. Discuss what the Statue of Liberty symbolises.
4. Write a paragraph for the blog *Symbols of America* entitled *Decoding the Statue of Liberty*.

UNCLE SAM

Uncle Sam, dressed in a top hat, striped trousers and a tailcoat, with his famous goatee beard, is a personification of the U.S government, indeed, of America as a whole.

But how did Uncle Sam become such an iconic symbol of America and its culture? Most people believe that the origins go way back to the war of 1812. Rations supplied to U.S. troops came from a meat packer[1] in New York named Sam Wilson, who stamped[2] the barrels[3] with the initials U.S. (United States). 'Good old Uncle Sam has sent our beef', the soldiers would say. And the name stuck.

As for Uncle Sam's attire, this was first seen in cartoons in the British magazine *Punch*, but it was Thomas Nast (1870s) who crystallised the image further.

However, the most well-known version, in James Flagg's World War One and Two recruitment posters, has a stern[4] Uncle Sam pointing his finger and staring straight at the observer to encourage him/her to join the U.S. forces in the war effort, thus making Uncle Sam an emblem of patriotism too.

Uncle Sam Day, celebrated every year since 1989 on September 13th to coincide with Sam Wilson's birthday, symbolises American strength, as well as ideals such as liberty.

1. person who prepares and packs meat – 2. marked with a sign (U.S.) – 3. container for meat, holding about 100 kilos – 4. unsmiling, severe

B | Student 1

Culture Tip

1812 war

The U.S. declared war on Great Britain on June 18th, 1812, due mainly to British restrictions on U.S. trade and America's desire for territory further north. The Royal Navy's blockade almost bankrupted the U.S. by 1814. However, being tired of war in Europe against Napoleon, Britain signed the Treaty of Ghent on February 18th, 1815, ending the war.

THE STAR-SPANGLED **BANNER**

On September 14, 1814, Francis Scott Key pens[1] a poem which is later set to music and in 1931 becomes America's national anthem, *"The Star-Spangled Banner."* The poem, originally titled "The Defence of Fort M'Henry," was written after Key witnessed[2] the Maryland fort being bombarded by the British during the War of 1812. Key was inspired by the sight of a lone[3] U.S. flag still flying over Fort McHenry at daybreak, as reflected in the now-famous words of the "*Star-Spangled Banner*": "*And the rocket's red glare, the bombs bursting in air, Gave proof through the night that our flag was still there.*" [...]

On June 18, 1812, America declared war on Great Britain after a series of trade disagreements. In August 1814, British troops invaded Washington, D.C., and burned the White House, Capitol Building and Library of Congress. Their next target was Baltimore. [...] Key watched the bombing campaign unfold from aboard a ship located about eight miles away. After a day, the British were unable to destroy the fort and gave up. Key was relieved to see the American flag still flying over Fort McHenry and quickly penned a few lines in tribute[4] to what he had witnessed.

superbowl 50, lady gaga

history.com

1. writes – 2. saw – 3. isolated – 4. respect and admiration

C **Student 2**

1. Gather information about your symbol (B or C): its origins • the history behind it

PAIR WORK
2. Explain why your symbol is the most significant. Convince the other student.

3. Film yourself presenting your symbol for *American Week* at school.

4. Grammar In document C, pick out the verbs in the past perfect. How is it formed? What does it express?

WORD BOX

- an anniver**sa**ry
- a **du**ty
- a de**pic**tion = **a** por**tray**al
- en**light**enment = under**stand**ing, illumi**na**tion
- de**ter**mined ≠ **he**sitant
- spread **li**berty
- be sy**no**nymous with sth

MEMORY CHALLENGE

Get your classmate to guess a symbol in less than 10 seconds.

Remember how to

Interpret symbols

Utilisez :

- **des verbes au présent simple :**
  → *stand for sth, represent sth, symbolise sth, embody/ personify sth...*
- **des noms** → *an allegory, a symbol/an emblem for sth*
- **des adjectifs** → *iconic, symbolic of sth, emblematic of sth*
  → *The torch is* ***symbolic of*** *enlightenment and knowledge.*
- N'oubliez pas qu'en anglais, les notions et les abstractions sont précédées de l'article Ø :
  → *The bald eagle symbolises* ***Ø freedom****,* ***Ø strength****,* ***Ø honesty****,* ***Ø wisdom****, and* ***Ø power****.*

PREPARE YOUR PROJECT

Radio phone-in

NPR is organising a radio phone-in to find out what people think is the most iconic symbol of the USA. Choose the symbol you would like to vote for and record your participation.

2 Rethinking American symbols

1. Look at the cartoon. Identify the symbols featured and what they represent.
2. Describe their actions and facial expressions.
3. Note down what you think are the cartoonist's intentions on his Facebook page.

A

B Levi Stadium, October 2, 2016 - Santa Clara, California

Video 23lmu2903

Culture Tip Colin Kaepernick is an American football quarterback and civil rights activist. He is renowned for kneeling during the national anthem at the start of matches in 2016 to protest racial injustice and police brutality against African Americans. Very soon, his teammates and other athletes supported his actions.

1. Read the Culture tip and watch the video. Identify the speaker and outline her point of view on kneeling during a football match.
2. Pick out what the speaker says about protesting.
3. Tweet on the subject of protesting at football matches. Use emojis and hastags.

WORD BOX

- a **pro**test
- **ra**cial in**jus**tice
- res**pect**ful ≠ disres**pect**ful
- split = di**vi**ded
- be **trea**ted (un)**fair**ly
- be**lieve** in sth
- make a stand = de**fend** a cause
- raise a**ware**ness
- kneel /niːl/ = take the knee
- de**nounce** sth = **cri**ticise sth
- pro**test**
- patri**o**tic ≠ unpatri**o**tic
- strike **some**one = at**tack** **some**one

Is kneeling during the national anthem an appropriate form of protest?

PRO

When one believes the United States is not living up to its ideals of freedom, liberty, and justice for all, kneeling during the national anthem is appropriate and justified.

Colin Kaepernick said, "I'm not going to stand up to show pride in a flag for a country that oppresses black people and people of color… To me, this is bigger than football and it would be selfish on my part to look the other way. There are bodies in the street and people getting paid leave and getting away with murder."

Many other athletes have since refused to stand for the national anthem for similar reasons. Denver Broncos linebacker Brandon Marshall, who also has knelt during the national anthem, said, "the message is I'm against social injustice… I'm not against the military or police or America at all." […]

CON

Kneeling during the national anthem shows disrespect for the flag and members of the armed forces.

The national anthem pays respect to the people who have risked their lives, been injured, or died defending the United States. Carole Isham, a great-great-great-granddaughter of the writer of the national anthem (Francis Scott Key) stated that "it just blows my mind[1] that somebody like (Kaepernick) would do what he does to dishonor the flag of this country and the national anthem when we have young men and women overseas fighting for this country, people that have died for this country." […]

On June 5, 2020, President Trump tweeted, "OLD GLORY is to be revered[2], cherished, and flown high… We should be standing up straight and tall, ideally with a salute, or a hand on heart. There are other things you can protest, but not our Great American Flag – NO KNEELING!"

www.procon.org

1. I'm amazed – 2. have deep respect for

C

Americans Divided on Athlete Protests

% of U.S. adults saying kneeling during the national anthem to protest racial discrimination is…

■ An acceptable form of protest ■ An unacceptable form of protest

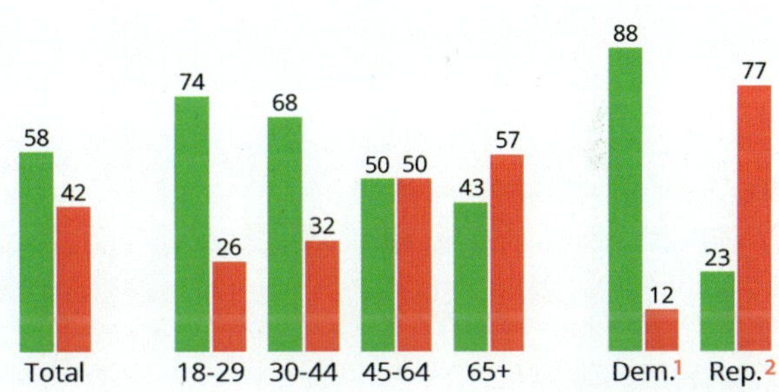

Based on a survey of 2,008 U.S. adults conducted July 21-24, 2020
Sources: CBS News, YouGov

1. Democrats – 2. Republicans

statista

D

PAIR WORK Student A is pro / Student B is con.

1. Analyse the infographic (Doc D) focusing on the data for your camp: pro or con.
2. Pick out the arguments from your text (Doc C) and support them with data from the infographic (Doc D).
3. Present your arguments to your partner. Convince him/her you are right.

Pronunciation In the following words, cross out the silent consonants: *knelt*, *writer*, *dishonor*. Do you know any other words containing the same silent letters?

PREPARE YOUR PROJECT

In-class debate

"Is kneeling during the national anthem an appropriate form of protest?"

- Split into 2 teams of 2/3 students. One team is for, the other against.
- Defend your point of view.

IMPROVE YOUR Grammar

Activités en ligne
23lmu2904

Le *past perfect*

Tyron's Tips
23lmu2905

- Le *past perfect* (ou *pluperfect*) se forme au moyen de l'**auxiliaire** ***had*** et du **participe passé.**

Forme affirmative	Forme négative	Forme interrogative
*I **had** worked*	*I **had not (hadn't)** worked*	***Had** she worked...?*

- On utilise le *past perfect* quand on veut repérer deux événements passés l'un par rapport à l'autre : le *past perfect* marque une antériorité par rapport à un autre événement passé qui, lui, est au prétérit :
  → *When I **arrived** at the ceremony, the President **had already given** a speech.* (le discours est antérieur à mon arrivée)
- On trouve souvent le *past perfect* **dans un contexte passé** avec des compléments de temps qui expriment une antériorité : ***previously*** (auparavant), ***already*** (déjà), ***earlier, a few weeks/days before***, etc.
  → *He criticised the athletes who **had taken** the knee **a few weeks before.***
- Il est souvent utilisé dans **les propositions de temps introduites par *after*** :
  → *After the athletes **had taken** the knee, some politicians sharply criticised them.*

> Précis p. 265

Exprimer la concession et la contradiction

- **La conjonction de coordination *but*** (mais) permet de relier deux phrases contradictoires.
  → *The Statue of Liberty is located in New York, **but** it was built in France.*
- **Les adverbes *however*** et ***nevertheless*** (cependant ou toutefois) sont souvent placés en début ou en fin de phrase.
  → *The Statue of Liberty is located in New York. **However/Nevertheless,** it was built in France.*
- **Les conjonctions de subordination *although*** /ɔːl'ðəʊ/ (bien que) et (***even***) ***though*** /ðəʊ/ (même si) introduisent une proposition subordonnée de concession.
  On les utilise pour exprimer une contradiction ou quand un fait n'entraîne pas la conséquence attendue.
  → ***Although the protesters were peaceful and nonviolent,** incidents broke out.*

1 Dans chaque phrase, repérez le complément de temps qui justifie l'emploi du *past perfect.* Puis mettez les verbes entre parenthèses au *past perfect.*

1. Several activists were arrested yesterday. Earlier in the day, several hundred protesters ... *(gather)* in the city centre.
2. After the audience ... *(sing)* the anthem, the match kicked off.
3. By the age of 15, I ... *(already/visit)* the Statue of Liberty twice!

2 Mettez les verbes entre parenthèses au prétérit simple ou au *past perfect.*

Francis Scott Key ... *(write)* the lyrics of *the Star-Spangled banner* in 1814, after he ... *(witness)* the bombardment of Fort McHenry. A few months before, the United States ... *(declare)* war on Britain. A few years later, Scott's poem ... *(be set)* to music. It ... *(become)* the American national anthem in 1931.

3 Reliez les deux phrases au moyen du mot entre parenthèses. Attention à la ponctuation !

a. Your arguments are convincing. I don't agree with you. *(even though)*
b. A large majority of Americans don't support the government's policy. The president was reelected. *(although)*
c. President George Washington oversaw the construction of the White House. He never lived there. *(however)*
d. Betsy Ross is credited with making the first American flag in 1776. There's no evidence this story is true. *(nevertheless)*
e. The journalist made a stand against racism and discrimination. She condemned the protesters. *(although)*

IMPROVE YOUR Pronunciation

Les consonnes muettes Audio 23lmu2906

- En anglais, certaines consonnes sont muettes quand elles apparaissent dans les contextes suivants :

b dans ***mb***	*bom**b**, thum**b**, dum**b***
k dans ***kn***	***k**now, **k**neel, **k**nife*
n dans ***mn***	*dam**n**, condem**n**, hym**n***
t dans ***sten, ften*** et ***stle***	*lis**t**en, whis**t**le, of**t**en*
w dans ***wr***	***w**rite, **w**rong*
l dans la ***alk, alf*** et ***alm***	*wa**l**k, ha**l**f, ca**l**m*

On ne prononce pas non plus le ***l*** dans les modaux *cou**l**d, wou**l**d* et *shou**l**d*.

- La consonne *h* n'est pas aspirée et est donc muette dans quatre mots : ***h**our, (dis)**h**onest, **h**onour* et ***h**eir* (héritier) ainsi que leurs dérivés.

1 a) **Recopiez ces mots et rayez les consonnes muettes.**

knee • knowledge • Palm Beach • climb • calm • talk • calf (veau) • half • knit (tricoter) • autumn

b) **Écoutez l'enregistrement pour vérifier vos réponses et répétez.** Audio 23lmu2907

2 **Donnez les homophones des mots suivants (des mots qui se prononcent de la même façon mais qui s'écrivent différemment).** Audio 23lmu2908

no • him • knew • night • knot • write • Neal (name) • would • (she) knows

La prononciation du *r* Audio 23lmu2909

- En anglais, la consonne ***r*** (représentée par le symbole /r/) se prononce en dirigeant la pointe de la langue vers le palais.

Le son *r* prononcé « à la française » n'existe pas en anglais.

Lorsque la graphie ***r*** suit une voyelle dans une même syllabe, **elle n'est pas prononcée** en anglais britannique : *pa**r**k* *New Yo**r**k* *Sta**r**-spangled banner*

En revanche, la plupart des Américains prononcent le ***r*** dans cette position.

3 **Écoutez les mots suivants puis répétez-les à l'identique en étant attentif à la prononciation de la consonne /r/.** Audio 23lmu2910

red • rally • really • agree • American • protest • parade

4 **Vous allez entendre les mots suivants prononcés par un locuteur britannique puis par un locuteur américain. Soyez attentif à la prononciation du /r/. Répétez les mots avec l'accent que vous aurez choisi.** Audio 23lmu2911

short • star • support • first • burn • mark • favour • torch • determined

IMPROVE YOUR Vocabulary

Activités en ligne
23lmu2912

American symbols

SYMBOLS

Audio 23lmu2913

- the Star-spangled banner
- a seal = *un sceau*
- a bald eagle
- a Native American
- a Pilgrim Father
- symbolise sth /ˈsɪmbəlaɪz/
- depict sth = illustrate, portray sth
- embody sth = represent, stand for sth
- express sth
- originate from/in sth = come from sth
- well-known = famous, renowned

EVENTS

Audio 23lmu2914

- a celebration
- a tribute
- a demonstration
- a street parade
- sports events
- the Super Bowl
- Independence Day
- kneeling
- march
- a protest
- hold a rally/ a demonstration/ a protest
- gather
- take to the streets

Debating

FOR

Audio 23lmu2915

- approve of sth
- be all for sth
- be in favour of sth
- endorse sth
- regard highly
- support sth
- I'm convinced
- I totally agree
- I must stress
- I'd like to focus on sth

UNSURE

Audio 23lmu2916

- be undecided
- have doubts /daʊts/
- be on the fence
- have misgivings

AGAINST

Audio 23lmu2917

- be debatable
- be disrespectful
- be divisive
- be opposed to sth
- disapprove of sth
- I can't believe that...
- it's a shame that...
- I can't quite agree with sth

1 The race is on! In teams, find 3:
- symbols of the USA
- synonyms for *represent*
- ways of protesting
- sentences to give your point of view
- events where you can see the U.S. flag
- expressions to use in a debate

2 Find 2 arguments for and against:

Kneeling during the national anthem

The U.S. flag

The Statue of Liberty is the most iconic symbol

3 Play *Last Person Standing*

In groups of 4, name a category of vocabulary associated with the unit. Then each person takes turns to give a word until someone is stuck. That person sits down and a new category is chosen. Play until there is only one player left standing; [s]he has won!

Let's RECAP

Faites le point ! Complétez la fiche bilan avec les documents que vous avez étudiés. Fiche 23lmu2918

AXE 8

The past in the present

Do American symbols still represent the USA?

#pastandpresent

What are the most iconic symbols of the USA?

#changingattitudes

How have attitudes towards certain symbols evolved?

 # iconicsymbols

Why are Uncle Sam, the Statue of Liberty and the Star-Spangled Banner so iconic?

#kneeling

Why do some athletes kneel during the National Anthem?

GROUP WORK Choose a question and discuss.

Quiz 23lmu2919

Become AN EXPERT

Lisez et écoutez de l'anglais en dehors de la classe

Books

- *Inventing the Flag*, Henry W. Moeller vers AMC

- *The United symbolism of America*, Robert Hieronimus vers AMC

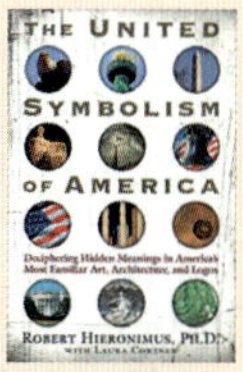

Music

- *The Star-Spangled Banner at Woodstock in 1969*, Jimi Hendrix
- *Born in the USA*, Bruce Springsteen

Films

vers LLCER

Series

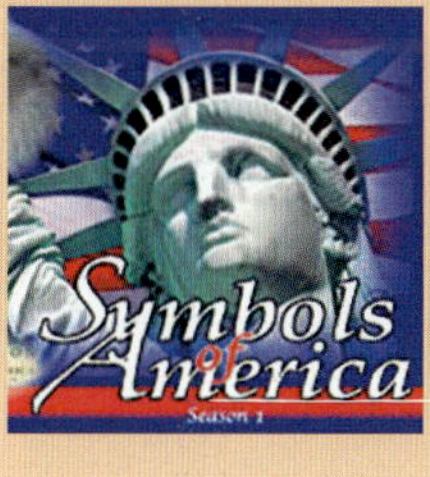

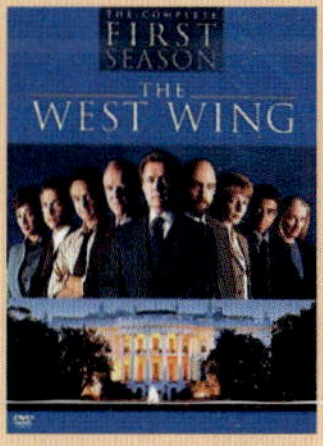

Documentaries

- *Liberty: Mother of Exiles*, HBO vers AMC

YOUR PROJECTS

Take part in a televised debate

Motion: 'The Star-Spangled Banner' should be replaced with a new US national anthem.
Musicians and historians suggest the anthem, which was written by a 19th-century slave owner, should not be America's national song.

- Create your character:
  - an expert in traditional American symbols,
  or
  - a member of an organisation that promotes the evolution of American symbols.

  Prepare your character: name, job, personality, etc.

- Refresh your memory.

  Go through the unit for information on the Star-Spangled Banner to use in the introduction to the debate. You can also do some research and find fresh arguments.

- Find out why some Americans want to change the national anthem.

  Prepare new arguments depending on your character.

- Revise debate vocabulary and review your arguments.
- Debate! May the best team win!

OR

Write a letter to the editor

You feel very strongly about the subject of kneeling during the American anthem. Write to the *Letters to the Editor* page of the New York Times International, expressing your view: for or against.

- Gather information.

  Review the documents in the unit on kneeling. Decide whether you are for or against.

- Use *Letters to the Editor* format.

  Start with *Dear Sir* or *Madam* and end with your name, your town and your county.

- Plan your letter.

  Order your main arguments in bullet points.

- Write and post.

  - Use expressions to convince the reader.
  - Write the letter in full, check spelling and grammar.

Relire un devoir écrit p. 282

BUILD UP YOUR SKILLS

How to
Debate and win!

REGARDEZ CETTE VIDÉO (→ 3'24) ET VÉRIFIEZ SI LES INTERVENANTS ONT BIEN RESPECTÉ LES RÈGLES D'UN DÉBAT !

Video 23lmu2920

Should schools teach the national anthem?

1. Pour se préparer

- Assurez-vous que vous avez bien compris le sujet du débat, ou *motion*.
- Rassemblez vos idées et documentez-vous pour nourrir vos arguments : en relisant le chapitre, en faisant quelques recherches complémentaires si besoin.
- Listez des arguments en fonction de votre position : For / Against
- Essayez d'anticiper les arguments de vos opposants pour pouvoir y répondre.
- Renforcez vos arguments par des exemples précis.
- Utilisez des tournures pour persuader et convaincre. [→ *Improve your vocabulary* p. 102]

2. Pour participer

- En introduction, présentez le sujet.
- Exposez clairement votre point de vue et écoutez attentivement celui de vos opposants pour comprendre leur raisonnement.
- Critiquez leurs arguments de manière nuancée.
- Citez vos exemples pour appuyer vos idées.

Rappelez-vous que le débat est un échange, pas un affrontement !

Are you ready?

+ prof
Évaluation

Entraînement à l'évaluation

Compréhension orale

marinashutup

Supreme Court Justice Ruth Bader Ginsburg's comments about Colin Kaepernick Video 23lmu2921

1. Explain Colin Kaepernick's action and why he was protesting.
2. Outline Ruth Bader Ginsburg's view of Colin Kaepernick, then pick out another form of protest she mentions.
3. Find out if Ginsburg believes such protests to be reprehensible by law.
4. Describe the video blogger's reaction to Ginsburg's comments.

Culture Tip

Ruth Bader Ginsburg (1933-2020)

Also known as R.B.G., was an American lawyer and jurist who became the second woman to serve on the Supreme Court where she fought for gender equality.

Production écrite

Add a comment to the video blogger's (Marina) site. First, give your opinion on Ruth Bader Ginsburg's views and then on Marina's video.

Compréhension écrite

The Seattle Times

Our flag tells a lot about who we are

By TYRONE BEASON – July 7, 2015

The six U.S. flags astronauts planted proudly on the moon in the Apollo missions are the same as the countless ones horrified Americans hung from balconies and porches the day of the Sept. 11 terrorist attacks and the same as the ones saluted by military personnel in the subsequent Afghan and Iraq wars. We fly the flag at parades, recite the Pledge of Allegiance to it in home room and lower it to half-staff for fallen soldiers and dignitaries. [...]

It is the banner we salute at events big and small, from citizenship ceremonies to sports events. [...]

And yet, study after study suggests that the flag flies over a nation that is not as patriotic as it used to be, at least not in the way that we're used to thinking about patriotism. [...]

The flag has continued to serve as a potent[1] tool in street protests in Seattle, from the World Trade Organization demonstrations in 1999 to countless May Day rallies by everyone from immigrant-rights advocates to anarchists.

At the most recent May Day rally and march for immigrants' and workers' rights, Antonio Diaz moves through the crowd of about 500 people gathered in Seattle's Central District, hoisting[2] a U.S. flag he hangs upside down to protest immigration laws and right-side up to show affection for a country to which he doesn't legally belong. Diaz, 42, says he's an undocumented[3] worker from Mexico who arrived here 14 years ago to work for a better life. Each year he comes to the May Day rally with his flag in tow. He says he dreams of becoming a citizen, that by going public with his plight[4] he might affect change in the country's immigration laws.

seattletimes.com

1. important – 2. holding – 3. illegal – 4. difficult situation

1. Identify when the American flag is used as a symbol of pride and then of protest.
2. Find information about Antonio Diaz.
3. Explain why Mr. Diaz is holding the flag upside down.
4. Comment on how Mr. Diaz uses the flag to get his message across.

> Avant de lire le texte : analysez la source de l'article et l'image qui l'accompagne.
> Après votre lecture : relevez les symboles, les évènements et les dates mentionnées.

Production écrite

Write a short article entitled: *Stars and Stripes, a symbol of pride and of protest*. [100 words]

Vivre entre générations

UNIT 10 Being Irish

▶ How is the Irish heritage passed on?

YOUR PROJECTS

Create an infographic about Irishness.

OR

Shoot a video to talk about Irish teenagers.

Capital City: Dublin

Name in Irish (Gaelic): Éire

Official languages: Irish, English

National Day: Saint Patrick's Day (March 17)

Proclamation of the Republic: 1916

War for independence: 1919-1921

Currency: Euro

Politics: Republic since 1937. Member state of the European Union since 1973.

A What it means to be Irish Video 23lmu21001

1. Watch the video and pick out 3 keywords defining Charlotte's Irish identity.
2. List the 3 elements she uses to illustrate the keywords and the final word she uses.
3. Prepare a one-minute oral presentation about Charlotte and her vision of what it means to be Irish.

Pronunciation Listen and repeat: *descendants, heritage, happiness*. Are the underlined vowels stressed or unstressed? Audio 23lmu21002

WORD BOX

- an **Uill**ean /ˈɪlən/ pipe
- a **Lep**rechaun /ˈleprəkɔːn/ = a small **elf**like **crea**ture of Irish **folk**lore
- a pa**rade**
- pride
- a sense of be**long**ing
- **cul**tural roots = a **cul**tural **her**itage
- em**brace** sth /ɪmˈbreɪs/
- be bi**lin**gual /baɪˈlɪŋgwəl/
- pass a**long** = trans**mit**
- **cel**ebrate sth
- have a strong sig**nif**icance = mean sth im**por**tant

Group A

Group B

Group C

B Group work

FICHE GROUP WORK

1. Read the information card on p. 108 then observe and describe your group's pictures. Identify as many Irish symbols as you can.
   Use Fiche 23lmu21003

2. Explain to the other groups what aspect of Irish culture your pictures represent.

3. Write an Instagram post with your 3 favourite pictures. Add a comment for each.

Culture Tip

Gaelic /ˈgeɪlɪk/ (or Irish) is a Celtic language that is older than English. It is the first official language in Ireland (before English). Its use has known a revival in today's Ireland and is spoken by approximately 39% of the population.

1 Irish Identity

GROUP WORK

DIFFÉRENCIATION

www.irishtimes.com

Ola Majekodunmi

Broadcaster[1] and journalist

You would laugh at the number of times people have asked me how I speak Irish or why I even speak it. I struggle[2] to understand at times what is it that is so surprising about a person of immigrant background speaking the first official language? Not only that, but why is it threatening[3] to some that I do? There are complexities within Irishness. We are not proud of who we are as a nation, yet we have this beautiful, cultural heritage. I fear it may all slip from our hands one day without us realising that now is the time to cherish[4] what we have.

1. someone hosting a show – 2. have difficulties – 3. menacing – 4. love

A Group 1

www.hotpress.com

Niall Horan

Former member of the band 'One Direction'

There are nights when I'm in New York or Sydney or wherever and just want to jump on a plane back to Ireland to see my friends and family. The longer I spend away from Mullingar* the more I want to come home. I'm going to make it a thing to get back a lot more this year when there are gaps in my schedule. [...] I was lucky enough to go on a couple of stadium tours with One Direction and play to 80,000 [...] people at Croke Park, which was one of the best nights of my life. Right now, though, what's most amazing is discovering that I'm one of only four Irish artists who've got to number one in America. I'm just going to make that phone call to my mum...

* Mullingar is Niall Horan's hometown, in the middle of Ireland

B Group 2

Culture Tip

Croke Park is a stadium in Dublin which is the home of Gaelic Sports (hurling, Gaelic football, Camogie). It was also the place of the first 'Bloody Sunday' in 1920 where 14 Irish people were killed by the British Army.

WORD BOX

- a com**mu**nity
- an **imm**igrant
- an **ath**lete
- a **cit**izen
- tra**di**tions
- multi**cul**turalism
- di**ver**sity /daɪˈvɜːrsɪti/
- world**wide** = all a**round** the world
- open-**mind**ed ≠ **nar**row-**mind**ed
- sup**port**ive
- **home**sick

www.irishtimes.com

Mary Lou McDonald

Leader of Sinn Féin

There is no one way to be Irish or to feel Irish, any more than there is one way to be human. For me, what it has meant to be Irish has changed over time. My experience of being an Irish woman began as an Irish girl born into a very different Ireland. In many ways Ireland at that time could be quite an austere and judgmental place to live if you were seen as being "other". [...] Throughout my lifetime, Ireland has embraced many changes which have improved our society for the better.

C Group 3

www.irishtimes.com

Sonia O'Sullivan

Former world champion and track-and-field[1] Olympian

Wherever I went to the farthest[2] corners of Earth, there was always at least one Irish flag in the stadium. [...] You begin to realise there are more Irish people living outside Ireland and, when there is a reason to connect, they are the first in line. I still experience the Irish welcome wherever I go. [...] I am proud to be Irish. It is true that when you live abroad, you tend to emphasise[3] the good things. For the people who live in Ireland, the view can be negative sometimes. And there has been negative news in recent years. I was so impressed by and proud of the equal marriage campaign[4] and the numbers of (mostly young) Irish who flew home to vote.

1. athletics – 2. most distant – 3. underline –
4. the equal marriage campaign asked for the right for same-sex couples to marry

D Group 4

Culture Tip Sinn Féin is an Irish political party that wants Northern Ireland (still part of the UK) to become part of the Republic of Ireland.

FICHE GROUP WORK

1. Work on one of these individuals.
Sum up: their vision of Ireland • their Irish identity • possible problems
Use Fiche 23lmu21004

2. Share your work with the other groups and find the common points between each vision.

3. Choose the personality who represents the aspect of being Irish that you most admire and explain your choice.

PREPARE YOUR **PROJECT**

Create a mind map

Create a mind map with the word "IRELAND" in the middle. List the values expressed by the people in the texts.

2 A new heritage?

1. Watch the video. Identify:
   - the different activities the teenagers have,
   - the reasons why they are doing them.
2. Find elements coming from their Irish heritage and more modern ones.
3. Focus on the part between 1'53 and 2'27 and explain why the girls are conflicted.
4. You are one of the teenagers in the video. Answer the question: *"Do you consider yourself a traditional or modern Irish teenager?"*

A What's it like to be a 16-year-old in Dublin today?

Video 23lmu21005

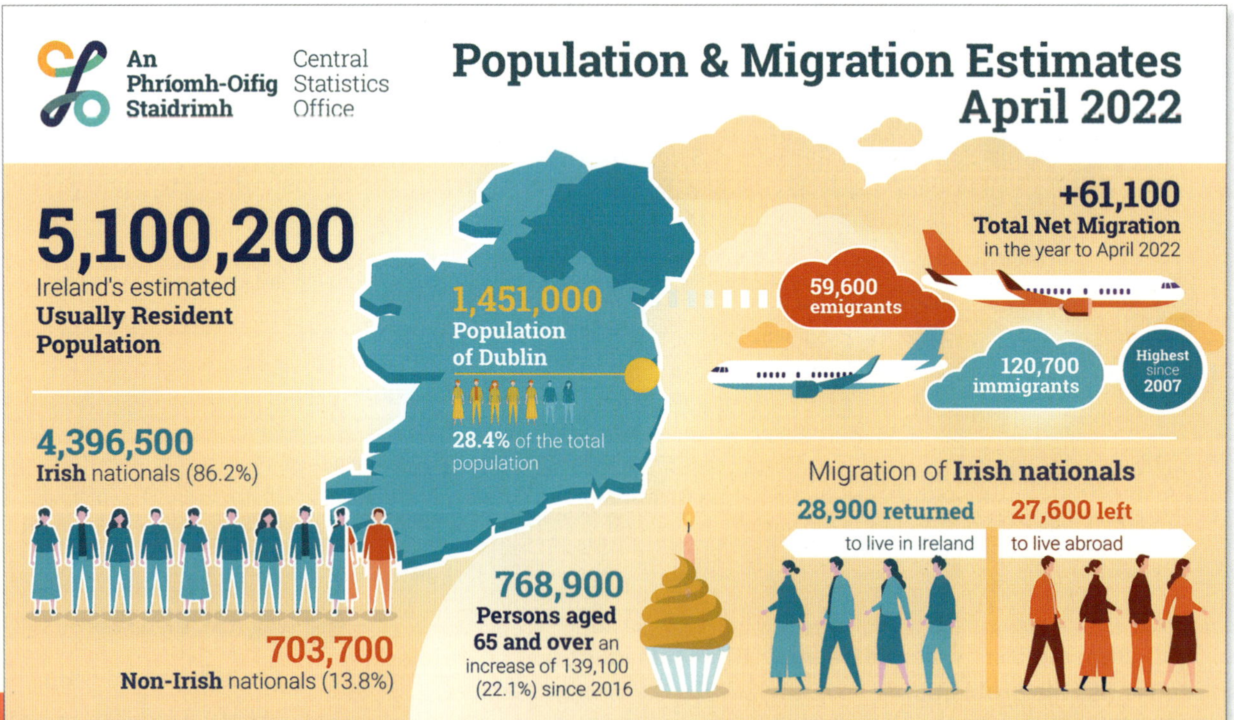

B

1. Observe the infographic and explain how Ireland is changing.
2. Focus on the planes and say what it reveals about today's Ireland.
3. Explain to your history teacher what this infographic reveals about the Irish population.

The real Ireland

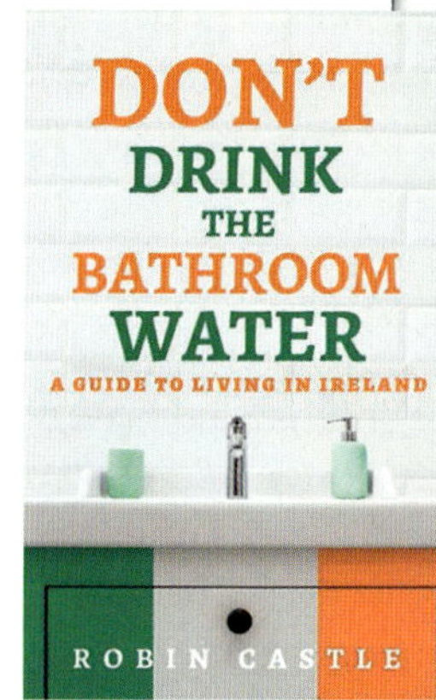

Obviously, you have excellent taste because you have taken an interest in one of the most beautiful, unspoiled[1] countries on earth. In Ireland, a drive in any direction will quickly lead you to rolling lush green hills, rivers, gardens, plant life of all varieties (even palm trees!), the sea, and an obscure pond[2] known as the Atlantic. Ireland has become a modern country embracing all mod cons (modern conveniences) without losing her identity, her culture, her heritage. That is what makes Ireland distinct. No big box stores, only a handful of drive-throughs[3], and a real preference for local produce and locally made goods have kept Ireland Irish.

Many items which are advertised in other countries as being Irish, such as Irish spring soap[4], corned beef and cabbage, and green beer are no more Irish than French fries are French. Celebrating Saint Patrick's Day in Ireland is a quiet family affair, marked by a parade in City Centre.

What is truly Irish? Meals with three different potato dishes […]. Roads designed for medieval carts and not since updated, disdain for bragging[5], the immersion, a widespread love of reading, and a cultural flexibility which allows Ireland to make massive social changes in one generation where other nations stumble: that is the real Ireland. Ireland is more than a beauty. She's smart too. And so are you for being interested in her.

But first, a bit of history. Don't worry, it's only a paragraph. There was no widespread access to electricity in Ireland until fifty years ago and every Irish person over forty grew up without a phone in their home or even in their village. Yet today, Google, Microsoft, LinkedIn, Facebook and all the other tech giants have large operations on Irish soil[6] Ireland is fast on its feet.

Robin Castle, *Don't Drink the Bathroom Water: A Guide to Living in Ireland*, 2020

1. intact – **2.** lake – **3** drive-in – **4.** American deodorant soap – **5.** talking loud – **6.** ground

C

1. Read the first sentence and find who "you" refers to.

2. Read the rest of the text and find the only question mentioned. Give a reason why the author asks it.

3. Create a grid and fill it with elements from the text: what is typically Irish • what is not • tradition • modernity

4. Write 5 reasons why people should visit Ireland that you would include in *"A guide to living in Ireland"*.

Grammar *"Celebrating Saint Patrick's Day"* (l. 16). What is the underlined verb form called? Find other examples.

WORD BOX

- a **cliché** /ˈkliːʃeɪ/ = a **stere**otype /ˈsteriətaɪp/
- youth /ˈjuːθ/
- an oppor**tu**nity
- a com**mit**ment
- camogie /kəˈməʊgi/ = an **I**rish sport
- **hope**ful
- **i**ronic = sar**cas**tic
- be in**volved** in +V-ing = be com**mit**ted to +V-ing
- trans**mit**
- start a new life
- grow **old**er

Remember how to

Present and discuss data

- En anglais, les décimales sont séparées par un point : ***1.5%*** *(one **point** five percent).*
- Pour décrire une augmentation : ***increase***, ***rise*** ou ***go up by X%***.
  → *The number of immigrants **increased / rose by 10% in 2022**.*
- Pour une diminution : ***decrease*** ou ***drop by X%***.
- Quand on arrondit un chiffre, on utilise ***about*** ou ***approximately*** :
  → *The population of Dublin represents **about/approximately** 28% of the country's population.*

PREPARE YOUR PROJECT

Radio phone-in

Rté Radio 1 (the Irish national radio) has just asked the following question in the morning show: *"Is Ireland changing today?"*. Record your one-minute participation to the show.

IMPROVE YOUR Grammar

Activités en ligne
23lmu21006

Les comparatifs

Tyron's Tips
23lmu21007

- **Les comparatifs de supériorité** des adjectifs et des adverbes se forment de la façon suivante :

Adjectifs courts (une syllabe)	Adjectifs longs (deux syllabes ou plus)
adjectif + ***-er*** *proud → prouder*	***more*** adjective *interesting → **more** interesting*

Les adjectifs en ***-y*** de deux syllabes forment le plus souvent leur comparatif en ***-ier*** : *happy → happier*. Il existe des formes irrégulières : *good → better, bad → worse.*

- Le complément du comparatif (ce à quoi on compare) est introduit par ***than*** :
  → *Dublin is **larger and more populated than** Belfast.*
- **Le comparatif d'égalité** se construit avec ***as* + adjectif + *as...*** (aussi... que...) :
  → *Irish culture is **as diverse as** British society.*
- **Le comparatif d'infériorité** se construit avec ***less* + adjectif + *than...*** (moins... que...)
  → *The west of the country is **less** densely populated **than** the east.*

> Précis p. 254

1 Mettez les adjectifs entre parenthèses au comparatif de supériorité :

a. Irish music is ... (*popular*) than ever.
b. Some people think that English is ... (*easy*) to learn than Gaelic.
c. Irish society is probably ... (*tolerant*) and ... (*multicultural*) nowadays than it used to be.
d. The Irish economy is much ... (*strong*) and ... (*wealthy*) today than it was 20 years ago.

2 Mettez les adjectifs à la forme du comparatif demandée.

a. Living in Ireland is ... in the rest of Europe. (*expensive* – infériorité)
b. Irish literature is ... British literature. (*rich and interesting* – égalité)
c. The weather in Ireland is ... you think. (*good* – supériorité)

Le gérondif

- Le gérondif est **la forme nominalisée** du verbe. On le forme en ajoutant ***-ing*** au verbe.
- On l'utilise par exemple quand on veut faire d'un verbe ou d'une proposition **le sujet d'une phrase**. Dans ce cas, on le traduit par un infinitif français :
  → *__**Celebrating**__ __Saint Patrick's Day in Ireland__ is a great experience.* (***Fêter*** *la Saint Patrick en Irlande est une expérience fabuleuse*).
- On trouve souvent le gérondif après des prépositions telles que ***of, for, in, with*** ou ***from...***
  → *Niall Horan is famous **for __being__** a former member of the boy band 'One Direction'.*
  → *I'm interested **in __working__** in Ireland.*
- ***Without*** est souvent suivi du gérondif :
  → *Ireland has become a modern country **without __losing__** her identity.* (__*sans perdre*__ *son identité...*)

3 Complétez ces phrases en employant un gérondif. Produisez deux phrases à chaque fois.

a. You can't go to Ireland without...
b. Dublin is famous for...
c. Most Irish young people are interested in...
d. A lot of Irish teenagers are involved in...

4 a) Mettez les verbes suivants au gérondif.

grow up in Ireland • listen to Irish folk music • immigrate to Ireland • learn Gaelic

b) Produisez des phrases où ce gérondif est en position sujet.

Ex. *visit Ireland → __**Visiting Ireland**__ is a great way to explore your own Irish heritage and history.*

IMPROVE YOUR Pronunciation

La consonne *h*

Tyron's Tips 23lmu21008

- En anglais, **la consonne *h* est généralement aspirée.** Ne pas la prononcer peut créer des problèmes de compréhension.

  Les mots commençant par un *h* aspiré sont précédés de **l'article *a*** : *a hero*. On ne fait pas la liaison devant un mot commençant par *h*.

- Dans certains mots, le *h* initial est **muet** : *honour, hour, honest* et *heir* (héritier).

  Ces mots sont alors précédés de **l'article *an*** (*an honest man*).

- Il est aussi le plus souvent muet dans les **mots grammaticaux : les pronoms** *he, him, his* et *her*, **l'auxiliaire *have / had*** du *present* et *past perfect*. On fait la liaison avant ces mots.

  → *Ireland has become a modern country*.

1 **Écoutez et répétez ces paires de mots.** Audio 23lmu21009

a. hat / at
b. all / hall
c. air / hair / heir
d. eight / hate
e. hi / eye

2 a) **Recopiez les phrases suivantes. Soulignez les *h* aspirés en rouge et les *h* muets en vert.**

a. We booked a hotel room in Dublin an hour ago.
b. It's an honour to visit his homeland.
c. Ireland has become a modern country without losing her identity and her heritage.

b) **Écoutez pour vérifier et répétez.** Audio 23lmu21010

La prononciation des terminaisons inaccentuées Audio 23lmu21011

Certaines terminaisons sont **inaccentuées :** leur voyelle est donc souvent **réduite**, c'est-à-dire prononcées avec la voyelle schwa /ə/ (comme dans *the*) ou /ɪ/ (comme dans *big*).

-ent, -ant /ənt/	*important*
-age /ɪʤ/	*heritage*
-dom /dəm/	*kingdom*
-ment /mənt/	*commitment*
-ous /əs/	*famous*
-ness /nəs/	*madness*
-ful /fəl/	*handful*
-or, -our, -er /ə[r]/	*honour*

3 **Écoutez et répétez les mots suivants en faisant attention à la prononciation de la voyelle en gras.** Audio 23lmu21012

ancestors • *tolerant* • *immigrant* • *freedom* • *message* • *image* • *dangerous* • *Irishness* • *illness*

IMPROVE YOUR Vocabulary

Activités en ligne 23lmu21013

Irishness

CULTURE

Audio 23lmu21014

- language
- Irish folklore
- Gaelic /'geɪlɪk/ = Celtic /'keltɪk/ language spoken in Ireland
- a landscape = scenery
- be bilingual /baɪ'lɪŋgwəl/
- pass along = transmit
- preserve sth
- be culturally rich
- embrace /ɪm'breɪs/ your culture = welcome your culture

HERITAGE

Audio 23lmu21015

- roots = origins
- homeland = country of origin
- history
- a custom = a tradition
- an ancestor ≠ a descendant
- a legacy
- respectful
- honour
- respect traditions
- symbolise

Identity

MIGRATION

Audio 23lmu21016

- a diaspora /daɪ'æspərə/ = a group of people from the same country
- a native /'neɪtɪv/
- emigration
- immigration
- settle = start living somewhere
- go abroad = go to another country, emigrate
- look backward ≠ look forward
- share a cultural background

BELONGING

Audio 23lmu21017

- a sense of unity
- a community
- similarity ≠ diversity
- citizenship
- otherness
- show pride
- maintain sth = keep in existence
- identify /aɪ'dentɪfaɪ/ as sth
- assert sth /ə'sɜːt/ = insist on sth

YOUTH

Audio 23lmu21018

- a transition year
- a cliché /'kliːʃeɪ/
- a stereotype /'steriətaɪp/
- an activist
- a commitment = an implication
- a determination
- a meaning
- hopeful

1 Use the letters I.R.E.L.A.N.D to create an acrostic poem with words from the mind map above.

IRISH — RESPECT — EMIGRATION — ETC.

2 *Play in groups of 4.* Choose a word from the mind map and say it to your group. Your neighbour's challenge is to say which category it belongs to. If they make a mistake they are out of the game.

3 Use 10 words from the mind map to show how the Irish heritage can be passed on.

Let's RECAP

Faites le point ! Complétez la fiche bilan avec les documents que vous avez étudiés. Fiche 23lmu21019

AXE 1

Intergenerational relationship

How is the Irish Heritage passed on?

#Irelandmylreland

Why do Irish people feel so proud of their country today?

#Irelandtheyoung

To what extent do young Irish people have the same perception of Ireland today?

#Irelandthegreen

How do Irish traditions continue to live on today?

#anewIreland

Is Ireland changing?

GROUP WORK Choose a question and discuss.

Quiz 23lmu21020

Become AN EXPERT

Lisez et écoutez de l'anglais en dehors de la classe

Podcasts

- Shared Ireland podcasts vers AMC

Movies

vers LLCER

vers LLCER

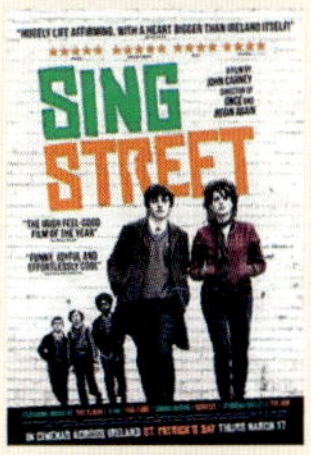

vers LLCER

vers LLCER

vers LLCER

Podcasts

- *The Bog Road*, Barry Keegan (2018) vers LLCER
- *Normal People*, Sally Rooney (2020) vers LLCER
- *A New Ireland: How Europe's Most Conservative Country Became Its Most Liberal*, Niall O'Dowd (2020) vers AMC
- *The Rise and Fall of Christian Ireland*, Crawford Gribben (2021) vers AMC

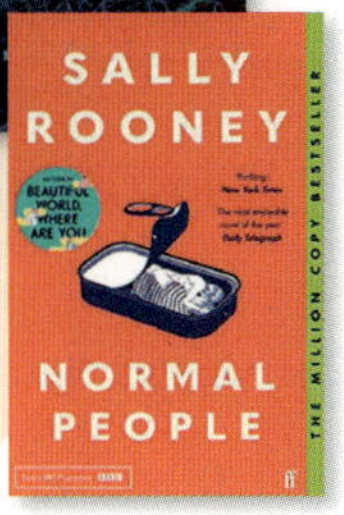

Music

- The Cranberries
- The Dubliners
- The Pogues
- U2
- Hozier

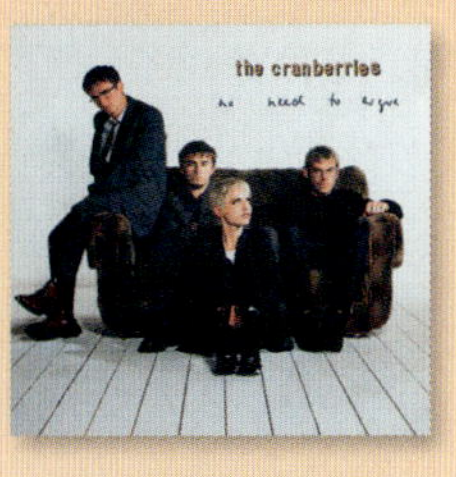

YOUR PROJECTS

Create an infographic about Irishness

The website cultureireland.ie has launched the event "Ireland Forever!". They want to select the best infographic celebrating Irishness.

- Find a strong catchphrase to start.
  - Sound Irish! Go online and find an Irish saying in Gaelic. Don't forget to write the translation in English!
- Select some information related to Irish culture and identity.
  - Make sure the information comes from a source you can trust like this unit or an encyclopaedia.
  - Do not copy everything from a website!
- Detail the reasons why you chose this information.
  - Describe how it best represents Ireland.
- Organise your findings.
  - Find fun facts to make your infographic appealing. Use eye-catching keywords or titles and superlatives.
- Create your infographic.
  - Go online to find a template. Pay attention to the colours and the way you present the information. Use typical Irish pictures.

OR

Shoot a video

On your 'Youth of the World ' Youtube Channel, create a new video entitled *'What does it mean to be a young Irish person today? '*

- Greet your followers and explain the goal of your video.
  - Say why you have posted the video in the introduction.
- Organise your video.
  - Firstly explain Irishness. Secondly, explain the life of Irish teens today.
- Give examples.
  - Talk about the Irish teenagers you have met in the chapter.
- Conclude your video.
  - Give a final answer and tell your followers about your reaction and/or what you discovered.

How to shoot a video p. 139

BUILD UP YOUR SKILLS

How to
Create an infographic

Saint Patrick's Day

LÁ FHÉILE PÁDRAIG SONA DHUIT!*

* "Happy St. Patrick's Day to you!"

St. Patrick's Day, celebrated on March 17, honors Ireland's patron saint who died on that day in 461.

The shamrock
Irish legend says Saint Patrick used the three-leafed clover to explain the Holy Trinity to non-believers.

The Irish flag
Green stands for Catholics; orange for Protestants; white for their wish for harmony.

Leprechauns
If you catch one, he will show you his treasure!

The Uillean pipe
Irish woodwind instrument still in use today. It's often played indoors and sitting down.

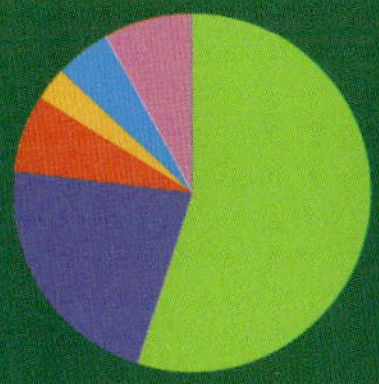

The global Irish Diaspora
- United States 55%
- Britain 22%
- Canada 7%
- Australia 3%
- Mainland Europe 5%
- Rest of World 8%

70 million people around the world claim Irish ancestry.

Today, St. Patrick's Day is celebrated all around the world. The largest St. Patrick's Day parade is held in New York City with over 2 million participants.

1. Pour la préparer

- Définissez le thème de votre infographie et son objectif :
  - évoquer un événement, une région ou un pays,
  - donner des informations sur sa population, des éléments culturels ou historiques...
- Faites des recherches pour rassembler des informations dans les documents de l'unité, en ligne ou au CDI, en étant attentifs à la qualité de vos sources :
  - données chiffrées
  - informations culturelles
  - faits surprenants
  - etc.
- Réfléchissez à la forme que vous voulez donner à votre infographie pour qu'elle soit très attractive ! Vous pouvez y inclure :
  - des chiffres bruts ou des pourcentages
  - des graphiques
  - des cartes
  - des illustrations

2. Pour la réaliser

- Sélectionner les informations qui vous paraissent les plus pertinentes.
- Organisez-les et soignez la présentation !
- Pensez aux applications gratuites pour créer des infographies spectaculaires, comme Canva ou Venngage.

Are you ready?

+ prof
Évaluation

Entraînement à l'évaluation

Compréhension orale

Faites un compte-rendu en français du document audio.

#IAmIrish Audio 23lmu21021

- Dessinez un tableau avec plusieurs colonnes qui retracent les moments importants de la vie de Lorraine Maher. Donnez un titre à chaque colonne.
- Ne traduisez pas mot-à-mot, essayez de retranscrire les idées avec vos propres mots.
- Ajoutez une dernière colonne pour détailler son point de vue sur son héritage et son identité irlandaise.

Production écrite

You work for *The Irish Times*, Ireland's most read newspaper. Interview Lorraine Maher about her Irishness. (120 word)

Compréhension écrite

GROWING UP IRISH

TRADITIONS OF AN IRISH-AMERICAN FAMILY

March 17, 2013 by Maggie Fitzgibbon

What does it mean to grow up Irish? When I posed this question to my three daughters and a few cousins, each shared with me their reflections on what being Irish means to them, and their childhood recollections[1]. [...]

Being Irish is not something one just celebrates on St. Patrick's Day but it's part of one's self-identity. Just ask my cousin, Bridget Culhane, Eileen's oldest daughter: "It's about listening to the uncles, their stories of Ireland and how they arrived in the United States. Or when the family is together at gatherings at McGinnity's[2]. It's about attending fundraisers for the Irish Children's Program, and many other Irish charity organizations. Or watching my Mom when she performed with her Irish dance group," Culhane said. [...]

Cousin Sheila Waters-Olin describes being Irish as more than genetic; it's part of who she is. "Coming from a father who is an Irish immigrant and a mother whose parents were Irish immigrants, being Irish is in my genes, my soul and most of all, in my heart," Olin said.

Olin said that being Irish is much more than celebrating on March 17. It's about family, sharing memories, telling stories and laughing.

"I have such great memories of our family reunions in Mendon, watching my cousins compete in a Feis[3] [...] or going to the Catskill Mountains for the Irish Festival. There is the memory of going to Ireland to visit aunts, uncles and cousins that I didn't know but leaving with a bond that can never be broken. It's the times when our family is together that makes me appreciate what we have. When we are laughing, telling stories and singing Irish songs, that's what being Irish is about," Olin said.

westsidenewsny.com

1. memories – 2. a typical Irish restaurant in Rochester, NY – 3. /fɛʃ/ a competition of Irish traditional dances.

1. Identify the characters in the text.
2. Sum up what they say about what it is to be Irish American.
3. Comment on their memories.
4. Analyse the general tone of the article.

Faites un tableau de trois colonnes avec :
- **la liste des personnes qui s'expriment,**
- **les souvenirs qu'ils évoquent,**
- **le regard qu'ils ont sur ces souvenirs (positif ou négatif).**

Production écrite

As an Irish American teenager, you describe your Saint Patrick's Day with your family. (120 words)

Flash UNIT 11

La création et le rapport aux arts

Art for all

▶ To what extent is Kadir Nelson making African American art accessible to all?

YOUR PROJECT

Present Kadir Nelson in a video for Black History Month.

Culture Tip **Black History Month** has been celebrated since 1976 to mark the achievements of African Americans.

Remember how to

Analyse a picture > Doc B

Analyser une image, ce n'est pas simplement la décrire. Il s'agit d'utiliser les éléments visuels explicites comme indices d'interprétation de l'implicite.

- Étape 1 **Présentation du document :** origine, nature, contexte, sujet général... Fiche Méthode > p. 284
- Étape 2 **Description :** on utilise ***there is/are...*** et **le présent en *be + -ing***
- Étape 3 **Analyse et interprétation :** ambiance, message de l'artiste, sentiment que l'œuvre suscite... On peut utiliser ces verbes **au présent simple** : *stand for = represent, symbolise, embody (incarner), mean (signifier), criticise/ denounce, suggest, insist on sth = emphasise sth...*

1 Art with a heart

A Kadir Nelson: the birth of the artist Video 23lmu21101

1. Watch the video until 1'25 and pick out information about the artist: location • artworks • musical tastes. Present him.
2. Focus on memories and events. Explain why he decided to become an artist.
3. Identify the people and the topics that inspire him.
4. Your school's art club prepares a blog post for Black History Month. Write a short post presenting the artist.

WORD BOX

- a **paint**ing / a **can**vas
- an illus**tra**tion
- a sketch = a first try
- a represen**ta**tion
- a **char**acter
- a role **mod**el = a **men**tor
- ar**tis**tic
- key = **cen**tral
- **cel**ebrate
- **il**lustrate
- raise one's fist
- **rec**ognise

Award-winning artist, author Kadir Nelson to speak at Norman Rockwell Museum

Jul. 20, 2022, By Anne-Gerard Flynn

Award-winning painter, illustrator and author Kadir Nelson [...] will speak Saturday at the Norman Rockwell Museum.

The exhibit, on view through Oct. 30, includes *Say Their Names*, a representation of George Floyd[1] that incorporates the faces of other Black victims of racial violence and discrimination, as well as *American Uprising*[2] that the artist has called "a tribute[3] to what Black women are doing to address[4] systemic barriers to equality".

[...] Nelson has said *American Uprising*, with its strong image of a modern African-American woman leading a civil rights protest with raised arm, was inspired by Eugene Delacroix's famous work, *Liberty Leading the People*, that was done in 1830 and shows a female figure in similar position embodying[5] the spirit of the French Revolution. "I wanted something that would be very hopeful and inspirational," Nelson said. He added one of the "favorite parts of the painting is the woman's face and the scarf, the American flag around her neck, which is showing how patriotic she is. This woman loves America."

masslive.com

American Uprising, 2020, Cover illustration for the magazine Rolling Stone, July 2020

1. see Culture tip – 2. political revolt – 3. homage – 4. deal with, give attention – 5. incarnating

B

1. Read the text and identify Nelson's main sources of inspiration for the two paintings mentioned.
2. Find two reasons why women are central in his art.
3. Pick out the different symbols of patriotism in the painting and their effect on the viewer.
4. Present *American Uprising* to a friend and explain its goal and message.

Culture Tip

George Perry Floyd Jr. (1973 -2020) was an African American man who was murdered by a white police officer. Many people then protested to denounce racial insecurity in the USA.

C

Painting their story Video 23lmu21102

1. Watch part 1. Focus on key words and explain his concept of "connection".
2. Watch part 2 and read the Culture tip below. Pick out what Kadir Nelson says about Norman Rockwell's art.
3. Write down three reasons why artists are trying to tell "their story".
4. Write an imaginary dialogue between Norman Rockwell and Kadir Nelson as they speak about the messages of their paintings.

Culture Tip

Norman Rockwell (1894-1978) was an American illustrator best known for his covers for the journal *The Saturday Evening Post*. He is famous for representing everyday life details realistically and with humour.

2 The unstoppable artist

KADIR NELSON: PROUDLY BLACK, POINTEDLY POSITIVE

By ELEFTHERIA PARPIS, FEB 07, 2020

Artist Kadir Nelson, Illustration Jury Chair[1] of the ADC 99th Annual Awards, was visiting the United States Capitol building in Washington, D.C. when he noticed something striking about the collection of paintings hanging in the rotunda. [...] "I saw the paintings that told the story of the beginnings of America, and those paintings leave African Americans out of that visual story," recalls Nelson. "I thought, wow, that's really unfortunate for all the school kids who come through here. They are left out of that story. How does that make them feel? In the story of freedom, they are not in it?" That trip to D.C. compelled[2] Nelson to write "*Heart and Soul: The Story of America and African Americans*," a picture book for young adults that tells the story of the nation and African Americans. [...] "I'm a painter by trade[3] and an author by necessity," explains Nelson, [...] I look for a really good story and the opportunity to create imaging[4] that will allow me to grow as an artist, do something new or different," he says. [...]

oneclub.org

1. President – 2. forced – 3. profession – 4. visual representations

A

1. Read the first sentence and find which other activity Kadir Nelson practises.
2. Read lines 1-13 and explain what shocked K. Nelson when he visited the Capitol.
3. Pick out elements showing K. Nelson had a "call of duty".
4. Share this article on twitter and add a comment on African Americans' visibility. Use hashtags.

Remember how to

Express your feelings and emotions

Pour donner son opinion sur une œuvre, il est important de le faire sur le moment afin de prendre en compte ses émotions spontanées.

- Utiliser des expressions pour indiquer un point de vue subjectif :
  → *in my opinion ... / to my mind ... / as I see it ... / I do believe that ... / to me ...*
- Utiliser des adjectifs pour dire ce que suscite une œuvre :
  → *This painting makes me feel* ***uncomfortable / sad / angry / happy...***
  → *This painting is* ***thought-provoking / interesting / beautiful / moving...***

PAIR WORK

DIFFÉRENCIATION

"*The Undefeated*," is a collaboration between author Kwame Alexander and Kadir Nelson. This picture book for young adults tells the story of the USA with key African American figures such as Jesse Owens, who won several medals at the 1936 Olympic Games in Berlin, at the time of Nazi Germany. It also gives an account of the 54th Massachusetts Regiment which was the first regiment of African Americans to serve during the Civil War and many others.

BBC Scotland

B **Kwame Alexander reads *The Undefeated***

Video 23lmu21103

In this video Kwame Alexander is the guest of "Authors' live", a Scottish TV show on the BBC.

PAIR WORK

1. Watch the beginning of the video (00-0'27) then work on your part of the video.
Use Fiche 23lmu21104

2. Watch the video again without the sound and comment on the students' change of facial expression.

3. You both work for the *BBC Teen Magazine online*. Write a 50-word post in which you explain how *The Undefeated* helps to share African American History around the world.

A teacher who attended Kwame Alexander's performance tells us about the experience she had with her students.

C **The audience reacts** Audio 23lmu21105

1. Write down elements about the speaker's opinion on the book: message • impact • icons • historical elements

2. Identify two moments when the image and the poem are complementary in her opinion.

3. Explain why the performance made them want to know more.

4. Think about your favourite moment of the performance and get ready to share it with the class: moment in the poem • corresponding image • your feelings and opinion...

WORD BOX

- committed art = art defending a cause
- a storyteller
- an audience = spectators
- a call of duty = a feeling that you should do sth
- cheerful = happy
- be surprised / amazed / captivated / fascinated
- be committed = be involved
- give sb a platform = give visibility to sb

IMPROVE YOUR Grammar

Activités en ligne 23lmu21107

Le présent en *be* + V-*ing*

Tyron's Tips 23lmu21106

- Il se forme au moyen de l'auxiliaire *be* au présent et du verbe auquel on rajoute la terminaison *-ing* :

Forme affirmative	Forme négative
→ *I'm* (ou *am*) *working* → *You/we/they're* (ou *are*) *working* → *She/he's* (ou *is*) *working*	→ *I'm not* (ou *am not*) *working* → *You/we/they aren't* (ou *are not*) *working* → *She/he isn't* (ou *is not*) *working*

- On utilise le présent en *be* + V-*ing* pour **décrire ou commenter une scène dont on est le témoin**. C'est aussi cette forme que l'on utilise **pour décrire une image**.
  → *In this drawing by Kadir Nelson, a man* ***is raising*** *his fist in protest.*
- Il est utilisé aussi pour parler d'un événement qui est **en cours** au moment où l'on parle et qui n'a pas encore atteint son terme.
  → *My daughter* ***is painting*** *a portrait in her bedroom.*

Certains verbes ne sont en principe pas employés avec *be* + V-*ing*: *like, hate, know, want...*

> Précis p. 259

1 Mettez les verbes entre parenthèses au présent simple ou en *be* + V-*ing* :

a. A lot of people ... (*gather*) in front of the city hall now. They ... (*protest*) against police brutality. Some of them ... (*wave*) signs and ... (*shout*) slogans.
b. My cousin is an artist: he ... (*paint/usually*) landscapes, but at the moment he ... (*paint*) portraits.
c. I ... (*not/understand*) why she ... (*not/like*) Kadir Nelson's paintings.

2 Faites une description de *American Uprising* de Kadir Nelson (p. 123). Produisez 5 phrases. Vous pouvez utiliser les verbes suivants :

stand • wear sth • raise one's fist • look at sth • protest against sth • wave an Americain flag

IMPROVE YOUR Pronunciation

La voyelle longue /ɑː/ Audio 23lmu21108

- La voyelle de ***art*** et de ***star*** est **la voyelle longue** /ɑː/. Ce son ressemble au *â* du français *pâte*. La bouche doit être bien ouverte.
- Le plus souvent, le son /ɑː/ est représenté par **la graphie *a* quand elle est suivie d'un *r*** en position accentuée : ***art****, part, scarf, arm*.
- Chez de nombreux Britanniques, la graphie *a* se prononce /ɑː/ dans les contextes suivants :

ass, ask, ast	*pass, class, ask, last*
ath	*father, rather*
ans, ance	*chance, dance, answer*

Il ne faut pas confondre la voyelle /ɑː/ avec la voyelle /æ/, un son plus bref (la bouche est légèrement plus fermée). Cette voyelle est elle aussi représentée par la graphie ***a*** dans *cat* ou *back*.

1 a) Dans les paires suivantes, identifiez le mot où la voyelle *a* se prononce /ɑː/ (aidez-vous de la graphie).

a. at/art
b. park/pack
c. had/hard
d. match/March

b) Vérifiez en écoutant l'enregistrement puis répétez. Audio 23lmu21109

2 a) Recopiez la phrase suivante et soulignez les mots contenant le son /ɑː/.

This article deals with young American artists who took part in an avant-garde exhibition in Chicago last year.

b) Vérifiez en écoutant l'enregistrement puis répétez. Audio 23lmu21110

IMPROVE YOUR Vocabulary

Activités en ligne 23lmu21115

Art for all

Inspiration & heritage

Audio 23lmu21113

- a role **mod**el = a **men**tor
- a uni**ver**sal **mess**age
- a **land**mark = a trace
- be in**spired**
- rep**re**sent
- in**her**it
- to leave your mark

Making things change

Audio 23lmu21114

- com**mit**ted art = art de**fend**ing a cause
- a demon**stra**tion = a **pro**test
- be com**mit**ted = be in**volved**
- de**nounce** sth
- **cri**ticise sth/**cri**ticize sth (US)
- im**ply** sth = im**pli**citly refer to
- give sb a **plat**form = give visi**bil**ity to sb
- be a pio**neer**

Artistic skills

Audio 23lmu21111

- paint
- sketch
- **high**light
- **il**lustrate

Artworks

Audio 23lmu21112

- a **paint**ing = a **can**vas
- a book
- an illus**tra**tion
- an exhi**bi**tion
- a sketch = a first try
- fine art
- a shade of + **col**our
- a shape
- a cold/warm **col**our
- a **char**acter

Let's RECAP

Faites le point ! Complétez la fiche bilan avec les documents que vous avez étudiés. Fiche 23lmu21116

AXE 6

Creation and relation to arts

To what extent is Kadir Nelson making African American art accessible to all ?

#inspiration

What are Kadir Nelson's main sources of inspiration for his paintings?

#storytelling

How and why does Kadir Nelson tell his story in his artworks?

#visiblity

How does Kadir Nelson make African Americans more visible?

#books

How can books help spread Kadir Nelson's message?

GROUP WORK Choose a question and discuss.

Quiz 23lmu21117

YOUR PROJECT

Shoot a video

To celebrate Black History Month, film a 2-minute video about Kadir Nelson.

- **A** for Accessibility.
  Explain who he is and list the most important aspects of his life. Show how he gives more visibility to his community.
- **R** for Reaction.
  Include at least one of his works of art. Comment on its message and how it makes you feel.
- **T** for Talent.
  Show he is a great artist. Underline how art can convey messages.

How to shoot a video p. 139

Sports et société

UNIT 12 Australia: winning together

▶ How is sport bridging the gap between communities in Australia?

YOUR PROJECTS

Record a video for the Australian Book of Records.

OR

Write an article about sport and reconciliation in Australia for your school website.

Warwick Keen

Sports fans visiting the Shoalhaven Sports Center in Bomaderry will be greeted by a mural designed by celebrated local Indigenous artist Warwick Keen. Entitled "Coming together", it celebrates the ideals of participation, inclusivity, diversity and community. It features local Indigenous former rugby player Andrew Walker in a celebration of local identity and talent.

Culture Tip Aboriginal and Torres Strait Islanders people have faced discrimination for centuries. Australians are acknowledging the wrongs of the past and are trying to move forward through different means, including sport inclusion.

A

1. Read the short text and explain the situation:
   artwork • artist • location
2. Pick out elements from the photo showing the importance of sport in the community and comment on the athlete's body language.
3. Warwick Keen organises a contest on your favourite social network. Post the mural in a story and explain its title in your own words.

Sporting legend and NBA champion Patty Mills became the first Indigenous Australian to carry the flag into an Olympic Games opening ceremony. A proud Kokatha, Naghiralgal and Dauareb-Meriam man*, Mills once again made history heading into his fourth Olympic Games, being the first Indigenous player to represent Australian Men's Basketball at four consecutive Olympic Games in 2020.

Adapted from nit.com.au

* a person from the Torres Strait and from the west coast of South Australia

B Patty Mills: Aboriginal and proud

Audio 23lmu21201

1. Look at the image and identify the flags around the athlete. Guess what they represent for him.
2. Read the text and pick out elements about Patty Mills: origins • sport • records • international events
3. Listen to the audio document and write down the reason(s) why Mills is so proud.
4. Explain why Patty Mills's story shows sport can bridge communities in Australia.

Remember how to

Express cause > Docs A/B

On peut utiliser :

- ***because*** (parce que), ***as*** (comme) ou ***since*** (puisque) :
  → ***As / because** he was an Aboriginal, he was often treated differently at school.*
  Proposition subordonnée
- ***because of*** et ***owing to*** (à cause de) ou encore ***thanks to*** (grâce à) :
  → *At school, he was sometimes bullied **because of** his brown skin.*
  Groupe nominal
  → ***Thanks to** his hard work, he won the championship.*
  Groupe nominal
- ***make sb do sth*** (faire faire qc à qn) ou ***make sb*** + **adjectif** (rendre qn + adjectif) :
  → *His son's fight against racism **made him so proud!***

WORD BOX

- **un**ity
- a u**nit**ed **na**tion
- **tell**ing = re**veal**ing
- **catch**y = **mem**orable
- repre**sent** sth = de**pict** sth
- pro**mote** sth
- raise a**ware**ness
- be repre**sent**ative of sth
- bridge your **diff**erences = be **rec**onciled
- **gath**er = as**sem**ble

1 From outsiders to game changers

GROUP WORK

DIFFÉRENCIATION

Johnny Mullagh, an Indigenous sports icon

Geoffrey Atherden • The Guardian, Jan 2020

"I'm not playing cricket with someone who won't eat lunch with me." This is how Johnny Mullagh explained his walk-off from the field at York on 13 July 1868. The Gentlemen of York had just denied him access to their luncheon tent, so he left the field in protest. Mullagh was a Jardwadjali man[1] from western Victoria and he was in England with an all-Aboriginal cricket team. They were the first Australian team to tour internationally. [...]

In England, Mullagh had to do more than play cricket. After every match, he and the team were exhibited for a curious English audience who paid to see them dressed in concocted native costumes made of possum[2] skins and emu feathers. They staged[3] mock battles and put on displays of spear[4] and boomerang throwing. [...]

Mullagh and the team returned to a changed country. In their absence, the colonial authorities had taken Aboriginal people "under their protection" and forced them off their lands and onto reserves and missions. Mullagh, though, defied this rule, and stayed living in the country where he was born.

He earned an income doing farm work and went on playing cricket. He was the star batsman[5] for the Harrow team. When he died in 1891, money was raised to put up a monument to celebrate his life and the Harrow cricket ground was renamed the Johnny Mullagh Oval.

It's an important story, a part of the shared history between black and white Australia. It deserves to be told, and told truthfully. We all should be proud of Australia's first Indigenous sporting hero, Johnny Mullagh.

1. Aboriginal people – 2. Australian animal – 3. acted out – 4. piercing weapon – 5. player who is batting / using a bat

A All class

1. Look at the image and read the first paragraph (l. 1-10). Explain how the Australian cricket team made history in 1868.
2. Pick out elements showing there was discrimination and how Johnny Mullagh reacted.
3. Identify what had changed while in England and how Mullagh reacted in protest (l. 20-27).
4. Present Johnny Mullagh in a short speech during National Reconciliation Week. Explain why he was a game-changer on and off the cricket pitch.

WORD BOX

- a pioneer = a trailblazer
- the winds of change: influence causing change
- narrow-minded ≠ open-minded
- take action
- advocate a cause = to defend/promote
- be discriminated against = face discrimination
- overcome obstacles

B Student 1 Lionel Rose, SKY NEWS Video 23lmu21202

1. Student 1. Watch the video and pick out biographical elements referring to Lionel Rose: sport • people he is compared to • origins • context. Use Fiche 23lmu21203

2. Comment on Lionel Rose's impact on the nation.

3. Identify the contrast the TV host makes between Rose's childhood and his career.

C Student 2 Cathy Freeman Video 23lmu21204

1. Student 2. Watch the video and pick out as many biographical elements as possible: sport • first medal • origins • dreams as a child • teenage revelation
Use Fiche 23lmu21205

2. Identify the challenges Cathy Freeman had to face, the support she had, and her achievements.

3. Explain how she used the 2000 Olympic Games as a platform to bring about unity in Australia.

PAIR WORK 4. Debate about the athlete who would most deserve to be in the Book of Records.

PREPARE YOUR PROJECT

Record a podcast

Introduce your favourite Aboriginal or Torres Strait Islander sportsperson. Mention biographical elements, important steps in the athlete's career, and how he/she managed to bridge communities.

2 Reconciling in victory

Culture Tip Reconciliation aims at building relationships, trust and respect between the wider Australian community and Aboriginal and Torres Strait Islander peoples. After centuries of discrimination and racism, it is a pledge to honour their culture and create real opportunities for them.

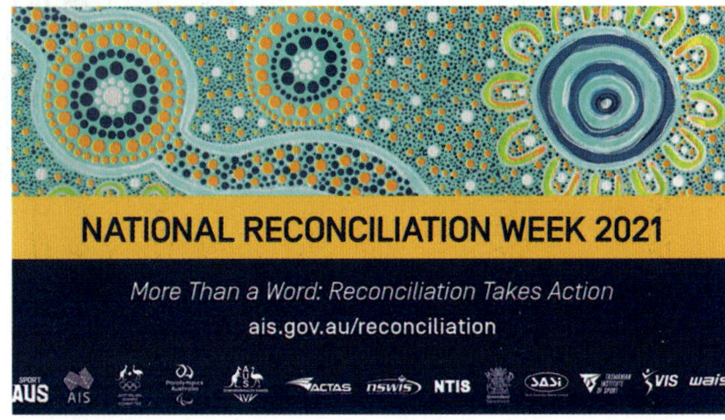

sportaus.gov.au

A Our reconciliation statement **Video** 23lmu21206

1. Read the Culture tip and watch the video. Pick out adjectives linked to "inclusion" and explain the goal of this project.
2. Identify words related to the world of sport, and comment on its specific role in this initiative.
3. Pick out action verbs to explain the theme "*More Than a Word: Reconciliation Takes Action*".
4. Create a mind map around the theme "*Reconciliation in sport*".

Cricket Australia
@CricketAus • Follow

Designed by Kirrae Whurrong woman Aunty Fiona Clarke & Butchulla and Gubbi Gubbi woman Courtney Hagen, the shirt continues the storytelling of the 1868 cricket team! 👏 #NAIDOC2022
Nov 11, 2020

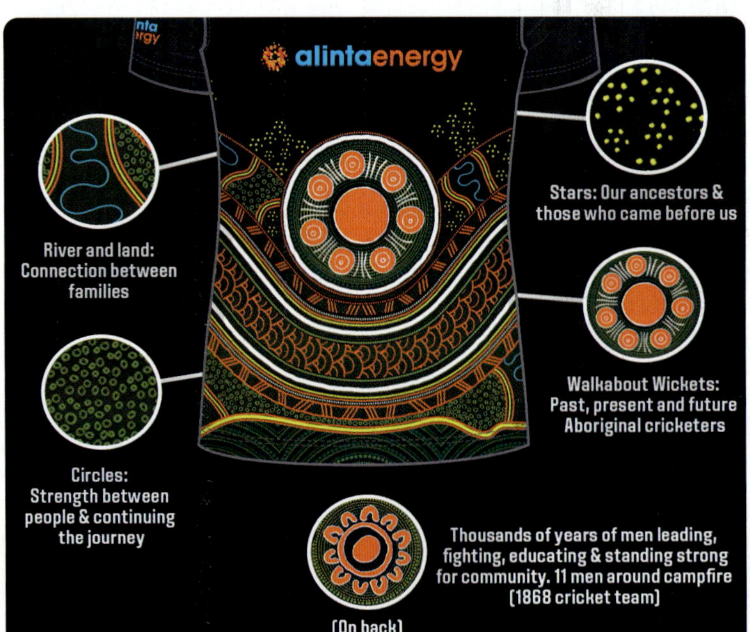

B

1. Focus on the jersey and identify symbols showing a link between past and present.
2. Explain the importance of art in this initiative (colours, patterns...).
3. Imagine how wearing this shirt could have an impact both in Australia and internationally.
4. Write a tweet to react to this announcement.

1. A walkabout: a journey in the Australian bush made by an Aboriginal person.
2. A wicket: in cricket, a set of 3 sticks defended by the batsman

• SPORT

Football Australia launches Indigenous Reconciliation Action Plan (RAP)

By Samantha Lewis • Tuesday 22 Feb 2022 • abc.net.au

Through its three core pillars of relationships, respect, and opportunities, Football Australia's "Reflect" RAP sets out a long-term framework that will empower and educate those within the sport about issues that continue to face First Nations people[1] in the pursuit of reconciliation.
Despite the long history of First Nations involvement in and contribution to football – stemming[2] all the way back to pre-colonisation days – the game has often failed to provide genuine, practical, and sustainable[3] opportunities and platforms for these crucial voices and experiences.

For NIAG (National Indigenous Advisory Group) co-chair Jade North, the RAP is the first step in rectifying that historical neglect and creating a path forward for the entire game.
"I'm greatly encouraged by the decisive action Football Australia is taking towards meaningful reconciliation with Indigenous people," he said.
"Now, as Australian Football are bringing full focus into this work, this action plan is just the first step of many to connect to community and embed[4] equity into the delivery and function of football more broadly."

1. indigenous people, the earliest known inhabitants of an area – 2. coming from – 3. which will last a long time – 4. integrate

C

1. Read lines 1-12 and list words with negative connotation. Explain what the 'issues' were.

2. Read the end of the text and pick out verbs showing the positive initiative of Football Australia. Comment on the RAP.

3. Imagine and present 3 actions that Football Australia can put in place.

WORD BOX

- an **in**itiative = a **pro**ject
- bring to**geth**er = **u**nify /ˈjuːnɪfaɪ/
- **cel**ebrate sb/sth = pay **tri**bute to sb/sth
- com**mit** to sth = **ful**ly en**gage** in sth
- be in**clu**ded in sth = be part of sth
- ad**dress** an **is**sue /ˈɪʃuː/ = **tack**le an **is**sue

PREPARE YOUR PROJECT

Create an infographic entitled "Reconciliation thanks to sport in Australia"

Your art teacher wants you to share what you have learnt about reconciliation through sport in Australia. Create an infographic about the role of sport, focusing on:
initiatives • sportspeople • Aboriginal art • key words

IMPROVE YOUR Grammar

Activités en ligne
23lmu21207

L'expression de la capacité

- Pour exprimer une capacité, on utilise **le modal *can* + V au présent** et ***could* + V au passé** :

Forme affirmative	Forme négative	Forme interrogative
*They **can** win* *They **could** win*	*They **cannot** / **can't** win* *They **could** / **couldn't** win*	***Can** they win?* ***Could** they win?*

La forme négative ***cannot*** s'écrit en un seul mot.
On ne prononce pas le *l* de *could* /kʊd/.

- On peut souvent employer ***(not) be able to*** **+ V** à la place de *can* : → *They **are able to** win.*

Be able to est obligatoire quand il n'est pas possible d'employer *can*, en particulier après un autre modal (*will, would, must*...) :
→ *Our team **will be able to win** the match.*

- On peut aussi utiliser les verbes suivants :

manage to +V (parvenir à)	*Cathy Freeman **managed to** win a silver medal.*
succeed in +V-ing (réussir à)	*The athlete **succeeded in** breaking a world record.*

> Précis p. 268

1 Complétez avec *can, could* ou *be able to* en mettant *be* à la forme qui convient. Plusieurs solutions sont parfois possibles.

a. Kate runs very fast: she ... cross the finish line in just four minutes.
b. One day, he will ... play for Australia.
c. She might ... win tomorrow's race.
d. When they were younger, they ... speak their minds freely.

2 Dites ce que les sportifs de l'unité ont réussi à accomplir dans leur carrière sportive. Produisez 3 phrases utilisant les structures suivantes :

be able to + V • *manage to* + V • *succeed in* V-ing

Ex. *Those athletes **were able to** overcome racial prejudice.*

By + gérondif

- Pour dire **comment** accomplir une action, on peut utiliser ***by*** + V-***ing*** (= gérondif) :
→ *In 1968 Lionel Rose made history **by** becoming the first Aboriginal boxing champion.*
→ *Cathy Freeman celebrated her victory **by** carrying the Aboriginal flag and the Australian national flag.*

On traduit cette structure par ***en*** **+ participe présent** (V + *ant*) : « ***en devenant*** *le premier champion de boxe aborigène* ».

3 Répondez à ces questions en utilisant *by* + gérondif. Vous pouvez utiliser les propositions en italique ci-dessous.

a. How can we pay tribute to Cathy Freeman?
b. How can I support the Aboriginal cause?
c. How can I get in touch with Patty Mills?
d. How can I learn about Aboriginal culture and identity?

send an e-mail to his press attaché • read books about Aboriginal traditions • donate to an Aboriginal organisation • name a school after her

IMPROVE YOUR Pronunciation

La dipthongue /eɪ/

Tyron's Tips 23lmu21208

- Le son voyelle présent dans *day* ou *Australia* est représenté par le symbole /eɪ/. Il peut être représenté par les graphies suivantes :

ai (en milieu de mot) ou ***ay*** (en fin de mot)	*explain, way, play* (exceptions : *said* /e/, *again* /e/)
ei dans quelques mots	*eight, neighbour, weigh*
dans ***ange***	*change, angel, strange*
dans la terminaison ***ation***	*infomation, nation*
ea dans quelques mots	*break, steak, great*

- Quand **la graphie *a*** est suivie d'une consonne unique (autre que le *r*) elle-même suivie d'un *e***,** celle-ci se prononce /eɪ/ : *game, place, make*. Le verbe *have* est une exception.

1 a) **Prononcez ces paires de mots en distinguant bien le son /eɪ/ de *say* du son /e/ de *bed*.**

a. *let - late*
b. *waste - west*
c. *gate - get*
d. *pen - pain*
e. *sell - sale*

b) **Écoutez et vérifiez.**
Audio 23lmu21209

2 **Identifiez les mots dans lesquels la graphie *a* se prononce /eɪ/.**
Audio 23lmu21210

discrimination • Australia • game changer • flag • brave • match • battle • strange

Les liaisons

Audio 23lmu21211

- Lorsqu'on prononce une phrase en anglais, comme en français, on fait des liaisons entre les mots se terminant par un son consonne et ceux commençant par un son voyelle :
→ *We are all very proud of our champion.*
- Quand un mot commence par un *h* aspiré, on ne fait pas la liaison :
→ *Patty Mills hopes to raise awareness.*

Il existe quelques mots où le *h* initial n'est pas prononcé : *honest, hour, heir* et *honour*. C'est aussi le cas dans certains mots grammaticaux : *he*, *him*, *her*, *his*, l'auxiliaire *has* / *has*. Il faut donc faire la liaison avec ces mots :
→ *They denied him access to their luncheon tent.*

3 a) **Recopiez les phrases suivantes et indiquez les liaisons au moyen du symbole ◡.**

a. She lives in Australia.
b. Her grandfather was not only a trailblazer but also influenced her own sporting career.
c. A lot of Aboriginals are discriminated against.
d. This athlete has made history.
e. When he died in 1891, money was raised to put up a monument to celebrate his life.

b) **Écoutez l'enregistrement pour vérifier vos réponses et répétez.**
Audio 23lmu21212

IMPROVE YOUR Vocabulary

Activités en ligne 23lmu21213

Towards reconciliation

EQUALITY AND INCLUSION

Audio 23lmu21217

- a healed and **peace**ful **coun**try /'kʌntri/
- di**ver**sity
- to**geth**erness = **close**ness
- **pow**erful
- come to**geth**er
- feel **e**qual
- feel safe /'seɪf/
- bring **peo**ple to**geth**er

PROTECTING RIGHTS

Audio 23lmu21218

- an i**ni**tiative
- a com**mit**ment
- a sub**stan**tive **ac**tion
- **safe**guard sth = pro**tect** from having **pro**blems
- speak up = say what you think
- take **ac**tion
- make change /'tʃeɪndʒ/
- right a wrong = cor**rect some**thing bad or wrong
- move **for**ward
- pro**mote** sth

DISCRIMINATION

Audio 23lmu21216

- **pre**judice /'predʒədɪs/ = dis**crim**ination
- **ra**cism /'reɪsɪzəm/
- ex**clu**sion
- **suf**fer from sth
- be dis**crim**inated a**gainst**
- be a **vic**tim of sth

Sports in Australia

SPORT

Audio 23lmu21214

- the staff = the team
- a team mate
- a **play**ing field /'fi:ld/
- **ath**letes /'æθli:ts/
- a set of rules
- a **jer**sey /'dʒ3:zi/
- green and gold = the **col**ours of the Aus**tra**lian sports **jer**sey

ABORIGENES

Audio 23lmu21215

- o**rig**inal cus**to**dians /kʌ'stəʊdiən/ of the land = **care**takers of the land
- First **Na**tions **peo**ple
- an **an**cestor
- a re**serve**
- re**sil**ience

1 **Memorise as many words from the mind map as possible in 2 minutes. Write them down and compare with your friends!**

1 **Use 10 words from the mind map to explain the concept of *Reconciliation* in Australia.**

3 **You have just watched a video of Cathy Freeman's famous Olympic race in 2000 on YouTube. Write a comment to say how sport has changed Australian society.**

Let's RECAP

Faites le point ! Complétez la fiche bilan avec les documents que vous avez étudiés. Fiche 23lmu21219

AXE 5

Sports and society

How is sport bridging the gap between communities in Australia?

#allaustralians
How can sport celebrate all cultures and traditions?

#unityinsport
To what extent can sport unite communities?

#reconciliation
To what extent can sport bring about reconciliation?

#changewithsport
How can sport promote change in society?

#iconicsportspersons
Who are the Indigenous Australian sports pioneers?

GROUP WORK Choose a question and discuss.

Quiz 23lmu21220

Become AN EXPERT

Lisez et écoutez de l'anglais en dehors de la classe

Books

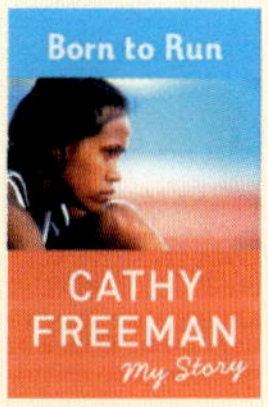

- *Born to Run*, Cathy Freeman vers LLCER
- *Deadly, Unna?* Phillip Gwynne vers LLCE
- *Black + White -Race, Politics and Changing Australia*, Warren Mundine vers AMC
- *Black Pearls, the Aboriginal and Islander Sports Hall of Fame*, Colin Tatz and Paul Tat vers AMC

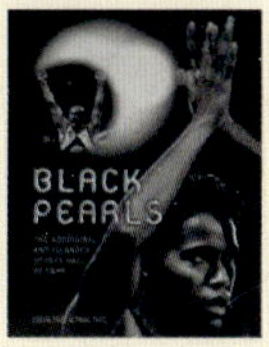

Aboriginal traditions

- Dance: the Watarrka Foundation
  Site 23lmu21221
- Games: The Yulunga Games
  Site 23lmu21222

Films & documentaries

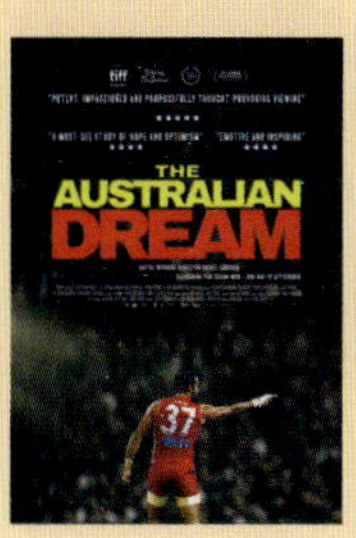

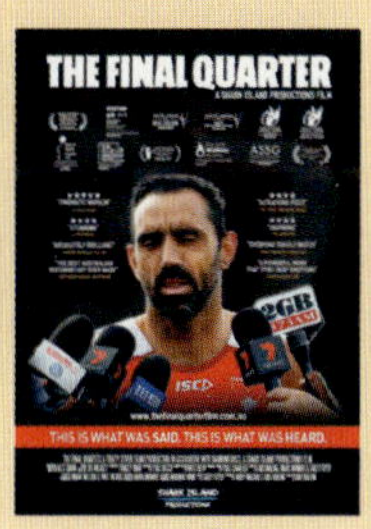

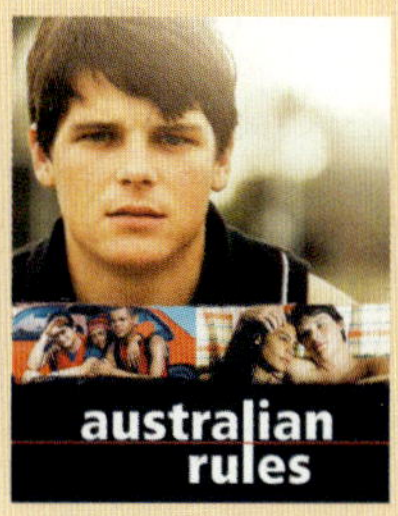

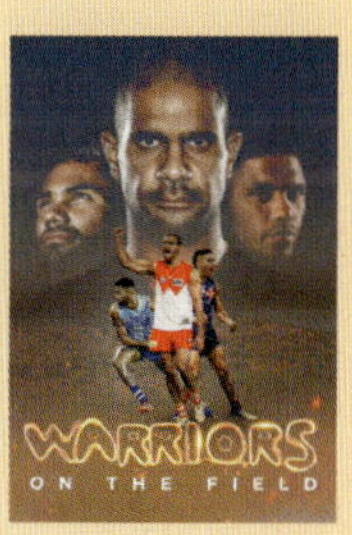

YOUR PROJECTS

Record a video for the Australian Book of Records

Promote the Aboriginal athlete who, for you, best represents unity in the country.

- Find information about the Aboriginal athlete you have chosen (studied in this unit or not).
  - List your findings in two columns: life • career
- ***Part 1*** **– LIFE:** Select the different pieces of information you will include.
  - Prefer elements that had an impact on the athlete's career.
- ***Part 2*** **– CAREER:** Select the athlete's key achievements.
  - Why he/she was a game changer: actions • records • impact.
  - Add historical elements that confirm how big the achievements were.
- Conclude.
  - Give three reasons why the chosen athlete deserves to be put in the Australian Book of Records.

OR

Write an article for your school website

You are celebrating Indigenous Sport Month in your school. Write a text for the website, explaining how sport can be a powerful tool towards reconciliation.

- Choose a title that will attract your readers.
  - Use key words and keep the title short.
- Think about the ideas you want to convey.
  - Use what you have learnt and organise your ideas
- Draft an outline of your ideas.
  - Focus on the commitment to support the Australian Aboriginals' cause and use adjectives and words to express concession and contrast.
- Choose iconic sportspersons who changed society and sports in Australia.
  - Find examples in the chapter and/or search the Internet.
- Select pictures of people and events.
  - Make some research on the Internet and find powerful and meaningful images.

Why not share your article with your sports teacher?

How to write an article p. 173

BUILD UP YOUR SKILLS

How to shoot a video

Cathy Freeman Video 23lmu21204

1. Pour la préparer

C **comme *commencer*** : faites un *brainstorming* des idées qui vous viennent spontanément ou après des recherches.

Vous pouvez les noter sous forme de *mind map*.

A **comme *articuler*** : sélectionnez les informations principales et trouvez les images correspondantes – elles serviront d'illustrations lors du montage.

Vous pouvez utiliser un story board pour vous aider, par exemple : www.canva.com/create/storyboards/

T **comme *titrer*** : imaginez les grandes étapes de la vidéo sous forme de titres.

Dans la vidéo ci-dessus, les titres pourraient être "*Her childhood*", "*Her dreams*" et "*Her achievements*".

C **comme *choisir* et *captiver*** : choisissez les informations de chaque partie en les variant pour mieux captiver votre auditoire.

Citations fortes, commentaire sur une image incontournable, rappel d'un événement historique, etc.

H **comme *harmoniser*** : équilibrez la durée des différentes parties.

Yeah! Vous êtes fin prêt.e à filmer !

2. Pour la réaliser

- Vous pouvez filmer avec votre téléphone ou avec un ordinateur portable avec une bonne webcam. Soyez vigilant à la lumière et au bruit.
- Pour monter votre vidéo : PowerDirector Essential, Canva, Imovie, Windows Movie Maker...
- Quelques expressions utiles pour le tournage :

1 Introduction	2 Developpement	3 Conclusion
• *Hello everyone / Hi* • *You're watching* (+ Présentation) • *This video is meant to* + BV • *Today my goal is to* + BV	• *What first comes to mind is ...* • *On the one hand...* • *On the other hand...* • *Which leads me to my next point...* • *Needless to say that...*	• *At the end of the day...* • *All in all...* • *To wrap this up we can say...* • *In the end...*

Are you ready?

+ prof Évaluation

Entraînement à l'évaluation

Compréhension orale

Faites un compte rendu en français de l'audio.

Reconciliation through sport Audio 23lmu21223

- Lisez attentivement le titre et observez l'image pour comprendre le sujet et repérer les intervenants et leurs métiers.
- Concentrez-vous sur les mots clés (notamment les adjectifs) pour pouvoir expliquer les initiatives qui sont prises.
- Repérez les conseils qui sont donnés pour consruire la réconciliation.

Production écrite

Do you think Reconciliation Week is the only moment when such an event should take place? Write a 100-word paragraph in which you give your opinion and support it with precise examples.

Compréhension écrite

'HE TRAIL-BLAZED FOR ME TOO': CATHY FREEMAN'S TRIBUTE TO GRANDDAD

Brad Walter / Mon 4 Jul 2022, 11:57 AM

Cathy Freeman's grandfather **Frank Fisher**

Olympic great Cathy Freeman believes her grandfather Frank Fisher was not only a trailblazer[1] for Indigenous rugby league players but also influenced her own sporting career.

Freeman, who was awarded the honour of lighting the cauldron at the opening ceremony of the 2000 Sydney Olympics and later won the 400m gold medal in one of Australia's greatest and most iconic sporting moments, told NRL.com[2] of her pride at Fisher's achievements on and off the field. [...]

Lions captain[3] Jim Brough, who described Fisher as the best country footballer he had seen, was so impressed that he convinced Salford[4] to offer him a contract to play in England. However, the Queensland Government rejected Fisher's application to travel under the Aboriginals Protection Act in place at the time and he continued to play for Cherbourg[5] until his 40s.

Despite the obstacles he faced, Fisher created a path to the top for the likes of Renouf, who grew up in nearby Murgon, and players from Cherbourg, including Willie and Esi Tonga, Chris Sandow and teenage Broncos sensation Selwyn Cobbo.

Earning the nickname "Big Shot", Fisher was honoured with the naming of the Frank Big Shot Fisher Bridge on the road between Cherbourg and Murgon in 1996. Yet because Fisher did not play in Sydney or Brisbane many are only now beginning to learn of his story and his struggles with racism.

Fisher's contribution to the game was also recognised with his selection in the Indigenous Team of the Century, alongside the likes of Renouf, Arthur Beetson, Laurie Daley, Johnathan Thurston, Greg Inglis, Cliff Lyons, Eric Simms and John Ferguson.

"Knowing that my Grandad was picked in the Indigenous Team of the Century totally fills my heart with pride," Freeman said.

"Seeing my Grandad recognised in this way and so long after his passing just gives me a sense of the genuine respect that NRL devotees have for him, and the significance of his contribution to the great game. I am proud to be part of his legacy."

nrl.com

1. a pioneer – 2. NRL: National Rugby League – 3. the Lions = the British national team – 4. Salford = a rugby club in Manchester, UK – 5. Cherbourg = an Aboriginal reserve near Brisbane, Queensland

1. Explain the relationship and common points between Franck Fisher and Cathy Freeman.
2. Comment on the obstacles that Franck Fisher faced.
3. Note the different ways in which he is now honoured.
4. Say how he became a role-model to other sportspersons.

- **Identifiez les personnes, les lieux et les équipes sportives.**
- **Soyez attentifs à la ponctuation : elle vous aide à comprendre qui parle et à identifier les points de vue exprimés.**
- **Relevez les mots appartenant au champ lexical du sport et de la réconciliation.**

Production écrite

The National Rugby League organises a ceremony in which Cathy Freeman represents her grandfather. Write her 100-word thank you speech, using the last sentence of the article as a starting point. You will explain why her grandfather opened the way for Aboriginal athletes today.

Création et rapport aux arts

UNIT 13 Let's get musical!

▶ How do musicals mirror society?

YOUR PROJECTS

Rap to promote a musical on your social media account.

OR

Create a brochure for a musical.

A

1. Observe document A and identify these elements:
   character • words in blue • words in white.
   Spot the adjectives, then state the goal of the document.

PAIR WORK

2. Student A works on texts (1) and (3) on p. 143 (Doc B).
   Student B works on texts (2) and (4).
   Give the names of the musicals. Find adjectives that describe:
   a show • a performance • the cast • a theatrical experience.
   Define the nature of the texts, then state their goal.

3. Exchange your findings with a classmate.

4. Create a poster for one of these musicals.

1 "*From & Juliet*" is exactly the show Broadway needs right now: fun, exuberant, supremely joyful, hilarious, and excellently performed by a talented and diverse cast*.

variety.com

* group of actors in a show

2 *Hamilton* lives up to the hype[1] as it is engaging, high-energy and an emotionally thrilling theatrical experience. It is an opera, a rap show, and an accurate history lesson that presents as dazzling[2] entertainment.

chicagocritic.com

1. meets expectations
2. amazing

3 **Dear Evan Hansen' review: Ben Platt gives captivating, vulnerable performance**

Platt is giving one of the most vulnerable and shaded[1] performances you've ever seen. He is terrified, enigmatic and completely believable. Except for a few comical and romantic moments, this is a serious and often uncomfortable portrait of contemporary domestic life. It is meant for[2] teens, parents and virtually anyone who has identified as an outsider.

amny.com

1. well-balanced - 2. intended for

4 **The Color Purple review – a musical with heart, spirit and soul.**

★★★★★

Curve, Leicester
Alice Walker's novel is transformed into an exuberant celebration of community and female empowerment*.

theguardian.com

* emancipation

B

What if Shakespeare's Juliet didn't kill herself at the end of the play? This musical gives Juliet her own empowered voice back and a clear desire to take control. The characters reflect the diversity of the world around us including gender, age, body type, ethnicity and sexual orientation.

nytimes.com

C

WORD BOX

- a show
- a cast
- a stage = a place where actors perform
- scenery = stage/ theatre set
- a close-up
- a burning issue = a current problem
- promote = publicise
- tackle sth = deal with sth

1. Read the text and describe the scene [Doc C]. Show the musical tackles societal issues.

2. Your friend doesn't like musicals – (s)he thinks they are frivolous. Write a mail to convince him/her to see a show.

Grammar Rewrite text 2 [Doc B] using indirect speech. Begin the sentence with: *"A critic wrote that..."*

MEMORY CHALLENGE

How many adjectives can you remember? Play in groups "*I went to a musical; it was...* (+ adjective)".

1 Music mimics society

The musical follows the story of Alexander Hamilton, an immigrant and one of the founding fathers of the United States.

"Shows like *Hamilton* are showing us that the musical can be all things to all audiences – relevant, accessible to young and old."

backstage.com

A *Hamilton*, official song clip Video 23lmu21301

1. Watch the clip with the sound off. Pick out: the components of a musical • the written elements • the costumes

2. Watch with the sound on, focusing on the lyrics of the songs. Find out what you can about Alexander Hamilton: background • parents • personality • his future
Deduce the topic and the time period of this musical.

3. Make a 30-second audio clip to promote this musical.

www.brightstarmusical.com

THE POWER OF MUSICAL THEATRE

Musical theatre is a performing arts genre in which the story is conveyed[1] through song and dance. It is often considered to be a frivolous and unnecessary art form, but it can actually be quite useful in conveying messages and emotions. Musical theatre can be used to address serious topics in a way that is both entertaining[2] and educational. It can also be used to explore the human condition and to promote social change. In a world that is often filled with negativity, musical theatre can be a breath of fresh air. It can be a source of hope and inspiration, and it can remind us of the power of love and compassion. So, while some may consider musical theatre to be useless, it is actually a powerful tool that can be used to make a difference in the world.

1. communicated – 2. enjoyable

B

1. List the positive and negative elements associated with musicals.
2. Explain how the text illustrates the title of this page: *Music mimics society*.
3. Post a Tweet about the power of musicals.

C The Color Purple Video 23lmu21302

The musical *The Color Purple*, adapted from Alice Walker's novel, is about the life-long struggles of Celie, a poor, uneducated African American woman, living in the Deep South during the early 1900s.

"A GLORIOUS, IMMENSELY MOVING CELEBRATION OF TRIUMPH OVER ADVERSITY"

wmc.org.uk

1. Read the text. Guess the topic of the musical and identify its serious issues.

2. Watch the clip, focusing on the written elements and pinpoint what is said about this musical: production • songs/singing • performance • cast • script

PAIR WORK 3. Médiation Compare notes with a partner and together come up with 3 reasons to persuade classmates to see a performance of *The Color Purple*.

WORD BOX

- **lyr**ics
- a chore**og**raphy
- a **cos**tume
- stand up for sth = de**fend** sth
- **mim**ic sb = **im**itate sb
- im**pov**erished = poor
- de**ter**mined
- am**bi**tious

Remember how to

Express enthusiasm

Pour exprimer votre enthousiasme pour un spectacle, utilisez :

- ***what a/an*** + nom → ***What an awesome musical*** Hamilton *is!*
- ***how*** + adjectif/adverbe → ***How fantastic*** *the choreography is!*
- ***so*** + adjectif/adverbe → *This musical is* ***so cool!***
- **des superlatifs** → *This musical is the* ***best***, *the* ***most brilliant!***

PREPARE YOUR PROJECT

Shoot a video

You are full of enthusiasm for a musical you have just seen. Make a video to promote it on your social media account.

2 Updating *West Side Story*

A ***West Side Story*, 1961 film poster**

Set in New York city, *West Side Story* updates Shakespeare's *Romeo and Juliet* to the 1950s. After the Broadway stage musical, a film was released in 1961, with Robert Wise and Jerome Robbins as co-directors. The show focuses on Maria and Tony's love story within the context of gang wars for territory in the Upper West Side. Their love story results in tragedy as the two rival gangs, the white Jets and the Puerto Rican Sharks, violently oppose it.

PAIR WORK

1. **Observe the poster and read the text. Define:**
the setting • the main characters • the main subject • other topics

2. **Share your findings with your partner. Discuss what makes *West Side Story* both universal and modern.**

3. Write a short review explaining:
- what inspired *West Side Story*;
- what the musical is about;
- what makes it modern.

B *West Side Story*, Steven Spielberg's remake, 2021 **Video** 23lmu21303

1. Watch the video (Doc B) with the sound off. Focus on the scenes from the musical and guess the following:
setting • characters • plot
Use **Fiche** 23lmu21304

2. Watch with the sound on and write down the words Spielberg insists on. Sum up: Spielberg's choice • the musical's theme • the importance of its message today.

3. Imagine and act out an interview between a journalist and Steven Spielberg about the relevance of the musical to today's audience.

1. Watch the video (Doc C) paying special attention to the *America* scene. Choose the words that best summarise the mood and justify your choice:
movement • violence • sadness • fun • brightness • darkness • mixing

2. Focus on what the two actors say and identify:
who they are • the reasons for the appeal of *America* • the message of the song

3. Pay attention to the lyrics and present the two visions of life in America.
Use **Fiche** 23lmu21306

4. Write a short article for your school newspaper, commenting on the message of *America*.

C **Living in America?** **Video** 23lmu21305

PREPARE YOUR PROJECT

Create a poster about *West Side Story*

It should include:
- a drawing / picture,
- a short review,
- key words about the plot / the topics.

IMPROVE YOUR Grammar

Activités en ligne
23lmu21307

Le discours rapporté

Il existe deux façons de rapporter les paroles ou les pensées d'autrui.

- **Au discours direct**, on cite ses paroles entre guillemets :
  → *"It's a great show," he said.*

En anglais, les guillemets ont la forme '...' ou "...", jamais « ... ».

- **Au discours indirect**, on rapporte les paroles d'autrui au moyen d'un verbe de parole suivi d'une proposition en *that*. *That* est souvent omis.
  → *He **said (that)** it was a great show.*
- Il est parfois nécessaire de changer les pronoms et de faire la concordance des temps, surtout si le verbe de parole est au passé (*He **said** that...*).

Discours direct		Discours indirect
présent *"I **like** the musical," he said.*	→	**prétérit** *He said that he **liked** the musical.*
prétérit *"I **met** the producer," he said.*	→	***past perfect*** (*had* + participe passé) *He said that he **had met** the producer.*
will + V *"I will **meet** her," he said.*	→	***would*** + V *He said that he **would meet** her.*

Les adjectifs

- En anglais, les adjectifs sont **invariables.** L'adjectif épithète est toujours placé **avant le nom.**
  → *a **talented** artist*
- Ils peuvent être précédés par des adverbes de degré, qui donnent une indication sur l'intensité de la qualité exprimée par l'adjectif :

Bas degré	Degré moyen	Haut degré
a little, a bit, slightly	*quite, rather, pretty, fairly*	*very, really, extremely, incredibly*

→ *His perfomance was **a bit / quite / really** boring.*

On place l'article indéfini ***a(n)*** **après** ***quite*** :
→ *He's **quite a good** actor.*

- Quand plusieurs adjectifs épithètes se suivent, ils apparaissent dans cet ordre :

	Opinion	Taille	Âge	Couleur	Origine	Matière	
a	*famous*		*old*		*English*		*song*
a	*nice*	*large*		*blue*		*velvet*	*costume*

On utilise parfois l'acronyme **OTACOM** comme moyen mnémotechnique pour se souvenir de cet ordre.

> **Précis p. 252**

1 **Mettez ces phrases au discours indirect.**

a. "Tonight's show is sold out," she said. → *She said that...*
b. "We are rehearsing a lot to be ready for the premiere," they told us. → *They told us that...*
c. "The producer invested about $10 million in advertising," he declared. → *He declared that...*
d. "She will become a star," the journalist predicted. → *The journalist predicted that...*
e. "His new musical will be a flop," he warned us. → *He warned us that...*

2 **Faites un compte rendu des propos de Steven Spielberg (vidéo B p. 147) en utilisant le discours indirect.**

In this interview, Steven Spielberg said that…

3 **Mettez les adjectifs entre parenthèses dans le bon ordre.**

a. Ariana DeBose is a (*young, famous, American*) singer.
b. The action of *Billy Eliot* is set in a (*small, English*) industrial town in the 1980s.
c. She came on stage in a beautiful (*red, silk, long*) dress.

4 **Remplacez l'adverbe de degré souligné par un adverbe équivalent.**

a. The show's staging was <u>a bit</u> disappointing.
b. The music is not only <u>very</u> inventive but also <u>very</u> catchy.
c. She gave a <u>pretty</u> good performance.

IMPROVE YOUR Pronunciation

La diphtongue /əʊ/

Tyron's Tips 23lmu21308

- Le son voyelle que l'on trouve dans ***no***, ***show*** ou ***boat*** est représenté par le symbole /əʊ/.
- Cette diphtongue est représentée, entre autres, par les graphies suivantes :

o en fin de mot	*no, Puerto-Rico, go*
ow	*show, low, follow*
oa	*goal, boat, soap* Exception : *Broadway*
ol + consonne	*cold, roll, sold-out*
ost dans quelques mots	*most, ghost, poster*

La graphie ***ow*** a deux prononciations possibles : /əʊ/ (*show, own*) ou /aʊ/ comme dans ***out*** (*down, now*). Il n'y a pas de règle pour prédire sa prononciation.

- Quand la graphie ***o*** est suivie d'une consonne unique puis d'un ***e*** final, elle se prononce /əʊ/ : *oppose, note, hope, promote*. Exceptions : *love, come, done, some* (prononcés /ʌ/ comme dans *duck*) ou *move, prove* (prononcés /uː/ comme dans *moon*).

1 a) **Dans les listes suivantes, chassez l'intrus (il ne se prononce pas avec la diphtongue /əʊ/).**

a. show – slow – down – know
b. goal – boat – Broadway – load
c. done – stone – bone – alone
a. yellow – town – blow – own

b) **Écoutez pour vérifier vos réponses et répétez.**

Audio 23lmu21309

2 a) **Relevez les mots contenant la diphtongue /əʊ/.**

They told me that 2,000 tickets had been sold for tomorrow's show.

b) **Écoutez l'enregistrement pour vérifier vos réponses et répétez.**

Audio 23lmu21310

L'accent emphatique

Audio 23lmu21311

- **Dans une phrase ou un groupe de mots, une syllabe est toujours prononcée avec plus de force et de conviction que les autres** : on parle d'« accent de phrase ». Il s'agit en principe de la syllabe accentuée du dernier mot lexical (nom, adjectif ou verbe) de la phrase :
→ *The show was very **bor**ing.*
- Afin d'être plus expressif, il est possible de déplacer cet accent et d'attirer ainsi l'attention sur un autre élément. On parle alors d'**accent emphatique**.
- Les adverbes de degré sont par exemple souvent porteurs d'un accent emphatique :
→ *The show was **very** boring.*
- Parfois, l'accent emphatique est utilisé pour exprimer un contraste, ou apporter une correction :
→ *I didn't buy the tickets. **She** bought the tickets.*

3 **Écoutez ces énoncés et repérez la syllabe qui porte l'accent de phrase. Est-elle à sa place attendue ou l'énoncé est-il emphatique ? Répétez.**

Audio 23lmu21312

a. The tickets for the show are expensive.
b. The tickets for the show are so expensive!
c. You absolutely must see *West Side Story*.
d. You absolutely must see *West Side Story*.
e. *Evita* isn't an American musical. It's a British musical!

IMPROVE YOUR Vocabulary

Activités en ligne 23lmu21313

Musicals

PEOPLE

Audio 23lmu21314

- the cast = the performers
- actors
- a producer
- a choreographer
- a lyricist
- a musical director
- a script writer
- a costume designer
- a composer
- talented = gifted

THEATRE

Audio 23lmu21315

- a show
- a stage
- the staging
- a costume /'kɒstjʊm/
- the audience = the spectators
- the box office
- a production = a show, a performance
- the venue = the place where shows are run

PROMOTION

Audio 23lmu21316

- a poster
- a flyer
- a publicity = an advert
- a review = a critique
- a bestseller
- promote sth = advertise sth

Describing shows

SOCIAL ISSUES

Audio 23lmu21317

- an outsider = someone who does not fit in
- a dark theme
- a mistreatment
- prejudice
- intolerance
- hardship
- poverty
- loneliness
- rivalry
- friendship
- freedom
- suffer from
- be shunned = be ignored

REVIEWING

Audio 23lmu21318

- a flop = a fail
- a blockbuster = a success
- breathtaking = astounding
- unbelievable
- entertaining
- well-acted
- amazing = awesome = terrific
- dreadful = awful
- grim = somber
- disappointing
- dreary /'drɪəri/ = boring
- acting, singing, choreography
- tackle an issue
- be out of this world = be extremely good

1 ***Play Quiz, Quiz Trade***
In groups. Make a small card: on one side, write a word from the mind map above and on the other, its definition. Quiz a peer, (s)he will then quiz you. Trade cards and find another partner.

2 **Challenge your peers!** Form 2 teams. Shout out a category from the mind map. The teams have to write down 3 words from that category on the white board. The first team to finish, spelling the 3 words correctly, wins a point.

3 **In pairs.** Describe a musical and get your classmate to guess which one it is. Give one clue at a time: *'It's a story about...'; 'it tackles the issue of...'; 'one of the characters is...'.*

Let's RECAP

Faites le point ! Complétez la fiche bilan avec les documents que vous avez étudiés. Fiche 23lmu21319

AXE 6

Creation and relation to arts

How do musicals mirror society?

#components
What does a musical consist of?

#reviews
Why do some people enjoy or dislike musicals?

#seriousness
How do musicals tackle deep issues?

#hottopics
Which societal problems are present in musicals?

#hype
How are musicals promoted?

#update
Why remake musicals?

GROUP WORK Choose a question and discuss.

Quiz 23lmu21320

Become AN EXPERT

Lisez et écoutez de l'anglais en dehors de la classe

Books

- *Alexander Hamilton*, Chernow (2004) vers LLCER
- *The Color Purple*, Alice Walker (1982) vers LLCER
- *Romeo & Juliet*, William Shakespeare (1591-1596) – graphic novel (2009) vers LLCER

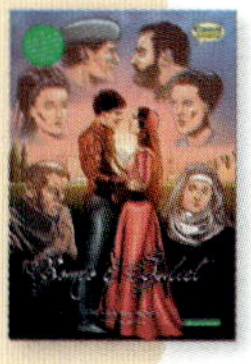

Popular songs

- Love Thy Neighbor, *The Prom* (2020)
- Another day of Sun, *La La Land* (2016)
- Dancing Queen, *Mama Mia* (2008)
- That's how you know, *Enchanted* (2007)
- Dearly Beloved, *Rent* (2005)
- All that Jazz, *Chicago* (2002)
- The Circle of Life, *The Lion King* (1997)
- Singing in the Rain, *Singing in the Rain* (1952)

Musicals

- For teens: *Everybody's Talking about Jamie* – *High School Musical* – *Billy Elliot*
- Popular: *Matilda* – *The Greatest Showman* – *Mama Mia* – *La La Land*
- Classics: *My Fair Lady* – *Singing in the Rain* – *Cabaret* – *Jesus Christ Superstar* – *Hair* – *Grease* – *Cats*
- About the 19th century: *Oliver!* – *The King and I* – *Hello Dolly!* – *Sweeney Todd*

YOUR PROJECTS

Rap to promote a musical!

GROUP WORK

Shoot a promotional video to be posted on your social media account.

- Choose a musical from this unit and a meaningful song.
  - Review the information in this unit.
  - Do some research online.
- Take notes about its societal issues.
  - Message, relevance today, appeal...
- Share roles:
  – one or two will be commenting on the musical/song (as a director, actor or reviewer);
  – the others will be rapping / slamming / singing the song. You can even create a choreography!
  - Watch this video and pay attention to what the director says. Video 23lmu21321
  - Find the song lyrics and select a passage you can rap, sing or dance to.
  - Watch this video (→ 3'04) and focus on the musical numbers with the girls. Video 23lmu21322
- Practise your part.
- Film both parts separately and mix them to make a promotion video (2 to 3 min.).
  - Keep the best passages from each part and mix them.

OR

Create a brochure for a musical

You work for a communication company. You have been tasked to create flyers for musicals.

- Choose a musical and decide on the layout.
  - Work on a musical from this unit.
  - Take a look at pages 142 and 143 for inspiration.
- Select a character or a scene.
  - Choose someone or something memorable from the musical.
- Invent some reviews.
- Give an indication of the topic.
  - Use adjectives and superlatives to promote the show.
  - Add (fake) spectators' reviews.
- Add useful information for spectators and make the presentation appealing!
  - Time, dates, place, photos...

How to create a brochure p. 207

BUILD UP YOUR SKILLS

How to
Rap a song for a musical

1. Pour se préparer

Glasgow girls trailer Video 23lmu21322

- Choisissez une bande son. Vous pouvez aussi slammer sur la vraie mélodie, en karaoké (sites *CurtainUp musical theatre / King of karaoke / Sing King,* etc.).

Il s'agira de dire le texte en rythme et non de le chanter.

- Faites un petit échauffement.

→ Massages du cou et du visage, bâillements, faire le son /i :/ en étirant les lèvres vers les oreilles...

→ Répétez quelques *tongue twisters,* en exagérant le mouvement des lèvres : fresh fried fish greek grapes the three trees red lorry, yellow lorry orange jello, lemon jello

- Travaillez l'accentuation.

→ Dans la chanson, repérez les mots ou syllabes accentuées (plus longues, claires et fortes que les autres).

→ Entraînez-vous à dire le texte en rythme : battez la mesure en frappant dans vos mains sur les syllabes accentuées.
Exemple :

I	***want** to*	***go** to*	***town***	***again.***
I	***want** you to*	***go** to*	***London***	***again.***
I	***wanted** you to*	***go** to*	***Birmingham***	***again.***

- Associez le texte et la musique.

→ Commencez par « bourdonner » (en faisant « *mmm...* »), en essayant de « coller » à votre bande son pour donner le rythme et le flow.
→ Puis essayez avec les paroles de la chanson, en insistant sur les mots/syllabes accentués.

Vous voilà prêts / prêtes pour le show !

2. Pour réaliser votre rap

Vous pouvez rapper une partie de la chanson comme un dialogue (à deux), faire un chœur, introduire des répétitions de mots ou de sons...

- Laissez libre cours à votre fantaisie !
- Répétez plusieurs fois pour avoir bien en tête la musique de la langue.
- Trouvez une petite chorégraphie, gestuelle ou des déplacements pour accompagner le rap.

→ Si certains savent danser, utilisez leurs talents !
→ Sinon, trouvez quelques gestes ou déplacements pour accompagner le texte : par exemple, se répartir sur l'espace puis se rapprocher pour former des paires ou de petits groupes.

Are you ready?

+ prof
Évaluation

Entraînement à l'évaluation

Compréhension orale

Faites un compte-rendu en français de la vidéo.

In the Heights review Video 23lmu21323

Avant l'écoute
Observez l'image, lisez le titre et commencez à émettre des hypothèses sur le contenu.

Pendant l'écoute :
Complétez ou corrigez vos hypothèses :
- relevez les informations sur les personnages, leur origine, le lieu où ils vivent ;
- identifiez les thèmes sociaux traités.

Après l'écoute :
Faites-vous votre propre opinion sur ce spectacle : aspects positifs/négatifs.

Production écrite

Write a short post about the issues in this musical for the American blog *Broadway World*. [100 words]

Compréhension écrite

STRUGGLING TO SURVIVE IN NEW YORK CITY

Rent[1] is a musical set in urban Lower Manhattan, where several artists struggle to make ends meet[2]. They all live within an apartment complex in the East Village and live under the shadow of the AIDS/HIV epidemic.

A lot of the songs and production numbers give a sense of urgency appropriate to the situation. One of the themes they explore is the virtue of not wasting time and living every moment like it's your last. Many of the main characters are already affected by AIDS in different manners. One of the characters, Mimi, sings about the desire to go out and live through the night. Through the song, she seeks[3] to entice[4] another main character, Roger, to go out with her. [...] His friends beckon[5] him to let go and live in the moment with them. The tragedy of the AIDs epidemic is marked when the character, Angel, passes away from the disease.

The musical explores other themes such as poverty, sexuality, and substance abuse. The main characters protest against the looming threat[6] of rent that they were promised wouldn't be a problem. At least in the movie, it is made clear that homelessness persists around the setting. Due to the staggering[7] rent, many people are unable to succeed given their socio-economic status. A couple of the main characters are also homosexual and take a liking to each other. In an excellent move of progressiveness, the musical gives the two characters the chance to have a duet to describe the future they can have together. One of the main characters, Mimi, is also shown to have an addiction that sends her life through a downward spiral. In Act II, she goes missing for months. When the main characters find her, she almost passes away, to their dismay. She holds on when her love interest, Roger, reprises a song they sang together (Columbus). Many musicals act as a mirror to political and social issues that are fresh in the minds of those watching.

digitalcommons.csumb.edu

1. *loyer* – 2. earn just enough to live on – 3. tries – 4. incite – 5. ask – 6. menacing problem – 7. very high

1. Identify the name and setting of the musical.
2. Pick out the characters and the problems they face.
3. State how the article is related to the question 'how do musicals mirror society?'.

Production écrite

"*What is the point of musicals?*" Use what you have learned in this unit to answer the question. [100 words]

Flash UNIT 14

Sports et société

The Uniting States of football

▶ How is American football bringing people together?

YOUR PROJECT

Take part in a discussion on an NFL online forum.

1 The Super Bowl: an American show

1. Look at the photograph and list as many elements as you can. Explain what the people are doing and why.
2. Watch the video and comment on the public: clothes • behaviour • mood
3. PAIR WORK Focus on the key words and create a word cloud with the different representations the Super Bowl has. Then explain what the Super Bowl means to people.
4. You are the BBC journalist. Write a caption for your video post on Twitter to report what supporters think of the Super Bowl.

A **Super Bowl: What does it mean to Americans?**
BBC News Video 23lmu21401

On this picture, Mickey Guyton sings the national anthem before the Super Bowl 2022 between the Los Angeles Rams and the Bengals of Cincinnati in Inglewood, California.

Culture Tip NFL stands for National Football League. It is composed of 32 teams that compete against each other every year.

WHAT'S SO SUPER ABOUT THE SUPER BOWL?

Each winter, millions of Americans gather around their televisions for Super Bowl Sunday. The Super Bowl is the final championship game of the National Football League (NFL).

NFL teams compete throughout the fall for the honor of being one of the top two teams who get to play in the biggest game of the year: the Super Bowl.

Super Bowl Sunday is considered an unofficial holiday in the United States. In fact, after Thanksgiving, more food is eaten on Super Bowl Sunday than any other day of the year.

Most years the Super Bowl is the most-watched program on television in America and the second most-watched program worldwide. In February 2015, the Seattle Seahawks and the New England Patriots played in the Super Bowl. More than 168 million people tuned in for the game, making it the most viewed program in history in the U.S.

Due to the high number of viewers during the Super Bowl, companies interested in buying commercial airtime pay a high price. In fact, if advertisers want to buy commercial time during the Super Bowl, they can expect to pay more than they would at any other time of the year. [...] By 2015, [the cost of a 30-second commercial] had risen to approximately $4.5 million. That's about $150,000 for every second!

wonderopolis.org

B

1. Focus on adjectives to describe how the Super Bowl brings people together.
2. Pick out dates and numbers and explain the importance of the Super Bowl for the US society and economy.
3. You have just watched the Super Bowl with your friends: record a short video explaining "what's so super about the Super Bowl".

Remember how to

Express your enthusiasm

Pour exprimer l'admiration ou l'enthousiasme, on peut utiliser :

- **des adjectifs :**
  → *great, amazing, fantastic, awesome, spectacular, terrific...*
- **Le superlatif + *ever* :**
  → *It was **the best** game **ever**!*
  → *The food was **the most delicious ever**!*
- **des interjections :**
  → *Oh my Gosh!, Oh my!, Wow!* /waʊ/

MEMORY CHALLENGE

Using all the words from the wordbox, explain what the Superbowl is.

WORD BOX

- a bank **holi**day
- a cele**bration**
- pride /'praɪd/
- a **cheer**leader
- spec**tac**ular
- a **nat**ional **an**them
- **unite** = come to**geth**er
- share **values**

2 A spectacular platform

PAIR WORK

DIFFÉRENCIATION

1. Work on one of the videos (A or B). Identify your protagonist and his symbolic gesture.
2. Pick out adjectives explaining how your protagonist is a game changer.

A Colin Kaepernick Video 23lmu21402

B Carl Nassib (→ 1'27) Video 23lmu21403

3. Focus on the values expressed to show how football can promote a more respectful society.

PAIR WORK 3. Exchange what you have learnt about your sportsman with your partner.

Pronunciation Listen to the word *visibility*. Which syllable carries the main stress? Audio 23lmu21404

Remember how to

Express your opinion

- **Verbes et expressions :**
  → ***As far as I'm concerned***, *I totally* ***agree/disagree*** *with this political gesture. It's* ***just my opinion****.*
  → ***I believe*** *he is very courageous.*
- **Modaux:**
  → *I* ***would like*** *them* ***to*** *change their view.*
  → *I think that they* ***could/should*** *listen to his opinion.*

WORD BOX

- a **ges**ture
- a com**mu**nity
- bi**ra**cial /baɪ'reɪʃəl/
- Cau**ca**sian = white-**skinned**
- take a knee = kneel
- cou**ra**geous /kə'reɪdʒəs/ = brave
- come out = an**nounce** you are part of the LGBTQ com**mu**nity

reach3insights.com

Eminem, Kendrick Lamar, Dr. Dre, Mary J. Blige, 50 Cent, and Snoop Dogg, February 2022

REACTIONS TO THE 2022 HALF-TIME SHOW

February 17, 2022 • Lianne Frick - Research consultant

The 2022 Super Bowl halftime show brought together hip-hop legends, and it was one of the best performances in history. However, the NFL faces allegations of racism, leading some to question its intentions.

→ A LEGITIMATE INCLUSION INITIATIVE?

1 "I enjoyed the music in the performers; it was the first time that rappers ever headlined the Super Bowl halftime show and it was awesome." She/Her, 35-44, White and Black/African American

2 "It felt like the NFL went out of their element by getting black hip-hop artists. I think a lot of white Americans would not like this, but the NFL did it anyway" — He/Him, 25-34, Black/African American

→ WAS EMINEM THE TOKEN[1] WHITE GUY?

3 "I liked how Eminem at the end of his performance took a knee like Colin Kaepernick. I thought it was a powerful moment." He/Him, 25–34, Black/African American

4 "Why put a white rapper in the lineup with other black singers? [...] I feel like they didn't want to do a full black lineup because they were afraid of getting backlash[2]. That's just my opinion." She/Her, 25-34, Hispanic

→ MAKING SURE THE PERFORMANCE ISN'T JUST PERFORMATIVE[3]

5 "They could have had white performers but instead they were mostly black. I'd still like to see more black coaches in the league but it's a start." He/Him, 25-34, Black/African American

6 "While I loved that the half time show featured black performers, it will take more for the NFL to convince me that they are trying to be more inclusive[4]." — She/Her, 25-34, Black/African American

1. symbolic, for the sake of form – 2. negative reaction – 3. just words – 4. including people, open to all

C

1. Read reactions 1 to 4. Pick out verbs and adjectives showing the opinions of the people interviewed and recap.

2. Read reactions 5 and 6. Focus on words showing the disappointment expressed by the interviewees and recap.

3. Act out an interview.
Student 1: you are the journalist;
Student 2: you are a fan who has just watched the halftime show.
Imagine the questions and the fan's reaction and point of view.

WHY NOT WATCH THE HALFTIME SHOW 2022 ON LINE?

IMPROVE YOUR Grammar

Activités en ligne 23lmu21405

La phrase exclamative

- Pour exprimer **une vive émotion** (négative ou positive), il existe plusieurs structures exclamatives.
  - Si l'exclamation porte sur **un groupe nominal** :
    what* + *a(n) + (adj.) + nom : → ***What an*** *amazing match!*
    such* + *a(n) + (adj.) + nom : → *They make* ***such a*** *great team!*

    On n'emploie pas l'article *a(n)* avec les noms indénombrables ou les noms au pluriel :
    → ***What*** *awesome players!*
  - Si l'exclamation porte sur **un adjectif ou un adverbe** :
    how **+ adjectif/adverbe** (+ sujet + verbe) :
    → ***How beautifully*** *she sings!*
    so **+ adjectif/adverbe** : → *She is* ***so talented!***

1 **Transformez ces phrases en exclamatives en utilisant l'amorce proposée.**

a. Ben is a popular cheerleader.
→ Ben is such…

b. This game is exciting.
→ What…

c. This player is agile.
→ This player is so…

d. This player runs quickly.
→ How…

e. They have a bad coach.
→ They have such…

f. The half-time show was boring.
→ How…

2 **Vous venez d'assister à la performance de Rihanna à la mi-temps du Super Bowl ! Produisez quatre phrases exclamatives en utilisant différentes structures.**

IMPROVE YOUR Pronunciation

L'accentuation des mots en *-ity* et *-ety*

Tyron's Tips 23lmu21406

- Ces mots portent leur accent principal sur **la syllabe qui précède cette terminaison** :

community ○◯○○ *diversity* ○◯○○ *unity* ◯○○
society ○◯○○ *variety* ○◯○○

La voyelle *i* se prononce /aɪ/ (comme dans *my*) dans la terminaison *-iety* : *propriety* /prəˈpraɪəti/, *society* /səˈsaɪəti/.

1 a) **Recopiez les mots suivants et soulignez la syllabe qui porte l'accent principal.**

authority • diversity • loyalty • capacity • opportunity • solidarity • personality • variety • university • visibility

b) **Écoutez l'enregistrement pour vérifier vos réponses et répétez.**

Audio 23lmu21407

IMPROVE YOUR Vocabulary

Activités en ligne 23lmu21408

Unity in sports

UNITY

Audio 23lmu21409

- a unifying force
- solidarity
- a gesture
- diversity
- unite = unify, bring together
- share value
- support

POLITICAL STATEMENT

Audio 23lmu21410

- dignity
- respect
- injustice, oppression
- racism, discrimination
- respectful ≠ disrespectful
- stand up for one's rights
- kneel, take a knee ≠ stand

PATRIOTISM

Audio 23lmu21411

- a national anthem
- a bank holiday
- a celebration
- a value
- pride
- loyalty
- honour
- commemorate sth

AMERICAN FOOTBALL

Audio 23lmu21412

- a coach
- a team
- a player
- a cheerleader
- a quarterback
- a stadium
- a commercial = an advert
- a playing field
- a competition, a tournament
- attend a game
- advertise
- broadcast sth = transmit sth on TV

Let's RECAP

Faites le point ! Complétez la fiche bilan avec les documents que vous avez étudiés. Fiche 23lmu21413

AXE 5

Sport and society

Does American Football bring people together?

#hypermediatised

How big is the Super Bowl in American media?

#nationalunity

To what extent does American football symbolise national unity?

#socialevent

Why is the Super Bowl such an important social event?

#political statement

How has the stadium been used as a platform for political statements?

GROUP WORK Choose a question and discuss.

Quiz 23lmu21414

YOUR PROJECT

Participate in an online Forum

Take part in a discussion on an NFL online forum about whether the Super Bowl brings Americans together.

In groups of 4, interact on line and give your point of view. Each person will give a different argument, and you can ask questions and answer each other.
You can use Etherpad, Learningapps or Cryptpad.

- Prepare your arguments and examples.
  Look for persuasive elements from the documents.
- Be ready to express your opinion.
  Use expressions to agree or disagree.
- Your answers must be short and impactful.
  To be convincing, express your enthusiasm!

Vivre entre générations

UNIT 15 Being born-free in South Africa

▶ How is the new generation building post-apartheid South Africa?

YOUR PROJECTS

Write an article about the South African youth.

OR

Deliver a speech on South Africa's future.

After the detection of the Omicron variant of the COVID-19 virus, several countries had imposed travel restrictions on South Africa in 2021. In this video, the journalists expose the reaction of President Cyril Ramaphosa and the other challenges South Africa has had to endure in its recent history.

Sky News Australia, 2021

A **'The Rainbow Nation': South Africa's troubled past and uncertain future** Video 23lmu21501

1. Watch the beginning of the video (→ 1'40). Identify reasons why South Africa has been divided.

2. Watch again. Find what the involvement of the African National Congress (A.N.C.) was and identify one of its members.

3. Watch the end of the video. Explain whether change is considered positive in the country.

4. Record a one-minute audio where you recap both South Africa's challenges and hopes.

Pronunciation Listen and repeat these words, paying attention to the *th* sound: *Sou**th** Africa*, *ano**th**er*, *apar**th**eid*, *wi**th***, *pa**th***.

B **Students at Tom Naudé High School in Polokwane, walking from one classroom to the next between classes.**

1948 – Apartheid (separateness), a legal system that separates people of different "races" in South Africa, is adopted when the National Party takes power. Black citizens are considered lesser citizens.

1950's – The African National Congress (ANC) responds with a campaign of civil disobedience.

1970s – 3 million people are forced to move back to black 'homelands'. More than 600 black protesters are killed in clashes with the security forces in Soweto.

1990 – Nelson Mandela is pardoned and freed from prison by President F.W. De Klerk.

1991-1994 – De Klerk revokes apartheid laws. ANC wins first non-racial elections. Mandela becomes president.

Adapted from bbc.com/news

C

1. Look at the picture. Describe: the scene • the people • the atmosphere
2. Read the Country Files > p. 300 and the timeline. List the events which made this situation possible.
3. Indicate to what extent this photograph portrays South African youth.

4. Create another caption for this photograph with the following words: *united • school • Soweto • apartheid*

Remember how to

Express certainty and hypotheses in the past > Docs B/C

- **Pour exprimer une forte probabilité concernant un événement passé : *must* + *have* + participe passé** (V + *-ed* ou 3e colonne des verbes irréguliers).
  → *It **must have been** impossible for black and white children to go to the same schools during the apartheid era.*
- **Pour parler d'un événement qui n'aurait pas été possible dans le passé : *could not* + *have* + participe passé.**
  → *They **could not have gone** to the same schools during the apartheid.*

WORD BOX

- apartheid /ə'pɑːtaɪt/
- segregation
- citizenship
- a privilege
- a boycott
- a clash = a fight
- an uprising = a rebellion
- harmonious
- prosperous
- be segregated = be discriminated against
- deny rights = refuse rights
- get arrested
- repeal = revoke
- get along with sb = be friends

1 Mandela's Rainbow Nation?

GROUP WORK

DIFFÉRENCIATION

Ilvy Njiokiktjien, 2019

A All class Mandela's Generation of Hope Video 23lmu21502

1. Watch the beginning of the video [→ 0'32] and describe the interviewed people: social background • ethnicity • gender • nationality • ...

2. Explain what the challenge of this generation is.

3. Watch the end of the video and pick out words expressing how this generation feels about being born-free. Make a sentence to explain their situation.

4. Prepare a one-minute speech about what being 'born-free' means.

Star Khulu – by Lebo Lukewarm

LEBO LUKEWARM PHOTOGRAPHS THE CHANGING YOUTH OF SOUTH AFRICA

Today marks 40 years since students in Soweto took to the streets to march against the apartheid government's implementation[1] of Afrikaans as the main language in schools. To commemorate the 40th anniversary of the Soweto Uprising, Lebo Lukewarm invited young South Africans to get their photo taken and reflect on how much has changed in the 40 years since 1976. "And to see if people remember the importance of being a youth and the power we, as the youth have."

What does it mean to you, to be part of the youth of South Africa today?

Nthabiseng Sechoaro

"It means having the creative footprint[2] of South African people in my hands, as my responsibility. It means different battles, but probably easier ones because the blood was taken from our mothers. It means audacity, it means chance, it means [why not?]"

South Africa's Youth in 16 Portraits, Lebo Lukewarm, 16/06/16

1. application – 2. impact

B Group 1

Being part of a new generation

Ballet dancer Thabang Mabaso grew up in Orange Farm, a poor township[1] outside Johannesburg, before going to art school. There he started to train as a dancer and is now a professional dancer in the Johannesburg ballet company. He gives ballet lessons in the townships and knows his life would have been very different under apartheid. "If we hadn't gained democracy in 1994," he says, "I'd have been perhaps a gardener but definitely not a ballet dancer." He readily[2] acknowledges[3] that few blacks attend[4] his performances and adds that there has been opposition to his chosen profession closer to home. "My mum never saw my ballet as a proper[5] job or career, she would always say: 'Oh you're going to go play ballet now?'" However, Thabang believes that South Africa has the diversity and the potential to develop like the United States.

bbc.com, April 25, 2014

1. segregated area for non-white people during apartheid – 2. easily – 3. admits – 4. go to – 5. real

C Group 2

Zakithi Buthelezi, 27, quickly noticed that people often treat him differently once they find out he has a white girlfriend. Friendlier, more interested. For Wilmarie Deetlefs, 24, it's often the other way around[1]. "Go get yourself a man of your own color," she said a taxi driver once snarled[2] at her.
Such remarks frustrate the couple. […] But those comments do not amount to prosecution[3], which is what they could have faced under apartheid laws that prohibited interracial relationships. […]
Five months into their relationship, Deetlefs hadn't yet told her parents about it. "The previous relationship I had with someone who wasn't white — my dad took it so weirdly, strangely personal," she said, blaming his reaction on the conservative mentality in the small rural town where she grew up.
"We're the generation that's going to completely move away from how South Africa lived," Buthelezi said. "For people in the older generation, everything is still so racialist[4], and apartheid is still thrown into debates. That is over, guys. It's just time to move on."

Born Free – Mandela's Generation of Hope, Ilvy Njiokiktjien, 2019

1. opposite situation – 2. expressed angrily – 3. official accusation of committing a crime – 4. racist

D Group 3

GROUP WORK

1. Work on your document (Doc B, C or D).
Introduce the people portrayed with one sentence.

2. List the positive aspects that came with the end of apartheid, and the difficulties this generation still faces.

3. Compare the people's lives with those of their parents.

4. Together, discuss these people's lives and their hopes for the future in South Africa.

Grammar *"...apartheid laws **that** prohibited interracial relationships"*: replace *that* with an equivalent word. What is this type of word called?

WORD BOX

- **rac**ism
- a **view**point = a point of view
- con**flic**ted
- inter**ra**cial
- opti**mis**tic = **hope**ful
- pay **tri**bute = to **ho**nor and praise
- **strug**gle = fight

PREPARE YOUR PROJECT

Celebrate the Rainbow nation

Choose a picture that best represents the rainbow nation and explain what being born-free means for this generation.
Post it on your favourite social media.

2 Building the future together

Culture Tip In South Africa they call it 'black tax', where young black professionals are often expected to support their families financially and therefore pay back for their family's sacrifices.

A Is 'black tax' help or a burden? **Video** 23lmu21503

1. Look at the title of the document and imagine definitions for 'a burden' and 'black tax'. Then read the Culture tip to check your guesses.
2. Watch the video (→ 1'50) and pick out words the speakers use to define the 'black tax'.
3. Clarify why the 'black tax' is considered both positive and negative.
4. List the pros and cons of the 'black tax'.

In 2021, as South Africa commemorated the 45th anniversary of the June 16 Soweto youth uprising, various events took place throughout the country celebrating the resistant youth of 1976.

- **fees:** university admission charges
- **Gender-Based Violence (GBV)** can take many shapes such as domestic and sexual violence against women, girls and LGBTQ+ people.

B Happy Youth Day

Bethuel Mangena, African News Agency, Jun 17, 2021

1. Read the engraving on the cartoon's stage ("*To honour...*") and explain how people usually commemorate an event.
2. Describe the young people's attitude on the stage and contrast it with the title "Happy Youth Day".
3. Read the introduction in blue, the placards in the cartoon and explain the students' demands.
4. **Médiation** Explain how demonstrating is another way of commemorating the Soweto rebellion.

"A shelter from reality"

As apartheid was coming to an end, South Africa's elite private schools started accepting children of all colors. My mother's company offered bursaries, scholarships[1] for underprivileged families, and she managed to get me into Maryvale College, an expensive private Catholic school. Classes taught by nuns[2]. Mass[3] on Fridays. The whole bit. I started preschool there when I was three, primary school when I was five.

In my class we had all kinds of kids. Black kids, white kids, Indian kids, colored kids. Most of the white kids were pretty well off[4]. Every child of color pretty much wasn't. But because of scholarships we all sat at the same table. We wore the same maroon blazers, the same gray slacks[5] and skirts. We had the same books. We had the same teachers. There was no racial separation. Every clique was racially mixed.

Kids still got teased and bullied, but it was over usual kid stuff: being fat or being skinny, being tall or being short, being smart or being dumb. I don't remember anybody being teased about their race. I didn't learn to put limits on what I was supposed to like or not like. I had a wide berth[6] to explore myself. I had crushes on white girls. I had crushes on black girls. Nobody asked me what I was. I was Trevor.

It was a wonderful experience to have, but the downside was that it sheltered me from reality. Maryvale was an oasis that kept me from the truth, a comfortable place where I could avoid making a tough decision. But the real world doesn't go away. Racism exists. People are getting hurt, and just because it's not happening to you doesn't mean it's not happening. And at some point, you have to choose. Black or white.

Born a Crime: Stories From a South African Childhood,
Trevor Noah, 2019

1. money for studies – **2.** religious women – **3.** church service – **4.** rich – **5.** trousers – **6.** place

C

1. Read lines 1-16. Focus on adjectives and find who could join this elite school.

2. Read the rest of the text and spot one thing for which students were not bullied for in the author's school.

3. Clarify what the author means when writing:

"It was a wonderful experience to have, but the downside was that it sheltered me from reality." (l. 31-32)

4. Write the end of the chapter explaining one challenge Trevor had to face when he finished school.

Remember how to

Describe past habits > Docs A/C

Pour exprimer un fait habituel dans le passé, il est possible d'utiliser l'auxiliaire modal ***would*** + **V**.

→ *Before the apartheid ended, they* ***would be segregated*** *because of their skin colour and* ***would not have access*** *to the same opportunities.*

WORD BOX

- **rac**ial segre**ga**tion
- an **is**sue /ˈɪʃuː/ = a **pro**blem
- **foot**steps = tra**di**tions
- **boun**daries = **li**mits
- a tui**tion** /tjuˈɪʃən/ = a **school** fee
- de**ter**mined = firm, **res**olute
- **de**monstrate = pro**test**
- af**ford** sth = have **mon**ey to buy sth
- **car**ry
- sup**port** sb = help sb

PREPARE YOUR PROJECT

Record a short speech

To celebrate South Africa's History, give a one-minute speech for your school's radio station.
Talk about the future of the country and the challenges it faces to come together as a united nation.

IMPROVE YOUR **Grammar**

+ Activités en ligne
23lmu21504

Les propositions relatives

- Une proposition relative permet d'apporter une information sur un nom appelé « antécédent ». Elle est introduite par **un pronom relatif (*who*, *which* ou *that*).**
- Quand l'antécédent renvoie à **une personne**, on utilise ***who*** :
  → ***Nelson Mandela, who spent 27 years in prison,*** *became president in 1994.*
- Quand l'antécédent renvoie à **un inanimé** (une chose ou une abstraction), on utilise ***which*** :
  → *The ANC was **a political party which fought against apartheid**.*
- **Le pronom relatif *that*** peut souvent être employé à la place de *who* ou de *which*.
  → *Soweto is **a black township which/that was established near Johannesburg in South Africa**.*

Le pronom relatif peut être omis quand l'antécédent est complément d'objet du verbe de la relative :
→ *Unemployment is **the main problem Ø young black people face nowadays**.*

> Précis p. 274

1 a) Complétez avec *which*, *who* ou *that*. Si plusieurs réponses sont possibles, donnez-les toutes.

a. In South Africa, the children ... were born after 1994 are called 'the born-free generation'.
b. Young South Africans can now choose the jobs ... they like.
c. The laws ... prohibited interracial relationships were repealed in 1985.
d. There is a wide generation gap between the younger generation and their parents, ... experienced apartheid.

b) Dites à chaque fois si le pronom relatif peut être supprimé ou non.

Exprimer l'interdiction

- Pour exprimer **une interdiction au présent**, on peut employer **les modaux *mustn't*** et ***can't***, ou bien dans une langue plus formelle ***may not*** :
  → *You **mustn't / can't disobey** your parents.*
- Pour exprimer **une interdiction au passé**, on utilise ***couldn't* + V** :
  → *During apartheid, black people **couldn't marry** white people.*
- ***(Not) be allowed to* + V** /əˈlaʊd/ est employé à tous les temps ou après un modal (*will*, *would*...) :
  → *During apartheid, black people **were not allowed to marry** white people.*
- Pour exprimer l'interdiction, on utilise aussi les verbes suivants :

be forbidden to do sth	→ *Black people **were forbidden to use** the same facilities as whites.*
be prohibited/banned from doing sth	→ *Black people **were prohibited from voting**.*

> Précis p. 267

2 Reformulez les phrases en utilisant les expressions entre parenthèses.

a. Black people were not allowed to live in affluent white neighbourhoods. *(be forbidden)*
b. As a child, my mother couldn't speak her mind. *(be allowed)*
c. "You can't date a white girl," my father said. (*must*)
d. During apartheid, black people couldn't run for election. (*be prohibited*)

3 Imaginez ce que les parents des enfants de la *born-free generation* étaient ou non autorisés à faire durant l'apartheid. Produisez 3 phrases. Utilisez à chaque fois une structure différente.

IMPROVE YOUR Pronunciation

La prononciation de *th*

- La graphie ***th*** se prononce toujours **en mettant la langue entre les dents**.
  Elle représente deux sons :

Tyron's Tips 23lmu21505

/ð/ comme dans *this*	Entre deux voyelles : ***rather***, ***other***, ***father***. Exceptions : ***Catholic***, ***cathedral*** /θ/
	Au début des mots grammaticaux : ***the***, ***this***, ***then***, ***though***...
/θ/ comme dans *think*	En début ou en fin des mots lexicaux (verbes, noms, adjectifs) : ***South***, ***throw***, ***Commonwealth***, ***thing***

Dans quelques mots, *th* se prononce /t/ : *Thomas*, *the Thames* (la Tamise), *apartheid* /əˈpɑːtaɪt/...

La prononciation de la terminaison *-ate*

Audio 23lmu21508

- La terminaison ***-ate*** peut se prononcer de deux façons différentes :

Si le mot est un nom ou un adjectif	Si le mot est un verbe
/ət/ (rime avec *quiet*): ***private***	/eɪt/ (rime avec *eight*): ***commemorate***

Les adjectifs et noms **d'une syllabe** en *-ate* ne suivent pas cette règle et se prononcent /eɪt/ : ***date***, ***United States***, ***late***, ***gate***... Il en va de même de ***debate*** et ***candidate***, qui sont des exceptions.

- **Les adverbes en *-ately*** étant dérivés d'adjectifs, ils se prononcent eux aussi /ət/ : ***unfortunately***, ***immediately***, ***deliberately***.

1 **Écoutez et prononcez les paires de mots suivantes. Distinguez bien le son /θ/ de *thing* du son /s/ de *sing*.**
Audio 23lmu21506

a. *thin – sin*
b. *thick – sick*
c. *mouse – mouth*
d. *sought – thought*
e. *path – pass*

2 **Écoutez ces mots et classez-les dans un tableau en fonction de la prononciation de *th* : /ð/ comme dans *this* ou /θ/ comme dans *think*.**
Audio 23lmu51507

Thursday • together • these • mother • truth • they • Catholic • though • there • thrive

3 a) **Dites si les mots suivants sont des verbes, des adjectifs ou des noms. Puis classez-les dans un tableau en fonction de la prononciation de *-ate* (/ət/ comme *quiet* ou /eɪt/ comme dans *eight*).**

educate • segregate • celebrate • climate • debate • appropriate • senate • illustrate • rate

b) **Vérifiez en écoutant l'enregistrement puis répétez.**
Audio 23lmu21509

4 **Écoutez l'enregistrement. Le mot *separate* est-il prononcé de la même manière dans les phrases suivantes ? Expliquez pourquoi.**
Audio 23lmu21510

a. During apartheid, black and white people lived in separate areas.
b. Laws were passed to separate black people from white people.

IMPROVE YOUR Vocabulary

+ Activités en ligne 23lmu21511

Legacy

TRADITION
Audio 23lmu21512

- a heritage = a legacy
- footsteps = traditions
- a multicultural society
- identify sb/sth as sth
- pay tribute to sb = show respect to sb
- a generation gap

YOUNG GENERATION
Audio 23lmu21513

- the born-free generation
- the Rainbow nation
- boundaries = limits
- interracial
- post-apartheid
- carry on = continue
- get along with sb = be friends with sb
- support sb = help sb financially

Challenges and successes

POLITICS
Audio 23lmu21514

- apartheid /ə'pɑːtaɪt/
- a boycott
- a clash = a fight
- an uprising = a rebellion
- a democracy
- freedom
- reconciliation
- a viewpoint
- an activist
- a means of expression
- convey a message
- express oneself
- denounce sth
- repeal sth = revoke sth
- deny rights = refuse rights

TRIUMPH
Audio 23lmu21515

- an opportunity
- harmonious
- optimistic = hopeful
- prosperous
- afford sth
  = have money to buy sth
- thrive = succeed

OBSTACLES
Audio 23lmu21516

- an issue /'ɪʃuː/ = a problem
- a discrimination
- racism
- segregation
- living-conditions
- unemployment
- education
- a tuition /tju'ɪʃən/
  = a school fee
- a privilege
- annoyed = angry
- feel conflicted about sth
  = feel unsure about sth
- lose hope
- struggle = fight

1 ***Pair Up!*** **Choose 5 words in the mind map above. Be the first one to finish writing a definition for each word and win the challenge.**

2 **Use the mind map to describe this picture and explain the message it conveys.**

3 **The Model U.N. Club in your high school is looking for volunteers to write an opinion piece on South Africa's development. Write a short paragraph to speak about its future using at least 10 words from this mind map.**

Let's RECAP

Faites le point ! Complétez la fiche bilan avec les documents que vous avez étudiés. Fiche 23lmu21517

AXE 1

Intergenerational relationships

How are South Africans building their nation together?

#legacy

To what extent has the end of the apartheid changed the country?

#unity

To what extent is South Africa united for a better future?

#intergenerational

How do new generations see themselves in comparison with their parents' generation?

#bornfreegeneration

What does it mean to be part of the born-free generation?

#battles

What are the challenges new generations have inherited from their parents?

#hopefulgenerations

What are the opportunities and challenges for these generations?

GROUP WORK Choose a question and discuss.

Quiz 23lmu21518

Become AN EXPERT

Lisez et écoutez de l'anglais en dehors de la classe

Books

- *Born-Free – Mandela's Generation of Hope,* Ilvy Njiokiktjien (2019) vers AMC

- *The Hidden Star,* K. Sello Duiker (2006) vers LLCER

- *No Turning Back,* Berveley Naidoo (1995) vers LLCER
- *Born a crime, Stories from a South African childhood*, Trevor Noah (2016)
- *July's People,* Nadine Gordimer (1981) vers LLCER

Films

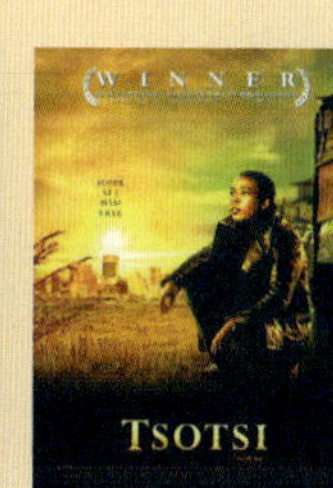

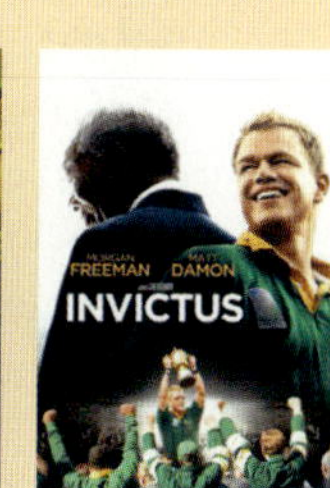

YOUR PROJECTS

Write an article

Write an article for your school's newspaper, where you reveal the challenges that South Africans must face together to build a better future.

- Introduce the born-free generation.
  Mention people you've gotten to know in the unit as examples.
- Explain what changes the end of the apartheid brought to people's lives.
  Use the present perfect for something that started in the past and continues in the present.
- Clarify what challenges the born-free generation still faces today.
  Use *'have to'* in order to show that the obligation comes from outside this generation.
- Conclude by showing how this generation is longing for a better future.
  Use the verb *hope* to express their optimism.

OR

Deliver a speech

As a member of the Model U.N. club in your school, report on South Africa's future.

- Introduce yourself and then South Africa's born-free Generation.
  Mention Nelson Mandela's legacy and dream for a Rainbow nation.
- Use the history of South Africa to prepare a presentation of the country.
  Use dates and mention events using the simple past to provide context.
- List the ongoing challenges this generation has inherited from the past and the new ones they must face today.
  Use comparatives to explain how this generation's experience is different from their parents'.
- Use examples of situations you have encountered in the unit and end on a positive note.
  Use *must* + V to express what necessary steps have to be taken towards a brighter future for all.

How to deliver a speech p. 85

BUILD UP YOUR SKILLS

FICHE GROUP WORK

1. Work on your document on p. 178 (Doc A or B). Look at the photo of your document and read its title. Guess what it is about.
Use **Fiche** 23lmu21602

2. Explain the cause the activist is fighting for and what means he/she uses. Share the information with your classmates.

3. Discuss the common points and differences between these activists.

4. You have decided to join one of these activists' movements. Send a message to your classmates to convince them to join too.

C Young activists on why they march, 2018 **Video** 23lmu21603

Culture Tip

On February 14, 2018, a former student of Marjory Stoneman Douglas High School in Parkland, Florida, entered the school, murdered 17 people and injured 17 others. This was the deadliest high school shooting in the history of the United States. In 2022, at least 639 mass shootings took place in the USA.

1. Look at the picture and read the Culture tip. Make hypotheses about the reasons for this protest.

2. Watch the video and explain why these people are protesting and in what way they decided to do it.

3. "*I'm marching so that generations after us don't have to*" : explain this sentence with your own words.

PAIR WORK

4. You have a conversation with one of these activists. Imagine the arguments they would use to explain their fight. Enact the dialogue.

WORD BOX

- carbon **emission**
- **cli**mate change /ˈklaɪmɪt ˌtʃeɪndʒ/
- eco-an**xi**ety /æŋˈzaɪəti/
- **gen**der e**qual**ity
- gun con**trol**
- gun **vio**lence /ˈvaɪələns/
- **pre**judice: discrimi**na**tion
- **stan**dards
- **stri**king /ˈstraɪkɪŋ/ = im**pres**sive
- de**mand** sth = ask for sth very **firm**ly
- ad**dress** /əˈdres/ an **is**sue = give at**ten**tion to a spe**cif**ic **is**sue
- con**vey** /kənˈveɪ/ (a **mes**sage) = trans**mit** (a **mes**sage)
- con**vince** sb to do sth

PREPARE YOUR PROJECT

Shoot a video

You want to join one of these causes. Prepare a video you will send to the activist of your choice explaining the impact they had on you. Give arguments to convince them to take you onboard.

2 Empowered youth

The fate of the world is in their hands

The youngest generations may feel that they have the smallest ability to impact the devastating effects of climate change at the moment but also shoulder the burden[1] of its future effects. This responsibility [...] has caused widespread psychological distress among young people. Many say they don't trust their leaders to make the right decisions for them and the planet. They are frustrated with older generations for putting them in this position and they are scared about the future of the planet – about what living conditions will look like decades from now.

But it has also sparked[2] a camaraderie among young people, who are using their collective voices and actions to become the most vocal generation to fight for the planet in recorded history. "The climate emergency is already here," 19-year-old Jeeva Senthilnathan, an engineering student at the Colorado School of Mines, told ABC News. "We're seeing the entire climate emergency in front of our eyes." Older generations have a responsibility to foster[3] and encourage young people's goals to conserve the planet as well, Lise Van Susteren, [...] told ABC News. "We have to listen," [she] said.

www.abcnews.go.com, 22/01/2022

1. something that is difficult to carry – 2. promoted – 3. take care

A

1. Describe the picture and rephrase the words on the placard *"We'll take it from here"*.
2. Read the text and find the cause youngest generations are fighting for and who they blame for inaction.
3. List 4 negative consequences caused by this lack of action and one positive effect.
4. Explain what young people would like older generations to do.
5. Create 3 other placards young people may want to show to adults and explain each message with two sentences.

B Supporting a teen activist. Milou Albrecht and her mum, Susie, NPR Audio 23lmu21604

Culture Tip "School Strike for Climate", also known variously as Fridays for Future (FFF), Youth for Climate, Climate Strike or Youth Strike for Climate, is an international movement of school students who skip Friday classes to participate in demonstrations to demand action from political leaders.

WORD BOX

- a com**mit**ment /kə'mɪtmənt/ = an en**gage**ment
- a **du**ty = an obli**ga**tion
- a **le**gacy = a **her**itage
- **ded**icated to sth
- **threat**ening
- be/get in**volved** in sth
- be com**mit**ted to sth
- e**man**cipate
- trust sb/sth
- perse**vere**

1. Read the Culture tip and listen to the audio. Collect information on Milou Albrecht's cause and on her family.
2. List the reasons why Milou's mother think her daughter's activism is good for her.
3. Identify the qualities that are developed when you are a young activist and a parent supporting one, according to the journalist.
4. PAIR WORK Milou listened to the interview and wants to thank her mum for her support. Write and act the dialogue.

Pronunciation Listen to the following words: *getting, supporting.* Audio 23lmu21620

Pay attention to the American pronunciation of the ***t*** sound. What do you notice?

Remember how to

Express blame > Docs A et B

Pour dire qu'on reproche quelque chose à quelqu'un, on peut utiliser différentes structures :

- ***blame someone for*** + V-ing.
  → *She **blames** adults **for** not understanding her.* (understanding = V-ing)
- ***accuse someone of*** + V-ing.
  → *They **accuse the oil industry of** contributing to climate change.* (contributing = V-ing)

PREPARE YOUR PROJECT

Create an identity card

Choose a young American activist and create his/her identity card:
name • age • location
Explain his/her cause in a short paragraph.

IMPROVE YOUR Grammar

Activités en ligne
23lmu21605

Exprimer le conseil

Tyron's Tips
23lmu21606

- Pour donner un conseil ou dire que quelque chose est souhaitable, on utilise le modal ***should* + V** (forme négative : *should not* ou *shouldn't*) :
  → *Industrialised countries **should reduce** carbon emissions.*

Le *l* de *should* est muet (comme celui de *could* et de *would*).

- On peut aussi employer ***ought (not) to* + V** (prononcé /ɔːt/), dont le sens est très proche :
  → *Industrialised countries **ought to reduce** carbon emissions.*
- Dans une langue plus familière, on emploie ***had better (not)* + V**. *Had* est souvent contracté en *'d* :
  → *You**'d** / **had better** go on strike.*
- On peut employer le verbe ***suggest*** ou ***recommend*** suivi d'une proposition en *that* :
  → ***I suggest / recommend that** you go on strike.*

> Précis p. 270

1 Reformulez les phrases suivantes en utilisant les mots entre parenthèses.

a. I suggest that you take part in the demonstration. *(should)*

b. I advise you to create your own website to increase your visibility. *(had better)*

c. Why don't you use social media to raise awareness of gun violence? *(should)*

d. Guns should be banned in the United States. *(ought to)*

2 Dites quatre choses que devraient faire les gouvernements pour rendre le monde plus juste. Utilisez ces expressions : *ought to, should, had better, I suggest that...*

Les propositions infinitives

- En anglais, de nombreux verbes sont suivis d'un **verbe à l'infinitif en *to*** : *want*, *expect* (s'attendre à), *need*, *would like*, *decide*, *hope*, *refuse*, *agree* (accepter de), *promise*, *demand* (exiger)...
  → *A lot of teenagers **hope to change the world**.*
- Avec les verbes ***want, need, expect*** et ***would like***, quand le sujet du verbe à l'infinitif en *to* est différent, il est placé avant *to*.
  → *We want / need **the government** to take action.*
- Si le sujet est un pronom personnel, il est à la forme complément (*him, them, me*...) :
  → *We want / need **them** to take action.*

Attention, *want*, *need* et *would like* ne sont jamais suivis d'une proposition en *that*. « *Je veux qu'il vienne* » se traduit donc par "*I want **him to come***".

3 Complétez ces phrases en employant un infinitif en *to*.

a. The protesters demanded...

b. Some teenagers would like...

c. The police decided...

d. His parents promised...

e. The government agreed...

4 Reformulez les phrases suivantes au moyen d'une proposition infinitive en commençant par l'amorce proposée.

a. Please, could you sign this petition? → *I would like...*

b. This project must be abandoned! → *We want...*

c. I'm sure that the police will arrest us. → *I expect...*

IMPROVE YOUR Pronunciation

L'anglais américain 🇺🇸 Audio 23lmu21607

- La plupart des Américains **prononcent <u>tous</u> les *r***, y compris après des voyelles (ce que ne font pas de nombreux Britanniques) : *park, girl, store.*
- Quand la **consonne *t*** apparaît entre deux voyelles, elle se prononce comme **un *d* très rapide** (on appelle ce son un *flap*) : *matter*, *city*.
- La voyelle de *hot*, *lot* ou *not* est plus longue qu'en anglais britannique. La bouche est plus ouverte (ce son ressemble davantage à un *a*).
- Le son /ju:/ de *new* est prononcé /u:/ dans de nombreux mots (surtout après les consonnes *d*, *n*, *t*, *s* et *l*) : *dude*, *attitude*, *student.*

> Précis p. 281

1 **Les mots suivants vont être prononcés par un locuteur britannique puis américain. Écoutez et répétez chaque mot avec l'accent que vous avez choisi.** Audio 23lmu21608

a. new
b. hot
c. duty
d. march
e. part
f. short
g. better
h. later

2 **L'information suivante est-elle prononcée par un locuteur américain ou britannique ? Sur quels indices pouvez-vous vous appuyer ?** Audio 23lmu21609

In 2018, a former student of Marjory Stoneman Douglas High School in Parkland, Florida, entered the school and murdered 17 people. This was the deadliest high school shooting in the history of the United States.

Les mots inaccentués Audio 23lmu21610

- **Les mots grammaticaux d'une syllabe** ne sont pas accentués dans la phrase. Il s'agit :

des articles	*the, a(n)*
des auxiliaires	*is, was, has, can, must...*
des prépositions	*from, of, to, for, with...*
des conjonctions	*and, or, that, as...*
des pronoms personnels	*we, me, them, us, they*
des possessifs	*my, your, his, our...*

- Leur voyelle est donc parfois réduite, c'est-à-dire prononcées avec la voyelle schwa /ə/ (comme dans *th**e*** ou ***a**n*).
- Parfois, des sons (consonnes ou voyelles) disparaissent même dans ces mots ! C'est pour cette raison que certains d'entre eux sont contractés à l'écrit pour refléter cette prononciation :
(I am → I'm   rock and roll → rock 'n roll).

3 **Recopiez ces phrases et soulignez les mots grammaticaux inaccentués. Écoutez l'enregistrement pour vérifier vos réponses.** Audio 23lmu21611

a. I have signed your petition.
b. Guns should be banned in the United States.
c. We want the government to take action.
d. A lot of teenagers are involved in the fight against climate change.

IMPROVE YOUR Vocabulary

+ Activités en ligne 23lmu21612

Emancipating

GROWING UP

Audio 23lmu21613

- the youth /yu:θ/ = young **peo**ple
- a **leg**acy = a **her**itage
- em**pow**erment = emanci**pa**tion
- pro**tec**tive
- brave = cou**ra**geous, bold
- feel con**cern** a**bout** sth
- be **ded**icated to sth = be de**vot**ed to sth
- take responsi**bil**ities

OBSTACLES

Audio 23lmu21614

- eco-anx**i**ety /æŋˈzaɪəti/
- **bul**lying
- be **rad**icalised /ˈrædɪkəlaɪzd/
- a**gree** ≠ disa**gree**
- cope with sth = face sth
- be over**whelmed** /əʊvəˈwelmd/ = have too much work or **feel**ings

Taking actions

CAUSES

Audio 23lmu21615

- **cli**mate change /ˈklaɪmɪt ˌtʃeindʒ/
- gender e**qual**ity
- LGBTQ+
- gun con**trol**
- gun **vi**olence /ˈvaɪələns/
- **car**bon e**mis**sion
- **prej**udice = bias, discrimi**na**tion
- **om**inous /ˈɒmɪnəs/ = **threat**ening

ACTIONS

Audio 23lmu21616

- a **pro**test
- a com**mit**ment /kəˈmɪtmənt/ = an en**gage**ment
- a march
- a strike /straɪk/ = a work **stop**page
- go on strike
- hold a demon**stra**tion = **or**ganise a demon**stra**tion
- in**volve** in sth, take part in sth
- con**vey**/trans**mit** a **mes**sage

TOOLS OF PROTEST

Audio 23lmu21617

- a social **net**work /ˌsəʊʃəl ˈnetwɜːk/
- a **ban**ner = a **plac**ard /ˈplækɑːd/
- a **head**line = a **slo**gan
- a **law**suit = *un procès*
- make a stand a**gainst** sth
- be an **ac**tivist
- fight for sth = **strug**gle for sth = stand up for sth
- ad**dress** an **is**sue /əˈdres/ = give at**ten**tion to a spe**cif**ic **is**sue
- raise a**ware**ness /əˈweənəs/
- be con**vinc**ing

1 ***Play Taboo!*** **In teams of 2-3, pick a word and make your classmates guess it using only synonyms or a definition.**

2 **Choose a young activist from the unit and describe him/her using 5 words from the mind map above.**

3 **Use at least 10 words from the mind map above to explain why youth activism is so strong in the United States.**

Let's RECAP

Faites le point ! Complétez la fiche bilan avec les documents que vous avez étudiés. Fiche 23lmu21618

AXE 4

Self-representation and relationship to others

How are American teens fighting to be heard?

#pickyourfight

What are some of the most important fights for American teens?

#voiceyouropinion

What tools do young Americans use to make their voice heard?

#haveanimpact

What is the impact of youth activism on the country?

#different generations

What differences and similarities are there between this generation and the previous ones?

GROUP WORK Choose a question and discuss.

Quiz 23lmu21619

Become AN EXPERT

Lisez et écoutez de l'anglais en dehors de la classe

Films

Books

- *Yes You Can! Your Guide to Becoming an Activist*, Jane Drake and Ann Love vers LLCER/AMC

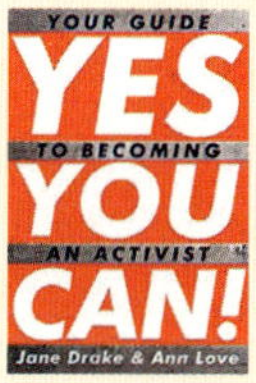

- *Watch Us Rise*, Renée Watson vers LLCER/AMC

- *The Hate U Give*, Angie Thomas Vers vers LLCER/AMC
- *This Is My America*, Kim Johnsoni vers LLCER/AMC

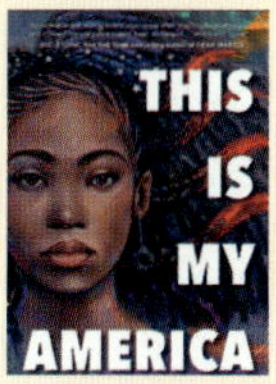

Documentaries

- *Generation Activism* – BBC vers AMC
- *Silence Sam* – by UNC Students vers AMC
- *Changing the Game* – by Michael Barnett vers AMC
- *This Changes Everything* by Naomi Klein vers AMC

YOUR PROJECTS

Take part in an interview

Student 1 As a young activist in the USA, you want to raise awareness on a cause that deeply matters to you.

- Collect information about your cause and choose efficient examples.
  - Go through documents of the unit and research the internet.
  - Write down the arguments that you're going to use.
- Use link words.
  - Work on the logic of your speech: *first, second, then, moreover, however, finally, for example...*
- Show your passion.
  - Show this cause matters to you and the world!

Student 2 As a journalist, question the young activist's commitment to her/his cause.

- Find out the cause your interviewee will defend and imagine counter-arguments.
  - Go through documents of the unit and research the internet.
  - Get prepared to ask questions (Précis p. 272).
- Introduce your program.
  - Be polite and welcoming with your interviewee: *"Welcome to..." ; "Today, our guest is..."*
  - Ask your questions.
- Conclude the show.
  - *"Thank you for joining us today."*

Convaincre à l'écrit et à l'oral p. 290

OR

Write a teen activist's profile story

Choose a young American activist and write a profile feature article for your high school newspaper.

- Choose the young activist.
  - It may be someone studied in this unit or one of your choice.
- Explain why he/she is of interest to your readers.
  - Maybe they are in the news, they have achieved something remarkable, or they have a moving personal story to tell.
- Decide on the content.
  - Do background research.
  - List facts and figures about their causes and provide examples of their actions.
- Focus on the connection he/she has with your readers.
  - How is their fight the fight of a generation?

How to write an article p. 173

BUILD UP YOUR SKILLS

How to
Take part in an interview

1. Pour se préparer

How to be a meddling kid with Isabel Hope, Activist, You! Audio 23lmu21621

Journaliste	Invité(e)
• Rassemblez des informations sur votre invité(e) : son identité — ce qu'il ou elle a accompli ses idées — ses modèles • Préparez des questions qui permettront de comprendre le sujet discuté et de découvrir la personne invitée : – choisissez les informations les plus significatives, – préparez des questions précises, – selon vos opinions, préparez des arguments pour contrer ou soutenir les idées de votre invité(e). • Préparez quelques mots clés pour pouvoir guider l'interview… et révisez les questions ! Précis > p. 272	• Rassemblez vos idées : – la manière dont vous allez vous présenter, – les sujets que vous voulez défendre, – cherchez des exemples, des anecdotes, des chiffres, pour appuyer vos idées et convaincre les auditeurs. 

Notez les mots qui vous seront utiles selon le sujet traité, et vérifiez la manière dont on les prononce sur un dictionnaire en ligne, par exemple wordreference.com

2. Pour participer

- **Journaliste :** c'est vous qui menez l'interview ! Présentez votre invité(e) et posez vos questions. Faites en sorte que l'interview soit dynamique et vivante.
- **Invité(e)** : répondez aux questions en donnant des exemples, des arguments ou contre-arguments, en racontant des anecdotes pour rendre votre prestation convaincante.

1 Introduction	2 Interview	3 Conclusion
Journalist: • *Hello, welcome to our program…* • *I'm your host* + name • *Today, my guest is…*	**Journalist:** • *What does it mean to you… ? / What/who inspired you… ?* • *Do you remember the first time you… ?* • *Can you give an example of… ?*	**Journalist:** • *Well, thank you for coming today.*
Interviewee: • *Hi, my name is… / I am…* • *It's nice to be with you today!*	**Interviewee:** • *For me, being an activist means…* • *I think that / I'm a strong believer of…*	**Interviewee:** • *Thank you for inviting me!*

Are you ready? + prof Évaluation

Entraînement à l'évaluation

Compréhension orale

Faites un compte-rendu en français de la vidéo.

An interview with teen climate activist, Jamie Margolin (8'43 - 9'44)
Video 23lmu21622

- Relevez les mots-clés et résumez la question de la journaliste.
- Repérez l'adjectif utilisé par Jamie Margolin au début de sa réponse. Cela vous aidera à résumer la suite.
- Identifiez ses gestes et le ton de sa voix : cela vous aidera à résumer sa décision.

Production écrite

Complete the interview by writing Jamie Margolin's answer to the journalist's question: *"What is your advice to a young activist who wants to do like you?"*. (100 words)

Compréhension écrite

"X GONZÁLEZ ABOUT TO SNAP"

X González is an American activist and advocate for gun control. In 2018, they survived the Stoneman Douglas High School shooting. They identify as non-binary, hence the use of 'they/them/their'

By Elaine Godfrey • JUNE 11, 2022

Godfrey: In 2018, you were a kid. You're still super young—you're 22! How has all of the attention from the world, all the political attention, affected you over the last four years?

González: It's really similar to how a lot of child stars will say, "Well, I had no privacy, and it really impacted me growing up." Except it was one of those situations where we were looking to bring attention to the issue, but then everybody started paying attention to *us* personally. There are people all over the country that see the Parkland survivors and are like, "That's my child!" And then there's other people that are like, "I will kill them if I see them." So it's really weird to deal with that. On a given day, you're like: *'I just want to be home and hang out. I don't want anybody to hate me. I don't even care if anybody likes me at this point. I just want to hang out by myself.'*

Godfrey: Has that gotten better?

González: I think it's gotten better because I've done a lot of stepping back during college. I've just tried to really focus on learning everything, instead of trying to talk too much to the world. Because I knew that I didn't know all the answers, and I didn't want to come off as though I did know the answers.

Godfrey: The answers to gun violence?

González: Well, yeah, but gun violence is connected to a lot of things, and I wanted to make sure that if I ended up coming back into the gun-violence-prevention scene, that I would have the information and I wouldn't come into it ignorantly or hoping for something that would never happen.

www.theatlantic.com

1. Identify the comparison X González makes at the beginning of the interview and explain it in your own words.
2. What was the students' intention at first? What were the effects on their mental health?
3. What did X González decide to do when she went to college? Why?
4. At the end of the interview, would you say that X González appears to be hopeful or hopeless? Explain your choice.

- **Identifiez l'expression utilisée pour se comparer à d'autres jeunes au début de sa prise de parole (l. 5-7).**
- **Repérez les pronoms personnels pour savoir quand X González parle pour elle / pour le mouvement *March for Our Lives*.**
- **Repérez la répétition de certains mots dans ses réponses pour parler de son état psychologique (l. 5-18).**
- **Repérez l'utilisation des temps pour comprendre la chronologie des événements.**

Production écrite

Write 10 entries on a leaflet entitled: "10 tips to live your teen activism healthily". (100 words)

Flash UNIT 17

La création et le rapport aux arts

Jammin' in Jamaica

▶ To what extent does reggae represent Jamaican culture?

YOUR PROJECT

Shoot a video to promote "International Reggae Day"

1 One love, one heart

Country: Jamaica

Population: 2,9 million

Capital city: Kingston

Independence: 1962 (UK)

Languages: English (official) and Jamaican Patois

Politics: constitutional monarchy with a parliamentary system

Leaders of the country: the British Monarch and the Prime Minister

visitjamaica.com

A Roots, rock, reggae **Vidéo** 23lmu21701

1. Watch the beginning of the video (→ 0'54). Pick out verbs, names and places. Identify: the effects reggae has on people • its birthplace • who made it popular
2. Watch 0'55 → 1'24. Focus on stressed words and use them to write 2 sentences about what reggae teaches people.
3. Watch until 2'00. Pick out words ending in *-ing* and explain the power of reggae.
4. Convince your friend in a voice message to come watch the documentary and explain why Reggae is so special.

Bob Marley Museum, Kingston, Jamaica

SOUL REBELS

Originally, this music style gets its name from the Jamaican phrase "rege-rege" which means "rags[1]" (of clothing). In reggae music, you can hear Jamaican history and Jamaicans' centuries-long struggle[2] for peace, freedom, and independence through protest and perseverance. This music tells the story of people living in rags who never give up on fighting for their freedom; it is a music style with a message of social change. That is why UNESCO's recently added reggae to its cultural heritage list. [...]

Reggae is the voice of the people, that is why the world reacted so positively to Marley's music. There are people all over the globe living an underprivileged life. These people relate to the messages in reggae.

02/10/2019, diggitmagazine.com

1. very used clothes – 2. a fight

B

1. Read the text and explain the origin of the word "reggae".
2. Make a list of the different themes you can find in reggae lyrics.
3. Explain why "people living in rags" (l. 6-7) find reggae helpful.
4. You are visiting the Bob Marley Museum. Answer the question: *"Why did UNESCO add reggae to their cultural heritage list?"*.

Culture Tip

United Nations Educational, Scientific, and Cultural Organization (UNESCO) is a department of the United Nations that aims to encourage peace between countries through education, science, and culture.

Remember how to

Make a statement > Doc B

- **Organiser** :
  - → *Firstly / Secondly / Finally*
  - → *But / on the other hand...*
  - → *For example / for instance*
  - → *This is the reason why... / therefore...*
- **Expliquer et justifier :**
  - → *Reggae music is the best way to talk about Jamaican hardships **as / since...***
  - → *Bob Marley was a prophet on a mission **because...***

WORD BOX

- a **mus**ical **gen**re
- **lyr**ics
- **rhy**thm /'rɪðəm/
- **pov**erty
- **hard**ship = se**vere** pri**va**tion
- in**jus**tice
- op**pres**sion
- slums = **ghet**tos
- in**spire** /ɪn'spaɪə/
- raise a**ware**ness
- ex**pose** /ɪk'spəʊz/ sth = de**nounce** sth

2 Get up, stand up

Culture Tip **Bob Marley** /ˌbɒb ˈmɑːli/ (1945-1981) Jamaican singer and writer who formed the Wailers group in 1965 and made reggae and its messages widely known around the world. In 1978, he led a campaign for peace after years of political violence in order to build a better Jamaica.

Bob Marley performing on stage, in a concert at Grona Lund, Stockholm, Sweden, 1978

A

1. Describe picture A in 3 sentences.
2. Read the Culture tip and imagine why Bob Marley raises his fist and closes his eyes.
3. Imagine the words Bob Marley was pronouncing when the picture was taken.

LISTEN TO *GET UP, STAND UP* LIVE!
Video 23lmu21702

Get Up, Stand Up

Get up, stand up
Stand up for your rights
Get up, stand up
Don't give up the fight
Get up, stand up
Stand up for your rights
Get up, stand up
Don't give up the fight
[…]

Most people think
Great God will come from the sky
Take away everything
And make everybody feel high
But if you know what life is worth
You would look for yours on earth
And now you see the light
You stand up for your rights
[…]

Bob Marley and the Wailers, 1973

B

1. Observe the chorus (l. 1-8) and imagine what Bob Marley means when he sings: *"Stand up for your rights"*.
2. Rephrase what *"Most people think"* (l. 10) and explain the message in the verse (l. 10-17).
3. Show the effects the song may have on listeners.
4. Write another verse of the song *Get Up, Stand Up* and explain it in a one-minute presentation.

Grammar Identify as many phrasal verbs in the song as you can (e.g. *get up*). Translate them into French.

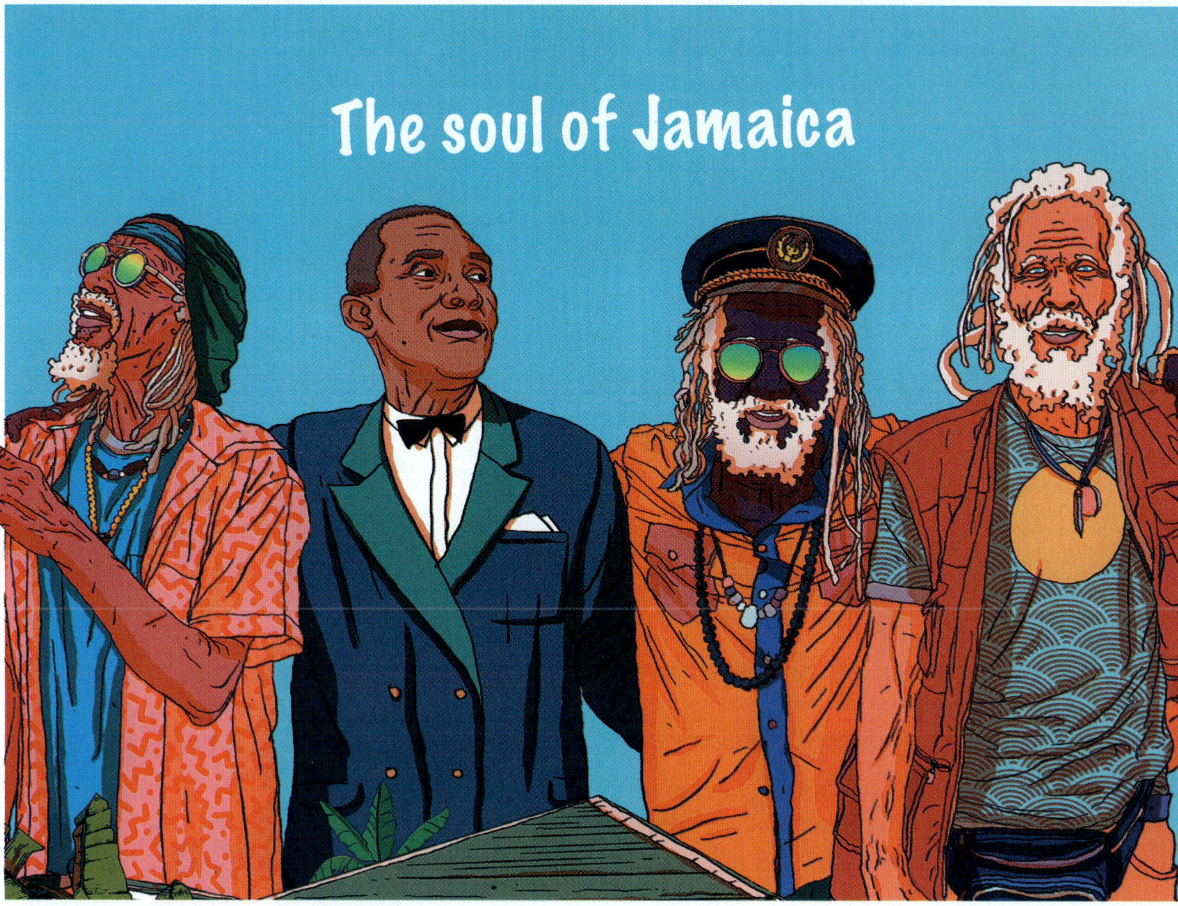

C **Trailer of the documentary about the legendary group Inna da Yard**

Video 23lmu21703

Culture Tip

A Rastafarian /ræstəˈfeəriən/ or a "Rasta" is someone who believes in Rastafarianism, a religious and rebellious movement which considers Haile Selassie, the former Emperor of Ethiopia, to be divine. Rastafarians often have long hair which they wear in a hairstyle called dreadlocks.

WORD BOX

- a **cho**rus /ˈkɔːrəs/
- a verse
- a com**mit**ment /kəˈmɪtmənt/
- **u**nity /ˈjuːnəti/
- a bond = a strong con**nec**tion
- **unique**
- **i**conic
- **gath**er /ˈgæðər/ = as**sem**ble
- **pro**test a**gainst** sth
- stand up a**gainst** sth = op**pose** to sth **ac**tively
- voice/ ex**press** one's o**pin**ion
- con**vey** a **mes**sage

1. Watch the video with the sound off and give your impressions on the atmosphere and the people.
2. Watch the beginning of the video with the sound on [→ 0'35]. Explain what the "Inna De Yard" project is about.
3. Watch from 0'35 to 0'54 and give an account of what reggae music means to the musicians.
4. Write a review of the documentary for your school's newspaper using the following key words: *Rastafarian* • *message* • *reality* • *language*.

MEMORY CHALLENGE

Play *word ping pong*. Write a word connected to reggae on a piece of paper and pass it to your partner who will do the same. Play until one of you can't think of one.

IMPROVE YOUR Grammar

+ Activités en ligne 23lmu21704

Les verbes à particule

Tyron's Tips 23lmu21705

- Une particule (*up, down, on, in, away, out*...) modifie le sens d'un verbe : *give* (donner) + *up* → *give up* (arrêter, renoncer à, abandonner).
- Voici quelques verbes à particule très courants :

grow ***up*** (grandir)	*pass* ***away*** (mourir)
bring sb ***up*** (élever)	*hang* ***out*** (flâner, traîner)
find ***out*** (découvrir, apprendre)	*go* ***on***, *carry* ***on*** (+ V-ing) (continuer)
call sth ***off*** (annuler)	*stand* ***up*** *for sth* (défendre)

La particule est mobile : elle peut être placée avant ou après le complément d'objet. → *We had to call* ***off the concert****.* = *We had to call* ***the concert off****.*

- Quand le complément d'objet direct est **un pronom**, la particule est obligatoirement placée **après celui-ci**. → *Don't give* ***it up****.*

1 Complétez avec la particule qui convient puis traduisez en français.

a. Bob Marley grew ... and was brought ... in Nine Miles, Jamaica.
b. Last summer, I used to hang ... in a bar that played reggae music.
d. I've just found ... that reggae music comes from Jamaica.

2 Reformulez ces phrases en remplaçant les verbes soulignés par des verbes à particule.

a. On May 11, 1981, Bob Marley died in Miami, Florida, at the age of 36.
b. They continued singing until the age of 70.
c. You should defend your rights.
d. I regret to inform you that the festival has been cancelled.

IMPROVE YOUR Pronunciation

La voyelle brève /ʌ/ Audio 23lmu1708

- La voyelle de *fun* est représentée par le symbole /ʌ/. C'est une voyelle brève qui ressemble à celle du français *jeune*. La bouche est légèrement plus ouverte.
- La voyelle /ʌ/ est le plus souvent représentée par la graphie ***u***, surtout quand elle est suivie de **deux consonnes** (*culture*, *injustice*) ou d'**une consonne unique en fin de mot** (*up*, *cut*, *slum*).

Les mots *push, put, pull* sont des exceptions où *u* est prononcé /ʊ/ (comme dans *look*).

- Elle est aussi représentée par **la graphie *o*** dans quelques mots courants qu'il faut apprendre :

come	*son*	*other*	*mother*	*one*
love	*some*	*none*	*brother*	*done*

- Elle est représentée par **la graphie *oo*** uniquement dans deux mots : *blood* et *flood*.

1 Les mots suivants existent en français. Écoutez leur prononciation en anglais en prêtant attention à la prononciation de la voyelle /ʌ/, puis essayez de les répéter à l'identique. Audio 23lmu21706

club • brunch • mug • must • rush • bluff

2 a) Chassez l'intrus (le mot qui ne rime pas avec les autres) dans les listes suivantes et identifiez les mots qui se prononcent avec la voyelle /ʌ/.

a. cut – but – put – shut
b. some – come – home
c. blood – flood – mood
d. bone – done – son – none

b) Écoutez pour vérifier vos réponses et répétez. Audio 23lmu21707

IMPROVE YOUR Vocabulary

Activités en ligne 23lmu21709

Reggae

MUSIC

Audio 23lmu21711

- a band
- a **mu**sical **gen**re /ˈʒɑnrə/
- **ly**rics
- a verse
- a **cho**rus = a re**frain**
- **fa**mous = well known
- i**con**ic
- re**cord** a song / an **al**bum
- at**tend** a **con**cert / a **fes**tival

EXPRESSING

Audio 23lmu21712

- a bond = a strong con**nec**tion
- libe**ra**tion
- to**geth**erness = being u**ni**ted with **oth**er **peo**ple
- a com**mit**ment = an in**volve**ment
- **gath**er /ˈgæðə/ = as**sem**ble
- voice/ex**press** one's o**pin**ion
- con**vey** / trans**mit** a **mes**sage
- ac**know**ledge sth /əkˈnɒlɪdʒ/ = ad**mit**, **rec**ognise sth /ˈrekəgnaɪz/

JAMAICA

Audio 23lmu21713

- a Carib**be**an **is**land
- a rich **cul**ture
- a **ras**tafari = a rasta
- **dread**locks = rasta**fa**rian **hair**style
- **land**scapes
- **bea**ches
- **pa**tois /ˈpætwɑː/

DENOUNCING

Audio 23lmu21710

- coloni**sa**tion
- **hard**ships = se**vere** pri**va**tions
- a slum = a de**prived ur**ban **ar**ea
- po**lit**ical op**pres**sion
- live in **po**verty
- **pro**test a**gainst** sth
- stand up a**gainst** sth = op**pose** to sth **ac**tively

Let's RECAP

Faites le point ! Complétez la fiche bilan avec les documents que vous avez étudiés. Fiche 23lmu21714

AXE 6

Creation and relations to arts

To what extent does reggae represent Jamaican Culture?

#music
What are the messages reggae music conveys?

#unity
To what extent does reggae music allow Jamaicans to be united?

#protest
To what extent is reggae music political?

#recognition
To what extent is Bob Marley considered iconic in Jamaica?

GROUP WORK Choose a question and discuss.

Quiz 23lmu21715

YOUR PROJECT

Shoot a video to promote 'International Reggae Day'

Give a motivational pitch to convince the United Nations to recognise 'International Reggae Day'.

- Prepare a dynamic introduction.
  - Give a definition of reggae music.
  - Present its culture: Bob Marley, Rastafarians...
- Prepare your arguments.
  - List what makes reggae music unique: message, music, lyrics, influence...
- Shoot your video.
  - Give examples and lyrics from songs.
  - Conclude with energy and conviction!

How to shoot a video p. 139

Le village, le quartier, la ville

UNIT 18 The London Tube

► What is the role of the Tube in Londoners' lives?

YOUR PROJECTS

Prepare a presentation for the reopening of a Tube station.

OR

Create a brochure about art events in the Underground.

Xavi Garcia

A The Underground brand, BBC News Video 23lmu21801

Culture Tip **TfL (Transport for London)** is the government body which is responsible for most of the transport network in London (tube, taxis, buses, river services...). Its chairman is the Mayor of London.

1863
The first underground railway, the Metropolitan Railway, opens between Paddington and Farringdon, connecting 6 stations.

Today
- 11 lines covering 402 kms and serving 272 stations.
- 5 million passenger journeys a day.

1. a. Watch the video (→ 0'44). Pick out the words used to describe the London Underground.
b. Use them to write a definition of "the Tube" and its brand.

2. Pick out the three elements which make the Tube such a marketing success.

3. Focus on one element from question 2 and pick out information about it.

4. Using the elements from the video, create a short audio guide about the painting saying how well it illustrates the Tube.

A MULTICOLOURED TUBE

> *Turn em red, turn em yellow, turn em any colour you want. But this is Turnham Green.*
> London Tube Driver over the PA

triptide.london

B

1. Read the Culture tip on p. 196 and explain what TfL does.
2. Look at the poster (doc B). Say what the names on the roundels refer to. Name four of them and imagine why there are so many colours.
3. Indicate why the poster and the logos show difference but also unity.
4. Link the poster to the quote above and explain the play on words with the colours. (Turnham Green is a London Tube station.)

Remember how to

Pronounce dates > Doc A.

- Quand on dit une date, on utilise obligatoirement un numéral ordinal (*the first, the second, the third*, ou en ajoutant *-th*) :
  → *the seventeen**th** of October* OU *October (the) seventeenth*
- On lit les années en deux temps :
  → **1993** = *nineteen ninety-three*
  2022 = *twenty twenty-two*
  1901 = *nineteen o' one*

À partir des années 2000, on peut aussi dire : *Two thousand...*

- Quand on écrit une date, attention aux majuscules :
  → *Monday 17(th) October 2022* 🇬🇧
  Monday October 17, 2022 🇺🇸
- En abrégé : ***Day**/**Month**/Year: **17**/**10**/2022* 🇬🇧
  ***Month**/**Day**/Year: **10**/**17**/2022* 🇺🇸

WORD BOX

- means of **trans**port
- a **jour**ney = a trip
- a **trade**mark = a brand
- **mer**chandising = **mar**keting, sales pro**mo**tion
- **ur**ban /ˈɜːbən/ = of **ci**ties
- over**crow**ded /əʊvəˈkraʊdɪd/ ≠ **emp**ty
- i**den**tifiable /aɪˈdentəfaɪəbəl/
- i**co**nic = sym**bo**lic
- com**mute** = **tra**vel to work
- ride the **un**derground = ride the tube

MEMORY CHALLENGE

Form two teams. Each team has to name as many London Tube lines as they can.

1 London united

GROUP WORK

DIFFÉRENCIATION

www.blog.britishnewspaperarchive.co.uk

When the Blitz began on 7 September 1940, 'It was the people of London who took command... Men, women, and children went straight to the safest place they could think of – the Underground stations.' [...]

However, the government was not keen on the Underground being put to such use. An article in the *Hartlepool Northern Daily Mail*, 20 September 1940, reveals how 'Little heed[1] was paid last night to the appeal of the Ministries of Home Security and Transport asking the public to refrain from using the London Tube stations as air-raid shelters[2] except in the case of urgent necessity.'

Instead, Londoners of all classes flocked[3] to Underground platforms to keep themselves safe from the destruction that was being wrought[4] above the ground. [...]

So with eighty or so London tube stations crowded[5] with thousands of people – was the Underground system able to continue? The answer is yes – that with true Blitz spirit, both shelterers and Tube travellers were able to co-exist.

Rose Staveley-Wadham

1. attention
2. refuge
3. go as a group, rush
4. at work / in process
5. full of people

Londoners taking shelter in the Underground, 1940

A All class

1. Read lines 1-3 and the Culture tip. Tell about the historical context using: Germany • the UK • Blitz • war • safe • Underground station

2. Find information on how Londoners used the London Tube during the Blitz.

3. Explain the reaction of the government.

4. You are an intern at TfL. Present the historical situation and the consequences of the Blitz in a one-minute podcast.

Culture Tip

The Blitz (Blitzkrieg, in German = the lightning war) was the name given to the devastating German bombing attacks in the United Kingdom from Sept. 1940 until May 1941.

WORD BOX

- a **pass**enger
- a **turn**stile = *un tourniquet*
- a **life**time = the **per**iod of your life
- a **bus**tling street = a street with **ma**ny **peo**ple
- ex**pen**sive ≠ cheap
- be thrilled = be ex**cit**ed
- ex**per**ience = feel e**mo**tion
- sprawl = spread
- **in**augurate
- rule **o**ver the world = **gov**ern

B Group 1

Culture Tip

The British Empire
Between the late 16th century and the beginning of the 20th century, the British Empire was the largest colonial empire with India, Canada, Australia and a big part of East Africa.

C Group 2 Video 23lmu21802

Elizabeth Line officially opened by Her Majesty The Queen on Tuesday 17 May 2022 during Her Majesty The Queen's Platinum Jubilee.

The Elizabeth line, the new London's east-west metro service that we called Crossrail, finally opened on Tuesday. It is three years late, cost at least £18.9bn, some £4bn over budget, and arguably – given the fall* in commuting post-pandemic – is no longer really needed.

And yet, having ridden on it a few hours after it opened, I can report that it is really nice. It is a typical model of the urban railway systems that are being built in giant cities all around the world, and a top-end version at that. Not sure it is worth queuing through the night to ride on, but it makes travelling across London a much more pleasant experience. [...] Let's see in a year or two whether the Elizabeth line is bringing more business to London. My guess, despite the huge cost of the enterprise, is that it will pay back the investment by making the city a little bit nicer for everyone.

independent.co.uk,
Hamish McRae, 24 May 2022

* decrease

D Group 3

GROUP WORK **1.** Work on your document (Doc. B, C or D). Match the correct title with your document and make a written summary of what you understand.

Visiting the Empire — Experiencing a new line — Inaugurating Elizabeth line

2. Focus on the role of the Tube in your document and explain its importance.

3. Share your findings with students from the other groups.

PAIR WORK **4.** Share text messages with a friend about the Tube and its great importance in the lives of Londoners.

PREPARE YOUR PROJECT

The London Tube Podcast

With a friend, prepare a 90-second podcast for your school's radio station explaining the importance of the Tube in the lives of Londoners.

2 The art connection

Mind the gap: London Tube opens new doors

One of the delights of travelling on the Tube is the artwork installed in various stations, seen by millions of people each day, contributing to the ways in which people experience the city. The Tube has been one of London's pioneering public sector patrons[1] due to a commitment to the arts led by Frank Pick, its managing director in the early 20th century. Every aspect of its architecture, poster design, train livery and upholstery[2] as well as its site-specific art commissions in stations has been contributed by several artists, designers and craftspeople[3] over the decades, including large-scale commissions at Gloucester Road station.

Besides artwork and many finding love during regular commuter journeys, you also get to enjoy live music as you move around corridors underground.

The Busking Scheme[4] has long been a hit with performers and the travelling public. Passengers enjoy more than 100,000 hours of live music, performed every year by professional, talented buskers[5], enlivening their otherwise drab journeys through the network. Big names such as Ed Sheeran, Jessie J, Bob Geldof and Katherine Jenkins have performed on the Tube. Licensed buskers have a unique audience of millions of Tube passengers every day, with many showing their appreciation by dropping a few coins in the hat. […]

khaleejtimes.com, Prasun Sonwalkar, 30 Sept. 2021

1. *mécènes* – 2. furniture fabric – 3. *artisans* – 4. the organisation that selects and licences artists in the tube – 5. street musicians

A

1. Pick out the different art forms we can find in the Tube. Explain the relationship between the Tube and artists.
2. Show what effects and consequences this art can have on passengers.
3. You commute on the tube and see art works and singers. Write an Instagram post.

Grammar Identify a noun in the genitive (N's). How is it formed? With what types of nouns is it generally used?

B Art on the Underground Commission

Video 23lmu21803

1. Watch the video. Explain why the Tube is a good opportunity to exhibit one's art.
2. Pick out the reasons why Joy chose the salon painting for Brixton Station.
3. Indicate why Joy thinks art in the Tube is valuable.
4. Continue the interview of this artist. Discuss the importance of art in the Tube.

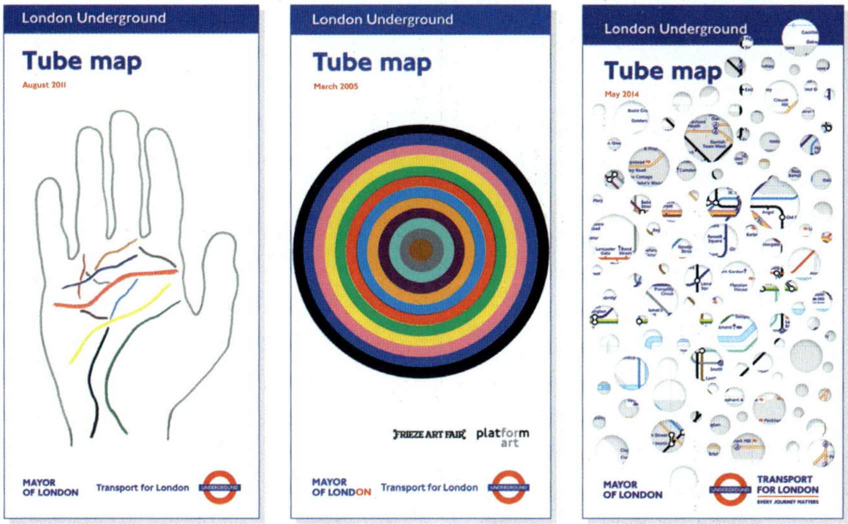

London Transport Museum

Culture Tip Since 2004, artworks have been specially commissioned for the cover of the pocket Tube map. In different ways, they respond to the map's design and function. The series has been commissioned by Art on the Underground, London Underground's public art programme.

C Tube map covers

Audio 23lmu21804

1. Read the Culture tip, then listen to the beginning of the audio [→ 0'26] and find information about the map cover project.
2. Pick out the constraints for artists and imagine two more.
3. Explain the objectives of these map covers. Show how they reflect the Commission's objectives.
4. Create a new version of the Tube map cover and write a paragraph to explain how your design fits in the project.

D

Poems on the Underground has helped to make journeys more stimulating and inspiring since 1986.

Poems Underground

As in the Underground there's no mistaking
the train's approach, it pushes air ahead,
whirls paper, the line sings, a sort-of dread[1]
suffusing longing[2] and my platform shaking[3] –
so it is before our every meeting
till you arrive. Hear how my heart is beating!

Our Meetings
by Andrew Waterman

1. fear – 2. desire – 3. trembling

1. Pick out words about "the Underground" and use them to explain the poem.
2. Show the emotions the speaker conveys in this poem.
3. You participate in the Tube poetry contest. Write a short poem.

WORD BOX

- a **sta**tion = a stop
- a com**mu**ter = a **dai**ly **tra**veller
- ex**po**sure = being **vi**sible
- a **sten**cil = a **tem**plate
- **lone**liness = **feel**ing a**lone**
- to**ge**therness = com**pan**ionship
- get **peo**ple **in**terested in sth
- **ce**lebrate = to com**mem**orate / to **ho**nour
- enter**tain** = to a**muse peo**ple
- spray = ap**ply** a fine mist

PREPARE YOUR PROJECT

Video 23lmu21805

Voice-over - "Rats" attack in the underground!

Watch this striking video showing Banksy in action. Then record a voice-over to explain the importance of street artists in the Underground and the impact of art on commuters.

IMPROVE YOUR Grammar

+ Activités en ligne
23lmu21806

Le génitif (N's N)

Tyron's Tips
23lmu21807

- Le génitif permet de mettre en relation deux noms (*my father's ticket*).
En français, on le traduit par *de* (le ticket **de** mon père).
On peut souvent remplacer un nom au génitif par un déterminant possessif (***his** ticket*).

N's N	avec des noms au singulier → *Anna**'s** car ; my teacher**'s** jacket*
	avec des noms propres se terminant par -s (prononcé /ɪz/) → *James**'s** book ; King Charles**'s** sons*
Ns' N	avec des noms au pluriel se terminant par un -s : → *the passengers**'** safety*

Quand le génitif est un nom propre, il n'est pas précédé de *the*.
→ *Tom's journey.*

- On l'emploie avec **des noms de personnes** (***Tom's** journey*), **de villes** (***London's** Tube*), **de pays** (***Britain's** most popular icon*) ou **d'institutions** (***the school's** reputation*).
- On l'emploie aussi avec **certains adverbes de temps** (*yesterday's accident*).
- Avec **des noms qui désignent des inanimés** (objets, abstractions, etc.), on utilise *of* : → *the driver **of the train**, a means **of transport**, the platform **of the station**...*

> Précis p. 248

1 **Recopiez et reliez les mots à l'aide d'un génitif ou d'une structure avec *of*. Si les deux structures sont possibles, précisez-le.**

a. the end / the journey
b. London / the suburbs
c. the tourists / the maps
d. the Tube station / the entrance
e. Emma / Oyster card
f. the inauguration / tomorrow

2 **Traduisez.**

a. Le bureau de David est situé en face de la station de métro.
b. Le train d'hier était en retard.
c. Je me suis perdu dans les couloirs de la station de métro.

Les prépositions *in*, *on* et *at*

- ***In*** se traduit souvent par *dans* (*in a house, in a pocket*).
On l'utilise aussi avec des noms **de pays et de villes** (***in** Britain, **in** London*) ou **des noms de rue** (*I live **in** Victoria Street*).

On dit ***in** the car* mais ***on** the bus/plane/train/Tube*.

- ***At*** est utilisée pour désigner **des endroits précis** (***at** the station*), **des adresses complètes** (***at** 10 Downing Street*), **des lieux publics** (***at** school, **at** the library, **at** the supermarket*) ou **des événement** (***at** the party*).
- On utilise aussi ces prépositions dans **des compléments de temps** :

in	on	at
• années (***in** 2022*), • mois (***in** January*), • siècles (***in** the 21st century*), • saisons (***in** summer*).	• jours (***on** Tuesday, **on** Father's Day*), • dates complètes (***on** September 7, 2022*)	• heures (***at** 5 o'clock*), • fêtes (***at** Christmas*), • repas (***at** lunch*)

3 **Complétez avec la préposition *in*, *on* ou *at* :**

a. The London Underground was built ... the 19th century.
b. I'll get off ... the next station.
c. There were a lot of tourists ... the train.
d. The Elizabeth line opened ... Tuesday 24 May 2022.
e. My cab arrives ... 2:55 pm sharp ... 11 St. James's street.
f. They met ... a party ... July ... London.

IMPROVE YOUR Pronunciation

La diphtongue /aʊ/ Audio 23lmu21808

- Le son-voyelle de ***now*** et ***out*** est représenté par le symbole /aʊ/.
- La diphtongue /aʊ/ est représentée par les graphies suivantes :

ou	*Underg**rou**nd, ab**ou**t, r**ou**nd*
ow	*n**ow**, d**ow**n, cr**ow**ded, all**ow***

La graphie ***ow*** peut se prononcer /aʊ/ (***now***, ***down***) ou /əʊ/ comme dans ***no*** (***slow***, ***blow***, ***show***). Il n'existe pas de règle : il faut vérifier la prononciation de ces mots dans le dictionnaire.

1 **Pour chaque série, écoutez l'enregistrement et chassez l'intrus (le mot qui ne se prononce pas avec la diphtongue /aʊ/).** Audio 23lmu21809

a. shout - south - youth - mouth
b. house - cloud - group - announcement
c. count - country - background - sound

2 a) **Recopiez ce tableau et classez les mots en fonction de la prononciation de la graphie *ow*.**

/aʊ/ (comme dans out)	/əʊ/ (comme dans no)

own • follow • allow • town • slow • know • how • crown • clown

b) **Écoutez l'enregistrement pour vérifier vos réponses et répétez.** Audio 23lmu21810

La prononciation de la terminaison -(e)s Audio 23lmu21811

- On trouve la terminaison **-(e)s** dans le pluriel des noms, dans la 3e personne du singulier des verbe (*she think**s***) ou dans le génitif (*Jack'**s** ticket*).
- Elle peut avoir **trois prononciations** en fonction du dernier son du mot auquel elle est ajoutée :

Après une voyelle ou les consonnes /b/, /g/, /v/, /ð/, /l/, /m/, /n/, /r/, /ŋ/	/z/	piano**s**, suburb**s**, station**s**
Après les consonnes /p/, /t/, /k/, /f/, /θ/	/s/	pack**s**, district**s**, stop**s**
Après les consonnes sifflantes /s/, /z/, /ʃ/, /ʧ/ et /ʤ/	/ɪz/	ros**es**, brush**es**, carriag**es**

3 a) **Recopiez ce tableau et classez les mots en fonction de la prononciation de la terminaison -s.**

/s/	/z/	/ɪz/

*ticket**s** • bag**s** • bus**es** • town**s** • Tom'**s** car • hotel**s** • class**es** • way**s** • map**s** • passenger**s** • card**s***

b) **Écoutez l'enregistrement pour vérifier vos réponses et répétez.** Audio 23lmu21812

IMPROVE YOUR Vocabulary

Activités en ligne 23lmu21813

The Tube

AT THE STATION

Audio 23lmu21814

- a Tube **station** = a stop
- a **carriage** = a train coach
- a **platform** = *un quai*
- a **turnstile** = *un tourniquet*
- a **corridor**
- an **escalator**
- a **ticket office**
- a one-day **ticket**
- an **Oyster** card = a **daily**, **weekly** or **monthly** pass
- an **announcement**

USING THE UNDERGROUND

Audio 23lmu21815

- a **metro** line
- a **journey** = a trip
- a route = an itinerary
- a **passenger**
- a commuter = a **daily traveller**
- a passer**by** (*plural:* passers**by**) = a pedestrian
- overcrowded ≠ **empty**
- take the Underground
- tap your card = **validate** your **ticket**
- **commute** = **travel** to work
- get on a train, plane, bus
- mind the gap = be **careful** of the gap
- take **shelter** = find a **refuge**

The network

BRANDING

Audio 23lmu21816

- a brand
- a **landmark** = a point of reference
- a **roundel** = a **circular** decoration
- an advertisement = an advert, an ad
- **merchandising** = **marketing**
- iconic = symbolic
- identifiable
- promote /prəˈməʊt/
- celebrate /ˈseləbreit/

PLACES IN THE CITY

Audio 23lmu21817

- **urban areas**
- a **city center**
- a **neighbourhood**
- a **suburb**
- a residential **area**
- an **office** = an **area** for work
- a place for **leisure**

CONNECTING

Audio 23lmu21818

- a means of **transport**
- an orientation
- a direction
- multicultural
- sprawl = **expand**
- **connect** = link
- piece together = assemble

ART FORMS

Audio 23lmu21819

- a **busker** /ˈbʌskə/ = a street musician
- a **painter**
- a **poet** /ˈpəʊɪt/
- a **mural**
- street art
- a composition
- a shape /ʃeip/ = a form
- a **motif** /məʊˈtiːf/
- a **stencil** /ˈstensəl/ = *un pochoir*
- **colourful** (US : **colorful**)

1 Fill the gaps with words from the mind map above (one blank = one word).

a. Juliet ... to Turnham Green every day. Her ... takes her 45 minutes.
b. The ... that the London Tube uses is a ... ... around the world.
c. "The Mind the ..." ... was first heard in 1969. It is also ... of the London Tube.
d. ... were stunned when they saw Ed Sheeran join street ...
e. In the Tube, after buying your ..., ... you need to ... your card and go through the ... then make it to the ....

2 You are an artist selected by the "Art in the Underground Commission". Write a thank you note and explain your artistic process using words from the mind map.

Let's RECAP

Faites le point ! Complétez la fiche bilan avec les documents que vous avez étudiés. Fiche 23lmu21820

AXE 3

Village, neighbourhood, city

What is the role of the Tube in Londoners' lives?

#undergroundbranding

How has the Underground branding become so successful?

#artists

How have artists shaped commuters' experience?

#artintheUnderground

To what extent is the Underground promoting art?

#lovemytube

Why are Londoners so fond of their Underground?

#Blitz

Why can we say that the Underground is more than a means of transportation?

GROUP WORK Choose a question and discuss.

Quiz 23lmu21821

Virtual Art

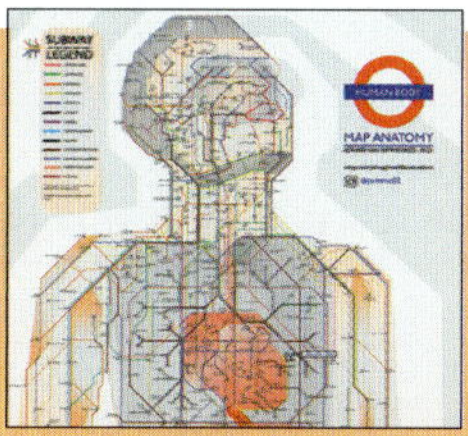

- *Doctor Reimagines the Human Body as a Subway Map*, My Modern Met

A journey through the human body. Basing his work on the traditional map of the London Underground. vers LLCER

Podcast

- *Mind the Gap Between Reality and Imagination*, The London Tube vers AMC

Audio 23lmu21822

Become AN EXPERT

Lisez et écoutez de l'anglais en dehors de la classe

Museum

- Visit the Museum of London and understand the Blitz vers LLCER/AMC

Site 23lmu21823

Books

- *Atonement*, Ian McEwan, 2001 vers LLCER
- *The Ministry of Fear*, Graham Green, 1943 vers LLCER

Films

vers LLCER/AMC

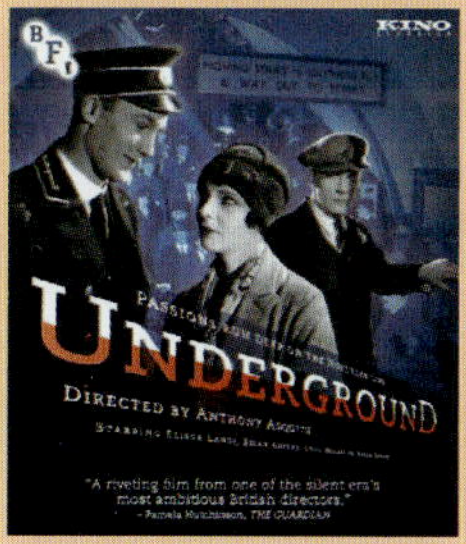

vers LLCER

vers LLCER

vers AMC

vers LLCER

YOUR PROJECTS

BUILD UP YOUR SKILLS

Create a brochure

Create a brochure about the different art events in the Underground.

- Think about all the art forms. — Visual art, music, poetry...
- Explain the importance of art in the Tube. — For commuters, tourists, employees, artists...
- Link art and history. — Think about different periods of time (Industrial Revolution, WWII, 21st century).
- Insist on the connecting and multicultural aspect of the London Tube. — You can evoke artists from different backgrounds in order to show the Tube is a place of inclusion.
- Gather the texts and illustrations and design your brochure.

OR

Prepare a presentation

You are an intern at the City Hall, London. Prepare a presentation to promote the reopening of a Tube station that was closed during the Second World War. It will be named "Lady Diana" to pay homage to the late Princess of Wales.

- Make further research on the Tube and the Blitz. — You can use this site: Site 23lmu21824
- Make research on Lady Diana. — You can use this site: Site 23lmu21825
- Prepare your presentation to convince the City and TfL to launch this project. — You can use words or expressions such as "*should*", "*why don't we...*".
- Note down the advantages of the reopening of the station. —
  - Advantages for the city, the commuters, the Londoners.
  - Use words and expressions from p. 204.
- Practise delivering your presentation from your notes. — Use a red pen to underline word stresses.

How to deliver a speech p. 85

How to
Create a brochure

1. Pour la préparer

- Délimitez les objectifs de votre document :
  - à qui est-il destiné ?
  - quel est son but ? [publicitaire ? informatif ? touristique ? ... ?]

Une brochure doit être facile à utiliser, claire et convaincante.

- Rassemblez les informations essentielles que vous souhaitez transmettre.
- Organisez ces informations en plusieurs thèmes, ou rubriques.
- Trouvez des titres accrocheurs pour chaque partie.
- Cherchez des illustrations en rapport avec le sujet.

2. Pour la réaliser

- Faites des paragraphes précis :
  - titre clair,
  - puces pour lister des éléments,
  - phrases courtes,
  - visuels, etc.
- Créez une page de titre qui attire l'attention : image, logo, contacts, phrase d'accroche...
- Choisissez des couleurs et polices de caractères qui auront de l'effet sur les lecteurs.

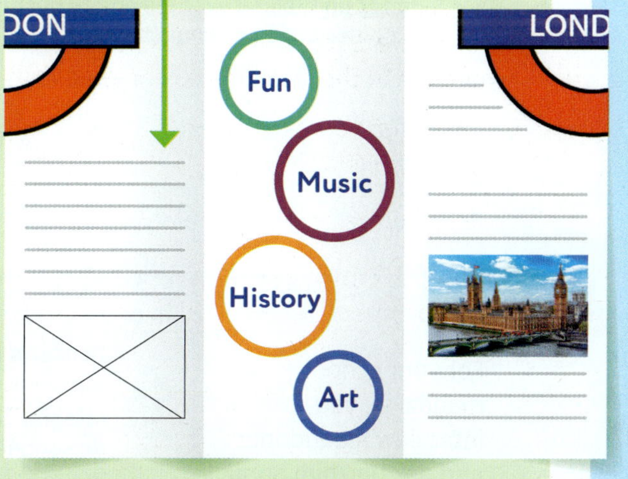

- Illustration de votre texte.
- Adressez-vous directement aux lecteurs [*you* / impératifs...].

Are you ready?

+ prof Évaluation

Entraînement à l'évaluation

Compréhension orale

Faites un compte rendu en français de l'audio.

What I (dis)like about the Tube Audio 23lmu2826

Avant l'écoute :
- observez l'image, lisez le titre et commencez à émettre des hypothèses sur le contenu et les mots que vous pourriez entendre ;
- faites un tableau avec les points positifs et négatifs qui pourraient être évoqués.

Lors des écoutes :
- complétez ou supprimez vos hypothèses ;
- n'hésitez pas à utiliser des abréviations et des symboles pour plus de rapidité !

Production écrite

For your school magazine, you interview a Londoner and ask her/him about what s/he thinks of the London Tube. Write down the interview. (150 words)

→ Pensez à mobiliser les connaissances culturelles et le lexique que vous avez acquis sur le métro de Londres.

→ Intégrez les salutations en début d'interview et les prises de congés à la fin.

→ Vérifiez les tournures de vos questions : ***do/does/did*** + Sujet + BV OU auxilliaire + Sujet (pour *be* et les modaux) :
- → *Do you often **use** the Underground?*
- → *You like this artwork, don't you?*

Compréhension écrite

London Underground: Fascinating facts you probably didn't know about busking at Tube stations

Emma Magnus – Jan. 6th, 2022

You've tapped your Oyster Card at Piccadilly Circus Tube station, and you step onto the escalator. You can hear something - a faint melody rising from the tunnels below. [...]

Although it might look like an informal arrangement, busking* on the Underground is an organised activity - and there's competition for pitches. [...]

How many buskers are there on the London Underground?

After auditions in 2017, 79 musicians were offered licences - one less than in 2015.

According to a freedom of information request, most buskers are between 18 and 39. Of the 49 buskers who completed the licence paperwork, only one person was over the age of 60.

How many pitches are available?

There are over 40 pitches across 30 central London stations. They're marked by a semi-circular floor graphic and a backdrop advert, and are located in highly visible spots. [...]

Which are the most popular pitches?

Busker Dan Hough writes on his blog that Southwark has good acoustics. At Chancery Lane, he says the wind coming from the tunnels carries his music all the way up the escalators.

Busker Wayne Myers told the Guardian that Piccadilly Circus is the big one in terms of pitches: "Piccadilly Circus has one of the few spots at the bottom of an escalator – everyone wants to play there."

mylondon.news

* playing music in the street

1. Explain how "organised" and "competitive" busking is.
2. Draw the portrait of the typical "busker".
3. Imagine where the photo might have been taken and justify your answer using the two buskers' testimonies. Explain what the other good spots are for buskers and why.

- Identifiez la source : à qui cet article s'adresse-t-il ?
- Relevez les mots de liaison afin de comprendre la logique interne de l'article.
- Relevez les chiffres, les dates et cherchez à quoi ils correspondent.
- Utilisez quelques adjectifs pour décrire le ton de l'article et l'intention du journaliste.

Production écrite

Why is art important in public places? (150 words)

Le village, le quartier, la ville

Flash UNIT 19

Bangalore, the city of tech

▶ How has Bangalore created a new urban identity?

YOUR PROJECT

Host a radio show about Bangalore.

1 India's Silicon Valley

Globaleconomics

A Bangalore: India's Silicon Valley?

Vidéo 23lmu21901

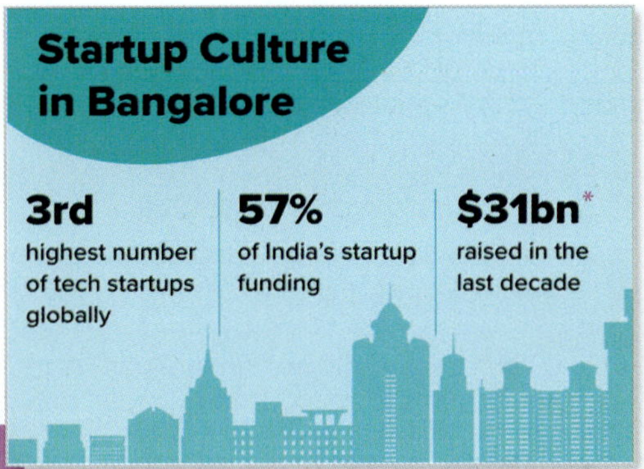

The Scalers

B

* Bn: billion

FICHE PAIR WORK **1.** Watch the video and find details about:
Student A: the original Silicon Valley • India's economy • the IT industry
Student B: university • post-independence reforms • electronic city • Texas instruments Fiche 23lmu21902

2. Swap information with your partner. Then discuss how document B validates Bangalore as India's Silicon Valley.

3. Write a short article entitled *'How did Bangalore become India's Silicon Valley?'* for an IT blog.

Remember how to

Compare the past with the present

- ***Used to*** + **V** permet d'insister sur le fait qu'une situation est totalement révolue :
  → *Bangalore **used to be called** the 'City of Gardens'.*
- Après *used to* + V, on utilise souvent ***but now***...
  → *A lot of retirees **used to live** in Bangalore, **but now** more and more young people are moving in.*

BANGALORE CITY OF HIGH TECH

The city of Bangalore is now home to one of the most highly educated workforces in the world. Known as "The Silicon Valley of India", this city of nearly 12 million rivals New York City in size. It is the third-largest city in India, a country of over a billion people. Bangalore is home to some of the most successful technology companies and leading universities in India. Offices of Microsoft, IBM, Infosys and Wipro – giants of the software and IT world – stand shoulder to shoulder[1] in towering glass structures within guarded, gated, pristine campuses on the outskirts[2] of the city. Their campuses keep their employees separated from the dusty roads, endless construction, noisy crowds, and wooden carts and cows that wander the city streets. Bangalore is one of the fastest growing cities in India, and city planners have predicted that Bangalore's population will continue to increase dramatically, reaching 20.3 million by 2031. Bangalore embodies[3] the post-1991 boom.

Bangalore is big, yes, but it's also hip and innovative. People flock to this city for the cosmopolitan lifestyle and global diversity they find here. Noted as one of the most liberal and progressive cities in India, it also has a history of religious pluralism. The city has had an LGBTQ pride march every year since 2008.

khanacademy.org

1. next to each other – 2. outer part of the city – 3. exemplifies

Bengaluru

- Bangalore was renamed "Bengaluru" in 2014
- Founded in 16th century
- Hub for headquarters of India's largest companies
- Hub for education and research
- 2nd fastest-growing city in India
- Called the City of gardens
- Home to Kannada Film Industry

1. Read the city's information card and the text from lines 1 to 4. Provide the characteristics of Bangalore: geographical location • population • size

2. Read the rest of the text. Find elements of modernity and tradition in Bangalore.

3. Focus on numbers and use them to show the city is evolving.

4. Join in a radio programme on Bangalore's new identity, giving a brief overview of the city.

MEMORY CHALLENGE

Play *Fact whiff-whaff* with a partner. Take it in turns to give a piece of information about Bangalore.

WORD BOX

- a **head**quarters
- a hub = a **cen**tre
- IT (infor**ma**tion tech**nol**ogy) world
- a lo**ca**tion = a situ**a**tion
- a side = a **fa**cet
- a **start**up
- a **tech**ie
- a way of **liv**ing = a **life**style
- **bu**sy /'bɪzi/
- **trend**y = hip
- **live**ly = **vi**brant
- **dirt**y = **grim**y
- open-**mind**ed = **tol**erant
- be on the up and up, boom = rise
- set sth up = cre**ate**, found sth

2 Urban identity

A Guide to living and working in Bangalore Vidéo 23lmu21903

FICHE PAIR WORK

1. Watch the video.
Student A: focus on • 'Garden City' • Old Bangalore • Challenges
Student B: focus on • The solution to rapid change
Use Fiche 23lmu21904

2. Exchange your findings and present the video in a paragraph.

3. Write a post on the split personality of Bangalore for Trip Advisor.

ART PROJECT: THE STORY OF BANGALORE

The Story of Bangalore captures the myriad communities that live and breathe in this vibrant, urban landscape. From migrant workers who have built the glass-facade buildings in the city's technology parks to the IT workforce that populate them – Bengaluru's "techies[1]" who have arrived here from different parts of the country and the world. The entire artwork visually weaves together[2] the stories of hundreds of people who have made Bangalore their home and reflects MAP's[3] vision of what the museum hopes to be – a space for a collection which unlocks stories that the community wants to hear and share and inspire each other with.

1. persons working in technology – 2. collects, assembles – 3. Museum of Art & Photography

The Aravani Art Project

B

1. Analyse the mural:
people and animals • professions • methods of transport • atmosphere

2. Write a definition of the city inspired by this artwork.

3. Read the text and explain the goal of the mural.

4. You work for the MAP. Present the mural in an audioguide.

www.vishwasmudagal.com

A PLACE CALLED HOME

Author Vishwas Mudagal on what Bengaluru means to him

Bengaluru has been home since 2003, when I came to the city as a student.The city has witnessed tremendous[1] growth in the past decade and a half. It has transformed from a sleepy town to a bustling[2] megapolis, full of life and energy. This has resulted in a multitude of job opportunities, an excellent talent pool and the city is seen as the country's answer to Silicon Valley. On the flipside[3], the boom has also resulted in unplanned growth and construction, a breakdown in infrastructure and nightmarish traffic. I hope the city authorities can overcome these issues in the near future.

However, what sets Bengaluru apart from other cities is the people. The city has the ability to make you feel at home instantly. Also, it is cosmopolitan in the true sense. We are a melting pot of different cultures, languages and a mix of industries, from IT to Biotech. You can never feel out of place here. The awesome weather is, of course, an added bonus.

I like walking in the Central Business District, especially on Brigade Road and MG Road. It transports me to a time when I discovered the city with my friends from college. Some of the best of times have been on these areas. I also like walking in the busy Jayanagar 4th Block market. It still has the old Bangalore charm that I miss.
I enjoy sampling[4] some delicacies from Bengaluru's fast food joints and darshinis[5]. I like trying out new things, so I often head out to new restaurants, hang out spaces, I think that it is very important to preserve and cherish this beautiful city.

1. very big – 2. full of activity – 3. on the other hand – 4. tasting – 5. fast food, self-service, vegetarian restaurant

C

1. Identify the positive and negative impacts of Bangalore's urban development.
2. Explain why Vishwas Mudagal feels at home in this city.
3. Pick out the reasons why he enjoys walking. Then find out what he says about food.
4. PAIR WORK Interview Vishwas Mudagal about his home city:
   Student A: plays the role of the journalist
   Student B: is Vishwas Mudagal

Remember how to

Describe an image

- **Localiser :**
  - → *In the top left-hand corner/ in the bottom right-hand corner*
  - → *On the right/left*
  - → *At the top/bottom*
- **Commenter :**
  - → *The overall impression...*
  - → *The atmosphere created is....*
  - → *The artist's message is...*

WORD BOX

- a **mem**ory
- an **up**side, an ad**van**tage ≠ a **down**side, a **draw**back
- har**mo**nious
- de**pict** = por**tray**, **il**lustrate, **dem**onstrate
- give the im**pres**sion of ...
- live to**geth**er side by side
- **fea**ture = take an im**por**tant part in
- aim to = in**tend** to + V
- **crit**icise sth = de**nounce** sth
- praise sth = ex**press** ap**prov**al or admi**ra**tion for sth
- remi**nisce** about sth = talk of past ex**pe**riences
- re**mem**ber **fond**ly = re**mem**ber with af**fec**tion

IMPROVE YOUR Grammar

Activités en ligne 23lmu21905

Le present perfect avec *for* et *since*

Tyron's Tips 23lmu21906

- **On traduit *for* et *since* par « depuis ».** Ces deux prépositions ne sont pas employées de la même manière :

for + durée	*since* + date ou événement
→ ***for*** 18 years, ***for*** 3 days, ***for*** 2 hours	→ ***since*** 2003, ***since*** Monday, ***since*** the independence of India

- Avec ***for*** et ***since***, on utilise en général le ***present perfect* en *be* + V-*ing* (*has/have been* + V-*ing*).**
Il est utilisé pour indiquer qu'un événement ou un état a commencé dans le passé et se poursuit jusqu'au moment présent. On le traduit par le présent en français.
→ ***I've been working*** *in Bangalore* *for 5 years.*
(Je **travaille** à Bangalore depuis 5 ans)

La forme simple du ***present perfect* (*have* + participe passé)** est parfois employée avec *for* et *since*.
→ ***I've known*** *this city* ***for*** *20 years.*

> Précis p. 262-264

1 Mettez le verbe entre parenthèses à la forme qui convient, puis choisissez entre *for* ou *since* :

a. India ... (*be*) independent from Britain **for / since** 1947.

b. They ... (*live*) in a wealthy district of New Delhi **for / since** 6 months.

c. **For / since** the past few decades, the population of Bangalore ... (*increase*) dramatically.

d. **For / since** 1990, the residents' living conditions ... (*improve*) a lot.

2 En quoi Bangalore a-t-elle changé ces dernières années ? Rédigez 3 phrases en utilisant le *present perfect* avec *for* ou *since*.

→ *Since the 1990s, Bangalore has become a major Information Technology (IT) hub.*

IMPROVE YOUR Pronunciation

La voyelle brève /ɪ/

Audio 23lmu21907

- La voyelle que l'on trouve dans *big*, *hip* ou *since* est représentée par le symbole /ɪ/. C'est **une voyelle brève** qui n'a pas d'équivalent en français : il s'agit d'un son intermédiaire entre le *i* de *petit* et le *é* de *père*.
La bouche est un peu plus ouverte qu'elle ne l'est quand on prononce le *i* français.

Il ne faut pas la confondre avec **la voyelle** /iː/ de ***see*** ou de *mean*. Cette voyelle est plus longue et très proche du *i* français de *rive*. Elle est le plus souvent représentée par **les graphies *ee* et *ea*.**

- La voyelle /ɪ/ est en général représentée :
– par la graphie ***i*** (*did*, *with*, *finish*) ou ***y*** (*system*)
– par *e* dans des syllabes inaccentuées (*become*, *result*, *economy*)
Notez qu'on la trouve aussi dans *busy*, *build* et *women*.

1 a) Recopiez les paires de mots suivantes et soulignez en bleu le mot qui contient /ɪ/ (comme dans *big*) et en rouge celui qui contient /iː/ (comme dans *mean*). Écoutez l'enregistrement et répétez.

Audio 23lmu21908

a. live / leave b. sheep / ship
c. cheap / chip d. feel / fill
e. bit / beat

2 Recopiez les mots suivants et soulignez la voyelle /ɪ/. Écoutez l'enregistrement pour vérifier et répétez.

Audio 23lmu21909

establish • *building* • *Silicon Valley* • *innovative* • *progressive* • *district* • *liberal* • *beginning* • *women*

IMPROVE YOUR Vocabulary

Activités en ligne 23lmu21915

Bangalore

DOWNSIDE

Audio 23lmu21911

- noisy
- heavy traffic
- fast growing

CITY

Audio 23lmu21912

- a residential area /ˈeəriə/
- a neighbourhood
- a city centre ≠ a suburb
- nightlife
- fun-filled = lively ≠ dull, boring
- peaceful = relaxing

MODERN

Audio 23lmu21913

- a CBD (US): a central business district
- a company
- headquarters
- a hub /hʌb/ = a center of activity
- IT = Information Technology
- a startup
- a techie

UPSIDE

Audio 23lmu21910

- diversity
- a melting pot
- a job opportunity
- a workforce
- a lifestyle
- an eatery = a fast food restaurant
- greenery = gardens, parks
- living conditions
- trendy, hip

TRADITIONAL

Audio 23lmu21914

- a crowd
- a pensioner
- a Tuk-Tuk
- a flower/spice market

Let's RECAP

Faites le point ! Complétez la fiche bilan avec les documents que vous avez étudiés. Fiche 23lmu21916

AXE 3

Village, neighbourhood, city

How has Bangalore created a new urban identity?

#siliconvalley
Why can Bangalore be called "India's Silicon Valley"?

#oldidentity
What was Bangalore like before the changes?

#newidentity
How has Bangalore changed?

#challenges
What difficulties has the new identity brought about?

GROUP WORK Choose a question and discuss.

Quiz 23lmu21917

YOUR PROJECT

Radio show

You have a 2-minute slot on the radio programme *IT world* to explain how Bangalore would be the ideal place to set up a startup.

- Look through the unit and gather positive information about Bangalore:
  – atmosphere of the city: people, lifestyle, etc.,
  – professional opportunities: universities, IT hub, talent, etc.

> • Use bullet points to order your notes.
> • Use persuasive structures:
> *You would be well advised to... – it's obvious that... – it's a great idea to... – let's not forget that...*

- Practice and check for pronunciation difficulties.

> You can use an online dictionary, like wordreference.com

- Present your show.

> Introduce yourself and your programme.
> End with a conclusion.

- Record and ace it!

Le passé dans le présent

UNIT 20 From Asia to America

▶ How have Asian immigrants been welcomed into the USA?

YOUR PROJECTS

Write a biography of a famous Asian American personality.

OR

Record a podcast on Asian immigration.

Angel Island and Ellis Island, 1910-1940: A comparison

Ellis Island
Location: New York Harbor
Immigration processed: 19 million
Number rejected: 1.2 million (6%)

Angel Island
Location: San Francisco Bay
Immigration processed: 150,000
Number rejected: 58,000 (33%)

U.S. Immigration and Naturalization Service

A Angel Island, the Ellis Island of the West — Video 23lmu22001

1. Watch the beginning of the video (→ 0'24) and pick out information about Don Lee: country of origin • dates • family
Present him in a sentence.
2. Watch the rest of the video and pick out numbers and dates. Say what you understand about Angel Island.
3. Focus on Don Lee's emotions and explain how he felt there.
4. Explain the statement *"You have to prove yourself"* in the video to better understand what happened on Angel Island.

B **Price of gold**

Culture Tip

Chinese people migrated to the USA for three main reasons:
- to build America's first Transcontinental railroads (1863-1869) where they worked in dreadful conditions;
- to join Americans in the quest for gold (Gold Rush);
- to be united with their families.

1. Read the Culture tip above, then look at the illustration. Spot the different elements and say what they may refer to.

2. Name the colours used and guess why the artist chose them.

3. Imagine the artist's intentions when he created this image.

WORD BOX

- a **new**comer = an **im**migrant
- **hard**ship = an **ob**stacle
- be **pro**cessed (through) **An**gel **Is**land
- be held in de**ten**tion = be in cap**tiv**ity, be de**tained**
- be in**tim**idated
- be in**ter**rogated = be **ques**tioned
- en**dure** = ex**pe**rience sth **dif**ficult
- prove your**self** = show you are good
- cross the **o**cean /'əʊʃən/
- disem**bark** = get off a boat

1 The untold story

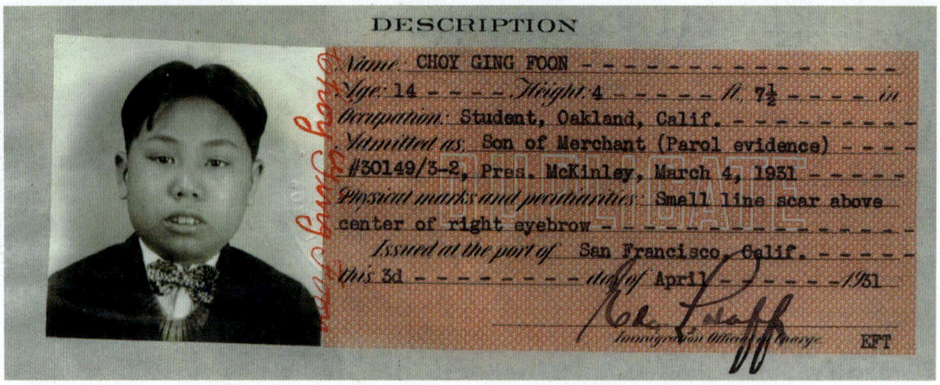
DESCRIPTION

Name: CHOY GING FOON
Age: 14 Height 4 ft. 7½ in
Occupation: Student, Oakland, Calif.
Admitted as: Son of Merchant (Parol evidence)
#30149/3-2, Pres. McKinley, March 4, 1931
Physical marks and peculiarities: Small line scar above center of right eyebrow
Issued at the port of San Francisco, Calif.
this 3d day of April 1931
Immigration Officer in Charge
EFT

A Paper daughters and sons Audio 23lmu22002

1. Listen and pick out information about who Erika Gee is talking about.
2. Explain what she discovered and list the consequences this revelation implied.
3. Say why the "paper children" system was invented.
4. Write a museum label for the document above.

① THE CHINESE EXCLUSION ACT [1882]

First significant law restricting immigration into the United States. Many Americans on the West Coast attributed declining wages and economic ills to Chinese workers. Although the Chinese composed only 0.002 percent of the nation's population, Congress passed the Chinese Exclusion Act to calm down worker demands and satisfy concerns about maintaining white "racial purity."

Adapted from history.com

② New U.S. Permanent Residents 1820-2019

Today, more than 5.4 million people of Chinese ancestry live in the U.S.A, an increase of 88% since 2000. Altogether, there are 20 million people of Asian ancestry in the U.S.A.

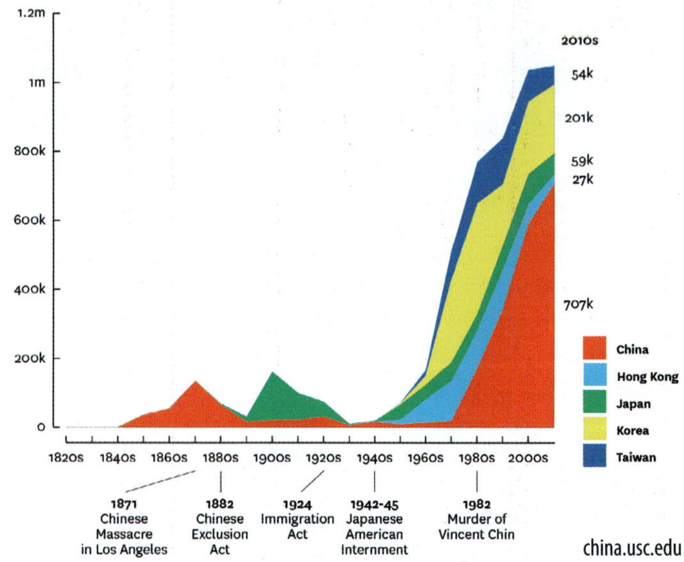

china.usc.edu

B

1. Find the period of time common to documents ① and ②. Explain the aim and specificity of the Exclusion Act.
2. Use figures from the graph ② to explain the consequences of the Exclusion Act.
3. Use documents ① and ② to compare the evolutions of Chinese and Japanese immigrations.

C Camps of shame – The early life of Aki Video 23lmu22003

1. Look at the Culture tip, the drawing and the title. Say what you expect to watch in the video.
2. Watch the beginning (→ 0'29). Say what the following dates and numbers refer to: 1941 – 1942 – 120,000 – 9066 – 50 – ⅓ . Use them to explain the drawing.
3. Watch the rest of the video (0'30-2'37) and say how the Japanese were seen and treated after Pearl Harbor.
4. Gather all the elements about the story of Akiko Kato in camp "Harmony" and record a one-minute teaser for a documentary about her.

Pronunciation Listen and repeat the following words: *confiscate*, *designated*, *desolate*. Focus on the stressed syllables. Audio 23lmu22004

Culture Tip

The U.S. navy base of Pearl Harbor was destroyed by Japanese fighter planes on December 7, 1941 which led President Franklin D. Roosevelt to ask Congress to declare war on Japan.

MEMORY CHALLENGE

In pairs, use five adjectives each to describe the experience of a paper child.

WORD BOX

- **a relative** = a **mem**ber of your **fam**ily
- a de**ten**tion **cen**ter
- **bar**racks = a **build**ing for **sol**diers
- barbed wires = *fils de fer barbelés*
- il**le**gally
- as**sume** or take a new i**den**tity
- be de**port**ed = be forced to leave a **coun**try
- be **prej**udiced (a**gainst**)
- be im**pris**oned = be de**prived** of one's **lib**erty
- be**tray** sb = be dis**loy**al to sb
- re**call** = re**mem**ber

PREPARE YOUR PROJECT

A diary to remember

You have found the diary of an Asian American teenager at the flea market. It dates back to December 1942 and was written by Akira, a 16-year-old boy. Write an email to a U.S. publisher explaining why it is important to publish it.

1 Towards recognition

Illinois Becomes First State to Mandate Teaching Asian American History

The move arrives amid a surge[1] in anti-Asian hate crimes across the country

Illinois is now the first state to require public schools to teach a unit of Asian American history. Governor J.B. Pritzker signed the Teaching Equitable Asian American Community History Act (TEAACH) into law last Friday. Per a statement, the legislation – set to take effect in elementary and high schools across the state in the 2022-23 school year – calls for instruction on Asian American history in Illinois and the Midwest, as well as contributions made by Asian Americans in such diverse fields as the arts, sciences and civil rights. […]

"Asian American history is American history. Yet we are often invisible," says State Representative Jennifer Gong-Gershowitz, who co-sponsored the legislation, in the statement. […]

Between March 2020 and March 2021, the Stop AAPI Hate coalition documented more than 6,600 hate incidents – including verbal harassment, physical assault and civil rights violations – across the country. In March, a gunman in Atlanta murdered eight people, six of whom were women of Asian descent. Lawmakers and activists hope the measure will help create a more inclusive environment, curb discrimination and empower Asian American students.

Research suggests that ethnic studies courses can boost students of color's morale and encourage them to learn about their heritage. In 2016, Stanford scholars found that enrollment in an ethnic studies class boosted attendance[2] and academic performance among high school students at risk of dropping out[3].

Isis Davis-Marks, smithsonianmag.com, July 14, 2021

1. sudden rush – 2. being present – 3. quitting school

A

1. Read the titles and lines 1 to 11. Pick out information about TEAACH. Explain why this acronym is humorous.
2. Find reasons why TEAACH is an important piece of legislation.
3. Read the end of the text and explain why this legislation can empower Asian American students.
4. Write an email to your history teacher to convince him/her to add a class on Asian American history.

Culture Tip
AAPI is an abbreviation that stands for *Asian American and Pacific Islander*.

WORD BOX

- a **pioneer**
- grit = determin**ation**
- har**ass**ment = **bull**y
- **pierc**ing = sharp, **pen**etrating
- defi**ant** = **stub**born, strong-willed
- glass **ceil**ing /ˈsiːlɪŋ/
- de**bunk** sth = decon**struct** sth
- be em**pow**ered

B The myth of the model minority
Video 23lmu22005

1. Watch part 1 of the video (→ 0'47). Create a word cloud with keywords from the conversation.
2. Watch part 2 (4'10 to the end). Explain why the notion of "model minority" is considered stereotypical.
3. Explain the concept of "model minority" to a friend.

C

people.com, 2022

Pioneering Movie Star Anna May Wong Will Be the First Asian American to Appear on U.S. Currency

1. Pick out two adjectives that are synonyms in the headline above. Explain the feeling conveyed by this repetition.
2. Read the Culture tip and observe the coin. Explain how symbolic it is (drawing and written elements).
3. Make a one-minute news report about the new quarter dollar coin for the celebrity channel *E!*

Culture Tip

Anna May Wong (1905-1961) is the first Chinese American movie star in Hollywood. She received her star on the Walk of Fame in 1960 and advocated for more diverse representation in the movie industry.

Remember how to

Describe and debunk stereotypes

- Pour dire **comment des personnes sont perçues ou caricaturées**, on peut utiliser *be perceived as / be stereotyped as* :
  → *Asians **are often perceived/stereotyped as** hard-working and successful (people).* (adj. ou groupe nominal)
- On peut employer **des structures passives** :
  → *Asian-Americans **are believed / thought / said to be** a privileged model community.* (infinitif en *to*)
- Pour déconstruire un stereotype, on peut dire :
  → ***Contrary to popular belief**, not all Asian Americans work in IT.*

PREPARE YOUR PROJECT

A flyer for AAPI Heritage Month

Make a flyer to promote Asian American and Pacific Islanders (AAPI) heritage month and fight against stereotypes. You will find some information here:
Site 23lmu22027

IMPROVE YOUR Grammar

Activités en ligne
23lmu22006

Present perfect ou prétérit ?

Tyron's Tips
23lmu22007

- **Le prétérit (V+ *-ed*)** et **le *present perfect* (*have* / *has* + participe passé)** ne sont pas équivalents.

Prétérit	- pour parler d'**un fait passé sans rapport** avec **le moment présent**, - pour évoquer des **faits historiques**, - pour **écrire une biographie**, - pour **écrire une fiction**.
Present perfect	- pour dire qu'**un fait passé a un résultat au moment présent**, - pour parler de **son expérience** ou faire **un bilan**, - pour dire qu'**un fait commencé dans le passé est toujours d'actualité**.

- **Le prétérit** est obligatoire avec les compléments de temps datant un événement du passé (*in 1880, yesterday, in the 19th century, ago, last week/month...*) :
  → *His family **immigrated** to the United States **in 1970** / **50 years ago**.*
- **Le *present perfect*** est utilisé quand on veut parler de **son expérience ou faire un bilan,** en utilisant des adverbes en lien avec le moment présent (*never/ever, always, already/yet* (déjà), *over/for the past few years*)**:**
  → *Ethnic minorities **have always faced** discrimination.*
  (= c'est le cas aujourd'hui encore)

> Précis p. 263

1 **Dans les phrases suivantes, repérez les compléments de temps, puis mettez le verbe au prétérit ou au *present perfect*.**

a. In the 19th century, a lot of Chinese people ... *(immigrate)* to the United States.
b. Asian immigrants ... *(always / play)* an essential role in California's economic growth.
c. On December 7, 1941, the Japanese Navy ... *(launch)* a surprise attack on the US naval base at Pearl Harbor, Hawaii. After this attack, the United States ... *(declare)* war on Japan.
d. Over the past few years, Asian immigration ... *(increase)* significantly.
e. ... *(you / ever / visit)* Chinatown in New York?

Les propositions de temps

- Elles peuvent être introduites par les conjonctions suivantes :

when	quand	***while***	pendant que
after	après que	***since***	depuis que
before	avant que	***until***	jusqu'à ce que
as	lorsque	***as soon as***	dès que

- Lorsque le sujet de la proposition de temps est le même que celui du verbe principal, il est fréquent d'omettre ce sujet et de mettre le verbe à la forme en *-ing* :
  → *After he **immigrated** to the United States, he started his own business.*
  → *After **immigrating** to the United States, he started his own business.*

2 **Complétez la biographie de la comédienne Margaret Chow en utilisant : *when, after, since, before.***

Margaret Cho was born in 1968 to a family of Korean origin in San Francisco, ... her parents had moved there from Seoul. Margaret Cho has been performing as a stand-up comedian ... she was 14. In the early 90s, ... moving to Los Angeles for better opportunities, she played minor roles in sitcoms. She struggled for years ... she came to prominence as an actress in 1994, ... she starred in the ABC sitcom *All-American Girl.*

IMPROVE YOUR Pronunciation

La consonne /ʒ/ Audio 23lmu22008

- Le son-consonne du français *je* ou *page* est représenté par le symbole /ʒ/.
- Ce son est rare en anglais. On le trouve surtout dans quelques terminaisons :

voyelle + *-sion*	*exclusion, decision*
-sure	*treasure, measure*
-sual	*usual, visual*

- On trouve aussi ce son-consonne dans quelques mots d'origine française : *massage, garage, genre*...

Le **s** de *Asia(n)* peut se prononcer de deux façons : /ʒ/ ou /ʃ/ (comme dans *nation*).

1 a) Recopiez les mots suivants et soulignez ceux qui contiennent la consonne /ʒ/.

invasion • occasion • conclusion • permission • precision • version • dimension

b) Écoutez l'enregistrement pour vérifier vos réponses et répétez les mots. Audio 23lmu22009

2 a) Classez les mots suivants en fonction de la prononciation de la consonne en gras : /ʒ/ (comme dans *deci<u>s</u>ion*) ou /ʃ/ (comme dans *<u>sh</u>ip*) ?

exposure • leisure • pleasure • censure • pressure • treasure

b) Écoutez l'enregistrement pour vérifier vos réponses et répétez les mots. Audio 23lmu22010

L'accentuation des mots en *-ate*

Tyron's Tips 23lmu22011

- Les mots de deux syllabes se terminant par *-ate* s'accentuent de la manière suivante :

Noms ou adjectifs de deux syllabes	Verbes de deux syllabes
Accent sur la 1re syllabe : *<u>pri</u>vate* Exception : *de<u>bate</u>*	Accent sur la 2nde syllabe : *cre<u>ate</u>*

En anglais américain, les verbes de deux syllabes en *-ate* sont accentués sur la 1re syllabe : ***cre**ate.*

- **Les mots de trois syllabes ou plus** sont accentués sur **l'avant-avant dernière syllabe** :
<u>im</u>migrate com<u>mu</u>nicate

La terminaison *-ate* se prononce /ət/ (comme dans *quiet*) dans un nom ou un adjectif : *immediate*. Elle se prononce /eɪt/ (comme dans *eight*) dans un verbe : *communicate*.

3 a) Recopiez les mots suivants et soulignez la syllabe qui porte l'accent principal.

approximate • discriminate • educate • relate • a mandate • immigrate • legitimate • climate

b) Écoutez l'enregistrement pour vérifier vos réponses. Audio 23lmu22012

c) Classez ces mots dans un tableau en fonction de la prononciation de la terminaison *-ate* :

/eɪt/ (comme dans *eight*)	/ət/ (comme dans *quiet*)

IMPROVE YOUR Vocabulary

Activités en ligne 23lmu22013

Asian-American

MIGRATION

Audio 23lmu22014

- a newcomer, a migrant
- hardship = obstacle
- migrate /maɪˈgreɪt/, emigrate /ˈemɪgreɪt/
- cross the ocean
- the Gold Rush, a gold seeker
- disembark
- be processed (through) Angel Island
- be intimidated
- endure sth = experience sth difficult

DETENTION

Audio 23lmu22015

- an immigration station
- a detention center
- barbed wires = *fils de fer barbelés*
- a curfew = *un couvre-feu*
- assume a new identity
- be held in detention = be in captivity
- be interrogated = be questioned
- be deported = be forced to leave a country

PAST AND PRESENT

Audio 23lmu22016

- a relative = a member of your family
- a commemoration
- intergenerational = sth that links generations
- pay tribute to sth = commemorate sth
- recall sth = remember sth

Recognition

COMMEMORATING

Audio 23lmu22017

- a shared experience an exhibition = an art display
- visibility
- acknowledge sth = recognise sth
- be perceived as
- represent
- mint a coin = manufacture money

PIONEERING

Audio 23lmu22019

- a trailblazer = a pioneer /ˌpaɪəˈnɪə/
- groundbreaking = making new important discoveries
- pave the way for sth = be a pioneer, be leading to

DETERMINATION

Audio 23lmu22018

- resilience /rɪˈzɪliəns/ = the ability to become strong after a difficult situation
- self-reliant = self-confident
- strong-willed = determined /dɪˈtɜːmɪnd/
- resolute /ˈrezəluːt/
- fierce /fɪəs/ = strong

STEREOTYPES

Audio 23lmu22020

- a model minority
- conformist /kənˈfɔːmɪst/
- debunk sth = show sth to be wrong, deconstruct sth
- be prejudiced (against)

1 Fill the gaps with words from the mind map above (one blank = one word).

a. Angel Island is an ... ... located on the West Coast of the USA.

b. Immigrants were held in ... and ... by officers.

c. Asian Americans ... many hardships: some Japanese Americans ... a new ... to escape from being sent to ... .

d. This model minority is perceived as ... and ... .

e. Thanks to their resilience, the Asian American community gained ... and ... .

2 Use one word from each of the seven categories of the mind map to explain how important Asian Americans have been in building the United States.

Let's RECAP

Faites le point ! Complétez la fiche bilan avec les documents que vous avez étudiés. Fiche 23lmu22021

AXE 8

The past in the present

How have Asian immigrants been welcomed into the USA?

#asianmigrants

How difficult was it for Asian newcomers to emigrate to the USA?

#campsofshame

How did Pearl Harbor change Japanese Americans' lives?

#identity

How has the past shaped the dual identity of Asian immigrants?

#asianvisibility

To what extent has the community gained positive visibility in the American society?

GROUP WORK Choose a question and discuss.

Quiz 23lmu22022

Become AN EXPERT

Lisez et écoutez de l'anglais en dehors de la classe

Museums

- Japanese American National Museum in LA vers AMC Lien 23lmu22023
- Dorothea Lange (photos) vers LLCER/AMC Lien 23lmu22024

Books

- *A Pho Love Story*, Loan Li vers LLCER
- *The Leavers*, Lisa Ko vers LLCER
- *How Much of These Hills Is Gold*, C. Pam Zhang vers LLCER
- *Asian American Dreams*, Helen Zia vers LLCER/AMC
- *No-No Boy*, John Okada vers LLCER

Series & films

vers LLCER/AMC

YOUR PROJECTS

Write a biography

Write a biography of a famous Asian American, focusing on his/her achievements and double-culture, for your school website. Here are some examples you may use:

Brayden Maniago [actor] Melissa Polinar [singer-songwriter]

Anne Akiko Meyers [violonist] Mazie Hirono [senator]

- Choose a famous Asian American.
  - Use the Internet if you don't know any.
  - Explain how he/she manages with his/her double-culture.
- Find one or two photographs that best represent him/her.
- Select what you want to put forward.
  - Use adjectives to qualify his/her strong points.
  - Explain how he/she best represents the Asian American community.
- Write two short paragraphs about him/her.
  - One paragraph about his/her early life and one about his/her today's activities.
  - Use link words [*First*, *then*, *finally*...].
- Pay attention to tenses.
  - Simple past or simple present to talk about his/her life.

OR

Record a podcast

To celebrate Asian American and Pacific Islander [AAPI] Heritage Month, record a podcast explaining the immigration history of the Chinese or Japanese communities.

- Using 2 or 3 different time periods, show the evolution of AAPI integration into U.S. society.
- Say why it is important to promote the AAPI's legacy.
  - Do some research about AAPI Heritage Month and show the importance of this minority in the US. Lien 23lmu22025
- Using migrants' personal accounts, explain the hardships they faced during their journey to the U.S.
  - You can include celebrities' accounts.
- Organise your ideas and rehearse your podcast.
  - Pay attention to intonation, pace, pronunciation and stress on words. Use an online dictionary to check your pronunciation.
- Find a jingle and prepare an introduction and conclusion to your podcast.

BUILD UP YOUR SKILLS

How to write a biography

Darren BARNET (1991 -)

An American actor, he was born on April, 27th, 1991 in Los Angeles, USA. His mother is of Japanese descent. He has got two sisters.
Darren Barnet attended Dr. Phillips High School and later, he graduated from Berry College with a Bachelor of Arts in 2013. He speaks Japanese fluently and has studied French in college, where he was part of the drama club. He first made his acting debut in 2017. Darren was primarily known for his appearance on *This is US* and *S.W.A.T.* Then, in 2020, he began starring in the Netflix teen comedy-drama series *Never Have I Ever*, as Paxton Hall-Yoshida. Following the series, news website EliteDaily noted "Barnet […] says starring on the show brought a greater focus to his Asian roots on a personal level. Not only did Barnet's Asian American ancestry influence Hall-Yoshida's part-Japanese background in the series, but the actor's identity has also influenced the show's storyline".
The rising star has recently been in the limelight for his appearance in the third season of *Never Have I Ever*. Finally, Darren is set to star in thriller drama film *Apophenia*. In five years, we can say that he has achieved a lot. Fun fact: in April 2022, Barnet became the first male brand ambassador for Victoria's Secret PINK.

1. Pour la préparer

- Rassemblez les informations qui vous intéressent :

Names	Dates (birth/death)	Nationality	Diplomas	Jobs	Achievements	...

Vous pouvez utiliser des sites tels que www.biography.com/people wikicelebs.com imdb.com

- Cherchez quelques anecdotes pour rendre votre biographie vivante.
- Organisez vos informations : dates et métier, puis jeunes années, carrière...
- Délimitez **les besoins lexicaux**. Peut-être aurez-vous besoin de verbes ou d'expressions précis, par exemple pour parler des études (*he graduated from*), des origines (*Japanese descent*), ou de la célébrité (*in the limelight*).
- Accordez les verbes aux temps qui conviennent : présent simple pour énoncer les caractéristiques de la personne et prétérit simple pour indiquer ce qu'il/elle a fait dans le passé.

2. Pour la rédiger

- Utilisez un dictionnaire en ligne pour vérifier l'orthographe, par exemple wordreference.com
- Utilisez des connecteurs logiques : *so, therefore, because, moreover,* ou pour marquer la chronologie : *first, second, then, later… finally*.
- Relisez attentivement votre texte (→ Relire un devoir écrit > p. 282) et choisissez quelques photos pour l'illustrer.

Are you ready?

+ prof
Évaluation

Entraînement à l'évaluation

Compréhension orale

Faites un compte-rendu en français de l'audio.

npr.org

Anna May Wong's legacy, NPR Audio 23lmu22026

- Identifiez le nombre d'intervenants et repérez qui ils sont.
- Repérez le ton de l'entretien : sérieux - humoristique - convivial - sarcastique...
- Essayez de comprendre le contexte de l'entretien et son intention : pourquoi ce sujet est-il abordé et quel est le but de l'entretien ?

Production écrite

How has the AAPI community's representation in Hollywood changed? Write a 150-words essay.

Compréhension écrite

This photograph was displayed in the Japanese American National Museum in Los Angeles. It is part of the exhibition (Asian Americans THEN and NOW) that tells the stories of two girls that were born in the late 1930s.

FAMILY NUMBERS:
ITASHIKI (Yoko/Mary Ann Yahiro) 19033
NAKAMOTO (Hideno/Helene Nakamoto Mihara) 19074

THEN Third-generation Japanese American Hideno Helene Nakamoto, 7, left, and second-generation Yoko Itashiki, 7, center, recite the Pledge of Alligiance at the Raphael Weill School in San Francisco before they went to Tanforan Assembly Center[1].

Both families were broken by incarceration. Hideno's father, Jitsuzo Nakamoto, who owned the American Fish Market at 1836 Buchanan St. in San Francisco's Japantown, was arrested by the FBI not long after Pearl Harbor, and incarcerated [...].
"These men in fedora hats came to the house and hurriedly took him out of the house," Hideno said. "I was at the top of the staircase, watching, and I remember the flashing lights and he was gone, that's it. [...]
Yoko's parents were also split up. Her father, Tarozimen, stayed with the children while her mother, Fuku Ogura, was taken to Camp Sharp Park, an internment facility in Pacifica. Yoko never saw her 51-year-old mother alive again. [...]

Photographer: Dorothea Lange, April 20, 1942, San Francisco, Calif.

NOW The Nakamoto family was released from Topaz[2] on Sept. 9, 1945. They moved to Salt Lake City and then returned to San Francisco, where Helene's father rented the same property he'd had before the war and re-established the American Fish Market. He eventually bought the property.

Helene's father, Jitsuzo Nakamoto, was offered the chance to be repatriated to Japan. He declined. "There was nothing back there in Japan. He didn't own any property," Helene said. [...] That was in 1946. In 1953, he received his American citizenship.

Mary Ann Yahiro (Yoko Itashiki) and her family followed her older sister out of Topaz and resettled on the North Side of Chicago where "I felt a little bit prejudiced against [...]." Mary Ann graduated from Mundelein College in Chicago. In looking back at her life, she said incarceration altered her forever. "You can't take freedom for granted, wherever you are," she said.

Japanese American National Museum in Los Angeles

1. an internment camp in California – 2. an internment camp in Utah

1. Give the name of the individuals and say what they have in common.
2. Show that Hideno Nakamoto's family had been fitting into the US society and had no more links with Japan (two items).
3. Show that the two families were broken. Give one example for each family.
4. Explain the USA's reactions towards Jitsuzo Nakamoto after the war (2 items).
5. Compare what both women think about the incarceration of their families. Quote elements from the texts.

Production écrite

You are at the Japanese American National Museum. Look at the photo of Hideno and Yoko above. You decide to write an email to them to meet up, so they can tell you their own story. You will also tell them the reasons why their stories touched you.

Escape Game

UNIT 21

Représentation de soi et rapport à autrui

ALICE'S QUEST

▶ How does Alice's journey through Wonderland help her grow up?

Fiche 23lmu22101
Le fichier d'activités

Listen to the Game Master before setting off on your journey with Alice!
Vidéo 23lmu22102

FOR IDENTITY

Help Alice find her true self while growing up! Follow her on her journey around Wonderland and meet many weird creatures. Deduce the passwords about what it is like to grow up; reconstruct the map of Wonderland and find your way out!

Curious Alice VR Experience by V&A and VIVE Arts

MEET ALICE

First of all, you need to know more about Alice, Lewis Carroll and Wonderland.

Look at and listen to the documents on these two pages and get ready to find the first clues.

Hurry Up, the clock is ticking!

Tick tock!
Tick tock!

The real Alice

Window at All Saint's Church, Daresbury, Cheshire, where Charles Dogson / Lewis Carroll was born in 1832.

Lewis Carroll and the story of Alice

Audio 23lmu22103

Show your findings to the Game Master to get the frame of the Wonderland map.

Escape Game

Read this poem by Lewis Carroll. Put your heads together and find out Alice's full name: it's hidden somewhere in the poem! Fiche 1 23lmu22104

A Boat Beneath a Sunny Sky

By Lewis Carroll

A boat beneath a sunny sky,
Lingering onward dreamily
In an evening of July —

Children three that nestle near,
Eager eye and willing ear,
Pleased a simple tale to hear —
Long had paled that sunny sky:
Echoes fade and memories die.
Autumn frosts have slain July.

Still she haunts me, phantomwise,
Alice moving under skies
Never seen by waking eyes.

Children yet, the tale to hear,
Eager eye and willing ear,
Lovingly shall nestle near.

In a Wonderland they lie,
Dreaming as the days go by,
Dreaming as the summers die:

Ever drifting down the stream —
Lingering in the golden gleam —
Life, what is it but a ....?

Give the password to the Game Master and you will get the first piece of the Wonderland map. Then move on to your next challenge!

MEET THE WHITE RABBIT

All of a sudden, you find yourself projected into the virtual world of *Wonderland*. You see Alice running after the White Rabbit and decide to follow them, when they disappear into a deep hole. Keep track of them and get ready for this new challenge.

In the illustration on the left, spot 3 of the items from the following list:

- A PEN
- A CLOCK
- A FAN
- A CROWN
- A BISCUIT
- A BOOK
- AN HOURGLASS
- A BABY PIG
- A POCKET WATCH
- A PINK FLAMINGO

Find out what these 3 elements symbolise and you will get the password.

Fiche 2 23lmu22105

Have you found the solution?
Go and see the Game Master.
Check you have the right answer
to escape the rabbit hole.

CHALLENGE 3

MEET THE CATERPILLAR

Escape Game

As you are walking in a strange forest, you can hear a voice: a weird-looking creature that resembles a caterpillar is talking to Alice who is complaining about changing sizes.

Pay attention to the conversation between Alice and the caterpillar. Complete the balloons with the sentences/words that keep coming back.

Fiche 3 23lmu22106

Extract from *Alice's Adventures in Wonderland* **Audio** 23lmu22107

In a minute or two the Caterpillar [...] got down off the mushroom, and crawled away in the grass, merely remarking as it went, "One side will make you grow taller, and the other side will make you grow shorter."

"One side of *what*? The other side of *what*?" thought Alice to herself.

"Of the mushroom," said the Caterpillar, just as if she had asked it aloud; and in another moment it was out of sight[1].

Alice remained looking thoughtfully at the mushroom for a minute, trying to make out which were the two sides of it; and as it was perfectly round, she found this a very difficult question. However, at last she stretched her arms round it as far as they would go and broke off a bit of the edge[2] with each hand.

"And now which is which?" she said to herself and nibbled[3] a little of the right-hand bit[4] to try the effect: the next moment she felt a violent blow underneath her chin[5]: it had struck[6] her foot!

She was a good deal frightened by this very sudden change, but she felt that there was no time to be lost, as she was shrinking[7] rapidly; so she set to work at once to eat some of the other bit. Her chin was pressed so closely against her foot, that there was hardly room to open her mouth; but she did it at last, and managed to swallow a morsel[8] of the lefthand bit.

Lewis CARROLL, *Alice's Adventures in Wonderland*, 1865

1. too far away to be seen – 2. side – 3. bit / ate – 4. piece – 5. part of the face under the mouth – 6. hit – 7. becoming shorter – 8. piece

Use your brain. Reorder the pictures in your worksheet according to the sequence of events in the extract.

Fiche 4 23lmu22108

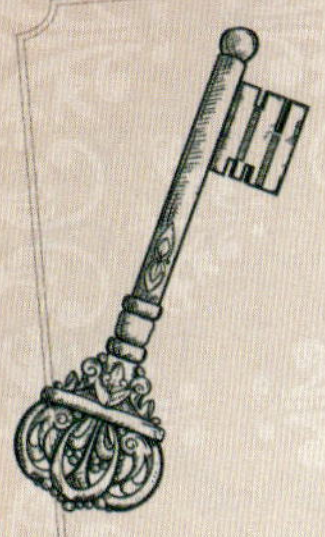

Have you found the passwords? Go and bring them to the Game Master. Now, you are ready for the next encounter!

1 Pronoms personnels, déterminants et pronoms possessifs

Pronoms personnels

Sujet	Complément
I	me
you	you
she	her
he	him
it	it
we	us
you	you
they	them

- Les pronoms de la première colonne sont employés quand ils sont sujets du verbe. Les pronoms de la seconde colonne sont utilisés quand ils sont compléments du verbe ou placés après une préposition.
→ ***We** brought Jamie's toys with **us. We**'ll put **them** in his bedroom.*
Nous avons apporté avec **nous** les jouets de Jamie. **Nous les** mettrons dans sa chambre.

He** / **him (masculin) et ***she** / **her*** (féminin) s'emploient uniquement pour désigner **des êtres humains** et parfois des animaux de compagnie. ***It*** s'emploie pour désigner des objets et des animaux qui ne sont pas domestiques.

Déterminants et pronoms possessifs

Déterminants	Pronoms
my	mine
your	yours
her	hers
his	his
its	–
our	ours
your	yours
their	theirs

- Les déterminants possessifs sont toujours suivis d'un nom (*my father, our house*).
Les pronoms possessifs remplacent des noms précédés d'un déterminant possessif. Ils permettent ainsi d'éviter une répétition. On les traduit par « le mien / la mienne / le sien, etc.».
→ *He forgot **his** key, so he had to use **mine** (= my key).*
Il a oublié **sa** clef. Il a donc dû utiliser **la mienne**.

Les possessifs anglais s'accordent avec « le possesseur », contrairement aux possessifs français, qui s'accordent en genre et en nombre avec « le possédé » (le nom qui suit le possessif).
→ ***My brother** lent me **his** car.*
Mon frère m'a prêté **sa voiture**.

- En français, on emploie souvent l'article défini pour désigner les parties du corps. En anglais, on utilise toujours un déterminant possessif.
→ *He raised **his** hand.* Il a levé **la** main.

1 Complétez avec les pronoms personnels qui conviennent.

a. **The neighbours** are getting on my nerves. ...'re making so much noise! Can you tell ... to be quiet?
b. My parents live in **a big house**. As ... is in bad condition, they have to renovate ... .
c. When **Kate** was 16, ... visited the USA. I met ... two years later.

2 Complétez avec le déterminant ou le pronom possessif qui convient.

a. The kids brushed ... teeth and went to bed.
b. My mother has lost ... car key.
c. The hotel has ... own swimming pool.
d. "Is this Brenda's room?" "Yes, it's ... ."
e. I paid for those sunglasses, so they're ... now!

2 Le pluriel des noms

- La plupart des noms forment leur pluriel de la manière suivante :

-S prononcé /s/ ou /z/	-ES prononcé /ɪz/ (mots qui se terminent par *s*, *ch*, *sh* ou *x*)
one apple → two apple**s**	one bus → two bus**es**
one dog → two dog**s**	one brush → two brush**es**
one cat → two cat**s**	one box → two box**es**

- Certains mots se terminant par *-o* forment leur pluriel en ***-es*** : *tomato**es**, hero**es**.* Quelques-uns forment leur pluriel avec un *-s* : c'est le cas de *piano**s**, radio**s**.*
- Les noms se terminant par *-y* font leur pluriel en ***-ies*** *: a pupp**y** → two pupp**ies**, a fl**y** → two fl**ies**.*
- La plupart des noms se terminant par *-f* font leur pluriel en ***-ves*** *: a wolf → two wol**ves**, a scarf → two scar**ves***. Il existe quelques exceptions : *a roof → two roof**s**, a chief → two chief**s**.*

Les pluriels irréguliers

- Quelques mots ont des pluriels totalement irréguliers.

*a m**a**n → two m**e**n*   *a wom**a**n → two wom**e**n*   *a child → two child**ren***

*a t**oo**th → two t**ee**th*   *a f**oo**t → two f**ee**t*   *a m**ouse** → two m**ice***

Bien sûr, les composés de *man* et de *woman* suivent la même règle (*a policem**a**n → two policem**e**n*).

Au pluriel, le *o* et le *e* de *women* /ˈwɪmɪn/ se prononcent /ɪ/ (comme le *i* de *big*).

Les noms invariables

- Quelques noms sont invariables :
  a sheep → two sheep   *a fish → two fish*   *a series → two series*
- On peut ajouter à cette liste *bison*, *trout* (truite), *salmon* (saumon), *shrimp* (crevette), *deer* (cerf)...

3 Mettez les mots entre parenthèses au pluriel.

a. I've bought ... *(tomato)*, ... *(peach)* and ... *(carrot)* at the supermarket.
b. Los Angeles is one of the world's largest ... *(city)*.
c. Several ... *(fisherman)* went out on the lake last night and caught a lot of ... *(fish)* and ... *(shrimp)*.
d. I brush my ... *(tooth)* three ... *(time)* a day.
e. ... *(mouse)* are small animals.
f. Plastic ... *(knife)* and ... *(fork)* are now banned in California.
g. Our menu includes a wide selection of vegetarian ... *(dish)*.

3 Dénombrables et indénombrables

- On divise souvent les noms en deux catégories :

Les noms dénombrables *Ex. : dog, house, ball*	• Ces mots ont un singulier *(one dog)* et un pluriel *(two dog**s**)*. • Ils peuvent être comptés avec précision et être employés avec l'article indéfini *a(n)*.
Les noms indénombrables *Ex. : bread, gold*	• Ils n'ont pas de forme au pluriel (on ne peut pas dire ~~golds~~ ou ~~breads~~). • Ils ne peuvent pas être comptés (on ne peut pas dire ~~one bread~~ ou ~~two golds~~) ni les employer avec l'article indéfini *a(n)*.

- De plus, on utilise ces deux catégories avec des quantifieurs différents (par exemple *much* et *many*, voir fiche 9, p. 250).

Quels noms sont indénombrables ?

Les noms indénombrables désignent...

des matières, des substances	des qualités, des abstractions	des activités
wool, butter, milk, apple juice	*joy, courage, beauty*	*knitting, swimming*

- Certains indénombrables en anglais se traduisent en français par des dénombrables :

advice (les conseils) — *luggage* (les bagages) — *furniture* (les meubles)
homework (les devoirs) — *information* (les renseignements) — *hair* (les cheveux)
news (les nouvelles) — *toast* (les toasts / tartines) — *pasta* (les pâtes)
underwear (les sous-vêtements) — *spinach* (les épinards)

- Cela signifie qu'en anglais, **ces mots ne sont jamais employés au pluriel et ne peuvent être précédés de l'article indéfini *a(n)*.** On les traduit parfois par des pluriels en français.
→ *He only gives **good advice**.* Il ne donne que de bon**s** conseil**s**.

Le mot *news*, bien qu'il se termine par un -s, est un indénombrable.
Il s'accorde donc avec le verbe au singulier.
→ ***News** travels fast.* Les nouvelles vont vite.

La structure *a piece of / piece(s) of...*

Certains indénombrables (en particulier *advice, luggage, news, information...*) peuvent être dénombrés de façon précise au moyen de la structure ***a piece of / piece(s) of...***
→ *I have **two pieces of news** for you.* J'ai **deux nouvelles** à t'annoncer.

4 Les noms en gras sont-ils dénombrables ou indénombrables ? Choisissez la forme correcte.

a. They have long **hair / hairs** and blue **eye / eyes**.
b. I had to carry my **luggage / luggages** to the car.
c. I eat a lot of **pasta / pastas**. I usually cook **it / them** with fresh **tomato / tomatoes** and **spinach / spinaches.**
d. The police gave us very detailed **information / informations** about what was happening.

4 L'article indéfini *a(n)*

La forme de l'article indéfini

- En anglais, l'article indéfini a la forme suivante :

A + nom commençant par un son consonne	**AN + nom commençant par un son voyelle**
a book **a c**at **a h**at	**an e**lephant **an a**rmchair **an i**dea

Les mots commençant par la consonne aspirée *h* sont précédés de *a* : ***a h**ouse*, ***a h**otel*.
On dira en revanche ***an** hour* car le *h* est muet dans ce mot.
Les mots commençant par le son consonne /j/ (comme dans ***you***) sont également précédés de *a* : ***a** university*, ***a** uniform*.

- Quand on souhaite traduire l'article indéfini pluriel français *des*, on a recours à l'article Ø (c'est-à-dire l'absence d'article, voir fiche 6, p. 247).
→ *There was **a** dog in her garden. There were **Ø** dog**s** in her garden.*
Il y avait **un** chien dans son jardin. Il y avait **des** chien**s** dans son jardin.

Quand doit-on l'utiliser ?

- L'article indéfini n'est employé qu'avec **des noms dénombrables singuliers** (voir fiche 3, p. 244). Son emploi est très similaire à celui de l'article indéfini « **un / une** » en français : on l'utilise en particulier quand on mentionne quelqu'un ou quelque chose pour la première fois dans un texte.
→ *I bought **a** magazine and **a** sandwich in **a** shop. I ate **the** sandwich but I forgot **the** magazine.*
J'ai acheté **un** magazine et **un** sandwich dans **un** magasin. J'ai mangé **le** sandwich mais j'ai oublié **le** magazine.

- On l'emploie aussi dans les cas suivants :

• quand on donne **la profession d'une personne**, surtout après un verbe d'état tel que *be* ou *become*.
→ *She is **a doctor**.* Elle est médecin.

• dans **des expressions temporelles** pour traduire « par » et **exprimer une fréquence**. Dans ce cas, on peut remplacer *a(n)* par la préposition *per*.
→ *She goes to the gym **three times a** (ou **per**) **week**.* Elle va à la salle de gym trois fois **par** semaine.

• dans **les phrases exclamatives en *what***.
→ *What **a lovely baby!*** Quel adorable bébé !

• après les prépositions ***without* (sans)** ou ***as* (en tant que, comme).**
→ *Last summer, he worked **as a waiter**.* L'été dernier, il a travaillé **comme serveur**.
→ *I can't work **without a computer**.* Je ne peux pas travailler **sans ordinateur**.

5 Complétez avec *a* ou *an*.
a. We stayed in ... hotel near the airport. The following day we rented ... car.
b. The babysitter charges $8 ... hour.
c. Marcia is ... university graduate. She works as ... engineer in ... IT company.

6 Produisez 4 phrases pour décrire votre routine quotidienne ou hebdomadaire. Utilisez des structures du type *three times a week / a day*.
Exemple : *I brush my teeth **three times a day**.*

5 L'article défini *the*

La prononciation de *the*

- En anglais, l'article défini est invariable. Il a en revanche deux prononciations possibles :

/ðə/ + nom commençant par un son consonne [*the* a la même voyelle que dans *an*]	/ði/ + nom commençant par un son voyelle [*the* a la même voyelle que dans *me*]
the book **the h**ouse	**the e**lephant **the I**nternet

Avant des mots commençant par un *h* aspiré, *the* est prononcé /ðə/ : ***the h**eart*, ***the h**otel.*
On dira en revanche ***the** hour* /ði/ car le *h* est muet dans ce mot.
Ceux commençant par le son consonne /j/ (comme dans ***you***) sont aussi précédés de /ðə/ : ***the** university.*

Quand emploie-t-on *the* ?

- On utilise l'article *the* pour signaler que quelqu'un ou quelque chose est **connu** ou **identifié**.

Parce qu'**on en a déjà parlé**
→ *I ordered a pizza and an iced tea.*
***The** pizza was delicious but **the** iced tea was yucky.*
J'ai commandé une pizza et un thé glacé.
La pizza était délicieuse mais **le** thé glacé était dégoûtant.

Parce qu'il est **familier** à celui qui parle
→ ***The** neighbour knocked at **the** door.*
Le voisin [le mien, celui que je connais bien] a frappé à la porte [la mienne].

Parce qu'il est **unique** ou **connu de tous**
→ ***the** Sun, **the** Earth, **the** Pope, **the** Internet*

- On utilise aussi l'article *the* :
  - quand le nom est suivi d'**un complément du nom** introduit par *of* ou par une relative.
    → ***the** size of the building* la taille du bâtiment
    → ***the** books which she bought* les livres qu'elle a achetés
  - avec **les superlatifs**.
    → *It was **the** most terrifying experience of my life.* Ce fut la plus terrifiante expérience de ma vie.
  - devant **les noms de mer ou d'océan** (***the** English Channel, **the** Pacific Ocean*) et **de rivière ou de fleuve** (***the** Thames, **the** Mississippi River*).

7 Complétez le texte suivant avec l'article défini *the* ou l'article indéfini *a(n)*.

... man has been killed by ... lion after breaking into its enclosure at ... zoo in Germany. ... man, who was in his 30s, was attacked and killed by ... lion after he had jumped over ... security fences of ... zoo. Zookeepers found ... man's body inside ... lion's enclosure on Monday morning. ... police officer who investigated ... case said ... man's conduct was ... most reckless she had ever seen.

6 L'article Ø (ou l'absence d'article)

Quand emploie-t-on l'article Ø ?

- On utilise l'article Ø (c'est-à-dire l'absence d'article) quand on veut désigner **des généralités**. Dans ce cas, on le rencontre :

• avec des **noms dénombrables pluriels**.
On désigne alors tous les membres de la catégorie concernée.
→ *I'm afraid of* ***Ø spiders.*** J'ai peur des araignées.

• avec des **noms indénombrables singuliers**.
Il peut s'agir de substances, de matières, d'abstractions.
→ ***Ø Mexican food*** *can be spicy.* La nourriture mexicaine peut être épicée.

- L'article Ø peut également être utilisé :
  • avec des dénombrables pluriels pour traduire l'article indéfini pluriel « **des** ».
  • avec des indénombrables pour traduire l'article partitif « **du / de la** ».

Dans ces emplois, il peut être remplacé par *some* (voir fiche 8, p. 249).
→ *I've bought* ***Ø / some*** *pears at the supermarket.* J'ai acheté **des** poires au supermarché.
→ *You've got* ***Ø / some*** *ketchup on your shirt.* Tu as **du** ketchup sur ta chemise.

Les cas particuliers

- On utilise aussi Ø dans les cas particuliers suivants :

devant les noms suivis d'un numéro	→ *Ø room 234, Ø page 8, Ø platform 8* (le quai n°8)
avec les noms de langue	→ *He speaks* ***Ø Spanish*** *fluently.* Il parle espagnol couramment.
avec les noms de repas (*lunch, dinner, breakfast*)	→ *What would you like for **Ø lunch**?* Qu'aimerais-tu pour le déjeuner ?
avec un titre suivi d'un nom propre	→ *Ø King Charles III, Ø President Biden, Ø Princess Ann* En revanche, on dira : ***the*** *President of the United States*
avec les noms de pays	→ *Ø France, Ø India, Ø Canada, Ø England* Exceptions : ***the*** *United Kingdom,* ***the*** *United States of America,* ***the*** *Netherlands* (les Pays Bas)

- On dit :

to go to → *Ø bed* / *Ø school / university* / *Ø work*

to be → *in Ø prison / jail* / *in Ø hospital* / *at Ø home*

8 Complétez avec *the, a(n)* ou Ø.

a. ... vegetarian is somebody who doesn't eat ... meat.
b. I don't care what ... people think.
c. I really like ... people who live in this neighbourhood.
d. Do you take ... sugar in your coffee?
e. Here is ... key to my hotel room. I'm staying in ... room 66.
f. ... President Kennedy was assassinated in 1963.
g. ... Northern Ireland is part of ... United Kingdom.
h. ... flight AB123 to New York City is now boarding at ... gate 13.

9 Traduisez ces phrases.

a. Il est allé au lit après le dîner.
b. Il a appris le portugais à l'université.
c. Son frère est en prison parce qu'il a dévalisé *(rob)* une banque.

7 Le génitif

- **Le génitif met en relation deux noms.** Il s'agit parfois d'une relation d'appartenance. On le traduit le plus souvent par la préposition « de » en français.
  → *Dana's glasses* les lunettes **de** Dana

Quand le nom au génitif est un nom propre, il n'est pas précédé de l'article *the* : on dira donc *Mike's house* et non ~~*the Mike's house*~~.

- Le génitif peut s'orthographier de deux façons différentes.

Règle générale : N's
→ *Kate's car* la voitude **de** Kate
→ *the president's office* le bureau **du** président

Nom au pluriel terminé par -(e)s : Ns'
→ *my neighbours' car* la voiture **de** mes voisins
→ *the witches' brooms* les balais **des** sorcières

- Les noms propres terminés par -s forment le plus souvent leur génitif en ajoutant 's (prononcé /ɪz/ comme dans *classes*) : *James's* /dʒeɪmɪz/ *umbrella.*

Génitif ou structure avec *of* ?

- On peut mettre au génitif des noms qui désignent :

des personnes, des animaux	→ ***Tom's*** *wallet,* ***the dog's*** *toy*
des pays, des villes	→ ***Britain's*** *army,* ***London's*** *tube*
des institutions, des entreprises	→ ***the school's*** *headmaster,* ***the company's*** *employees*
des moments (surtout *yesterday*, *tomorrow* et ceux contenant *last* ou *next*)	→ ***yesterday's*** *accident,* ***last week's*** *test*

- Les noms qui désignent des **inanimés** (des objets, des substances, des abstractions, etc.) se construisent en principe avec *of* : *the roof* ***of the house****, the end* ***of the film****, a glass* ***of milk****...*

Les génitifs elliptiques

- Parfois, pour éviter les répétitions, le nom qui suit le génitif est omis car il est sous-entendu. On parle alors **de génitif elliptique**.
  → *I forgot my phone, so I took* ***Monica's****.* [sous entendu : ***Monica's*** *phone*]
  J'ai oublié mon téléphone. J'ai donc pris **celui de Monica.**

- On utilise souvent des génitifs elliptiques pour traduire la préposition « **chez** » en français.
  → *He still lives at* ***his parents'****.* [sous entendu : ***his parents'*** *house*] Il vit encore **chez** ses parents.

- On utilise cette structure avec des noms de commerçants.
  → *I went to* ***the butcher's*** *this morning.* [sous entendu : ***the butcher's*** *shop*]
  Je suis allé **chez le boucher** ce matin.

10 Reliez les mots à l'aide d'un génitif ou d'une structure avec *of*. Si les deux sont possibles, précisez-le.

a. the children / Rachel
b. today / the meeting
c. the Earth / the orbit
d. Mrs. Higgins / the haircut
e. the garage / the door
f. the farm / his grandparents
g. tea / a cup
h. the book / the beginning

8 *Some, any, no* et leurs composés

Some et *any*

- ***Some* et *any*** permettent le plus souvent d'indiquer **une quantité vague ou indéterminée.** On les trouve alors avant des noms indénombrables ou dénombrables pluriels. On les traduit par l'article partitif **du / de la / des**.
  → *I've bought* ***some apples*** *at the supermarket.* J'ai acheté **des pommes** au supermarché.
- L'emploi de ***some* ou de *any*** dépend du type de phrases dans lesquelles ces mots apparaissent.

Phrase affirmative	Phrase négative	Phrase interrogative
SOME	*NOT … ANY*	*ANY*
→ *I have* ***some money.***	→ *I do**n't** have* ***any money.***	→ *Do you have* ***any money?***

Il peut arriver que *some* apparaisse dans des phrases interrogatives, en particulier quand on propose quelque chose.
→ *Would you like* ***some coffee****?* Veux-tu **du café** ?

No et *none*

- À la place de ***not… any* + nom**, il est possible d'utiliser ***no* + nom**. Le verbe est alors **à la forme affirmative.**
  → *I* ***don't*** *have* ***any money****. = I have* ***no money****.*
- À la place de *no* + nom, il est possible d'utiliser **le pronom *none*** /nʌn/ pour éviter des répétitions : le nom est alors sous-entendu.
  → *My wife has two brothers. I have* ***none****. [= no brother]* Ma femme a deux frères. Moi, je n'en ai pas.

Quand on veut associer *any*, *some* ou *none* avec un autre déterminant *(these, my…)* ou un pronom *(you, them…)*, il faut utiliser *of*.
→ ***None of my friends / them*** *helped me.* **Aucun de mes amis / d'entre eux** ne m'a aidé.

Les composés de *some*, *any* et *no*

quelqu'un / personne	quelque chose / rien	quelque part / nulle part
somebody / someone	something	somewhere
anybody / anyone	anything	anywhere
nobody / no one	nothing	nowhere

Ces composés obéissent aux mêmes règles que celles vues ci-dessus.
→ *I* ***didn't*** *buy* ***anything****. = I bought* ***nothing****.*

11 Complétez avec *some* ou *any*.

a. She took … headache tablets but they didn't have … effect.
b. Are there … eggs left in the fridge? I also need … butter for this recipe.
c. I haven't seen … of his movies.

12 Transformez ces phrases contenant *any* en utilisant *no* ou *none*.

a. I don't have any cash on me.
b. I didn't know anything about computers until I started this job.
c. They didn't invite any of us.

9 *Much, many* et la grande quantité

- Pour choisir entre *much* et *many*, il faut dans un premier temps examiner le nom qui suit : est-il dénombrable ou indénombrable (voir fiche 3, p. 244) ?

MUCH	*MANY*
NOM INDÉNOMBRABLE *(money, milk, luggage)*	NOM DÉNOMBRABLE AU PLURIEL *(dogs, houses, books)*

L'expression de la grande quantité (beaucoup de...)

- *Much* et *many* peuvent se traduire par « beaucoup de... » et sont synonymes de *a lot of*.
Notez que *much* et *many* sont plus souvent utilisés dans **les phrase négatives ou les questions.**

MUCH + nom indénombrable *Do you have **much money**?*	***MANY*** + nom dénombrable pluriel *Do you have **many friends**?*

Avec les deux types de noms :
a lot of / lots of / plenty of + nom dénombrable ou indénombrable
*She has **a lot of money / friends.***

Quand on veut associer un quantifieur avec un autre déterminant (*the, these, my...*) ou un pronom (*you, them...*), il faut utiliser *of.*
→ ***Many of my friends** know I'm allergic to dairy products.*
Beaucoup de mes amis savent que je suis allergique aux produits laitiers.

Autres emplois de *much* et *many*

- *Much* et *many* peuvent être associés à d'autres mots.

combien de... ?	***HOW MUCH*** **+ indénombrable** → ***How much money** do you need?* **De combien d'argent** as-tu besoin ?	***HOW MANY*** **+ dénombrable** → ***How many friends** do you have?* **Combien d'amis** as-tu ?
trop de...	***TOO MUCH*** **+ indénombrable** → *Sam has drunk **too much milk**.* Sam a bu **trop de lait**.	***TOO MANY*** **+ dénombrable** → *Sam has eaten **too many cookies.*** Sam a mangé **trop de cookies**.
tellement de...	***SO MUCH*** **+ indénombrable** → *She has so **much courage**!* Elle a **tellement de courage** !	***SO MANY*** **+ dénombrable** → *She has **so many friends**!* Elle a **tellement d'amis** !
autant de...	***AS MUCH*** **+ indénombrable + *AS...*** → *I earned **as much money as** you did.* J'ai gagné **autant d'argent que** toi.	***AS MANY*** **+ dénombrable + *AS...*** → *I have **as many friends as** you do.* J'ai **autant d'amis que** toi.

13 Le nom en gras est-il dénombrable ou indénombrable ? Complétez avec *much* ou *many*.

a. I don't have ... **clothes.**
b. How ... **languages** do you speak?
c. There isn't ... **time** left.
d. He took as ... **photos** as he could.
e. How ... **butter** should I use to make these cookies?
f. She was exhausted because she was carrying too ... **luggage**.
g. We can't talk here. There's too ... **noise**.

10 *(A) few, (a) little* et la petite quantité

L'expression de la petite quantité (un peu de / quelques...)

- Pour choisir entre *(a) few* et *(a) little*, il faut dans un premier temps examiner le nom qui suit : est-il dénombrable ou indénombrable (voir fiche 3, p. 244) ?

(A) LITTLE	*(A) FEW*
NOM INDÉNOMBRABLE *(money, milk, luggage)*	NOM DÉNOMBRABLE AU PLURIEL *(dogs, houses, books)*

Quand on veut associer ces quantifieurs avec un autre déterminant *(the, these, my...)* ou un pronom *(you, them...)*, il faut utiliser *of*.
→ ***Few of my friends / them** know I'm allergic to dairy products.*
Peu de mes amis / d'entre eux savent que je suis allergique aux produits laitiers.

- ***A** little* et ***a** few* indiquent qu'**une quantité est faible**. On les traduit par « un peu de » ou « quelques ».

A LITTLE + nom indénombrable	***A FEW*** + nom dénombrable pluriel
*Add **a little vinegar and salt**.*	*May I ask you **a few questions**?*
Ajoutez un **peu de vinaigre et de sel**.	Puis-je te poser **quelques questions** ?

- Il est possible d'utiliser *a little* seul, comme adverbe.
Dans ce cas, il peut aussi être remplacé par *a bit*, qui est plus familier.
→ *His hands were shaking **a little / a bit**.* Ses mains tremblaient **un peu**.

L'expression de la quantité insuffisante (peu de...)

- *Little* et *few* peuvent se traduire par « peu de... » : ils indiquent qu'**une quantité est jugée insuffisante**.

LITTLE + nom indénombrable	***FEW*** + nom dénombrable pluriel
*I'm happy even if I have **little money**.*	*She's hungry but she has **few biscuits** left.*
Je suis heureux même si j'ai **peu d'argent**.	Elle a faim mais il reste **peu de biscuits**.

- À la place de *few* et de *little*, il est courant d'utiliser *many* ou *much* dans des phrases négatives.
→ *I have **little** money. = I **don't** have **much** money.*
→ *I have **few** biscuits. = I **don't** have **many** biscuits.*

- Il est possible de renforcer *little* et *few* par *very*, *too* ou *so*.
→ *I have **so / very / too little** money.* J'ai **si / très / trop** peu d'argent.

14 Le nom en gras est-il dénombrable ou indénombrable ? Complétez avec *a little, little, a few* ou *few*.

a. Let's have a coffee. I have ... **time** before the train leaves.
b. Ben is very busy with his job. He has ... **time** for his family.
c. I'll be ... **minutes** late.
d. The exhibition was a flop: it was seen by very ... **visitors**.
e. With ... **luck**, you'll get the job.
f. Sarah called me ... **days** later.

11 Les adjectifs et les adverbes de degré

- Les adjectif sont rigoureusement **invariables** en anglais.
Ils ne s'accordent pas en nombre avec le nom qu'ils qualifient : *three **red** cars.*
- Les adjectifs épithètes sont toujours placés **avant le nom** qu'ils qualifient.

L'ordre des adjectifs épithètes

- Quand plusieurs adjectifs épithètes (c'est-à-dire placés avant le nom) se suivent, ils apparaissent dans l'ordre suivant :

	Opinion	**T**aille	**Â**ge	**C**ouleur	**O**rigine	**M**atière	
a	handsome		young		American		actor
a		large				gold	watch
a		big	old	red			car
an	amazing				British		novel

On utilise parfois l'acronyme OTACOM comme moyen mnémotechnique pour se souvenir de cet ordre.

Les adverbes de degré

- Les adverbes de degré sont des mots invariables qui se placent avant l'adjectif.
→ *You look **pretty / really / a bit / very** tired.* Tu as l'air **assez / vraiment / un peu / très** fatigué.

Ils donnent une indication sur l'intensité (ou le degré) de la qualité exprimée par l'adjectif :

bas degré (un peu)	**degré moyen (plutôt)**	**haut degré (très)**
a little	*quite* (plutôt, assez)	*very*
a bit [familier]	*rather* (plutôt, assez)	*really*
slightly (légèrement)	*pretty* (plutôt, assez)	*extremely*

- En revanche, l'adverbe *enough* (assez, suffisamment) /ɪ'nʌf/ se place directement **après** l'adjectif.
→ *Our teacher isn't **strict enough**.* Notre professeur n'est pas assez sévère.

15 Mettez les mots entre parenthèses dans le bon ordre.

a. She is a *(talented / young / very / British)* novelist.
b. I've bought *(cotton / long / blue)* socks.
c. He fell asleep on a *(comfortable / leather / large)* sofa.
d. There are lots of *(French / charming / little)* restaurants in the city centre.

16 Traduisez ces phrases en anglais.

a. Ces exercices sont un peu trop difficiles pour moi.
b. Les yeux de sa fille sont d'une couleur légèrement différente.
c. Mon appartement n'est pas assez grand.
d. Il a acheté une grande chemise bleue en coton.

12 La formation des adjectifs

Préfixes et suffixes

Il est possible de **former des adjectifs à partir de suffixes et de préfixes**.

- Certains **suffixes** permettent de transformer des noms en adjectifs.

-al	*origin → original*	***-ous, -eous* ou *-ious***	*courage → courageous*
-ful /fəl/ (qui a les qualités de…)	*respect → respectful*	***-less*** (marque l'absence de…)	*home → homeless*
-ic, -ical	*cube → cubic*	***-y***	*hair → hairy* (poilu)
-some /səm/	*trouble → troublesome*	***-ish***	*book → bookish* (studieux)

- **Les préfixes *un-* et *in-* / *im-*** permettent de former des adjectifs de sens contraire :
*comfortable → **un**comfortable* *happy → **un**happy* *possible → **im**possible* *visible → **in**visible*

Les adjectifs en *-ing* et en *-ed*

On peut **former un adjectif à partir d'un verbe** en lui rajoutant **la terminaison *-ing* ou *-ed*.**

Adjectif en *-ing* (ex. : *interesting, boring*)	Adjectif en *-ed* (ex. : *interested, bored*)
• indique que quelque chose ou quelqu'un **suscite, provoque** une qualité ou un sentiment (*this book is interesting* = ce livre **suscite** de l'intérêt). • se traduit souvent en français par **un participe présent en *-ant***, employé comme adjectif (ce livre est intéress**ant**).	• indique que quelqu'un **ressent** ou est affecté par un sentiment (*she's interested in literature* = elle **ressent** de l'intérêt pour la littérature). • se traduit souvent par un **participe passé français** (elle est intéress**ée**).

Tous les adjectifs en *-ed* ou *-ing* ne se traduisent pas par des participes : *boring* → ennuy**eux**.

Attention aussi à la traduction d'*excited* (« agité » ou « enthousiaste ») et d'*exciting* (« passionnant » ou « enthousiasmant »).

17 Transformez ces noms en adjectifs au moyen d'un suffixe. Attention, plusieurs solutions sont parfois possibles. Donnez une traduction à chaque fois.

power • pain • danger • child • success • wealth • poison • blood

18 Transformez le verbe entre parenthèses en adjectif en utilisant soit *-ing*, soit *-ed*. Traduisez les phrases ainsi obtenues en français.

a. His new book is really … *(disappoint)* and … *(bore)*.
b. He was so … *(disappoint)* that he didn't get the job!
c. I could listen to my history teacher for hours. She's so … *(interest)*!
d. Sarah is very … *(interest)* in biology.
e. The rugby match was really … *(excite)*.
f. My sister's coming home tomorrow – we're all very … *(excite)*.
g. The election results were … *(surprise)*.
h. I was … *(surprise)* she won the election.

13 Les comparatifs

Le comparatif de supériorité (plus... que...)

Adjectifs courts (d'une seule syllabe)	Adjectifs longs (deux syllabes ou plus)
ADJECTIF ***-er*** + ***THAN***... *Canada is **larger than** France.* Le Canada est **plus grand que** la France.	***MORE*** + ADJECTIF + ***THAN***... *Lucy is **more talented than** David.* Lucy est **plus talentueuse que** David.

- Les adjectifs en *-y* de deux syllabes forment leur comparatif en *-ier* : *happy* → *happier*.
- Les adjectifs en *-ow* et *-le* de deux syllabes forment souvent leur comparatif en *-er* : *narrow* → *narrower*, *simple* → *simpler*.
- Les adjectifs d'une syllabe qui se terminent par une voyelle unique suivie d'une consonne unique (V + C) doublent leur consonne : *big* → *bigger*, *hot* → *hotter*.

Il existe quelques **comparatifs irréguliers** :
good / well → *better*   *bad / badly* → *worse*   *far* → *farther / further*

Le comparatif d'égalité (aussi... que...)

AS + ADJECTIF + ***AS***...   *Beyoncé is **as popular as** Selena Gomez.*   Beyoncé est **aussi populaire que** Selena Gomez.

Dans une phrase négative, le premier *as* peut être remplacé par *so*.
*It's not **so** / **as hot as** yesterday.*

Le comparatif d'infériorité (moins... que...)

LESS + ADJECTIF + ***THAN***...   *An ice cream is **less expensive than** a hamburger.*   Une glace est **moins chère qu'**un hamburger.

L'emploi du comparatif d'infériorité en *less* est assez rare.
À la place, on préfère utiliser le **comparatif d'égalité à la forme négative**.
On dira donc plus volontiers : *An ice cream **isn't so / as expensive as** a hamburger.*

Le double comparatif

Pour traduire « de plus en plus », on utilise la structure ***more and more*** + **adjectif long** ou bien **adjectif-*er and* adjectif-*er*** si l'adjectif est court.
*Life is **more and more expensive.*** La vie est **de plus en plus chère.**
*It's getting **colder and colder.*** Il fait **de plus en plus froid.**

19 À partir des paires de phrases et des adjectifs entre parenthèses, produisez une phrase contenant un comparatif. Plusieurs solutions sont parfois possibles.

a. Big Ben is 96 meters tall. The Statue of Liberty is 93 meters high. *(high)*
b. Jane and Lucy are both 15 years old. *(young)*
c. In this restaurant, a burger costs £7. A pizza costs £10. *(cheap)*
d. I weigh 80kg. You weigh 72kg. *(heavy)*
e. The diameter of the Earth is 12,742km. The diameter of Mars is 6,779km. *(big)*

14 Les superlatifs

Le superlatif de supériorité (le / la plus...)

Adjectifs courts (d'une seule syllabe)	Adjectifs longs (deux syllabes ou plus)
THE* ADJECTIF *-est *Russia is **the** larg**est** country in the world.* La Russie est **le plus grand** pays au monde.	***THE MOST* + ADJECTIF** *She bought **the most** expensive car.* Elle a acheté la voiture **la plus chère.**

- Les adjectifs en *-y* de deux syllabes forment en général leur superlatif en *-iest* : *happy → happiest*.
- Les adjectifs en *-ow* et *-le* de deux syllabes forment souvent leur superlatif en *-est* : *narrow → narrowest*, *simple → simplest*.
- Les adjectifs d'une syllabe qui se terminent par une voyelle unique suivie d'une consonne unique (V + C) doublent leur consonne : *big → biggest*, *hot → hottest*

Il existe quelques **superlatifs irréguliers** :
good → best *bad → worst* *far → farthest / furthest*

Le superlatif d'infériorité (le / la moins...)

***THE LEAST* + ADJECTIF LONG OU COURT** *She bought **the least** expensive car.* Elle a acheté la voiture **la moins chère**.

Le choix de la préposition après un superlatif : *in* ou *of* ?

- En anglais, on utilise normalement ***in*** si le complément désigne **un lieu** ou **un groupe de personnes**.
*She is **the most brilliant** girl **in the class**.* C'est la fille **la plus brillante de la classe.**
- Si le complément désigne **une période**, on utilise ***of***.
*This is **the best** film **of the year 2023!*** C'est **le meilleur** film **de l'année 2023 !**

Parler de son expérience au moyen d'un superlatif

Le superlatif est souvent suivi d'une proposition relative (introduite par *that* ou par aucun pronom relatif) dont **le verbe est au *present perfect*** et est employé avec **l'adverbe *ever*.**
*This is **the funniest** film **that/Ø I've ever seen**.* C'est le film **le plus drôle que j'aie jamais vu.**

20 Mettez l'adjectif entre parenthèses au superlatif de supériorité. Choisissez le cas échéant la préposition qui convient (*of* ou *in*).

a. Brazil is the ... *(large)* country **in** / **of** South America.
b. Where is the ... *(near)* hospital?
c. It was the ... *(terrifying)* experience **in** / **of** my life.
d. Is Elon Musk still the ... *(rich)* man **in** / **of** the world?
e. He's one of the ... *(experienced)* players **in** / **of** the league.
f. He's the ... *(bad)* singer I have ever heard!
g. His bedroom is the ... *(dirty)* place **in** / **of** the house.

21 Produisez 5 phrases pour évoquer vos goûts en matière de cinéma, de musique ou de littérature. Utilisez une structure composée d'un superlatif suivi d'un verbe au *present perfect* employé avec *ever*. Utilisez les adjectifs suivants : *interesting* • *scary* • *bad* • *weird* • *boring*.

Exemple : Interstellar *is the most fascinating film I've ever seen.*

15 Le verbe *be*

Conjugaison

Présent			
Forme affirmative		Forme négative	
Forme pleine	Forme contractée	Forme pleine	Forme contractée
I **am**	I**'m**	I **am not**	I**'m not** (*ou* **'m not**)
you **are**	you**'re**	you **are not**	you **aren't** (*ou* **'re not**)
she/he/it **is**	she/he/it**'s**	she/he/it **is not**	she/he/it **isn't** (*ou* **'s not**)
we/you/they **are**	we/you/they**'re**	we/you/they **are not**	we/you/they **aren't** (*ou* **'re not**)

Prétérit		
Forme affirmative	Forme négative	
	Forme pleine	Forme contractée
I **was**	I **was not**	I **wasn't**
you **were**	you **were not**	you **weren't**
she/he/it **was**	she/he/it **was not**	she/he/it **wasn't**
we/you/they **were**	we/you/they **were not**	we/you/they **weren't**

- Au *present prefect* ou au *past perfect*, on utilise le participe passé *been* : *I have / had* ***been.***
- À l'impératif, sa forme est *be* et sa forme négative est ***don't be***.
  Be *nice to me!* Sois gentil avec moi !
  Don't be *so selfish!* Ne soyez pas si égoïstes !

Emplois

On utilise *be* dans les cas suivants :

lorsqu'il est suivi d'un adjectif.	*She* ***is*** *American.*
pour donner un âge.	*I* ***am*** *15 years old.*
dans l'expression *there is/are* (pour traduire « il y a… »). Attention à l'accord du verbe !	*There* ***is*** *a car in the driveway.* *There* ***are*** *a lot of cars in the car park.*
au passif (*be* est alors auxiliaire et est suivi d'un participe passé).	*The house* ***was destroyed*** *in 2022.*
pour construire les formes verbales en *be* + V-*ing*.	*The dog* ***is sleeping*** *in the garden.*

22 Mettez le verbe *be* à la forme indiquée entre parenthèses. Donnez la forme pleine et la forme contractée (si celle-ci est possible).

a. The party … *(présent)* on Friday.
b. I … *(présent, forme négative)* ready yet.
c. We … *(prétérit, forme négative)* pleased to see him.
d. I … *(present perfect avec* never*)* to San Francisco.
e. There … *(prétérit)* a glass on the table.
f. … *(impératif, forme négative)* so rude!
g. There … *(prétérit)* a lot of people in the restaurant.

23 Dites si *'s* correspond au verbe *is*, *has* ou est la marque du génitif. Traduisez les phrases.

a. Miranda**'s** 16 years old.
b. I've never met my neighbour**'s** wife.
c. Brenda**'s** bought a new car.
d. He**'s** in the kitchen.
e. He**'s** using my mobile.

16 Le verbe *have*

Quand *have* est un verbe lexical

- Lorsque *have* signifie « posséder », on construit **sa forme négative et interrogative** au présent et au prétérit simple au moyen de **l'auxiliaire *do / did*.**

Présent		
Forme affirmative	**Forme négative**	**Forme interrogative**
I/we/you/they **have**	I/we/you/they **do not have** (*ou* **don't have**)	**do** I/we/you/they **have**...?
she/he/it **has**	she/he/it **does not have** (*ou* **doesn't have**)	**does** she/he/it **have**...?
Prétérit		
Forme affirmative	**Forme négative**	**Forme interrogative**
I/you/he... **had**	I/you/he... **did not have** (*ou* **didn't have**)	**did** I/he/they... **have**...?

- La structure ***have to* + V** exprimant l'obligation construit aussi sa forme négative et interrogative au moyen de l'auxiliaire *do / did*.
*I **don't have** to go to work.* Je n'ai pas à aller travailler. / Je n'ai pas besoin d'aller au travail.

Quand *have* est un auxiliaire

- Quand *have* est **un auxiliaire**, il peut se contracter et on construit sa forme négative en ajoutant *not*.

Présent			
Forme affirmative		**Forme négative**	
Forme pleine	**Forme contractée**	**Forme pleine**	**Forme contractée**
I/we/you/they **have**	I/we/you/they**'ve**	I/we/you/they **have not**	I/we/you/they **haven't** (*ou* **'ve not**)
she/he/it **has**	she/he/it**'s**	she/he/it **has not**	she/he/it **hasn't** (*ou* **'s not**)
Prétérit			
Forme affirmative		**Forme négative**	
Forme pleine	**Forme contractée**	**Forme pleine**	**Forme contractée**
I/you/he... **had**	I/you/he...**'d**	I/you/he... **had not**	I/you/he... **hadn't** (*ou* **'d not**)

- On emploie l'auxiliaire *have* au *present perfect* et au *past perfect*.
Il est alors suivi d'un participe passé. *I**'ve eaten** too much.* J'ai trop mangé.

Dans l'expression ***have got*** (employée surtout en anglais britannique), *have* fonctionne comme un auxiliaire et peut donc se contracter.
*I**'ve got** an amazing family.* J'ai une famille extraordinaire.

24 Dans les phrases suivantes...

a) dites si *have* est un auxiliaire ou un verbe lexical. Sur quels indices vous êtes-vous appuyé ?
b) contractez ces formes si c'est possible puis mettez-les à la forme négative.

a. Her mother **has** brown hair.
b. They **have** a house in Brighton.
c. He **has** eaten all the cookies.
d. We almost **had** an accident on the highway.
e. I **had** to wait for two hours.
f. I **have got** a headache.

17 Le présent simple

Formation

Forme affirmative		Forme négative	Forme interrogative
Toutes les personnes sauf la 3e pers. du singulier	verbe + Ø I **work**	*do not / don't* + verbe I **don't work**	*do* + sujet + verbe **do** I **work**?
3e pers. du singulier	verbe + -s he **works**	*does not / doesn't* + verbe he **doesn't work**	*does* + sujet + verbe **does** he **work**?

Les verbes qui se terminent par *-s*, *-z*, *-sh*, *-ch* et *-o* prennent **-es à la 3e personne** (*she watch**es**, he finish**es**, he go**es***).
La 3e personne de *have* est *ha**s***.

Emplois

On utilise le présent simple dans les cas suivants :

- pour exprimer **une habitude.**
  *Monica **gets up** at 7 o'clock every morning.* Monica se lève à 7 heures tous les matins.
  Dans ce cas, le présent simple est utilisé avec **des adverbes** ou **des compléments de temps** qui expriment **la fréquence, la répétition** :

  often | *every day / every week / every year...* | *usually* (d'habitude) | *never* | *sometimes* | *always* | *rarely / seldom* (rarement) | *occasionally* | *in general / generally*

- pour exprimer **les vérités générales**, c'est-à-dire des vérités vraies en tout temps.
  *Water **boils** at 100°C.* L'eau bout à 100 degrés.
- pour donner **une caractéristique**.
  *She **works** in a university.* Elle travaille dans une université. [= C'est sa profession.]
- avec **des verbes qui décrivent des états** : **les verbes de goût** (*like, hate, dislike*), **de cognition** (*know, understand*), **d'opinion** (*think, believe, suppose*) ou **de volonté** (*want*).
  *I **think** that he **doesn't like** me.* Je crois qu'il ne m'aime pas.
- pour parler d'**un événement futur qui est planifié** (horaire, emploi du temps) et dont la réalisation est considérée comme certaine.
  *My plane **takes off** at 7 o'clock.* Mon avion décolle à 7 heures.
- comme **présent de narration** ou quand on résume une histoire (film, roman).
  In Harry Potter and the Chamber of Secrets, *Harry, Ron, and Hermione **return** to Hogwarts for their second year.* Dans *Harry Potter et la Chambre des Secrets*, Harry, Ron et Hermione retournent à Poudlard pour leur deuxième année d'étude.

25 a) **Justifiez l'emploi du présent simple dans chacune des phrases ci-contre : habitude ? Vérité générale ? Caractéristique ? Verbe d'état ?**

b) **Mettez ces phrases à la forme interrogative.**

a. Koalas sleep 18 hours a day.
b. They all know the truth.
c. I speak English fluently.
d. She goes to the post office every day.
e. Ice melts at 0°C.
f. I often watch television.
g. My train leaves at 5 o'clock.

18 Le présent en *be* + V-*ing*

Formation

- Le présent en *be* + V-*ing* se forme à l'aide de **l'auxiliaire *be* conjugué au présent**.
On ajoute **la terminaison -*ing* au verbe**.

Forme affirmative	Forme négative
I'**m** (*ou* **am**) work**ing** he/she/it'**s** (*ou* **is**) work**ing** you/we/they'**re** (*ou* **are**) work**ing**	I'**m not** (*ou* **am not**) work**ing** he/she/it **isn't** (*ou* **is not**) work**ing** you/we/they **aren't** (*ou* **are not**) work**ing**
Forme interrogative	
am I work**ing**? **is** he/she/it work**ing**? **are** you/we/they work**ing**?	

- On double la consonne finale avant -*ing* dans les verbes qui se terminent par **une voyelle unique suivie d'une consonne unique** (V + C) : *stop* → *sto**pp**ing*, *plan* → *pla**nn**ing* (mais *look* → *look**ing***, *write* → *writ**ing***).

Emplois

- Le présent en *be* + V-*ing* sert **à décrire ou à commenter un événement qui est en cours de déroulement** (et donc qui n'a pas atteint son terme) au moment même de la prise de parole.
*It'**s** rain**ing** today.* Il pleut aujourd'hui.

- Il est donc utilisé **pour décrire ce que l'on voit**. On l'utilise aussi pour décrire une image.
*Look! Timothy **is** runn**ing** in the schoolyard.* Regarde ! Timothy court dans la cour de l'école.

- On utilise également *be* + V-*ing* pour parler **d'un événement futur**. Il exprime alors **une intention.**
On le traduit souvent en français par un présent à valeur de futur.
***Are** you com**ing** tomorrow?* Est-ce que tu viens demain ?

- Il est aussi employé pour évoquer des situations temporaires (qui ne durent pas).
*He is out of work. So he'**s** liv**ing** at his parents' house at the moment.* Il est au chômage.
Il vit donc chez ses parents en ce moment.

> On **n'utilise** normalement **pas** le présent en *be* + V-*ing* avec les verbes qui expriment des états : les verbes de goût (*like, hate, dislike*), de cognition (*know*), d'opinion (*think, believe, suppose*), de volonté (*want*), etc.

26 Mettez le verbe au présent simple ou au présent en *be* + V-*ing*.

a. Please, be quiet. The children ... *(sleep)*.
b. Don't talk to me now! I ... *(write)* an important e-mail.
c. The Sun ... *(rise)* in the East.
d. He ... *(see)* his children every weekend and ... *(take)* them to dinner every Wednesday evening.
e. "Where are the girls?" "They ... *(do)* their homework in their bedrooms."
f. I ... *(feel)* like she ... *(not / like)* her boss. She ... *(often / criticise)* her.
g. Excuse me, I ... *(think)* you ... *(sit)* in my seat.
h. What ... *(you / wear)* today?

19 Le prétérit simple

Formation

Forme affirmative	Forme négative	Forme interrogative
Verbe régulier + *-ed* : *I work**ed*** OU **Forme irrégulière à apprendre (voir p. 275) :** *I **sang***	***did not / didn't*** + verbe *I **didn't work*** *I **didn't sing***	***did*** + sujet + verbe ***did** you **work**?* ***did** you **sing**?*

- On double la consonne finale avant *-ed* dans les verbes qui se terminent par **une voyelle unique suivie d'une consonne unique** (V + C) :
*stop → sto**pp**ed, plan → pla**nn**ed* (mais *hope → hoped*).

- Les verbes se terminant par *-y* forment leur prétérit **en *-ied*** :
*try → tr**ied**, justify → justif**ied***.

Emplois

- Le prétérit est avant tout **le temps du récit** : il s'agit de raconter des événements révolus, nettement détachés du moment présent. On l'utilise ainsi dans les romans, les contes, les livres d'histoire, les narrations de faits objectifs, etc.
*Queen Elizabeth II **died** on September 8, 2022, at the age of 96.*
La reine Elizabeth II est morte le 8 septembre 2022 à l'âge de 96 ans.

- Il est souvent accompagné **de compléments de temps qui datent un événement** (*yesterday, last year, in 2019, once, on Tuesday...*) ou bien d'adverbes qui marquent les différentes étapes d'un récit (*first, then, later...*).
*I **met** her **on Monday**. We **went** to the movies. **Then**, we **had** dinner in an Italian restaurant.*
Je l'ai rencontrée lundi. Nous sommes allés au cinéma. Puis, nous avons dîné dans un restaurant italien.

27 Mettez le verbe entre parenthèses au prétérit, puis mettez les phrases à la forme négative et interrogative.

a. Her plane ... *(land)* at 3 pm.
b. They ... *(grow up)* in London.
c. Manchester ... *(win)* the match.
d. They ... *(meet)* in Ireland last year.

28 Mettez le verbe au prétérit simple. Attention aux verbes irréguliers.

a. The police ... *(identify)* and ... *(arrest)* the murderer.
b. "Where ... *(buy / you)* those cookies?"
"I ... *(buy)* them at Tesco's."
c. We ... *(eat)* dinner at seven, then we ... *(go)* out.
d. I ... *(say)* goodbye to my grandmother at the airport. She ... *(kiss)* me and ... *(give)* me a big hug.
e. The moment we ... *(see)* this apartment, we ... *(know)* we ... *(want)* to buy it.
f. He ... *(find)* a ten-dollar bill on the sidewalk. He ... *(pick)* it up and ... *(put)* it in his pocket.
g. At 20 he ... *(leave)* school to find a job and support his family.

20 Le prétérit en *be* + V-*ing*

Formation

- Le prétérit en *be* + V-*ing* se forme de la même manière que le présent en *be* + V-*ing*, à la différence près que l'auxiliaire *be* est conjugué au prétérit *(was / were)*.

Forme affirmative	Forme négative
I/he/she **was** sleep**ing**	I/he/she **was not/wasn't** sleep**ing**
you/we/they **were** sleep**ing**	you/we/they **were not/weren't** sleep**ing**

- La forme interrogative se construit en plaçant le sujet après l'auxiliaire : ***Were** you sleeping?*
- On double la consonne finale avant *-ing* dans les verbes qui se terminent par **une voyelle unique suivie d'une consonne unique** (V + C) : *stop* → *sto**pping***, *plan* → *pla**nning*** (mais *look* → *look**ing***, *write* → *writ**ing***).

Certains verbes **ne s'emploient** en principe **pas** à la forme en *be* + V-*ing* : il s'agit de verbes de volonté *(want)*, de goût *(like, love, hate)*, d'opinion *(think, believe)*...

Emplois

- On utilise le prétérit en *be* + V-*ing* pour indiquer qu'à un certain moment du passé, un événement **était en cours de déroulement et n'était pas achevé.**
  → *I **was sleeping** when Marcia called.* Je **dormais** / J'**étais en train de dormir** quand Marcia a appelé.

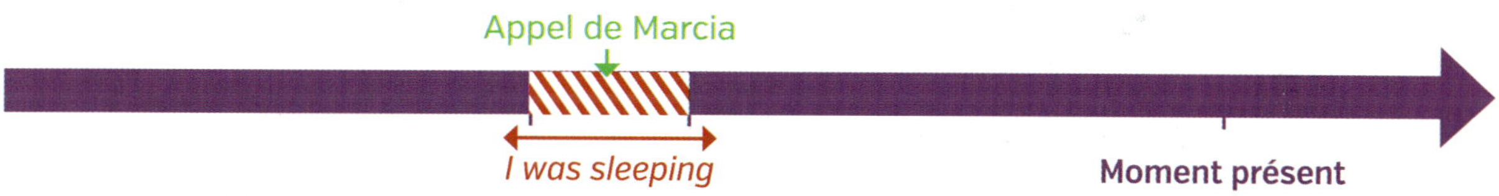

On peut le traduire en français par « était en train de... » (j'étais en train de dormir) ou par un imparfait (je dormais).

- On trouve souvent le prétérit en *be* + V-*ing* dans des phrases contenant une proposition introduite par ***when*** (quand), ***(just) as*** (lorsque, alors que) ou ***while*** (pendant que) : on indique alors qu'un événement ponctuel (au prétérit simple) est survenu pendant qu'un autre événement était en cours.
  → *A man **came** to talk to me while I **was having** lunch.*
  événement ponctuel (came) — **événement déjà en cours** (was having)
  Un homme **est venu** me parler pendant que je **déjeunais**.
- Le prétérit en *be* + V-*ing* est parfois employé **pour décrire, commenter ou justifier** une situation passée.
  → *It was clear from the beginning that he **was lying**.* Il était clair depuis le début qu'il mentait.
  → *The sun **was shining**. I knew it would be a good day.* Le soleil brillait. Je savais que cela allait être une belle journée.

29 Mettez le verbe au prétérit simple ou au prétérit en *be* + V-*ing*.

a. What ... *(you / do)* at 5pm when the accident ... *(happen)*?
b. Just as I ... *(leave)* the house, I ... *(realise)* that my wallet was upstairs.
c. Last night, I ... *(hear)* an explosion while I ... *(walk)* my dog.
d. I ... *(drive)* to work when my car ... *(break down)*.
e. I ... *(watch)* television when the lights ... *(go)* off.

21 Le *present perfect* simple (*have* + V-*en*)

Formation

- Le *present perfect* se forme à l'aide de **l'auxiliaire *have* conjugué au présent** suivi du participe passé (verbe régulier + V-*ed* ou forme irrégulière à apprendre, voir liste p. 275, 3e colonne).

Forme affirmative	Forme négative
I/you/we/they**'ve** (*ou* **have**) work**ed**	I/you/we/they **haven't** (*ou* **have not**) work**ed**
she/he/it**'s** (*ou* **has**) work**ed**	she/he/it **hasn't** (*ou* **has not**) work**ed**

- La forme interrogative se construit en plaçant le sujet après l'auxiliaire.
→ ***Have** you worked a lot?*

Emplois

Le *present perfect* permet de **mettre en relation un événement passé avec le moment présent.** On l'utilise en particulier :

- pour indiquer **un lien de cause à effet** entre un événement passé et une situation présente. Son emploi implique donc **un résultat au moment où l'on parle** (explicite ou implicite).

→ ***I've fixed** your computer. It's working now.* J'ai réparé ton ordinateur. Il fonctionne maintenant.
cause — conséquente présente

- pour **faire un bilan** et parler de **son expérience**. Dans ce cas, on l'utilise souvent avec certains adverbes tels que ***never*** / ***ever***, ***already***, ***yet*** (déjà), ***always***... (voir fiche 22, p. 263).
→ ***I've never seen** this film.* Je n'ai jamais vu ce film.
→ ***She's always liked** creative people.* Elle a toujours aimé les gens créatifs.

On le trouve aussi après ***it's the first time...***
→ ***It's the first time I've met** him*. C'est la première fois que je le rencontre.

- pour dire qu'un état ou une action a commencé dans le passé et se poursuit jusqu'au moment présent. On trouve cet emploi avec des compléments de temps introduits par ***for* et *since* (tous les deux traduits par « depuis »)** pour traduire **un présent français.**
→ ***I've known** him **for 10 years**.* Je le **connais** depuis 10 ans.

- avec **les adverbes *just*, *recently* ou *lately*** pour indiquer qu'**un événement est récent**.
→ ***I've just called** Marcia.* Je viens d'appeler Marcia.

En anglais américain, on utilise en général le prétérit avec ces adverbes : *I **just called** Marcia*.

30 Conjuguez les verbes suivants au *present perfect*. Attention aux verbes irréguliers.

a. He ... *(already / call)* the emergency services.
b. Who ... *(you / invite)* to the party?
c. I ... *(always / want)* to go to Scotland.
d. Don't worry! We ... *(already / buy)* the tickets.
e. It's the most absurd story I ... *(hear / ever)*.
f. The owner is ruined: his hotel ... *(go)* bankrupt.
g. I ... *(not / see)* him for ages.

22 Prétérit ou *present perfect* ?

Le prétérit…

- permet d'évoquer un fait passé **sans envisager de lien** avec le moment présent.
- permet de **raconter** une histoire, de relater des événements historiques.
- permet de **dater** un événement avec précision.

Le *present perfect*…

- **met en relation** un événement passé avec le moment présent.
- permet de parler de **son expérience** ou de faire **un bilan**.
- permet de dire qu'un fait commencé dans le passé **est toujours d'actualité**.

Le meilleur moyen d'utiliser la forme correcte est **d'examiner les compléments de temps**.

Cas où le prétérit est obligatoire

Le prétérit est obligatoire avec **un complément de temps qui date un événement de manière précise et ponctuelle** (hier, la semaine dernière, en 2016). On le trouve par exemple toujours avec les expressions suivantes :

yesterday | ***in 2016*** | ***in the 19th century*** | ***last week / month / year…*** | ***that day*** | les questions en ***when…*** | ***then*** | compléments de temps avec ***ago***

→ *She **arrived** in Miami **yesterday / last week / on Tuesday / 3 days ago.***
Elle est arrivée à Miami hier / la semaine dernière / mardi / il y a trois jours.

Cas où le *present perfect* est employé

- On utilise le *present perfect* quand on souhaite exprimer un bilan ou rendre compte de son expérience avec **des adverbes ou compléments de temps en rapport avec le moment présent** :

never / ever | ***always*** | ***already / yet*** | ***so far / up to now*** | ***over the past few years***

→ *I **have never seen** this film.* Je n'ai jamais vu ce film.
→ ***I've already read** that book.* J'ai déjà lu ce livre.

- Le *present perfect* est obligatoire avec *for* et *since* (dans le sens de « depuis ») **pour traduire un présent français.**

→ *She has been married **for 10 years.*** Elle **est** mariée **depuis 10 ans**.

On trouve parfois le prétérit avec *for* mais dans ce cas, on le traduit par « pendant ».
→ *He **worked** in a factory **for 10 years.*** Il a travaillé dans une usine **pendant 10 ans**.

31 Repérez les compléments de temps puis mettez les verbes entre parenthèses au prétérit ou au *present perfect*. Attention aux verbes irréguliers.

a. I … *(see)* them yesterday afternoon.
b. I … *(never / like)* sports.
c. My grandmother … *(retire)* 10 years ago.
d. So far we … *(collect)* over $3,000.
e. World War I … *(break out)* in August 1914.
f. When … *(you / leave)* Los Angeles?
g. They … *(not / have)* a vacation since last year.

23 Le *present perfect* en *be* + V-*ing*

- Le *present perfect* en *be* + V-*ing* se forme de la manière suivante :

Forme affirmative	Forme négative
I/you/we/they **'ve** (*ou* **have**) **been** work**ing**	I/you/we/they **haven't** (*ou* **have not**) **been** work**ing**
she/he/it**'s** (*ou* **has**) **been** work**ing**	she/he/it **hasn't** (*ou* **has not**) **been** work**ing**

- La forme interrogative se construit en plaçant le sujet après l'auxiliaire : ***Have** you **been** work**ing**?*

Certains verbes ne s'emploient en principe pas à la forme en *be* + V-*ing* : il s'agit de verbes de volonté *(want)*, de goût *(like, love, hate)*, d'opinion *(think, believe)*...

Quand utiliser la forme simple ?

- Le *present perfect* simple insiste **sur le résultat** (en particulier sur les conséquences sur le complément d'objet du verbe).
  → *Trevor has repaired **the car**.* (= ***The car** is working now.*)

- Le *present perfect* simple exprimant un bilan ou insistant sur un résultat, on utilise **la forme simple** avec des expressions qui expriment **la quantité** (ou dans des questions introduites par *how much / many*). Dans ce cas, *have been* + V-*ing* est normalement impossible.
  → ***How many** cups of coffee **have** you **drunk** today?* Combien de cafés as-tu bu aujourd'hui ?
  → *I **have drunk three** cups of coffee today.* J'ai bu trois cafés aujourd'hui.

Quand utiliser la forme en *be* + V-*ing* ?

- Le *present perfect* en *be* + V-*ing* met, quant à lui, l'accent sur **l'activité en elle-même** et ses conséquences sur le sujet du verbe.
  → ***Trevor** has been repairing the car.* (= ***Trevor** is tired, his clothes are dirty, etc.*)

- Le *present perfect* en *be* + V-*ing* est très souvent utilisé **avec *for* et *since* (tous les deux traduits par « depuis »)** : il s'agit en effet d'indiquer qu'une activité commencée dans le passé se poursuit au moment où l'on parle.
  → ***I've been working** for 2 hours.* Je travaille depuis deux heures.
  Ici, le résultat importe peu et on insiste plutôt sur ce que l'on a fait et combien de temps cela a duré.

- On l'utilise parfois pour **dire avec un ton accusateur que quelqu'un s'est adonné à une activité.**
  → *You**'ve been using** my computer again!* Toi, tu as encore utilisé mon ordinateur !

32 Mettez le verbe au *present perfect* simple ou en *be* + V-*ing*.

a. We ... *(peel and boil)* 5 kg of potatoes.
b. She ... *(look)* for her glasses for 15 minutes.
c. Jimmy's eyes are red. He... *(cry)*.
d. I ... *(know)* Daniel since 2017.
e. How much pasta ... *(you / cook)*?
f. I'm exhausted. I ... *(cook)* all day.
g. Don't lie to me. You ... *(watch)* horror movies again.

24 Le *past perfect*

Formation

On forme le *past perfect* simple à l'aide de **l'auxiliaire *have* conjugué au prétérit** (*had* ou *'d* à la forme contractée) et **du participe passé du verbe** (V+-*ed* ou forme irrégulière à apprendre voir liste p. 275, 3e colonne,). Sa forme est identique à toutes les personnes.

Forme affirmative	Forme négative	Forme interrogative
I'**d** / **had** work**ed**	I **hadn't** (*ou* **had not**) work**ed**	**Had** I work**ed**?

L'expression de l'antériorité

Le *past perfect* indique qu'**un événement passé est antérieur à un autre événement, lui aussi passé,** et conjugué au prétérit. Il correspond la plupart du temps **au plus-que-parfait français.**

→ *Anthony **bought** the book that the teacher **had recommended** to us.*
-1 -2
Anthony **a acheté** le livre que le professeur nous **avait conseillé**.

Emplois

On rencontre souvent le *past perfect* :

- dans **des propositions de temps introduites par *after***.
  → *I **called** the police after he**'d left**.* J'ai appelé la police après qu'il est parti.
  -1 -2
- mais également avec des adverbes tels que ***just, before, yet*** **ou** ***already*** qui marquent l'antériorité.
  → *When I **arrived** at the station, the train **had just left**.* Quand je suis arrivé à la gare, le train venait de partir.
  -1 -2
- **au discours indirect** après des verbes de parole ou de pensée au prétérit (*He **said** / **thought** that...*) afin de respecter **la concordance des temps**.
  → *Bruce **said** he **had been** absent the day before.* Bruce a dit qu'il **avait été** absent la veille.
  -1 -2

33 Conjuguez les verbes au *past perfect*. Attention aux verbes irréguliers.

a. We ... *[never / be]* to Wales before.
b. While she was talking to me, I suddenly realised that I ... *[see]* her somewhere before.
c. He panicked because he ... *[not / bring]* his ID card with him.
d. She told me she ... *[have]* a lovely day at the office.

34 Mettez les verbes au prétérit ou au *past perfect*.

a. I ... *[never / meet]* anyone from Leeds before I ... *[meet]* James.
b. We ... *[ask]* Rebecca if she ... *[want]* to go to the cinema, but she ... *[tell]* us she ... *[finish / not]* her homework yet.
c. She ... *[return]* home because she ... *[forget]* her purse.

25 L'expression du futur

Le modal *will*

Forme affirmative	Forme négative	Forme interrogative
I'**ll** / **will** work	I **won't** (*ou* **will not**) work	**Will** I work?

- On utilise le modal *will* pour faire **une prédiction** et dire qu'un fait a **toutes les chances de se produire**.
  → *I'm quite certain that she **will pass** her exam.* Je suis presque certain qu'elle réussira son examen.
- On l'utilise pour faire **une promesse**.
  → *I **will come** to your party.* Je viendrai à ta fête. [= Je m'y engage.]
- Il est employé quand on prend une **décision spontanée**, « sur le moment ».
  → *Don't move! I'**ll answer** the phone.* Ne bouge pas ! Je vais répondre au téléphone.

Be going to + V

- On emploie ***be going to*** **+ V** quand des indices indiquent que quelque chose va se produire.
  → *Look at the clouds! It looks like it'**s going to rain.*** Regarde les nuages ! On dirait qu'il va pleuvoir.
- On l'utilise pour exprimer **une intention** et dire qu'**une décision a été prise.**
  → *I'**m going to tell** him the truth.* Je vais lui dire la vérité. [= J'ai réfléchi.]

Be going to n'est pas nécessairement employé pour évoquer des événements proches dans le temps. Inversement, *will* n'exprime pas forcément un futur lointain.

Le présent en *be* + V-*ing*

On utilise parfois **le présent en *be* + V-*ing*** pour évoquer un événement à venir. Il s'agit souvent d'un projet, d'un événement qu'on a déjà planifié. On le traduit souvent par un présent en français.
→ *I'**m meeting** Bradley at 8pm.* Je vois Bradley à 20 heures.

L'expression du futur dans les propositions de temps

On n'utilise jamais le futur en *will* dans **les propositions de temps** introduites par ***when***, ***as soon as*** (dès que), ***until*** (jusqu'à ce que...), etc. À la place, il faut utiliser **le présent simple**.
→ *I'll call you **when / as soon** as I **get** home.* Je t'appellerai quand / dès que je rentrerai à la maison.

Le verbe principal *(call)* est en revanche employé avec *will*.

35 Mettez le verbe à la forme qui convient : *will* + V, présent en *be* + V-*ing* ou *be going to* + V.

a. Be careful! Your shoelaces are undone. You ... *(fall)*!
b. How old ... *(you / be)* on your next birthday?
c. We ... *(get)* married in July.
d. I can't see you this afternoon. I ... *(play)* tennis with Beverly.
e. Oh no, there's no more spaghetti left. I ... *(have)* the pizza instead then.

36 Imaginez la suite. Produisez deux phrases à chaque fois.

a. I'll wait until...
b. As soon as I get home...
c. Mum will be very upset when...

26 Les auxiliaires modaux

Les modaux sont **des auxiliaires**. Ils ont des propriétés que l'on ne trouve pas avec les verbes « ordinaires » (comme *play* ou *help*, par exemple).

- Ils sont suivis de **la base verbale** du verbe (l'infinitif sans *to*) : *She **must help** him.*
- Ils ne prennent pas de *-s* à la 3e personne du singulier : *He **can** swim.*
- On forme **les questions** en inversant l'auxiliaire et le sujet (et sans utiliser *do*) : *You **can** help him. **Can** you help him?*
- Ils portent directement **la marque *not* de la négation** (et se contractent souvent avec cette dernière) : *You must **not** (ou must**n't**) tell him the truth.*
- On les utilise dans **les réponses brèves ou les *tags*** : *"He can't swim, **can he**?" "Of course, he **can**!"*

Les 9 auxiliaires modaux

Modal	Forme négative pleine	Forme négative contractée
will ou *'ll*	*will not*	*won't* /wəʊnt/
would ou *'d* /wʊd/	*would not*	*wouldn't*
can	*cannot*	*can't* GB : /kɑːnt/, US : /kænt/
could /kʊd/	*could not*	*couldn't*
may	*may not*	*mayn't* (rare)
might	*might not*	*mightn't* (rare)
shall /ʃæl/	*shall not*	*shan't*
should /ʃʊd/	*should not*	*shouldn't*
must	*must not*	*mustn't* /'mʌsənt/

On ne prononce pas la lettre *l* dans *could* /kʊd/, *should* /ʃʊd/ et *would* /wʊd/. La forme négative « pleine » de *can* s'écrit en un seul mot : *cannot*.

Les substituts des modaux

Les modaux n'ont pas d'infinitif, ils ne peuvent pas suivre un autre modal (en particulier *will* et *would*), *must* n'a pas de forme passée, etc. On utilise alors des substituts tels que *be able to* ou *have to*.

Substitut	Remplace...	Exprime...	Exemple
be able to	*can*	la capacité (voir fiche 27)	*I'll **be able to come** on time.* Je pourrai venir à l'heure.
have to	*must*	l'obligation (voir fiche 28)	*I **had to get up** early this morning.* J'ai dû / Il a fallu me lever tôt ce matin.
be allowed to /ə'laʊd/	*may (not), can't, mustn't*	la permission ou l'interdiction (forme négative)	*You **are not allowed to smoke** here.* Tu n'es pas autorisé à fumer ici.

37 Choisissez le modal qui convient.

a. Geraniums **would / must / might** be watered regularly.
b. I **can't / wouldn't / couldn't** drive because I don't have a driving licence.
c. **Should / Would / May** I use your phone, please?
d. You look so pale. You **should / can / may** go to the doctor's.
e. When I was a child, I **might / could / can** run very fast.
f. You **must / shall / would** be tired after your long journey.

27 L'expression de la capacité

Les modaux *can* et *could*

- *Can* permet d'exprimer une capacité présente. *Could* permet d'exprimer une capacité passée (je pouvais) ou hypothétique (je pourrais).

Forme affirmative	Forme négative	Forme interrogative
I **can help** you	I **cannot / can't help** you	**Can** I **help** you?
I **could help** you	I **could not / couldn't help** you	**Could** I **help** you?

On ne prononce pas la lettre *l* dans *could* /kʊd/.
La forme négative de *can* s'écrit en un mot : *cannot*.

- En anglais, on utilise très souvent le modal *can / could* avec **les verbes de perception** *(hear, see, feel...).*
→ ***Can*** *you* ***hear*** *me?* M'entendez-vous ?

Be able to + V

On utilise *be able to* + V à la place de *can*, en particulier quand on ne peut pas utiliser ce dernier : après un modal (notamment *will*), à l'infinitif, au *present perfect*, etc.
→ *I don't know if I* ***will be able to*** *come.* Je ne sais pas si je pourrai venir.

Autres structures

D'autres structures ou verbes permettent d'exprimer la capacité.

manage to do sth (parvenir à faire qqc)	*He* ***managed to*** *persuade her to come.* Il est parvenu à la persuader de venir.
succeed in doing sth (réussir à faire qqc)	*He* ***succeeded in*** *persuad****ing*** *her to come.* Il est parvenu à la persuader de venir.
be unable to do sth (être incapable de faire qqc)	*He****'s unable to*** *win a medal.* Il est incapable de gagner une médaille.
be (in)capable of doing sth (être (in)capable de faire qqc)	*She****'s incapable of*** *ly****ing****.* Elle est incapable de mentir.

38 Complétez avec *can ou could*. Si ce n'est pas possible, utilisez *be able to* (mettez le verbe *be* à la forme qui convient).

a. Nina works at the European Parliament: she ... speak three languages.
b. The dentist is very busy but I'm sure she'll ... see you tomorrow.
c. I ... see by the look on his face that something was wrong.
d. I've never ... make friends at work.
e. It was so dark that we ... *(not)* see anything.

39 Reformulez les phrases en utilisant le verbe entre parenthèses.

a. The goalkeeper managed to catch the ball. *(succeed)*
b. Sam can't control his emotions. *(be unable)*
c. Matt can't hold his tongue. *(be incapable)*

28 L'expression de l'obligation

Le modal *must*

Le modal *must* + V exprime **une forte obligation**. On ne peut l'utiliser qu'au présent.
→ *Passengers **must fasten** their seatbelts.* Les passagers doivent boucler leur ceinture de sécurité.

La forme négative de *must* n'exprime pas l'absence d'obligation mais **l'interdiction**.
Elle est l'équivalent de *may not* ou de *can't*.
→ *You **musn't walk** on the lawn.* Tu ne dois pas / n'as pas le droit de marcher sur la pelouse.
Pour exprimer l'absence d'obligation, il conviendra d'utiliser *don't have to*.

Have (got) to

Si *must* ne s'emploie qu'au présent, ***have to*** **+ V** peut s'employer au prétérit et avec *will*.

	Obligation passée	Obligation présente	Obligation future
Forme affirmative	**had to + V** You **had to call** me.	**have to + V** **have / 've got to + V** You **have to call** him. You**'ve got to call** him.	**will / 'll have to + V** You**'ll have to call** him.
Forme négative = absence d'obligation	**didn't have to + V** You **didn't have to call** him.	**don't have to + V** **haven't got to + V** You **don't have to call** him. You **haven't got to call** him.	**will not / won't have to + V** You **won't have to call** him.
Forme interrogative	**Did + S + have to + V?** **Did** you **have to call** him?	**Do + S + have to + V?** **Have + S + got to + V?** **Do** you **have to call** him? **Have** you **got to call** him?	**Will + S + have to + V?** **Will** you **have to call** him?

La forme *have got to*, surtout employée en anglais britannique, ne s'emploie qu'au présent, contrairement à *have to*, qui peut exprimer une obligation passée ou future.

Autres moyens d'exprimer l'obligation

D'autres structures ou verbes permettent d'exprimer l'obligation.

be obliged /əˈblaɪdʒd/ ***to do sth*** (être obligé de faire qqc)	*His boss **is obliged to** pay the minimum wage.* Sa patronne est obligée de payer le salaire minimum.
be compelled to do sth (être obligé de faire qqc)	*He **was compelled to** resign because of the scandal.* Il a été contraint de démissionner à cause du scandale.
be required /rɪˈkwaɪəd/ ***to do sth*** (être tenu de faire qqc)	*Passengers **are required to** wear masks on planes.* Les passagers sont tenus de porter des masques dans les avions.

40 Complétez avec *must* ou *have* (ou *had*) *to* à la forme affirmative ou négative.

a. When I moved to Los Angeles in 2022, I ... buy a car.
b. If you earn more than $3,000 a month, you'll ... pay income tax.
c. You ... park in front of the store. It's forbidden!
d. We ... rush: the train leaves in two hours.

29 L'expression du conseil et de la suggestion

Le modal *should*

- L'auxiliaire modal *should* + V (prononcé /ʃʊd/) permet d'exprimer un conseil. On le traduit par le verbe « devoir » au conditionnel (« il devrait... »).

Forme affirmative	Forme négative	Forme interrogative
I **should** work	I **shouldn't** (*ou* **should not**) work	**Should** I work?

→ *You **should take** a rest.* Tu devrais te reposer.

- Quand *should* est suivi de ***have* + participe passé,** il exprime un reproche.
→ *He **should have said** thank you.* Il aurait dû dire merci.

Ought to + V

Plus rarement, on peut également employer *ought to* + V (prononcé /ɔːt/), dont le sens est très proche de celui de *should*.

Forme affirmative	Forme négative	Forme interrogative
I **ought to** work	I **oughtn't** (*ou* **ought not**) **to** work	**Ought** I **to** work?

→ *You **ought to take** a rest.* Tu devrais te reposer. / Il faudrait que tu te reposes.

Autres expressions

- Dans une langue plus familière, il est possible d'employer ***had better (not)* + V**. *Had* peut se contracter en *'d*.
→ *You**'d / had better** take a rest.* Tu ferais mieux de te reposer.

- Pour faire une suggestion ou donner un conseil, il est possible d'utiliser les expressions suivantes :

What / How about + V-***ing***...	***How / What about** tak**ing** a rest?* Que dirais-tu de te reposer ?
If I were you, I would + V...	***If I were you, I would** take a rest.* À ta place, je me reposerais.
suggest / recommend that...	***I suggest / recommend that** you take a rest.* Je te conseille / recommande de te reposer.
advise sb to + V	*I **advise you to take** a rest.* Je te conseille de te reposer.
Why not + V	***Why not take** a rest?* Pourquoi ne pas te reposer ?

41 Reformulez les phrases en utilisant les structures entre parenthèses.

a. Brenda should apologise to her neighbour. *(ought to)*
b. It's an amazing novel – you should read it. *(If I were you...)*
c. You shouldn't drive so fast. *(ought to)*
d. You should phone Garry to say you'll be late. *(had better)*
e. You should meet them. They're really nice. *(suggest)*

42 Donnez 5 conseils à un ami pour l'aider à se maintenir en forme. Utilisez les structures suivantes : *should, ought to, had better, If I were you..., I suggest that...*

Exemple : *You should eat healthy food.*

30 Le possible et le probable

En anglais, on peut exprimer le possible et le probable de différentes manières.

Les auxiliaires modaux

Impossible	Possible, vraisemblable	Incertain *(= I don't know)*	Très probable
CAN'T	COULD (NOT) MIGHT (NOT)	MAY (NOT)	MUST
That **can't** be true.	That **could / might** be true.	That **may** be true.	That **must** be true.

- Lorsqu'**un fait passé** est possible ou probable, on utilise la structure suivante :

modal + ***have* + participe passé**

Monica **must** **have told** the truth.
Monica **doit avoir dit / a probablement dit** la vérité.

- Lorsqu'**un fait encore en cours au moment où l'on parle** est possible ou probable, on utilise :

modal + ***be* + V-*ing***

The cat **must** **be sleeping** on the sofa.
Le chat **doit être en train de dormir** sur le canapé

Les adverbes

À la place d'un auxiliaire modal, il est possible d'utiliser **des adverbes.**

possible	probable
maybe, perhaps, possibly	*probably, certainly, undoubtedly*

→ *This story **must** be true.* = *This story is **probably / certainly** true.*

Be likely to + V

***Be likely to* + V** exprime une forte probabilité, en particulier pour parler d'un événement à venir. Quand un événement est improbable, on peut utiliser ***be unlikely to* + V.**
→ *Manchester United **is likely to win** the match.* Manchester United va probablement gagner le match.

43 Reformulez les phrases suivantes en utilisant un auxiliaire modal.

a. Perhaps he'll come Monday. I really can't tell.
b. She certainly missed the train.
c. There's a chance that the escaped prisoner is still alive.
d. Maybe he's right. I really don't know.
e. He isn't 52 years old. That's impossible: he looks so young!

44 Un crime vient d'être commis. Vous êtes enquêteur ou enquêtrice et venez de trouver les objets suivants : *a pair of sunglasses • a rope • an axe (covered with blood) • an anonymous love letter.* Grâce à ces indices, formulez 4 hypothèses sur les circonstances du crime. Utilisez les modaux *must, could, might, can't* et *may*.

31 Les questions

L'ordre des mots dans les questions

Dans une question, l'ordre des mots est le suivant :

(Mot interrogatif)	Auxiliaire	Sujet	Verbe
-	Have	you	finished?
Where	does	Emma	work?
What	will	you	tell her?

Au présent et au prétérit, on utilise **l'auxiliaire *do* / *did*** suivi du sujet, puis de **la base verbale** du verbe (l'infinitif sans *to*).

→ *What **did** you **do**?* Qu'as-tu fait ?

Quand la question porte sur le sujet de la phrase (en particulier quand on demande qui a fait quelque chose), l'auxiliaire *do* / *did* n'est pas utilisé.
*Who **broke** this vase?* Qui a cassé ce vase ?

Les mots interrogatifs

- Une question peut débuter par un mot interrogatif :

What (quoi) ***Who*** (qui) ***When*** (quand) ***Where*** (où) ***How*** (comment) ***Why*** (pourquoi)

Whose (à qui) ***What time*** (à quelle heure) ***What / Which* + nom** (quel(les) + nom)

- *Whose* permet de demander à qui appartient quelque chose. Il est directement suivi du nom.
→ ***Whose bag** is this?* À qui est ce sac ?

Les questions en *How* + adjectif ou adverbe

- Il est possible de former des questions en utilisant la structure ***how* + adjectif** ou ***how* + adverbe**.

How old...? (âge) ***How tall...?*** (taille) ***How long...?*** (durée ou longueur)

How deep...? (profondeur) ***How fast...?*** (vitesse) ***How often...?*** (tous les combien)

→ ***How deep** is Lake Ontario?* Quelle est la profondeur du lac Ontario ?
→ ***How tall** are you?* Combien mesures-tu ?

- Pour poser une question sur une quantité, on utilise ***How much...*** ou ***How many...***
(voir fiche 9, p. 250).

45 Transformez les phrases suivantes en questions fermées *(yes/no questions)*.

a. Drucilla works in a bank.
b. She used an oven to cook the potatoes.
c. Mark will talk to her.
d. They met Frank last week.
e. Ron is going to San Francisco next week.

46 Posez les questions qui appellent pour réponses les éléments soulignés.

a. Carl lives <u>in Liverpool</u>.
b. They were late <u>because the traffic was bad</u>.
c. Antony left <u>at 4 pm</u>.
d. She has bought <u>a new laptop</u>.
e. This book is <u>mine</u>.

32 La phrase passive

Le verbe passif

- La voix passive se construit de la manière suivante : ***be* + participe passé** du verbe.
L'auxiliaire *be* peut se conjuguer à tous les temps et tous les aspects.

Présent simple	I **am followed** (by a police car).
Prétérit simple	I **was followed** (by a police car).
Present perfect	I **have been followed** (by a police car).
Past perfect	I **had been followed** (by a police car).
Futur (ou modal)	I **will (can / may...) be followed** (by a police car).

- On peut aussi mettre les formes en *be* + V-*ing* **à la voix passive.**
Dans ce cas, *being* suit l'auxiliaire *be*.
→ *I **am being followed** by a police car*. Je **suis en train d'être suivi** par une voiture de police.

Le complément d'agent

- **Le complément d'agent** (la personne ou la chose qui est **à l'origine de l'action**) est introduit par ***by***. Il correspond au sujet de la phrase active équivalente.
→ ***My grandfather** built this house.* *This house was built **by my grandfather.***

- **L'agent est souvent omis**, soit parce qu'il n'a pas d'importance, soit parce qu'on ne sait pas qui est à l'origine de l'action, soit parce qu'il est évident.
→ *My purse has been stolen.*

Dans ce cas, on traduit souvent ces phrases passives en employant **le pronom « on »** en français : **On** a volé mon sac.

La voix passive des verbes à deux compléments

Quand un verbe **a deux compléments** *(give, say, show, tell, offer, ask...)*, ils sont tous les deux susceptibles de devenir le sujet de la phrase passive.
→ *They gave **him** a present.* ***He** was given a present.*
→ *They gave him **a present**.* ***A present** was given **to** him.*

47 Mettez le verbe entre parenthèses à la voix passive à la forme indiquée.

a. John Fitzgerald Kennedy ... *(assassinate, prétérit)* in Dallas in 1963.
b. Many languages ... *(speak, présent)* in India.
c. The conference ... *(organise, futur en will)* next month.
d. I ... *(invite, present perfect)* to his birthday party.
e. My computer ... *(repair, présent en be + V-ing)* right now.

48 Mettez les phrases suivantes à la voix passive en commençant pas l'amorce proposée. Exprimez le complement d'agent si nécessaire.

a. A famous law firm hired Mark and Stacy last month. → *Mark and Stacy...*
b. Somebody has stolen the bicycle.
→ *The bicycle...*
c. Dickens wrote *Oliver Twist* in 1838.
→ *Oliver Twist...*
d. We'll send you the report by midnight.
→ *The report...*
e. We'll send you the report by midnight.
→ *You...*

33 Les relatives

Une proposition relative permet d'apporter une information sur **un nom appelé antécédent**. Ces propositions sont introduites par **des pronoms relatifs** *(which, who, that...)*.

→ ***The man*** ***who*** ***sold me the car*** *is dishonest.* L'homme **qui m'a vendu la voiture** est malhonnête.

antécédent — pronom relatif — proposition relative

Les pronoms relatifs *who*, *which* et *that*

Antécédent humain	Antécédent non humain
who, that	*which, that*

- *Which et who* peuvent souvent être **remplacés par *that***. On l'utilise quand la relative nous permet d'identifier ce dont on parle.
  → ***The car*** ***which / that he bought yesterday*** *is in bad condition.* La voiture qu'il a achetée hier est en mauvais état.

- Le pronom relatif peut parfois être omis quand l'antécédent est le complément d'objet du verbe de la proposition relative.
  → ***The car*** Ø ***he bought yesterday*** *is in bad condition. [= He bought the car yesterday.]*

Les relatifs *where* et *when*

Le relatif français **« où »** se traduit :

- par ***where***, si l'antécédent désigne un lieu.
  → *In 2018, we moved to* ***London***, ***where my cousin lived.***
  En 2018, nous avons déménagé à Londres, **où** vivait mon cousin.
- par ***when***, si l'antécédent renvoie à un moment ou une période.
  → *Do you remember* ***the day*** ***when you met her****?* Te souviens-tu du jour **où** tu l'as rencontrée ?

Le relatif *whose*

Le relatif *whose* (prononcé /huːz/) est **directement suivi d'un nom**. Il permet de traduire « dont » et établit entre l'antécédent et le nom qui le suit un lien comparable à celui d'un génitif (N's) ou d'un possessif.

→ *Have you talked to* ***the man*** ***whose car is parked in the driveway****? [= The man****'s*** */* ***his*** *car is parked in the driveway.]* As-tu parlé à l'homme **dont** la voiture est garée dans l'allée ?

| On ne met jamais d'article après *whose* (on dira *whose car* et non *whose ~~the~~ car*).

49 Choisissez le ou les relatif(s) qui convien(nen)t.

a. The castle **who / that / Ø** we visited is haunted.
b. All the people **which / that / Ø** they have interviewed are unemployed.
c. The apartment **who / that / where** she lives overlooks Central Park.
d. Jamie married a girl **who / which / Ø** works for a big oil company.

50 Reliez les deux phrases au moyen du relatif *whose*.

a. The police interrogated the witness. Her identity will be kept secret.
b. Miranda donated $1 million to charity. Her family is very wealthy.
c. He wants to sell his company. Its profits have increased a lot lately.

Base verbale	Prétérit	Participe passé	Traduction
Verbes identiques aux trois formes			
burst	burst	burst	*éclater*
cost	cost	cost	*coûter*
cut	cut	cut	*couper*
hit	hit	hit	*frapper*
hurt	hurt	hurt	*blesser, faire mal*
let	let	let	*laisser*
put /ʊ/	put /ʊ/	put /ʊ/	*mettre*
quit	quit	quit	*cesser, démissionner*
read /iː/	read /e/	read /e/	*lire*
set	set	set	*poser*
shut	shut	shut	*fermer*
spread /e/	spread /e/	spread /e/	*(s')étaler, se répandre*
Prétérit et participe passé en *-ought* ou *-aught* /ɔːt/			
bring	brought	brought	*apporter*
buy	bought	bought	*acheter*
catch	caught	caught	*attraper*
fight	fought	fought	*se battre*
teach	taught	taught	*enseigner*
think	thought	thought	*penser*
Bases verbales en *-ee*			
bleed	bled	bled	*saigner*
feel	felt	felt	*ressentir*
feed	fed	fed	*nourrir*
keep	kept	kept	*garder*
meet	met	met	*rencontrer*
sleep	slept	slept	*dormir*
Bases verbales en *-ow*			
blow	blew	blown	*souffler*
grow	grew	grown	*pousser, augmenter*
know	knew	known	*savoir, connaître*
show	showed	shown	*montrer*
throw	threw	thrown	*jeter*
Prétérit et participe passé en *-t*			
build /ɪ/	built /ɪ/	built /ɪ/	*construire*
burn	burned *ou* burnt	burned *ou* burnt	*brûler*
deal /iː/	dealt /e/	dealt /e/	*distribuer*
dream /iː/	dreamed *ou* dreamt /e/	dreamed *ou* dreamt /e/	*rêver*
learn	learned *ou* learnt	learned *ou* learnt	*apprendre*
lend	lent	lent	*prêter*
lose /uː/	lost	lost	*perdre*
mean /iː/	meant /e/	meant /e/	*signifier*
send	sent	sent	*envoyer*
smell	smelt	smelt	*sentir*
spell	spelled *ou* spelt	spelled *ou* spelt	*épeler*
spend	spent	spent	*dépenser*
Changement de voyelle et participe passé en *-(e)n*			
bear	bore	borne	*porter*
beat	beat	beaten	*battre*
bite /aɪ/	bit /ɪ/	bitten /ɪ/	*mordre*
break /eɪ/	broke /əʊ/	broken /əʊ/	*construire*
choose	chose /əʊ/	chosen /əʊ/	*choisir*
draw	drew	drawn	*dessiner*
drive /aɪ/	drove /əʊ/	driven /ɪ/	*conduire*

Base verbale	Prétérit	Participe passé	Traduction
eat	ate	eaten	*manger*
fall	fell	fallen	*tomber*
fly	flew	flown /əʊ/	*voler*
forget	forgot	forgotten	*oublier*
freeze	froze	frozen	*geler*
give /ɪ/	gave	given /ɪ/	*donner*
hide /aɪ/	hid /ɪ/	hidden /ɪ/	*cacher*
ride /aɪ/	rode /əʊ/	ridden	*aller (à cheval ou à vélo)*
rise /aɪ/	rose /əʊ/	risen /ɪ/	*s'élever, augmenter*
shake /eɪ/	shook /ʊ/	shaken /eɪ/	*secouer*
shine /aɪ/	shone /ɒ/	shone /ɒ/	*briller*
speak	spoke /əʊ/	spoken /əʊ/	*parler*
steal	stole /əʊ/	stolen /əʊ/	*voler, dérober*
take /eɪ/	took /ʊ/	taken /eɪ/	*prendre*
wake /eɪ/	woke /əʊ/	woken /əʊ/	*réveiller*
wear /eə/	wore	worn	*porter (un vêtement)*
write /aɪ/	wrote /əʊ/	written /ɪ/	*écrire*
Changement de voyelle			
become /ʌ/	became	become /ʌ/	*devenir*
begin	began	begun	*commencer*
come /ʌ/	came	come /ʌ/	*venir*
drink	drank	drunk	*boire*
find /aɪ/	found /aʊ/	found /aʊ/	*trouver*
get	got	got *ou* gotten	*obtenir, devenir...*
hang	hung	hung	*pendre*
hold	held	held	*tenir*
ring	rang	rung	*sonner ou téléphoner*
run	ran	run	*courir*
shoot	shot	shot	*tirer*
sing	sang	sung	*chanter*
sit	sat	sat	*être assis*
stick	stuck	stuck	*coller*
stink	stank	stunk	*puer, sentir mauvais*
strike	struck	struck	*frapper*
swim	swam	swum	*nager*
win	won /ʌ/	won /ʌ/	*gagner*
Les inclassables			
be	was / were	been	*être*
do	did	done /ʌ/	*faire*
go	went	gone /ɒ/	*aller*
have	had	had	*avoir*
hear /ɪə/	heard /ɜː/	heard /ɜː/	*entendre*
lay	laid /eɪ/	laid /eɪ/	*poser*
leave	left	left	*laisser, quitter, partir*
lie	lay	lain	*être allongé*
light	lighted *ou* lit	lighted *ou* lit	*allumer*
make	made	made	*faire, fabriquer*
pay	paid /eɪ/	paid /eɪ/	*payer*
say	said /e/	said /e/	*dire*
see	saw /ɔː/	seen	*voir*
sell	sold /əʊ/	sold /əʊ/	*vendre*
stand	stood /ʊ/	stood /ʊ/	*être debout*
tell	told /əʊ/	told /əʊ/	*dire, raconter*
understand	understood /ʊ/	understood /ʊ/	*comprendre*

1 L'alphabet phonétique international

L'alphabet phonétique international (API) permet de représenter fidèlement la prononciation d'un mot. Par convention, la transcription d'un mot ou d'un son apparaît toujours entre barres obliques /…/. Les syllabes accentuées sont précédées du symbole ˈ (accent primaire) ou ˌ (accent secondaire d'une moindre intensité).

Les consonnes Audio 23lmu22201

/k/ **c**at	/ð/ **th**ere	/tʃ/ **ch**air	/ŋ/ ri**ng**
/θ/ mou**th**	/ʃ/ **sh**eep	/dʒ/ **j**uice	/j/ **y**ogurt
/z/ **z**ebra	/ʒ/ trea**s**ure		

Les autres consonnes sont représentées par les lettres de l'alphabet usuelles (/p/, /d/, /h/…).

Les voyelles brèves Audio 23lmu22202

/ɪ/ p**i**g	/ʊ/ b**oo**k	/ʌ/ b**u**s
/ɒ/ d**o**g	/æ/ c**a**t	/ə/ ang**e**l
/e/ b**e**d		

Les voyelles longues Audio 23lmu22203

/iː/ qu**ee**n	/ɔː/ f**or**k
/uː/ sh**oe**	/ɜː/ b**ir**d
/ɑː/ c**ar**	

Les diphtongues et les triphtongues Audio 23lmu22204

/aɪ/ fl**y**	/ɔɪ/ b**oy**	/ɪə/ d**eer**	/ʊə/ c**ure**	/aɪə/ f**ire**
/eɪ/ r**ai**n	/əʊ/ g**o** (US : /oʊ/)	/eə/ ch**air**		/aʊə/ p**ower**

1 Donnez le mot correspondant aux transcriptions suivantes. Dans les mots de deux syllabes ou plus, soulignez la syllabe accentuée. Puis écoutez et vérifiez. Audio 23lmu22205

a. /bed/ b. /kiːp/ c. /deɪ/ d. /fɪt/ e. /bʌs/ f. /ʃɪp/
g. /ðæt/ h. /bɪˈgɪn/ i. /ˈfriːdəm/ j. /fəˈget/ k. /sləʊ/

2 Les outils et ressources pour améliorer sa prononciation

Les dictionnaires en ligne

Wordreference est un dictionnaire bilingue qui propose d'écouter les mots prononcés avec différents accents : britannique standard, américain standard, irlandais, jamaïcain, écossais, américain du Sud des États-Unis…

Dans le dictionnaire ***Longman Dictionary of Contemporary English Online***, il est possible d'écouter les mots avec une prononciation américaine ou britannique. Le dictionnaire propose en outre de nombreuses phrases d'exemples qui permettent d'écouter les mots en contexte.

Les plateformes vidéo

Tous les sites de vidéo à la demande (Amazon Prime, Netflix, Disney+...) proposent leurs programmes en version originale. Il est possible d'activer les sous-titre français ou anglais. Un bon exercice pour habituer son oreille consiste à visionner un programme en version originale sous-titrée en anglais, puis sans sous-titres.

YouGlish (www.youglish.com) permet de rechercher un mot ou une phrase parmi de nombreuses vidéos YouTube afin de les entendre en contexte. Il est possible de sélectionner un accent : américain, britannique, irlandais, australien... On peut également visualiser une transcription des vidéos.

La BBC (www.bbc.com) propose une chaîne YouTube spécialisée dans l'apprentissage de l'anglais. La chaîne publie des vidéos de 6 minutes sur des sujets d'actualité, permettant ainsi de travailler sa compréhension orale. Il est à chaque fois possible d'activer les sous-titres anglais. On y touve aussi des vidéos sur des sujets divers : vocabulaire thématique, points de grammaire, points de phonologie, etc.

3 Prononciation et graphie : pièges et erreurs fréquentes

TIP 1 Se méfier des ressemblances orthographiques entre les deux langues

De nombreux mots anglais ressemblent aux mots français. Certains ont même des orthographes identiques : *nation*, *table*, *document*... Mais la prononciation des mots anglais est en général très différente de celle des mots français. Il faut donc vérifier la prononciation de ces mots dans un dictionnaire.

TIP 2 Bannir ces sons français qui n'existent pas en anglais

- **Certains sons français n'existent pas en anglais**. Il faut donc les bannir de votre prononciation. Il s'agit :
  - des voyelles nasales de *ball**on***, ***en**f**an**t* ou *lap**in***. Il faut garder à l'esprit que dans les graphies *in*, *an*, *en* ou *on*, le *n* se prononce toujours en anglais.
  - du son *u* dans ***du*** ou ***sur***.
- Par ailleurs, le *r* anglais n'est jamais prononcé comme en français. La langue se dirige vers la zone du palais, à l'arrière de la bouche.

TIP 3 Les voyelles inaccentuées sont souvent réduites en anglais Audio 23lmu22206

Quand une voyelle est en position inaccentuée, **elle est souvent réduite**, c'est-à-dire prononcée comme la voyelle *schwa* /ə/ (comme dans ***the*** ou ***an***). Il s'agit de la voyelle la plus fréquente en anglais. Elle peut donc être représentée par de très nombreuses graphies : *o, a, e, ai*...

arrogant /'ærəgənt/ ● ● ●   *support* /sə'pɔːt/ ● ●

TIP 4 Les consonnes muettes Audio 23lmu22207

Dans les cas suivants, certaines consonnes ne sont pas prononcées :

b* après *m	*bom**b**, dum**b**, thum**b***	***l* dans *alk* et *alf***	*wa**l**k, ta**l**k, ha**l**f*
k* avant *n	***k**now, **k**nife, **k**nee*	***t* dans *stle* et *sten***	*cas**t**le, whis**t**le, has**t**en*
w* avant *r	***w**rite, **w**rong, **w**rist*	***n* après *m***	*condem**n**, dam**n**, hym**n***

2 Les mots suivants sont orthographiés de la même manière dans les deux langues. Écoutez et répétez. Audio 23lmu22208

document • passion • ressemblance • observe • question • incident • invisible

Maintenant, recopiez-les et soulignez les consonnes qui ne sont pas prononcées de la même façon.

4 L'accent de mot

Qu'est-ce que l'accent de mot ?

En anglais, lorsqu'un mot contient deux syllabes ou plus, l'une d'entre elles est nécessairement accentuée. Une syllabe accentuée est prononcée avec **plus de force** que les autres.
Sa voyelle est également **légèrement plus longue**.

*for**get*** /fə'get/ ●● *__hus__band* /'hʌzbənd/ ●●

En anglais, l'**accentuation d'un mot est primordiale.**
Les anglophones ont souvent des difficultés à comprendre un mot mal accentué.

L'accent secondaire

Les mots de 3 syllabes ou plus ont souvent une seconde syllabe accentuée, de moindre intensité : on parlera alors **d'accent secondaire** (par opposition à l'accent principal, plus intense, appelé **accent primaire**).

revolution /ˌrevə'luːʃən/ ●●●● *pronunciation* /prəˌnʌnsi'eɪʃən/ ●●●●●

Comment connaître l'accentuation d'un mot ? Audio 23lmu22209

- La meilleure solution est **d'écouter le mot** ou, à défaut, de regarder sa transcription dans le dictionnaire. L'accent primaire est représenté par le symbole ˈ placé avant la syllabe accentuée. L'accent secondaire est représenté par un ˌ.
- Existe-t-il des règles pour prédire la place de l'accent ?
– **Les verbes de deux syllabes** sont en général accentués sur **la deuxième syllabe** ●● :
*ad**dress**, be**come**, dis**cuss***.
– **Les noms et adjectifs de deux syllabes** sont le plus souvent accentués sur **la première** ●● :
***sand**wich, **fa**ther, **re**cent, **cer**tain.*

• On peut aussi connaître l'accentuation d'un mot en examinant **sa terminaison**. Une terminaison qui détermine la place de l'accent est dite « **contraignante** ». Dans les exemples suivants, l'accent est placé sur la syllabe qui précède immédiatement la terminaison.

Terminaison	Exemples	Terminaison	Exemples
-ion	*revo**lu**tion, expe**di**tion, e**mo**tion* Exception : ***te**levision*	*-ic(al)*	*his**tor**ical, ath**let**ic, scien**tif**ic* Exception : ***Cath**olic, **Ar**abic, **pol**itics...*
-ity et *-ety*	*ca**pac**ity, a**bil**ity, so**ci**ety*	*-ia, -ian, -ial*	*Aus**tra**lia, poli**ti**cian, com**mer**cial*

3 **Recopiez les mots suivants et identifiez à chaque fois la terminaison contraignante, puis soulignez la syllabe qui porte l'accent principal. Écoutez l'enregistrement pour vérifier vos réponses et répétez.** Audio 23lmu22210

vegetarian • political • physician • reputation • repression • musical • musician • stupidity

5 L'intonation

• Une phrase n'est pas une suite de mots prononcés de façon monotone. Comme dans la mélodie d'une chanson, la voix peut varier en hauteur : c'est ce qu'on appelle **l'intonation.**

• L'intonation est à la fois porteuse **de sens et d'expressivité** : elle donne des indications sur les intentions ou les sentiments de l'énonciateur. Travailler son intonation permet d'adopter un débit naturel et surtout expressif.

L'intonation descendante Audio 23lmu22211

La voix peut suivre **une mélodie descendante ↘.** Cette intonation est utilisée :

- dans les phrases affirmatives — *I'm hungry.* ↘
- dans les questions ouvertes *(wh-questions)* — *What are you doing?* ↘
- dans les phrases à l'impératif — *Don't be so rude!* ↘
- dans les phrases exclamatives — *What a great book!* ↘

L'intonation montante Audio 23lmu22212

La voix peut suivre **une mélodie montante ↗.** Cette intonation est utilisée :

- dans les questions fermées *(yes/no-questions)* — *Are you happy?* ↗
- lorsqu'on demande de répéter — *Sorry?* ↗
- lorsqu'on demande une confirmation, surtout dans des *tags* — *You live in France, don't you?* ↗
- pour indiquer qu'une phrase ou une énumération n'est pas achevée. — *She bought tomatoes,* ↗ *apples* ↗ *and milk.* ↘

4 **L'intonation est-elle montante ↗ ou descendante ↘ dans les questions suivantes ? Écoutez l'enregistrement pour vérifier vos réponses, puis répétez.** Audio 23lmu22213

a. Have you seen the film? b. What time does the film finish? c. Were you travelling together? d. What have you been doing? e. What?! I beg your pardon? f. You play the piano, don't you?

6 Anglais britannique et anglais américain

• Il existe de nombreux accents dans le monde anglophone : britannique, américain, écossais, irlandais, australien, indien… et même des accents régionaux (accent du nord de l'Angleterre, du Texas, etc.). **Aucun accent n'est plus valable qu'un autre** : vous pouvez apprendre celui qui vous plaît, à condition de rester cohérent dans votre choix.

• Malgré tout, deux variétés sont plus représentées et enseignées que les autres : **l'accent britannique standard et l'accent américain standard**. Les ressources et les outils pour améliorer sa prononciation s'appuient souvent sur l'un des deux. Voici ce qui les différencie.

La prononciation du *r* Audio 23lmu22214

La plupart des Américains prononcent tous les *r* dans un mot. En revanche, la plupart des Britanniques ne prononcent pas les *r* quand ils suivent une voyelle dans une même syllabe.

	anglais britannique standard	anglais américain standard
park	/pɑːk/	/pɑːrk/
store	/stɔː/	/stɔːr/

La prononciation du *t* Audio 23lmu22215

• En anglais américain, le *t* situé entre deux voyelles se prononce comme un son qui ressemble à un *d* (appelé *flap t*) : *wa**t**er, be**tt**er, mee**t**ing…*

• Après la consonne *n*, le *t* semble souvent disparaître en anglais américain : *twe**nt**y, de**nt**ist, i**nt**erview, adva**nt**age…*

Voyelles et diphtongues Audio 23lmu22216

• La voyelle de *h**o**t* ou de *st**o**p* est plus longue et plus ouverte en anglais américain et ressemble au *a* de *car*.

• La diphtongue de *g**o*** ou *n**o*** est prononcée /əʊ/ en anglais britannique standard. En anglais américain, elle est plus arrondie et est prononcée /oʊ/.

• Le son /juː/ de *new* ou de *you* est prononcé /uː/ en anglais américain (comme dans *moon*), surtout après certaines consonnes (*n, d, t, s*) : *dude, k**n**ew, tune…*

Mots qui ont des prononciations différentes Audio 23lmu22217

	anglais britannique	anglais américain
advertisement	/ədˈvɜːtəsmənt/	/ˌædvərˈtaɪzmənt/
either	/ˈaɪðə/	/ˈiːðər/
squirrel	/ˈskwɪrəl/	/ˈskwɜːrəl/
terminaison *-ile*	/ˈməʊbaɪl/	/ˈmoʊbəl/
tomato	/təˈmɑːtəʊ/	/təˈmeɪtoʊ/

5 Les mots suivants vont être prononcés par un locuteur britannique puis par un locuteur américain. Écoutez et répétez chaque mot avec l'accent que vous avez choisi. Audio 23lmu22218

a. new b. due c. got d. so e. go f. meeting g. letter h. tomato i. painter j. twenty k. over l. short m. mark n. turn

1 Relire un devoir écrit

Règle d'or

Garder le temps nécessaire pour deux relectures (minimum 5 mn).

Une relecture en deux temps

Étape 1

Lisez une première fois pour revoir la cohérence globale, vos arguments et vos exemples, ainsi que l'enchaînement des idées.

Étape 2

Faites une seconde lecture en vous concentrant sur la langue (orthographe, grammaire), la mise en forme (paragraphes…) et la ponctuation (virgules, deux points, points finaux…).

Pensez à repérer tout au long de l'année les erreurs que vous avez tendance à faire et créez une fiche de relecture personnalisée.

« Mistakes are our teachers. They help us to learn! »

John Bradshaw

Ma Check List

- ☑ J'ai bien traité le **sujet**, tout le sujet et rien que le sujet.
- ☑ J'ai tenu compte des **consignes** : type de production (lettre, article, dialogue…), nombre de mots.
- ☑ J'ai fait l'effort de **structurer le devoir** en développant 2 ou 3 arguments principaux.
- ☑ Les idées s'enchaînent de façon logique avec des **mots de liaison**.
- ☑ J'ai illustré mon travail avec des **exemples concrets** et des **références culturelles**.
- ☑ J'ai fait des paragraphes en allant **à la ligne pour chaque nouvelle idée**.
- ☑ J'ai utilisé une **langue riche** (un vocabulaire et des structures variés, des propositions relatives…).
- ☑ J'ai vérifié l'**orthographe**.
- ☑ J'ai vérifié la **grammaire** (en me souvenant de mes erreurs passées : je n'oublie pas le *-s* du pluriel ou de la 3e personne du présent, je fais attention aux temps, à l'ordre des mots…).
- ☑ J'ai respecté la **ponctuation** (points, virgules…) et mis des **majuscules** en début de phrases et aux noms propres.
- ☑ J'ai écrit **proprement** et **lisiblement**.

Les *Grammy Awards* de la grammaire !

Écoutez les chansons sur Internet et mémorisez les refrains pour retenir les points de grammaire illustrés.

Pour vous aider à éviter les erreurs les plus courantes, voici notre top 10 des classiques de la pop anglo-saxonne

1. *Can't Take a Joke*, by Drake — Les auxiliaires modaux (*can, could, must, may, might, should, will, would*) sont toujours suivis de la base verbale.

2. *Why do I Feel so Sad?*, by Alicia Keys — Une question se forme selon le schéma suivant : (mot interrogatif) + auxiliaire + sujet + verbe, sauf quand *who* ou *what* sont sujets.

3. *Born to Run*, by Bruce Springsteen — Pour exprimer le but (pour + verbe), on utilise *to* + base verbale.

4. *I Forgot that you Existed*, by Taylor Swift — Quand vous racontez un fait passé et daté, il faut utiliser le prétérit.

5. *She Moves far away*, by Alle Farben — À la 3e personne du singulier du présent simple, le verbe prend un *-s*.

6. *I Want to Break Free*, by Queen — Pour dire « vouloir + verbe », on utilise *want* + *to* + base verbale.

7. *Single Ladies*, by Beyoncé — Les adjectifs ne prennent jamais de *-s* en anglais.

8. *Some People don't Change*, by Josh Tobias — Au pluriel, *person* devient *people*. *People* est un nom pluriel.

9. *Give Peace a Chance*, by John Lennon — Devant un nom employé dans un sens général, on ne met pas l'article *the*.

10. *The Man who Sold the World*, by David Bowie — *Who* renvoie à une personne. *Which* renvoie à une chose ou une idée.

2 Analyser et commenter une image

Identifier
- le type de document
- la date de création
- la source

Décrire
- les éléments (objets, personnages…)
- comment ils sont organisés

Interpréter
- le contexte, le titre, l'intention de l'auteur·e
- en donnant son opinion

Une image fixe

Identifier en repérant les informations données dans la légende *(the caption)* :

- le **nom** de l'artiste, le **titre** de l'œuvre et sa **date** de création.
- le **type de document** : *an advertisement* (une publicité), *a poster* (une affiche), *a painting, a cartoon* (un dessin humoristique), *a comic strip* (une bande dessinée), *a drawing* (un dessin), *a photograph, a screenshot, a still from a film* (une image tirée de…).

Exemple :
This painting is entitled American Uprising, *it was painted by Kadir Nelson in 2020.*

Situer les différents éléments de l'image et les **nommer**

people person light
character setting
colourful dark

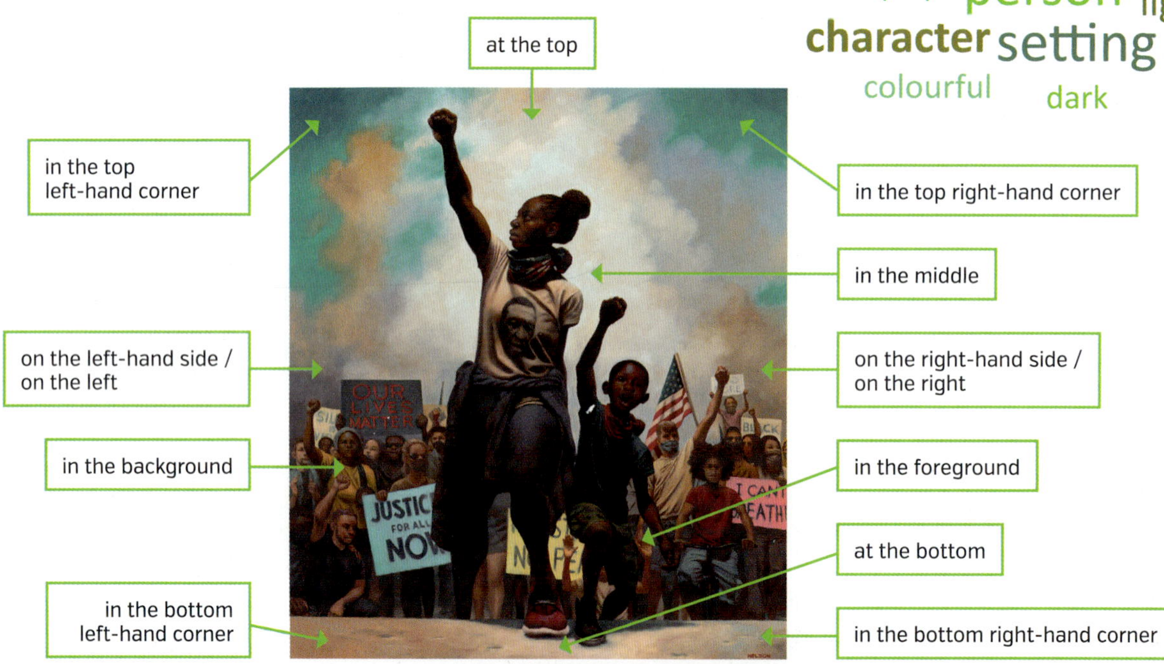

American Uprising, Kadir Nelson, 2020

Décrire ces éléments en utilisant des énoncés simples et des adjectifs.

***I can see** a young woman, **there is** a boy **next to** her. In the background, **there are** people who **are** hold**ing** signs. They **look** determined. **The focus is on** the symbolic gesture of the raised fist. It's a colourful and dynamic painting.*

Une image animée

Identifier

- la **source**.
- le **type de document** : *film, TikTok video, trailer, advert (= commercial), TV show, blockbuster, documentary, reel, news report.*
- le **genre** (si c'est un film) : *cartoon, science fiction, fantasy, horror, comedy, musical, disaster film.*

Prenez en compte votre ressenti et les émotions que procurent la dimension artistique, la bande son *(soundtrack)*, les changements de rythme, les couleurs, les jeux d'ombre et de lumière…

Décrire les éléments principaux

Who? *The characters / the people involved are…*

What? *This extract is about… It deals with…*

Where? *The scene was shot in… The setting is…*

When? *The story takes place in…*

Repérer les plans et angles de vue et les effets qu'ils peuvent produire.

*A **long shot** shows the setting of a scene.*

*A **low-angle shot** can convey superiority, threat, power.*

*A **high-angle shot** can suggest inferiority or weakness.*

*A **full shot** shows a character's entire body whereas a **close-up** will focus on a part of the body (hands, face…) to convey emotions.*

Interpréter une image fixe ou animée

Exprimer ses premières réactions

- *What strikes me most is…*
- *I think it is about…*
- *I find it interesting / surprising / funny / unusual / disturbing that…*
- *We get a feeling of…*

Interpréter

- *The artist's aim / goal / purpose is to…*
- *The atmosphere is tense / strained…*
- *It reminds me of…*
- *It illustrates / represents / shows / portrays…*
- *It is a symbol of…*
- *It criticises… / denounces…*

Formuler des hypothèses

- *It makes me think of…*
- *I have the feeling that…*
- *If we pay attention to… we can deduce that…*
- *For me, it's about… because…*

Expressions idiomatiques:

- *I was in stitches.*
- *It gave me food for thought.*
- *It made my blood run cold.*
- *It was like watching grass grow.*

3 Créer une présentation numérique avec PowerPoint

Règle d'or

Les diapositives illustrent vos propos : elles doivent être claires et attractives !

Pour quoi faire ?

- Un document bien conçu sera un **plus** pour votre public (grâce à son impact visuel) et un **atout** pour vous : cela vous apportera une bonne dose de confiance en vous !
- Vos diapositives vont être un **support** à votre présentation grâce aux éléments visuels que vous allez choisir de façon **judicieuse** : photos, schémas, graphiques, organigrammes, mots-clés...
- Tout cela viendra **appuyer** les éléments principaux de votre discours. Le public va ainsi **visualiser** les idées que vous exprimez, ce sera plus aisé de **suivre votre exposé** et de **prendre des notes**.

Ne surchargez pas vos diapositives, notamment en texte : votre public ne pourra pas lire et vous écouter en même temps ! Et si vous lisez tout ce qui est écrit sur une diapositive, cela peut vite devenir ennuyeux...

OUTILS

SlideLab – LibreOffice Impress – SmartSHOW 3D – PowerDirector – Microsoft PowerPoint – Google Slides – Keynote – Slidesgo – Prezi – Genially

Organiser les diapositives

Diapo 1 Indiquez le **titre** et/ou le **sous-titre** et/ou la **problématique**.

Diapo 2 Présentez le **plan** de votre présentation.

Diapos suivantes

- Proposez **1 à 2 idées par diapositive**, avec **1 à 2 illustrations** maximum.
- Les textes doivent être **synthétiques** et **cohérents**.

Dernières diapos **Conclusion** ainsi que **sources** et **ressources documentaires consultées** (bibliographie, webographie).

concision
charte graphique
clarté
visibilité
homogénéité

Concevoir une diapositive

- Choisissez **1 seule police d'écriture** (2 au maximum : une pour les titres, une pour le texte) plutôt classique et bien lisible.
- La **taille de la police** doit être comprise entre 24 et 30.
- Choisissez **2 ou 3 couleurs** de texte maximum, qui soient contrastées avec le fond (texte sombre sur fond clair).
- **L'arrière-plan ne doit pas être trop chargé**, pour améliorer le contraste.
- Évitez l'italique, les mots soulignés, les ombres.
- Pour aérer votre texte, faites **de courtes listes de mots-clés** (paragraphes / puces).

L'onglet « révision » vous aide pour corriger la grammaire et l'orthographe.

Les animations

- Elles rendent vos diapositives **dynamiques**, **accrocheuses** et **attrayantes**. Elles doivent être **utiles**, souligner ou révéler à un moment opportun un **élément percutant** de votre discours.
- **Pour créer une animation**, cliquez sur l'objet que vous voulez animer, puis sur l'option « animation ». Choisissez ensuite le type d'animation (apparition, entrée brusque, etc.), sa durée, sa direction, etc.
- Vous pouvez insérer et animer des vidéos, des fichiers son, des illustrations SmartArt, des objets en 3D... Enfin, il est possible de **créer des transitions entre chaque diapositive**.
- Mais restez modéré·e, il ne faudrait pas que votre public ait mal au cœur !
- Bien sûr, n'oubliez pas d'**enregistrer votre travail** au fur et à mesure...

Les objets en 3D peuvent être manipulés. En les dupliquant d'une diapo à la suivante puis en utilisant la transition « morphose », on obtient un bel effet d'enchaînement !

Vous pouvez utiliser l'option « conception » : laissez-vous guider par les propositions et petit à petit développez vos talents de graphiste et votre créativité !

You're the boss!

Même si votre présentation numérique est géniale, c'est bien vous qui allez l'animer !

Quelques derniers conseils...

- **maîtrisez** bien votre sujet ET votre document numérique.
- pour rendre votre exposé vivant et original, racontez une **anecdote** personnelle, avec une touche d'**humour**.
- travaillez votre **diction**, l'intensité de votre **voix**.
- soyez bien **présent physiquement** : regardez le public, soignez votre gestuelle qui va soutenir votre discours, déplacez-vous... et ne vous tenez pas devant la présentation !
- si possible, utilisez une **télécommande** ou une tablette numérique connectée pour ne pas être collé·e à l'ordinateur.

4 Publier sur les réseaux sociaux et repérer les *fake news*

Publier sur les réseaux sociaux

Instagram Images et vidéos courtes.
Quel conseil ? Choisissez les mots-clés pertinents précédés de #.
Quels avantages ? Partager ce qu'on voit et suivre les comptes qu'on aime.

Snapchat Photos et vidéos en messages éphémères. Possibilité de créer une story éphémère (24 heures).
Quel conseil ? Réglez les paramètres de confidentialité pour cibler les destinataires.
Quel avantage ? Partager en temps réel avec ses amis.

TikTok Courtes vidéos.
Quel conseil ? Mettez une limite de temps à son utilisation car cette application est très chronophage !
Quels avantages ? C'est un bon moyen de se divertir et le choix de vidéos est sans limite, ou presque.

Twitter Textes courts, images et vidéos. Possibilité de créer un fil de messages *(thread)*.
Quel conseil ? Utilisez les bons symboles : # pour mots-clés et @ pour les mentions.
Quels avantages ? Réagir en temps réel ou non. Possibilité de s'adresser à un large public (si vous avez beaucoup de *followers*). 😉

YouTube et Dailymotion Vidéos.
Quel conseil ? Réglez les paramètres de confidentialité pour une visibilité « privée » ou « publique ».
Quels avantages ? Suivre les comptes que l'on aime. Créer sa chaîne.

Facebook Tous types de documents (sauf PDF).
Quel conseil ? Réglez les paramètres de confidentialité pour cibler les destinataires.
Quel avantage ? Partager en temps réel avec ses amis.

QUELQUES CONSEILS

#Vigilance !

Le harcèlement en ligne est très courant et tous les utilisateurs ne sont pas bienveillants. En cas de problème, prévenez tout de suite un adulte.

#Respect !

Faites attention à bien éviter les propos agressifs ou blessants. Souvent, on dit des choses derrière son écran qu'on ne dirait jamais dans la « vraie » vie ! Vous pouvez aussi modérer les commentaires des internautes après une de vos publications.

#Droits !

Respectez le droit d'auteur et le droit à l'image en citant systématiquement vos sources et vérifiez que vous avez le droit d'utiliser tel ou tel document par exemple en préférant des licences *Creative Commons* (CC) gratuites.

#Netiquette !

N'écrivez pas en majuscule, car c'est comme CRIER sur quelqu'un, utilisez plutôt le **gras** ou l'*italique*.

#Sécurité !

Choisissez un mot de passe différent pour chaque réseau. Utilisez un pseudo, ne révélez aucune donnée personnelle et optez pour le mode « privé ». N'acceptez pas d'inconnus dans votre réseau d'amis.

#Autorisation !

Demandez toujours l'autorisation avant de publier une photo, une vidéo ou même l'enregistrement de la voix de quelqu'un.

#Selfies et photos !

Ne publiez pas n'importe quelle photo de vous ! Elle peut être téléchargée, copiée en capture d'écran et utilisée de façon malveillante.

#Pas d'infox !

Ne propagez pas de fausses informations (*fake news*).

6 astuces pour repérer une *fake news*

1 Le titre et le message
En majuscules ? Avec des points d'exclamation ? C'est louche ! Surtout si on vous incite à le partager et à le diffuser au plus grand nombre : cela peut indiquer qu'il s'agit d'une publicité ou d'une infox. Vérifiez aussi qu'il ne s'agit pas d'une blague ou d'un article satirique.

2 La source
Promenez-vous sur le site, jettez un œil à la rubrique « contact » et explorez les liens proposés : sont-ils en relation avec l'article ? Quel est le but de ce site ?

3 L'auteur·e
Faites une recherche rapide : existe-t-il ? Quelle est sa fonction, pour qui travaille-t-il ? Cela devrait vous permettre de juger de sa fiabilité.

4 La date
Un vieil article est parfois republié pour faire croire qu'il s'agit d'une information récente.

5 Les images
Décryptez la photo. Est-elle originale ou retouchée ? Quelle est sa source ? Si vous avez un doute, faites une recherche inversée sur un moteur de recherche en copiant l'URL de l'image (clic droit).

6 D'autres articles
Si l'information est vraie, alors d'autres articles en auront parlé. Une simple recherche vous permettra de recouper les informations.

Demandez aux expert·es ! En cas de doute, interrogez vos professeurs, un·e bibliothécaire, vos parents !

La vidéo *This is an apple* fait partie d'une campagne de la chaîne d'information en continu américaine CNN pour promouvoir la lutte contre les *fake news*. Video 23lmu22301

5 Être convaincant·e à l'écrit et à l'oral

Règle d'or

Pour chacun de vos arguments, développez un ou deux exemples.

Organisez vos arguments et structurez votre discours

- **Analysez le sujet de votre intervention**

  Pour bien cerner le sujet, considérez chaque terme et faites un *brainstorming* en créant une carte mentale. Mobilisez vos connaissances culturelles, les structures grammaticales vues en classe, ainsi qu'un vocabulaire riche appartenant au champ lexical du sujet.

- **Regroupez vos idées pour que votre intervention soit fluide et cohérente.**

  1) Préparez une courte **introduction** qui situe le sujet et le définit.

  2) Développez un **argument** puis soutenez votre idée avec un ou des **exemple**(s) concret(s).

  3) Terminez par une phrase de **conclusion** qui récapitule votre pensée et propose une ouverture vers d'autres questionnements.

Organisez vos notes dans l'ordre, en notant les mots-clés, quelques références, les chiffres et/ou dates. Utilisez **différentes couleurs, surlignez les mots** importants à accentuer.

Formulez un discours logique et cohérent

- Vos **arguments** doivent se succéder **logiquement** pour que votre public puisse vous suivre facilement. Votre **éloquence** repose en premier lieu sur votre capacité à être **clair·e dans le déroulement de vos pensées**.
- Utilisez **des expressions marquant des liens logiques**.

Pour une entrée en matière accrocheuse, il est judicieux de mentionner l'actualité ou de faire une référence culturelle pertinente

Pour commencer
first, firstly, let me just start by saying, to start with...

Pour ordonner vos idées
then, next, in fact, anyway, actually, indeed, to some extent...

Pour reformuler
the point I wanted to make is..., what I mean is..., on second thoughts...

Pour conclure
eventually, to conclude, finally, all in all...

- Utilisez des **mots de liaison** à bon escient.

Comparaison

likewise, similarly, **also**, compared to, in the same way, **whereas**, while

Contraste

unlike, **contrarily**, however, but, on the contrary, **conversely**, yet

Exprimez votre point de vue

Argumenter

The reason why...
That's why...
For this reason...
Most people think...
For example...
For instance...

S'opposer

I don't agree / I disagree with...
I don't think so!
Frankly, I doubt it.
The truth is...
I see your point but the problem is...

Donner son opinion

I think... / I suppose...
In my opinion, ...
To my mind, ...
The way I see it, ...
I'm sure / certain / convinced that...
I strongly believe that...
As far as I'm concerned...

Pour vous démarquer, n'hésitez pas à faire preuve d'**originalité**, d'**humour**, ou à associer à votre discours des **remarques personnelles** ou **inattendues** qui marqueront les esprits !

Conseils pour une intervention orale

- **Ne lisez pas vos notes,** ce qui rendrait votre présentation monotone et mécanique.
  N'ayez que des **mots-clés** sous les yeux !

- Soignez votre **élocution** pour qu'elle soit claire et intelligible.
  Parlez suffisamment **fort** pour être entendu·e de tout le monde, **articulez** et **accentuez** les mots-clés.

- **Regardez** vos interlocuteurs·trices et soignez votre **gestuelle** : soyez dynamique !
  Entraînez-vous devant un **miroir** ou **filmez-vous** pour pouvoir vous améliorer !

- Ajustez votre **débit** : n'allez pas trop vite, ou à l'inverse ne soyez pas trop lent·e.
  Utilisez des ***gap fillers*** pour rendre votre intervention plus fluide et spontanée : *So, well, I mean, You know, Let's see...*

- Ayez une **prononciation** authentique : accentuez les mots porteurs de sens et adaptez votre **intonation**.
  Vérifiez la prononciation **des mots nouveaux** ou difficiles grâce à un **dictionnaire en ligne**.

Lors d'un débat, respectez la parole de chacun, soyez cordial·e et à l'écoute des arguments de l'autre pour mieux les réfuter.

6 Améliorer sa compréhension orale

Règle d'or

Ne paniquez pas si vous ne comprenez pas tout !
Utilisez tous les indices à votre disposition et émettez des hypothèses à partir des mots que vous avez reconnus.

Principe : comprendre un document audio ou vidéo consiste à élucider les passages flous à partir de ce que l'on connaît : il s'agit d'inférer le sens, de le deviner. Pour cela, il faut prendre de bonnes habitudes. Prenons ici l'exemple de la vidéo *Super Bowl : What does it mean to Americans ? BBC News* (Unit 14, p. 243).

Les indices avant l'écoute pour anticiper

- **Le titre** apporte des informations sur le sujet, la thématique.
- **La légende** (source, date) éclaire le contexte.
- **L'image** aide à affiner vos intuitions.

Photo et légende : de nombreux emblèmes (drapeau, hymne national) soulignent l'importance de cet événement.

Titre : interrogation sur la signification du *Super Bowl* dans la culture américaine.

Source : analyse journalistique par un média britannique.

A **Super Bowl: What does it mean to Americans?**
BBC News Video 23lmu21401

Mickey Guyton sings the national anthem before the Super Bowl 2022 between the Los Angeles Rams and the Bengals of Cincinnati in Inglewood, California.

- **On peut en déduire que :**
  - le document, de type journalistique, va proposer les points de vue d'Américain·es sur le *Super Bowl*.
  - des informations objectives vont être présentées (activités lors de cet événement, traditions...).
  - les sentiments des protagonistes seront exposés (joie, excitation, patriotisme).

- **Que faire pour vous préparer à l'écoute ?**
  - Listez tous les mots que vous connaissez en rapport avec le sujet et créez une carte mentale.
  - Organisez votre brouillon, par exemple en dessinant des colonnes correspondant à chacune des 3 écoutes, que vous remplirez avec des couleurs différentes.
  - Émettez des hypothèses sur le contenu du document.

La première écoute pour une compréhension globale

- **Les indices sonores** (musique, bruit de fond), tout comme les **indices visuels** s'il s'agit d'une vidéo (gestuelle et expressions des personnes, bandeaux indiquant noms propres ou chiffres, lieux...), sont souvent révélateurs et d'une grande aide.

extrait de film bande-annonce
Nature du document
discours extrait de journal télévisé
interview publicité

noms
Personnes attitudes
métiers liens entre elles

âges
Chiffres dates
pourcentages
sommes

Relevez les mots-clés (qui en anglais sont accentués !) et utilisez des abréviations, des initiales... Notez tout ce que vous pouvez : ce que vous avez entendu ou vu.

- **Qu'avez-vous noté lors de cette première écoute ?**

Arizona, Washington, California, Tennessee, February, documentary, BBC, sporting event, Super Bowl, game, fun, good, happy, eat lots of food, drink, family, friends

- **Visual and sound elements**

2 reporters interviewing people, crowd, stadium, NFL logos and flags, football fans: smiling, laughing, wearing colourful clothes and jerseys, music: lively and catchy

Les écoutes suivantes pour une compréhension détaillée

- **Pour compléter vos notes, demandez-vous :**
  - **à qui** s'adresse le document ?
  - quel est **le ton** des personnes qui parlent ? neutre ? en colère ? passionné ? Cela vous aidera à comprendre **l'implicite** du document (ce qui n'est pas dit).
  - quels sont les **sujets**, les **enjeux**, le **but** du document ?

- **Qu'avez-vous noté des écoutes suivantes ?**

Arizona, Washington, California, Tennessee, February, documentary, BBC, noisy, sporting event, Super Bowl, drink beer, game, funny tone, important, national holiday, people from everywhere (and different religions), excited, quintessential American, fun, good, happy, competitive, eat lots of food, let loose, drink, family, friends, hanging out, reunion, fan fest, beautiful celebration

Après les écoutes

- **Relisez** vos notes, puis **rédigez** des phrases complètes en étant **synthétique** et en traitant **tous les éléments repérés**. Vous êtes maintenant capable de dire ce que vous avez compris du document !

Ce compte-rendu pourra être en **anglais** ou en **français** : dans les deux cas, il vous faudra prendre vos notes en anglais, puis traduire dans un second temps si besoin. Utilisez bien sûr des connecteurs logiques et un vocabulaire précis.

7 Améliorer sa compréhension écrite

Règle d'or

***Don't panic!* Comprendre un texte, ce n'est pas arriver à traduire chaque mot, mais repérer les éléments connus afin de saisir l'essentiel.**

Les indices avant la lecture pour anticiper

Analyse du paratexte → chapô / image / légende

Le **chapô** est constitué de quelques lignes qui « coiffent » le texte, c'est-à-dire qui l'introduisent.

- **Le titre**
  Que vous évoque-t-il ? Quelles hypothèses vous permet-il d'émettre ?
- **La date**
  d'écriture ou de parution : contexte historique pertinent ?
- **L'auteur·e**
  Connaissez-vous d'autres œuvres de cette personne ?
  Connaissez-vous le courant artistique auquel elle appartient ?
- **La source**
  D'où provient le document ? Que vous évoque cette origine ?

- Tous ces éléments vous permettent de déterminer la **nature du document** : article de journal, extrait de roman, poème...
- Le **chapô**, souvent en italique, vous apporte des informations importantes sur les personnages, l'intrigue, le contexte...
- S'il s'agit d'un **texte littéraire**, on parlera d'un·e auteur·e *(writer / author)*, plus précisément d'un·e dramaturge *(playwright)*, d'un·e romancier·ère *(novelist)*, etc.
- S'il s'agit d'un **texte journalistique**, on parlera d'un·e journaliste *(a journalist)*, d'un article de journal *(a newspaper article)*. Une analyse du sous-titre, du premier paragraphe (qui introduit le sujet) et du dernier (qui souvent le résume) vous sera d'une grande aide.

Lecture du texte

Il est essentiel de faire plusieurs lectures du texte.

- Lisez les questions **en amont**, pour savoir ce que vous allez devoir **repérer**. Choisissez la **méthode** qui vous convient le mieux : différentes couleurs de surligneurs, tableau à remplir, carte mentale...
- **Première lecture :** afin de comprendre le sens global, vérifier vos hypothèses et faire des repérages (chiffres, noms propres, mots transparents).
- **Lectures suivantes :** afin de comprendre les détails du texte, d'identifier les relations entre les personnages, les points de vue exprimés, les enjeux du texte.

Dans un extrait littéraire

Personnages
liens entre eux nombres
importance dans le récit

Lieux
villes pays
lieux publics

Dates
contexte
époque
période historique

Narration
interne externe omnisciente

Repérez les **pronoms personnels** sujets ou compléments : à qui correspondent-ils ?

ATTENTION **Ne confondez pas l'auteur·e (qui écrit) et le ou la narrateur·trice (qui s'exprime dans un texte). Il ne s'agit pas forcément de la même personne !**

Dans un article de presse

Personnes
nombre fonction
citations paroles rapportées

Nombres
années pourcentages
sommes

Objectifs
dénoncer annoncer alerter montrer

ATTENTION **Un article de presse n'est pas toujours objectif !**

Analyser la structure

Il est primordial de comprendre la logique du texte, sa progression du début à la fin.

Pour cela, il vous faut repérer les **mots de liaison**, les différents **paragraphes**, la **répartition des échanges** dans les dialogues.

Vous pouvez donner un titre à chaque paragraphe ou lister des thèmes principaux.

Deviner le sens d'un mot

- Vérifiez d'abord si une **aide lexicale** est apportée et si vous connaissez **un mot de la même famille**.
- La stratégie qui consiste à deviner le sens d'un mot s'appelle **l'inférence**. Inférer le sens d'un mot c'est chercher, enquêter à partir de divers éléments. Voici les étapes à suivre.
  → Trouvez le mot **racine** en enlevant le préfixe et/ou le suffixe.
  → Aidez-vous du **contexte** pour comprendre le sens du mot.
  → Analysez la **syntaxe** pour comprendre le **rôle** du mot dans la phrase, sa **fonction**.
- Exemple: *"Now, as Australian Football are bringing full focus into this work, this action plan is just the first step of many to connect to community and **embed** equity into the delivery and function of football more **broadly**."*

– Cette phrase possède de nombreux **mots transparents**, ce qui va vous aider à la comprendre. Une **aide lexicale** vous est donnée pour le mot ***embed*** *[=integrate]*. Il vous faudra analyser la **syntaxe** (l'ordre des mots) pour **reformuler** la phrase en la simplifiant : *this action plan is the first plan to... embed equity.*

– L'adverbe *broadly* est un adverbe classique construit à partir d'un mot **racine**, l'adjectif *broad*, et du **suffixe** *-ly*. Le **contexte** étant celui de l'équité, de la justice, de connecter différents membres d'une société, on peut supposer qu'il s'agira pour le football australien d'être le plus inclusif, le plus **large** *(broad)* possible.

TIMELINES

UK

History & society

2000 BC – **Stonehenge completed**

1337 – **Hundred years' war** with France begins

1605 – A group of English Catholics – among them **Guy Fawkes** – fails to assassinate **King James I**

1801 – **United Kingdom formed** by union of the Kingdoms of Great Britain and Ireland

Arts & Science and technology

1597 – **William Shakespeare** writes a tragedy entitled ***Romeo and Juliet***

1776 – James Watt invents his **Watt steam engine,** one of the driving forces of the industrial revolution

1816 – George Stephenson, known as "the Father of Railways", builds the **1st steam locomotive**

USA

History & society

1492 – **Christopher Columbus** reported to be the 1st European to set foot on the New World

1620 – **Pilgrim Fathers** sail to America on the ***Mayflower***

1621 – **First Thanksgiving**

4th July 1776 – **American Independence from the U.K.**

1861 - 1865 – **Civil War** following 11 states seceding from the Union

1882 – **Chinese Exclusion Act**

1920 – **Women get the right to vote**

Arts & Science and technology

1876 – Graham Bell invents **the telephone**

1927 – **1st sound movie** produced in Hollywood: *The Jazz Singer*

June 28, 1838

Queen Victoria's coronation

1928

British women obtain the right to vote

1948

The **British Nationality Act** grants citizenship to people from British colonies

1948

Arrival of the *HMT Empire Windrush* with people from the West Indies (including Jamaica) who come to rebuild Britain after WWII

June 2, 1953

Elizabeth II's coronation

2016

UK votes to leave the European Union in a referendum (**BREXIT**)

2023

Charles III 's coronation

1863

Construction of the **Metropolitan Railway**, the world's first underground railway, in London

1865

Alice's Adventures in Wonderland by Lewis Carroll is published

1950

Alan Turing publishes a landmark paper in which he speculates about **thinking machines**

1989

The English scientist Tim Berners-Lee invents the **World Wide Web**

1994

The **Channel Tunnel** which links London to Paris is inaugurated

1954

Beginning of the **Civil Rights Movements**

1955 – 1975

Vietnam War

August 28, 1963

Martin Luther King Jr. delivers his speech ***"I have a dream"***

April 4, 1968

Segregation abolished (Civil Rights Acts)

1991

Gulf War: BDCA coalition of 35 countries led by the US declares war on Iraq

11th September 2001

Terrorist Attack on the World Trade Center

2009

Barack Obama becomes the first African American President of the USA (44th)

2013

Black Lives Matter is created as a reaction to the acquittal of George Zimmerman in the murder of Trayvon Martin

January 6, 2021

Following Donald Trump's defeat in the 2020 presidential election, a mob of his supporters attacks the Capitol Building in Washington, D.C.

1958

NASA is created as a result of the space race between the USA and the Soviet Union

1969

Neil Armstrong and Buzz Aldrin become **the first men to land on the moon**

1969

Woodstock music Festival

1975

Bill Gates and Paul Allen found **Microsoft**

1976

Steve Jobs, Steve Wozniak and Ronald Wayne found **Apple** Computer

2004

Launching of **Facebook** by Mark Zuckerberg

2006

Twitter founded by Jack Dorsey, Evan Williams, Biz Stone and Noah Glass

2012

Tesla Model S becomes the best selling **electric car**

COUNTRY FILES

UK

Units 1, 2, 3, 5, 10, 13

Capital: London
Population: 68.8 million
The United Kingdom is made up of **four countries**: England (cap. London), Wales (cap. Cardiff), Scotland (cap. Edinburgh) and Northern Ireland (cap. Belfast).

DID YOU KNOW?

- The United Kingdom is a **constitutional monarchy.**
- It does not have a written, codified constitution but a set of rules and regulations constituted by jurisprudence and laws.

Monarch
= Head of State
(representative role)

Legislative power
(makes laws)

House of Commons
= 650 Members of Parliament (MPs) elected every 5 years

House of Lords
= more than 700 unelected members

Executive power
(puts laws into practice)

Prime Minister
= Head of Government, the leader of the majority party

Cabinet
= other ministers

USA

Units 3, 4, 7, 9, 11, 13, 14, 16, 20

Capital: Washington D.C.
Population: 334.2 million
The United States is a **federal republic divided into 50 states**.
It is a fairly "young" country (less than 250 years old).

DID YOU KNOW?

- The president is elected indirectly by an electoral college of 538 electors. Americans vote for their state's electors according to which president and vice president they promise to elect.
- The constitution provides a separation of powers.

Constitution

Legislative power
(makes laws)

House of Representatives
= 435 representatives according to each state's population

Senate
= 100 senators, two from each state

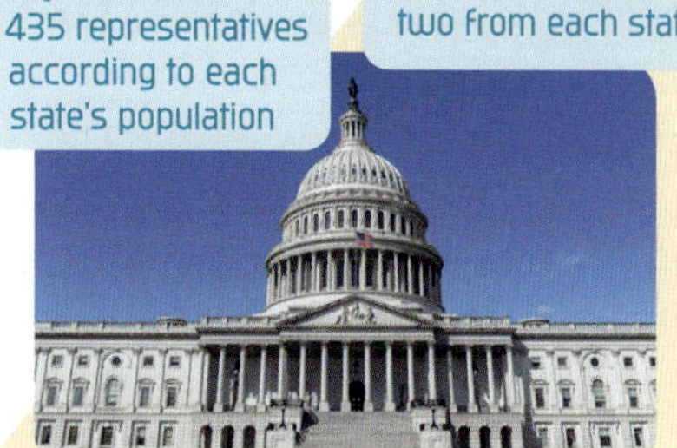

Executive power
(puts laws into practice)

President
= Head of Government, (elected every 4 years)

Vice President

Cabinet
= other ministers

Juridical power
(interprets laws)

Supreme Court
= nine justices nominated for life by the President with the consent of the Senate

Lower Courts

AUSTRALIA

Units 6, 12

Capital: Cambera
Population: 26.3 million
A megadiverse country, with a **wide variety of landscapes and climates**, deserts in the centre, tropical rainforests in the north-east, and mountain ranges in the south-east.
Politics: federal parliamentary constitutional monarchy

DID YOU KNOW?

- Australia is about the **same size as the USA**.
- When it was still a British colony, Australia was used as a prison for British convicts.
- 80% of the Australians live less than 50 km from the ocean.
- Between 300,000 and 1 million Aboriginal people inhabited the island in 1788.
- Today, the Aboriginal and Torres Strait Islander people make up **3,3% of the population**.

50,000 to **65,000** years ago Humans are believed to have arrived in Australia

1770 English Lieutenant James Cook's expedition charts the eastern coast and claims it for the British Crown

1787 13 May The first 11 ships depart from Great Britain for Australia to begin European colonisation

1788 26 January Captain Philipp formally proclaims British sovereignty. This day is now celebrated as Australia Day

1891 A National Australian Convention agrees on adopting the name " the Commonwealth of Australia ". It also drafts a constitution

1902 Right to vote in federal elections for women

1913 Canberra is named capital

1914 Soldiers sent to WWI to fight for the first time under the Australian Flag

1949 Australian citizenship is established

1953 Indigenous Australians gain the right to vote in the state of Queensland

1971 The Australian Aboriginal Flag is designed

2006 The Commonwealth Games are held in Melbourne

KENYA

Unit 8

Full name: Jamhuri Ya Kenya
Capital and largest city: Nairobi (4.5 million)
Kenya is the world's 48th largest country by area
Population: 56.9 million
Official Languages: Swahili and English, but there are over 60 different languages spoken in Kenya.
Politics: Presidential republic / unitary multiparty republic with two legislative houses (Senate and National Assembly)

DID YOU KNOW?

- It is known that human history in Kenya dates back millions of years, as some of the earliest fossilised remains were discovered there.
- **Nairobi** originated in the late 1890s as a colonial railway settlement, taking its name from a water hole known to the Maasai people as "Enkare Nairobi" ("Cold Water").
- The **Dandora dumpsite** collects 1,500 tons of garbage a day, polluting the soil and the surrounding rivers.

1000 BC Swahili people, Bantu groups migrate to the Great Lakes Region

1498 Vasco da Gama visits Mombasa

1850 European explorers begin mapping the interior of the territory

1875 - 1884 Peak of the slave plantation economy

1884 Britain claims Kenya and Uganda at the Berlin Conference

1890 - 1906 Nandi resistance against colonial rule

1909 Slavery is abolished in East Africa

1920 The British East African Protectorate is transformed into the Kenya Colony and Uganda Colony

1963 Kenya becomes a sovereign state and remains a member of the Commonwealth

1964 Kenya becomes a republic

2004 8 October Wangari Maathai becomes the first African woman and first environmentalist to win the Nobel Peace Prize

SOUTH AFRICA

Unit 15

Full name: the Republic of South Africa (RSA)
Capitals:
Pretoria (executive)
Cape Town (legislative)
Bloemfontein (judicial)
Population: 70 million
Language: 11 official languages

DID YOU KNOW?

- On April, 27th, South Africans celebrate **Freedom Day** (or Vryheidsdag in Afrikaans), which commemorates the first multiracial elections in 1994.
- **Rainbow nation** is a term that was originally coined by Archbishop Desmond Tutu to describe post-apartheid South Africa.
- **Lesotho** is a state that is completely surrounded by South Africa, without any access to the ocean.

1652 Jan van Riebeck, representing the Dutch East India Company, founds the Cape Colony at Table Bay

1880 - 1881 Boers rebel against the British, sparking the first Anglo-Boer war

1899 Second Anglo-Boer War begins

1912 Native National Congress is founded, later renamed the African National Congress (ANC)

1948 Policy of apartheid (separateness) is adopted by the National Party (NP)

1950 Group Areas Act is passed to segregate blacks and whites. ANC responds with campaign of civil disobedience, led by Nelson Mandela

1960 Seventy black demonstrators are killed at Sharperville. ANC banned.

1961 South Africa is declared a republic and leaves the Commonwealth

1964 ANC leader Nelson Mandela is sentenced to life imprisonment

1990 ANC unbanned, Mandela is released after 27 years in prison

April 1994 ANC wins first non-racial elections. Mandela becomes president

December 5th 2013 Nelson Mandela dies, aged 95

JAMAICA

Unit 17

Capital: Kingston is the country's capital and largest city.
Population: 2.9 million
Politics: Jamaica is a **parliamentary constitutional monarchy**
(Parliament of Jamaica = Senate + House of Representatives).
Heavily dependent on tourism; it has an average of **4.3 million tourists a year**.

DID YOU KNOW?

- **Meaning of the Jamaican Flag**: the black symbolises the strength and creativity of the people.
  The gold represents the natural beauty of sunlight, as well as the wealth of the country.
  The green signifies hope and agriculture.
- **Windrush Scandal in the UK** (2018): many West Indians, descendants of those who arrived undocumented on *HMT Empire Windrush*, were denied healthcare or were threatened with deportation as they couldn't provide legal documents. Some of them were even deported or illegally detained because of the government's "hostile environment" policies. The then-home secretary Amber Rudd resigned.

1494 Christopher Columbus' lands in Jamaica

1655 The British invade Jamaica

1838 Slavery is abolished

1865 Morant Bay rebellion

1938 Riots are caused by unemployment and British racial policies

1944 Universal suffrage is introduced

1962 Jamaica becomes independent within the British Commonwealth

1976 Bob Marley's assassination attempt

1981 Bob Marley dies, aged 36

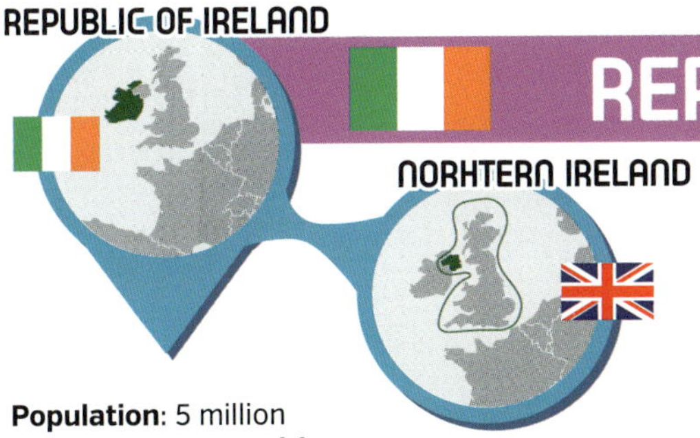

REPUBLIC OF IRELAND

Unit 18

Population: 5 million
Ireland is the **second-largest island of the British Isles**. It is divided between the Republic of Ireland (officially named Ireland) and Northern Ireland, which is part of the United Kingdom.
Politics: The **Republic of Ireland**, whose capital is **Dublin**, is a **parliamentary democracy** and is a member of the EU. The government is headed by a prime minister, the Taoiseach.
Northern Ireland, whose capital is **Belfast**, is **part of the United Kingdom** with a local council and assembly.

DID YOU KNOW?

- The **Irish culture** has had a significant influence across the world. This is due to the vast number of Irish who emigrated from Ireland in the 19th century (mainly because of the Great Famine from 1845 to 1849). Nowadays, for example, one third of the Australian population claim Irish descent!
- Ireland is the only country in the world to have a musical instrument, the harp, as its national symbol. It dates back to the 13th century.

445 St. Patrick founds a church at Armagh

1695 - 1728 Penal Laws are passed against Catholics

1800 Signing of the Act of Union

1845 - 1849 Great Potato Famine results in more than one million deaths; mass immigration to the United States

1919 - 1921 War between Ireland and Britain

1922 Partition. Six counties in the north of the island opt to stay in the United Kingdom while the rest of Ireland becomes independent and later a republic

1937 Voters approve a new constitution which proclaims "Éire" as a sovereign, independent, democratic state

1968 Civil rights movement. Catholics complain of unfair treatment at the hands of a largely Protestant political establishment

1970s - 1990s Terrorist groups on both sides commit attacks, including bombing bars and clubs, killing politicians, soldiers and civilians

30th January 1972 Bloody Sunday: British soldiers shoot 28 unarmed civilians during a peaceful protest march in Derry

1992 Ireland signs the Treaty on the European Union at Maastricht

1998 Good Friday agreement: creation of the Northern Ireland Assembly. The Republic of Ireland also agrees to drop its constitutional claim to the six counties which formed Northern Ireland

2002 Euro replaces punt as national currency

INDIA

Unit 19

Capital: New Delhi
Population: 1.43 billion
India is the **seventh largest country by area** and the **most populous democracy** in the world.
Languages: There is no national language. India has **22 recognised languages**. Hindi, with the largest number of speakers, is the official language of the government.
English is used in business and administration and has the status of a "subsidiary official language".
General dates of significance:
- Republic Day – January 26th
- Anniversary of Mahatma Gandhi's death – January 30th
- Independence Day – August 15th

DID YOU KNOW?

- **Diamonds** were first discovered in India.
- **Shampoo** originated in India.
- The **Taj Mahal** is the number one tourist site.
- **Holi** is one of the most colourful festivals in the world.
- **Cows** are considered sacred.
- Around 70% of the world's **spices** come from India.

VII century BC – III century *Ramayana* (one of the two major Sanskrit epics of ancient India)

IV century BC – IV century *Mahabbarata* (the other major Sanskrit epic of ancient India)

500 First temples are built and are still visible today: Sanchi (Madhya Pradesh), Dashavatara (Uttar Pradesh), Lad Khan (Karnataka)

1498 Vasco da Gama arrives in India

1856 The British control most of India

1857 Large-scale rebellion in northern and central India against the British East India Company rule

1876 Queen Victoria becomes Empress of India

1919 Satyagraha civil disobedience (launched by Mahatma Gandhi)

1947 India becomes free and independent from the British Empire

1947 Jawaharlal Nehru becomes India's Prime Minister

1948 Gandhi's assassination

1984 Indira Gandhi's assassination

2016 India launches its first space laboratory Astrosat

Table des illustrations

111-b ph © Mary Evans / Allstar / Stewart Kendall / SIPA
112-h © 'What's It Like to Be A 16-Year-Old In Dublin Today, i-D © 2023 VICE MEDIA GROUP, D.R.
112-b © Central Statistics Office, Ireland (CSO)
115 ph © Himertanz / Shutterstock
117-bd ph © Ben Molyneux / Alamy Stock Photo / © Andy Earl / Mercury Records
119 ph © Vector Tradition - stock.adobe.com
120 © Courtesy of Lorraine Maher
121 ph © Dm - stock.adobe.com
122 © Artist Kadir Nelson's illustrations of pride and soul © CBS Sunday Morning
123-h ph © Collection of the artist and THE JKBN GROUP. © 2020 Kadir Nelson
123-b ph © Underwood Archives / UIG / Bridgeman Images
124 © HarperCollins Publishers. All rights reserved. Illustrations © 2011 by Kadir Nelson
125 ph © Kwame Alexander reads from The Undefeated, Authors Live, 1 avr. 2020 © BBC Scotland
128 ph © Warwick Keen
129 ph © Matt Adekponya / Australian Olympic Committee via Getty Images
130 © Australia Post
131-h © Lionel Rose: "I think of myself as an Australian" © Sky News AUSTRALIA
131-b © Cathy Freeman, Trailblazers - Episode 3, 8 march 2021 © Eurosport
132-hg ph © dimensi design - stock.adobe.com
132-hd © Our reconciliation statement, 27 may 2021 © Australian Sports Commission, D.R
132-b ph © Designed by Kirrae Whurrong woman Aunty Fiona Clarke & Butchulla and Gubbi Gubbi woman Courtney Hagen. © Cricket Australia
133 ph © Ricardo Mazalan / AP / SIPA
135 ph © dimensi design - stock.adobe.com
139-h © Cathy Freeman, Trailblazers - Episode 3, 8 march 2021 © Eurosport
139-b ph © Thomas Kienzle / AP / SIPA
140 © National Reconciliation Week - Sport Business Snapshot, 3 june 2019 © Australian Sports Commission, D.R.
141 ph © Vock collection / The Cherboug Memory (Australia)
142 Coll. Christophel / © Universal Pictures - Marc Platt Productions - Perfect World Pictures
143 ph © Sara Krulwich / The New York Times - REDUX-REA
144-hg ph © Matthew Murphy
144-hd ph © Evan Agostini / AP / Sipa
145 ph © Peter Bennett / Citizen of the Planet / Alamy Stock Photo
146 ph © PictureLux / The Hollywood Archive / Alamy Stock Photo
147-h ph © 20th Century Studios / Amblin Entertainment / BBQ_DFY / Aurimages / Photo: Niko Tavernise
147-b ph © 20th Century Studios / Amblin Entertainment / Photo: Niko Tavernise
149 ph © nadia_bormotova / iStockphoto
153 © Backstage: Glasgow Girls - Interview with Cora Bissett, 17 october 2012 © National Theatre of Scotland
154 ph © IN THE HEIGHTS, Official Trailer, Quiara Alegría Hudes, Lin-Manuel Miranda, 2019 © Warner Bros Pictures
155 © Drew Hodges
156 ph © David Crane / MediaNews Group / Los Angeles Daily News via Getty Images
157 ph © Robert Deutschman / Digital vision / Getty Images
158-g Coll. Christophel © Triple Threat Television
158-d ph © Ethan Miller / Getty Images / AFP
159 ph © Gregory Shamus / Getty Images
160 ph © Dustin Bradford / Getty Images / AFP
162 ph © Ben Curtis / AP / SIPA / © John Adam (Artist)
163-h ph © Ilvy Njiokiktjien / VII Photo
163-mg ph © Betka82 / iStockphoto
163-md ph © Baluchis / iStockphoto
164-h ph © "BORN FREE - Mandela's Generation of Hope, Short Doc", Ilvy Njiokiktjien, 03/05/19 © Ilvy Njiokiktjien / VII Photo
164-b ph © Lebo Lukewarm
165-h ph © Thabang Mabaso (dancer) /Joburg Ballet / Photo by Lauge Sorensen (2019)
165-b ph © Ilvy Njiokiktjien / VII Photo
166-h © South Africa: Is 'black tax' help or a burden?, Produced and edited by Christian Parkinson, 12/10/20, BBC News - Africa
166-b ph © Bethuel Mangena / African News Agency (ANA)
169 ph © Baluchis / iStockphoto
170 ph © Horst Könemund - stock.adobe.com
174 ph © Ilvy Njiokiktjien / VII Photo
175 ph © Ilvy Njiokiktjien / VII Photo
176 ph © Dave Bledsoe, FreeVerse Photography
177-h ph © Greg Mionske for Rolling Stone
177-b ph © Ponomariova_Maria / iStockphoto
178-h ph © Luka Galle
178-b ph © Helen H. Richardson / The Denver Post via Getty Images
179 ph © Paul Marotta / REX / Shutterstock / SIPA
180 ph © Isabel Hope
181 ph © Susie Burke
188 © An interview with teen climate activist, Jamie Margolin - New Day Northwest, 27 november 2019 © KING 5 Seattle
189 ph © Kevin Mazur / Getty Images for March For Our Lives
190-h ph © Andy Martin Jr. / ZUMA Press, Inc. / Alamy Stock Photo
190-b ph © Balint Radu - stock.adobe.com
191-h ph © Alvaro Leiva - www.agefotostock.com
191-m ph © pict rider - stock.adobe.com
191-b ph © ZOO.BY / Shutterstock
192-h ph © Bridgeman Images
192-b ph © tribalium81 - stock.adobe.com
193 ph © Borsalino Productions / BBQ_DFY / Aurimages
194 ph © Vyacheslav Rakitskiy / iStockphoto
196-h © Xavi Garcia
196-bg ph © Keystone Pictures USA / ZUMA PRESS / Alamy Live News
196-bd ph © Images reproduced with permission of Transport for London (TfL). All rights reserved
197 ph © Images reproduced with permission of Transport for London (TfL). All rights reserved
198 ph © Shawshots / Alamy Stock Photo
199-g ph © Archivart / Alamy Stock Photo
199-d ph © Toby Melville / Reuters
200-h ph © Greg Balfour Evans / Alamy Stock Photo
200-b ph © Joy Labinjo, '5 more minutes', 2021. Brixton Underground station. Commissioned by Art on the Underground. Courtesy the artist and Tiwani Contemporary. Photo: Angus Mill, 2021
201-g ph © Michael Landy, 'All my lines in the palm of your hand', 2011. The 14th pocket Tube map cover. Commissioned by Art on the Underground.
201-m ph © Emma Kay, Tube Map cover, 2004. The 1st pocket Tube map cover. Commissioned by Art on the Underground
201-d ph © Rachel Whiteread, 'The Hole of London', 2014. The 20th pocket Tube map cover. Commissioned by Art on the Underground
203 ph © topvectors - stock.adobe.com
207-g ph © Delphotostock - stock.adobe.com
207-m ph © Panther Media GmbH / Alamy Stock Photo
207-d ph © Vladislav Zolotov / iStockphoto
208 ph © Dennis Ludlow / iStockphoto
209 ph © Facundo Arrizabalaga / Photoshot / MaxPPP
210-g ph © Amith Nag Photography / Getty Images
210-d ph © 2023 The Scalers
211 ph © gg-foto / Shutterstock
212-h ph © John Eccles / Alamy Stock Photo
212-b ph © The Aravani Art Project
213-h ph © Catalin Lazar / Shutterstock
213-m ph © Gary Cook - www.agefotostock.com
213-b ph © CamBuff / iStockphoto
215 ph © The Aravani Art Project
216 ph © The U.S. National Archives and Records Administration
217 ph © Illustration by Mojo Wang
218-h ph © Collection of Choy Ging Foon / AIISF
218-b © Chart: University of Southern California U.S.-China Institute, Data: U.S. Dept. of Homeland Security
219-h "Waiting in lines, Tanforan Assembly Center, San Bruno, California, 1942" by Miné Okubo / ph © Japanese American National Museum (Gift of Miné Okubo Estate, 2007.62.87)
219-b ph © Elen_Art - stock.adobe.com
220 ph © Tayfun Coskun / Anadolu Agency via AFP
221-h ph © Gary Conner / Alamy Stock Photo
221-bg ph © U.S. Mint via Getty Images
221-bm ph © Bettmann / Getty Images
222 ph © ABC / AJ Pics / Alamy Stock Photo
223 ph © KateDemianov / iStockphoto
227 ph © Rodin Eckenroth / Getty Images for The Artists Project
228 ph © Paramount / EVERETT / Aurimages
229 ph © Dorothea Lange / Library of Congress
230-231 © Still from 'Curious Alice', a VR experience created by the V&A and HTC Vive Arts. Featuring original artwork by Kristjana S Williams, 2020
232,234,235,236,237,238 (clock) ph © Hurst Photo / Shutterstock
232-hg Ill. by John Tenniel / ph © Andrew Howe / iStockphoto
232-hd ph © UtCon Collection / Alamy Stock Photo
232-md ph © Andrey Kuzmin - stock.adobe.com
232-bg Stained glass by Geoffrey Webb / ph © Tony Smith / Alamy Stock Photo
232-bd ph © Private Collection / Bridgeman Images
233-h © Courtesy of Michael Foreman and Chris Beetles Gallery, St James's London
233-b ph © BigJoy - stock.adobe.com
234-hd Ill. by John Tenniel / ph © Bridgeman Images
234-g ph © Svetlana Smirnova - stock.adobe.com
234-mh ph © Arcady - stock.adobe.com
234-mb ph © Burbuzin - stock.adobe.com
235 Ill. by John Tenniel / ph © Granger / Bridgeman Images
236-hd ph © Alexander Pokusay - stock.adobe.com
236-g Ill. by John Tenniel / ph © Bridgeman Images
236-md Coll. Christophel © Walt Disney Pictures
236-bd Alice In Wonderland (1999) - Dir: Nick Willing - Pers: Whoopi Goldberg / ph © Hallmark / NBC / EVERETT / Aurimages
236,237,238,239 (déco) ph © svetlanasmirnova - stock.adobe.com
237-m Ill. by John Tenniel / ph © Derek Bayes / Bridgeman Images
237-bd Ill. by John Tenniel / ph © Bridgeman Images
238-mg Ill. by John Tenniel / ph © Bridgeman Images
238-md ph © svetlanasmirnova - stock.adobe.com
238-239 ph © Mary Evans / AF Archive / Aurimages / © Disney
239-hd Ill. by John Tenniel / ph © Granger / Bridgeman Images
239-md ph © Don Arnold / WireImage via Getty Images
277-h © Longman Dictionary of Contemporary English (LDOCE)
277-b © Wordreference
278-h © YouGlish
278-b © BBC
284 ph © Collection of the artist and THE JKBN GROUP. © 2020 Kadir Nelson
285-1 ph © Jan Kranendonk - stock.adobe.com
285-2 ph © frimufilms - stock.adobe.com
285-3 ph © Nick Brundle - stock.adobe.com
285-4 ph © Ian Douglas / The New York Times-REDUX-REA
285-5 ph © Netflix / Courtesy Everett Collection / Aurimages
288 ph © Rawpixel Ltd. / Freepik
292 ph © David Crane / MediaNews Group / Los Angeles Daily News via Getty Images
296-h1 ph © vencav - stock.adobe.com
296-h2 ph © Bridgeman Images
296-b1 "The first Thanksgiving", c.1930 by Jean Leon Gerome Ferris / ph © Bridgeman Images
296-b2 "Fight For The Colors", 1985 (oil on canvas) by Don Troiani / ph © Bridgeman Images

296-b3	ph ©	Bridgeman Images
297-h1	ph ©	Alexander Bassano / Mary Evans / Bridgeman Images
297-h2	ph ©	SSPL / NMeM / Daily Herald Archive / UIG / Bridgeman Images
297-h3	ph ©	Hulton-Deutsch Collection / Corbis via Getty Images
297-h4	ph ©	Jane Barlow / POOL / AFP
297-h5	ph ©	Prismatic Pictures / Bridgeman Images
297-b1	ph ©	AP / SIPA
297-b2	ph ©	Sean Adair / Reuters
297-b3	ph ©	Brendan Smialowski / AFP
297-b4	©	Nasa
297-b5	ph ©	Charles Harbutt / GAMMA-RAPHO
298-h1	ph ©	luoman / iStockphoto
298-h2	ph ©	oversnap / iStockphoto
298-b1	ph ©	Brandon - stock.adobe.com
298-b2	ph ©	OlegAlbinsky - stock.adobe.com
299-h1	ph ©	Horizon International Images / Alamy Stock Photo
299-h2	ph ©	Issah - stock.adobe.com
299-h3	ph ©	jasonbennee / iStockphoto
299-h4	ph ©	National Maritime Museum, Greenwich / Bridgeman Images
299-b1	ph ©	hadynyah / iStockphoto
299-b2	ph ©	Eric Feferberg / AFP
300-h1	ph ©	Murgroup - stock.adobe.com
300-h2	ph ©	Per-Anders Pettersson / Getty Images
300-h3	ph ©	akg-images / African Pictures
300-h4	©	African National Congress (ANC)
300-h5	ph ©	Look and Learn / Illustrated Papers Collection / Bridgeman Images
300-b1	ph ©	akg-images / Jazz Archiv Hamburg / Hardy Schiffler
300-b2	ph ©	Luisa Ricciarini / Bridgeman Images
301-h1	ph ©	Ken Welsh / Bridgeman Images
301-h2	ph ©	The Stapleton Collection / Bridgeman Images
301-h3	ph ©	Mary Evans / Bridgeman Images
301-bg1	ph ©	olenatur - stock.adobe.com
301-bg2	ph ©	shunmugam - stock.adobe.com
301-bd1	©	Indian Space Research Organisation (ISRO)
301-bd2	ph ©	Granger / Bridgeman Images
301-bd3	ph ©	Baron / Hulton Archive / Getty Images
301-bd4	ph ©	Biblioteca Casanatense, Roma / Album / Oroñoz / akg-images
301-bd5	ph ©	Rafal Cichawa - stock.adobe.com

D.R. : Malgré nos efforts, il nous a été impossible de joindre certains auteurs ou leurs ayants-droit pour solliciter l'autorisation de reproduction, nous avons réservé en notre comptabilité les droits usuels

Iconographie : Véronique Foz / Hatier Illustration

Table des crédits texte

p. 28 : Cryptid Currency: How the Loch Ness Monster Became a Force in Scotland's Economy, by Michele Debczak, Sep 4, 2020 © Mental Floss
p. 29 : Kelpie, Myths and Legends, Dec 7, 2017 © spookyscotland.net, D.R.
p. 26/27 : 12 OF SCOTLAND'S MOST FAMOUS STORIES & TALES, Aldona Reyes Mallet, June 17, 2022 © VisitScotland 2022, www.visitscotland.com
p. 37 : SCOTTISH MYTHS, FOLKLORE AND LEGENDS, by Brand Scotland Contributor, 1 April 2015, scotland.org © VisitScotland 2022, www.visitscotland.com
p. 38 : Stranger Things Is Breaking One Dangerous (And Deadly) Hollywood Pattern, by Bianca Mercuri © 2022 Goalcast, 2022 D.R.
p. 40h : A quick curtain call. Then bed: Child actors in adult theatre", Maddy Costa, The Guardian, 05/05/10 © Guardian News & Media Ltd 2022
p. 40b : The not so cursed child: did Harry Potter mark the end of troubled young actors?", Ryan Gilbey, The Guardian, 22/10/21 © Guardian News & Media Ltd 2022
p. 41 : There is no book of rules: how theatres aim to safeguard child actors, David Jays, The Guardian, 13/12/21 © Guardian News & Media Ltd 2022
p. 58 : Meredith Grey, Greys Anatomy © 2021 CharacTour, All Rights Reserved
p. 58 : Richard Hendriks, SiliconValley © 2021 CharacTour, All Rights Reserved
p. 58 : Shuri, Black Panther © 2021 CharacTour, All Rights Reserved
p. 59 : Dr. Charles Edward Eppes, Numb3rs © ShareTV
p. 67 : LAB GIRL by Hope Jahren, copyright © 2016 by A. Hope Jahren. Used by permission of Alfred A. Knopf, an imprint of the Knopf Doubleday Publishing Group, a division of Penguin Random House LLC. All rights reserved
p. 68 : Wave goodbye: the battle to protect Australia's surf breaks by Narelle Towie, Jan 2022, The Guardian © Guardian News & Media Ltd 2022
p. 71 : Surfing to save the world, November 19, 2020 by James Taylor © 2022, Geelong Times
p. 75 : UK cities amongst best destinations in Europe for street food, by Sophie, 22/06/2022 © NCASS 2002
p. 76 : THE EVOLUTION OF STREET FOOD, February 15, 2014, By Samantha Kelly © samanthachristinekelly.wordpress.com, D.R.
p. 77 : Best Food Halls in England, by Lucas Oakeley, 15 July 2021 © Mouth Group Limited, D.R.
p. 78 : Reusing iconic buildings, © ilovemanchester.com, D.R.
p. 87 : These are the Best Neighborhoods for Foodies in London, August 8, 2022 © City Experiences, D.R.
p. 91 : Creating Green Spaces Amid Kenya's Largest Dumpsite, by Marie Mulli, August 3, 2022 © Next City
p. 97 : Francis Scott Key pens "The Star-Spangled Banner", September 11, 2020 © A&E Television Networks, D.R
p. 99 : Kneeling during the National Anthem: Top 3 Pros and Cons, 4/11/2022 © ProCon.org, D.R.
p. 107 : Our flag, used as a symbol of pride and protest, tells a lot about who we are, July 2, 2015, by Tyrone Beason © Seattle Times
p. 110b : Happy Birthday Niall Horan: Revisiting a Classic Interview, 13 September 22 © Hotpress
p. 110h/ 111 : What being Irish means to me, by Marie-Claire Logue, November 7th 2021 © The Irish Times, D.R.
p. 113 : Don't Drink the Bathroom Water: A Guide to Living In Ireland, Robin Castle © Robin Castle, D.R.
p. 121 : Growing up Irish – Traditions of an Irish-American family, March 17, 2013 by Maggie Fitzgibbon, Westside News © westsidenewsny.com
p. 123 : Award-winning artist, author Kadir Nelson to speak at Norman Rockwell Museum, Jul. 20, 2022, by Anne-Gerard Flynn © Advance Local Media, D.R. "
p. 124 : Kadir Nelson: Proudly Black, Pointedly Positive, by Eleftheria Parpis, February 07, 2020 © One Club, D.R.
p. 129 : Patty Mills becomes Olympics' first Indigenous flag bearer, by Teisha Cloos, July 8, 2021 © National Indigenous Times
p. 130 : Johnny Mullagh, an Indigenous sports icon, by Geoffrey Atherden, The Guardian, Jan 2020, © Guardian News & Media Ltd 2022
p. 133 : Football Australia launches Indigenous Reconciliation Action Plan, by Samantha Lewis Tuesday 22 Feb 2022 © ABC Australia, D.R
p. 141 : He trail-blazed for me too': Cathy Freeman's tribute to Granddad, by Brad Walter, 4 Jul 2022 © National Rugby League © Brad Walter, senior journalist, NRL.com
p. 144 : Why the British Musical Matters Now More Than Ever, by ELleanor Ross, December 6, 2018 © Backstage.
p. 144 : The Power Of Musical Theatre, by Katie Gutierrez © Bright Star Musical, D.R.
p. 145 : A Glorious, Immensely Moving Celebration Of Triumph Over Adversity © The Stage
p. 155 : Musical Perspective: An Analysis of How Musicals Reflect, Cultural Discourse, by Amosi Morgan, 5/21/2021 © California State Univ California State University, Monterey Bay, Digital Commons
p. 157 : What's So Super About Super Bowl Sunday? © Wonderpolis
p. 159 : No more (diversity) drama? Black viewers approve of the 2022 Super Bowl Halftime Show but want more action from the NFL, by Lianne Frick, February 17, 2022, D.R.
p. 164 : South Africa's Youth in 16 Portraits, Lebo Lukewarm, 16/06/16, Okay Africa, D.R.
p. 165h : South Africa's 'born-free' generation, 25 April 201 © BBC News
p. 165b : 'Born free', Just two people connected by Ilvy Njiokiktjien, 9/05/2019 © Ilvy Njiokiktjien / VII Photo
p. 167 : "BORN A CRIME: STORIES FROM A SOUTH AFRICAN CHILDHOOD by Trevor Noah, copyright © 2016 by Trevor Noah. Used by permission of Spiegel & Grau, an imprint of Random House, a division of Penguin Random House LLC. All rights reserved"
p. 173 : Why are South African cities still so segregated 25 years after apartheid?, Justice Malala in Johannesburg, 21/10/19 © Guardian News & Media Ltd
p. 175 : "No rainbow nation for today's youth", Sibonelo Mavuso, News / Politics / Opinion, Independent Online, 23/06/22, D.R.
p. 177 : The Power to Change the World: A Teaching Unit on Student Activism in History and Today, by Katherine Schulten, March 7, 2018 ©The New York Times
p. 178h : Luka Galle, Reconnecting with Femininity © Amplifier
p. 178b : The Next Generation - Youth "Artivist" and Environmental Advocate, Lena Eyen © SANTA CLARA UNIVERSITY
p. 180 : How young people can make effective change in the climate crisis, according to experts, by Julia Jacobo, January 22, 2022 © ABC News
p. 189 : 'I'm, Like, This Close to Snapping', by Elaine Godfrey, June 11, 2022 © 2022 The Atlantic Monthly Group, Inc. All rights reserved. Distributed by Tribune Content Agency
p. 191 : Reggae as a global culture scape, by Naomi Hofman, 02/10/2019, diggitmagazine.com © Department of Culture Studies of Tilburg University
p. 192 : Get Up Stand Up, de TOSH PETER et ROBERT MARLEY © Hal Leonard
p. 198 : The Blitz and The London Underground – Safety Beneath the Streets in the Second World War, by Rose Staveley-Wadham, November 6, 2019 © The British News Paper Archive
p. 199 : The Elizabeth line could be transformative for London – here's how, by Hamish McRae, 24 May 2022 © Hamish McRae/The Independent
p. 200 : Mind the gap: London tube opens new doors, by Prasun Sonwalkar, Thu 30 Sep 2021 © Khaleej Times, D.R.
p. 201 : Our Meetings by Andrew Waterman. Reprinted by permission of Carcanet from Collected Poems 1959-1999 © Carcanet Press
p. 209 : London Underground: Fascinating facts you probably didn't know about busking at Tube stations, by Emma Magnus 6 January 2022 © MyLondon/Reach Licensing
p. 211 : Bangalore: City of High Tech, by Dr. Whitney Howarth © 2023 Khan Academy, D.R
p. 212 : Aravani Art Project © The Aravani Art Project
p. 213 : A place called home, by Vishwas Mudagal © The Hindu
p. 218 : Chinese Exclusion Act, History.com, 24 august 2018 © A&E Television Networks
p. 220 : Illinois Becomes First State to Mandate Teaching Asian American History, by Isis Davis-Marks, July 14, 2021 © Smithsonian Magazine, D.R.
p. 229 : Japanese American National Museum in Los Angeles © Paul Kitagaki Jr.

PAPIER À BASE DE FIBRES CERTIFIÉES

Hatier s'engage pour l'environnement en réduisant l'empreinte carbone de ses livres. Celle de cet exemplaire est de : 1.4 kg éq. CO_2
Rendez-vous sur www.hatier-durable.fr

Achevé d'imprimer en France par Pollina - 13760
Dépôt légal : 09679-0/01 - Avril 2023

IMPRIM'VERT
Votre imprimeur agit pour l'environnement